1999
Arriva
Bus Handbc

British Bus Publishing

Type:

A	Articulated vehicle
B	Bus, either single-deck or double-deck
BC	Express - high-back seating in a bus body
C	Coach - high-back seating
CB	Contract - bus seats in a coach body
H	Heritage full-height double-deck
L	Heritage low-height double-deck with side gangway upstairs
M	Minibus with design capacity of 16 seats or less
N	Low-floor bus, either single-deck or double-deck
O	Open-top bus (CO = convertible - PO = Partial open-top)

Seating capacity is then shown. For double-decks the upper deck first,

Door position:-

C	Centre entrance/exit
D	Dual doorway
F	Front entrance/exit
R	Rear entrance/exit (no distinction between doored and open)
T	Three or more access points

Equipment:-

L	Lift for wheelchair
T	Toilet

e.g. - B32/28F is a double-deck bus with thirty-two seats upstairs, twenty-eight down and a front entrance/exit.
B43D is a bus with two doorways.

Re-registrations:-

Where a vehicle has gained new index marks the details are listed at the end of each fleet showing the current mark, followed in sequence by those previously carried starting with the original mark.

Other books in the series:

The Scottish Bus Handbook
The Ireland & Islands Bus Handbook
The North East Bus Handbook
The Yorkshire Bus Handbook
The Lancashire, Cumbria and Manchester Bus Handbook
The Merseyside and Cheshire Bus Handbook
The North and West Midlands Bus Handbook
The East Midlands Bus Handbook
The South Midlands Bus Handbook
The North and West Wales Bus Handbook
The South Wales Bus Handbook
The Chilterns and West Anglia Bus Handbook
The East Anglia Bus Handbook
The South East Bus Handbook
The South West Bus Handbook
The South Central Bus Handbook

Annual books are produced for the major groups:

The 1999 Stagecoach Bus Handbook
The 1999 FirstBus Bus Handbook
The 1999 Arriva Bus Handbook

Associated series:

The Hong Kong Bus Handbook
The Leyland Lynx Handbook
The Model Bus Handbook
The Postbus Handbook
The Toy & Model Bus Handbook - Volume 1 - Early Diecasts
The Fire Brigade Handbook (fleet list of each local authority fire brigade)
The Fire Brigade Handbook - Special Appliances Volume 1
The Fire Brigade Handbook - Special Appliances Volume 2
The Police Range Rover Handbook

1999 Arriva Bus Handbook

The 1999 Arriva Bus Handbook is a special edition of the Bus Handbook series which contains the various fleets of Arriva plc a year after group embarked on a major change on name and image. The Bus Handbook series is published by British Bus Publishing, an independent publisher of quality books for the industry and bus enthusiasts. Further information on these may be obtained from the address below.

Although this book has been produced with the encouragement of, and in co-operation with, Arriva plc management, it is not an official group fleet list and the vehicles included are subject to variation, particularly as the vehicle investment programme continues. Some vehicles listed are no longer in regular use on services but are retained for special purposes also out of use vehicles awaiting disposal are not all listed. The services operated and the allocation of vehicles to subsidiary companies are subject to variation at any time, although accurate at the time of going to print. Livery details given only aim to show significant variations from the group standard of aquamarine and cream. Minor variations or local identity and marketing schemes are not all included and older liveries being phased out are not shown.

To keep the fleet information up to date we recommend the Ian Allan publication Buses, published monthly, or for more detailed information, the PSV Circle monthly news sheets and LOTS publications.

Edited by David Donati and Bill Potter

Acknowledgements:
We are most grateful to Keith Grimes, Fred Huppertz, Mark Jameson, Colin Lloyd, Stuart Martin, John Rimmington, Steve Sanderson, Tony Wilson, LOTS, the PSV Circle and the management and officials of Arriva Group plc, and their operating companies, for their kind assistance and co-operation in the compilation of this book.

The front cover photo is by Richard Godfrey, frontispiece by Tony Wilson

All books in the series are available from our evening orderline 01952 255669 - ⬤ 𝘝𝘐𝘚𝘈 Fax:- 07070 660418
From January 1999 payments to British Bus Publishing may be made in Euro or British Pounds

ISBN 1 897990 72 3

Published by British Bus Publishing Ltd
The Vyne, 16 St Margarets Drive, Wellington,
Telford, Shropshire, TF1 3PH

Contents

ARRIVA plc

In August 1996 the Cowie Group completed the acquisition of British Bus plc and at a stroke became the second largest bus operating group in the United Kingdom, the move led to the reclassification of the enlarged group from being a motor trader to the Transport classification.

This introduction will chart the evolution of the elements of the grouping under their different historical strands which in itself will shed some light on the different trading names and types of vehicles to be found in the fleet. Full historical details will for the most case be found elsewhere in other published material reference to which is recommended for the serious student of the history of the British bus industry.

In 1997 the group started a bold rebranding of all its business interests under the new trading identity of 'ARRIVA'. The group livery and identity will replace the existing versions progressively over the next 12 to 18 months and therefore this second volume is a record of the change in the trading identities of the companies within the Bus Division of the Group.

The Arriva group is different from the Stagecoach and First Groups in that it has transformed into a major player in Public Transport from a previous core business in the Motor and Finance areas. Therefore the group identity applies to more than the bus business.

Readers will see the Arriva identity on over forty dealerships in the Motor Retailing division, these offer Ford, Vauxhall, BMW, Citroen, Daihatsu, Honda, Lexus, Nissan, Peugeot, Renault, Rover, and Toyota. As an echo of the origins of the Cowie group there is a motor cycle dealership in Bristol. The Motor Retailing division also includes Arriva Vehicle Rental at nearly 60 locations some under brands such as Willhire in East Anglia and U-Drive in Kent and Surrey, Bellamour in the West Country, and Lathom in the North West, in over 20 locations the Arriva branding is used, and explains vans and minibuses that readers may have seen carrying the Arriva name.

Arriva Automotive Solutions is the new name of the former Cowie Interleasing business, very much in the news in the latter half of 1998 as there was exploration of the disposal of this business. Automotive Solutions provides vehicles on contract hire to fleet customers, over 70,000 vehicles are in the current portfolio with well known names. Associated parts of the group are Broadwood Finance which offers instalment credit- 'hire purchase' to customers of Motor Retailing, and Arriva Finance Lease which specialises in the smaller business market. Offices of Automotive Solutions are to be found in Birmingham, Slough, Sunderland and Perth. International alliances offer multinational companies the opportunity of a one stop solution in markets such as North America, Australia, Europe, Scandinavia, and the former Soviet Union.

Since the last edition of this book Arriva has made acquisitions. In the UK The Original London Sightseeing Tour Ltd was acquired in December 1997 from its previous owners London Coaches.

Latest expansions into Europe

In Europe there have been significant developments. On 6 January a 75% stake in Vancom Nederland BV was acquired and quickly rebranded as Arriva Nederland, since when the minority holding has been acquired. The Vancom business, with an American parent, had established itself as the largest private sector bus operation in Holland, having the concession to operate the urban services in Groningen. Late in 1998 this position was greatly consolidated by the acquisition of Veonn and Hanze two subsidiaries of the state owned VSN group. A policy in the Dutch transportation market of moving to competitive tender for transport operations saw the need to reduce the market share of VSN companies to encourage competition for tenders in the future. There will be other disposals during 1999. The competitive tendering will also involve loss making rural rail lines, where bidders will be invited to submit the lowest subsidy requirement, in a bid to get best value for money, a process also being reflected in Germany. Arriva was able to acquire the two northern subsidiaries of VSN, some 3 500 employees have joined the group, 750 buses, along with a further 700 minibuses, taxis, and ambulances. These are based in over 60 locations in 30 towns and cities. In addition to these activities also acquired are two maintenance companies, small minibus and ambulance body building concerns, and remarkably a small ferry operation. This makes Arriva one of the key players in transport market in the Netherlands and well placed for the introduction of tendering in future years in the Public Transport market.

A link with the past was broken when the Group Headquarters relocated in the latter part of 1998 from Hylton Road in Sunderland to new purpose built premises on the Doxford International Business Park on the outskirts of Sunderland near the A19.

The end of 1998 saw the retirement of Gordon Hodgson as Chief Executive after a long period with the Group, he was suceeded in January 1999 by Bob Davies, whose most recent appointment was as Chief Executive at East Midlands Electricity.

Now to some historical background to a group with a complex pedigree.

The Cowie name - early years

Like other large transport names Cowie started from humble beginnings. In 1931 the Cowie family started a motorcycle repair business in Sunderland. In 1934 the first sales outlet opened on what became until recently the location of the Group Head Offices. By 1942 the effects of the war saw the business coming to a halt.

After the war in 1948 the business reopened and benefited from the boom in personal mobility offered by the motorcycle. A second motorcycle shop was opened in Newcastle in 1952. Further expansion occurred in 1955 with a another branch in Newcastle, and new branches in Durham and Stockton-on-Tees.

A move into the Scottish market was taken with the acquisition of the J R Alexander motorcycle dealerships in Edinburgh and Glasgow in 1960. However there were signs that the market was moving against the motorcycle, and in favour of the motor car which was becoming a more mass market item in availability and price.

In 1962 Cowie acquired its first car dealership in Sunderland, and such was the pace of change that by 1963 Motor Car sales constituted 80% of sales. On the back of this change a public company, T Cowie plc, was formed in 1965, the same year saw two more car dealerships acquired, one in Redcar and a second in Sunderland..

In 1967 there was investment in new car showrooms for the Ford franchise in Sunderland, there has been a long association with Ford over the years. In 1971 this was strengthened with the acquisition of Ford Blackburn and another Ford dealership in Middlesbrough. By 1971 as a measure of the development of the trading interests the group turnover reached £8m per annum.

Growing on the motor business

In 1972 a new business was set up in the form of Cowie Contract Hire, this and its successors have grown to be large element of the present group.

The first exposure to the bus and coach industry came in 1980. In that year Cowie took over The George Ewer Group which had various motor interests including Eastern Tractors. It also included the long established Grey Green Coach operation with its involvement in historic operations such as East Anglian Express, the Eastlander Pool, and joint services to Scotland with Scottish Bus Group. Private Hire coaching also played a large part in the business, operating bases at Stamford Hill and Dagenham in London and also Ipswich in East Anglia were assets bought with the business.

In 984 Cowie acquired the Hanger Group which brought Ford dealerships in Nottingham and Birmingham, and significantly, Interleasing, the contract hire business. The pace of expansion continued in 1987 when seven main dealerships were acquired from the Heron Group. On the leasing side of the business Marley Leasing was acquired. Further growth in this area of the business came in 1991 when RoyScot Drive and Ringway Leasing were acquired adding to the prominence of this activity.

1992 was the year that Cowie very nearly took another step into the bus and coach market narrowly failing to purchase Henlys which by that time had ownership of Plaxtons. Consolation came with the addition of a Ford dealership in Swindon, a Peugeot dealership in Middlesbrough, and a Toyota dealership in Wakefield. In 1993 the Keep Trust Group was acquired, the dealership network being boosted by 70%.

Another notable event in 1993 was the retirement of Sir Tom Cowie, the Chairmanship of the business being taken up by the present Chairman Sir James McKinnon in 1994.

Explosion into Buses!

The privatisation of the newly created subsidiaries of London Buses offered the opportunity to reinforce the favourable experience of Grey Green in the London bus market. Leaside was acquired in 1994 and was renamed Cowie Leaside. Later in 1995 the previously troubled South London company was purchased becoming Cowie South London. These two acquisitions made Cowie the largest single operator in the London Buses area when taken with the existing Grey Green business.

In 1994 the FMM contract hire and fleet management business was acquired continuing the growth in that sector.

1996 was the year that pushed Cowie in to the number two slot in the UK bus industry. County Bus was purchased from the National Express Group adding to the South East presence. The acquisition of British Bus added a whole raft of bus companies across the country and very nearly brought all the disparate elements of the former London Country company under one ownership including Green Line Travel. The final acquisition of 1996 brought another previously divided company back under common ownership being North East Bus. United Auto became a bedfellow of Northumbria which was split off from it in 1986.

There was a Monopolies and Mergers Commission inquiry into the acquisition of British Bus with particular focus on the situation in London and the South East however the report did not require any disinvestment, and the market for London Buses tenders remains highly competitive.

Grey Green into Arriva London North East

A most distinguished name in coaching has transformed itself into a major operator of London bus routes. The involvement in the East Anglian Express Pool transformed itself in the mid 1980's into National Express operation before withdrawal from this sector, along with the former Eastlander pool. Great opportunities were perceived in the 1980's in commuter coaching after the deregulation of coach services under the 1980 Act and there was subsequent absorption and expansion. An area again sold on to National Express was the operation of International Services. Early day success in London Bus tendering brought Grey Green operation into to the very heart of the City, notably on route 24 . Bus operation is now very much the key to the business and is reflected in the fleet composition which now has only 20 coaches.

The company was renamed Arriva London North East, and the vehicles operate under the branding 'Arriva serving London'. A recent development has been the vacation of the historic premises at Stamford Hill.

Arriva in London- generally!

It is appropriate here to cover the renaming of the two former London Transport companies into the Arriva family. Cowie Leaside has become Arriva London North, based at Wood Green taking into the business the Edmonton operation from Arriva East Herts and Essex. The former Kentish Bus operations at Cambridge Heath and Battersea have also been incorporated into Arriva London in a tidying up exercise after the take-over of British Bus. The Leaside Travel coach and bus contract hire fleet still retains a separate livery. Arriva London South is the former Cowie South. All three companies in London trade as 'Arriva serving London'.

Arriva is without doubt the largest provider of bus services in London. It is therefore appropriate that the branding adapted for The Original London Sightseeing Tour is 'Arriva presenting London'.

1999 will see the remainder of 89 low floor DAF Alexander double decks enter service, 20 being on the road so far, the first of the type in London.

County Bus and Coach into Arriva East Herts and Essex

This company is quite recent having come into being at the beginning of 1989 to carry on the eastern operations of the former London Country North East, which in itself was one of the four parts into which London Country was divided. Operations were carried out at Harlow, Hertford and Grays. Ownership had progressed through the AJS group in 1988, the South of England Travel group in 1989, the Lynton Travel group in 1990. The company was then purchased by the West Midlands Travel holding company, and then joined the National Express Group when WMT merged into NEG. A retraction into core business led NEG to sell County to Cowie in 1996. A significant acquisition in 1989 was the bus interests of a well known operator Sampsons of Hoddesdon together with their base at Hoddesdon, this allowed the Hertford operation to be relocated. A restructuring of responsibilities saw County Bus take over the controlling supervision of Southend Transport and Colchester Transport from London and Country, this responsibility has now passed to Arriva The Shires along with overall control of Arriva East Herts and Essex. The Edmonton operation has passed to Arriva London group in a rationalisation of responsibilities within London.

The growth of British Bus plc

British Bus was the other major component of the Cowie Group's bus interests. The acquisition of British Bus brought a quantum leap in the involvement in Public Transport.

Drawlane Ltd

The privatisation of the National Bus Company followed the 1985 Transport Act with the National Bus Company becoming a vendor unit selling its subsidiaries to pre qualified and interested parties. Endless Holdings Ltd was one of those interested parties being a group of companies based in the cleaning and building management sector with a head office on Endless Street in Salisbury. The prime mover in Endless was Ray McEnhill. Endless set up a subsidiary called Drawlane Ltd to bid for NBC companies as they were made ready for sale.

The first company bought by Drawlane was Shamrock and Rambler in July 1987. This was the major part of the coaching activities of Hants and Dorset and was based at a modern depot in Bournemouth. The business was heavily dependant on National Express contracts, although an NBC style minibus operation was set up to compete in the Bournemouth area with Yellow Buses. As Shamrock and Rambler did not have an ongoing existence it is necessary to record here that the bus operations were reduced in scale, though difficulties with the National Express contracts led to notice of termination being given to Shamrock and Rambler which sealed its fate. National Express set up a local joint venture company called Dorset Travel Services Ltd to take over the workings of Shamrock and Rambler using other vehicles and based as a tenant of Yellow Buses at Mallard Road. Yellow Buses eventually purchased Dorset Travel Services. The Shamrock and Rambler vehicles were dispersed as required around the then Drawlane Group and Shamrock and Rambler was wound up..

Drawlane was then preferred bidder for three more companies: Southern National, North Devon, and London Country (South West). Each purchaser was limited to three NBC companies in the first instance. However there was concern that Drawlane might be related to another bidder called Allied Bus which had been selected as preferred bidder for another three companies: Lincolnshire Road Car, East Midland Motor Services and Midland Red North. The concern was sufficient for the preferred bidder status to be withdrawn from both and offers reinvited.

Drawlane was successful in acquiring Midland Red (North) in January 1988 and at the time of purchase had 248 vehicles and 491 employees, for more detail see below. The following month London Country (South West) Ltd was purchased with 415 vehicles and 1250 employees, though here the garages were purchased separately to Speyhawk Properties who then leased them to the bus company with varying securities of tenure, reflecting the premium value of property in London and the South East. Finally in March 1988 Drawlane acquired the 'new' North Western Road Car Company Ltd with 340 vehicles and 870 staff.

Drawlane had also bought East Lancashire Coachbuilders from the industrial conglomerate John Brown. East Lancs was based in Blackburn and had a strong customer base in the local authority sector.

Further expansion for Drawlane would now come from acquiring bus operations from other sources. ATL (Western) Ltd had purchased Crosville Motor Services from NBC in March 1988 and in early 1989 was ready to sell. Drawlane purchased the company adding a further 470 vehicles. A quick overview of the future of Crosville would be appropriate here as it disappears before the present day. In an exercise to realise value from the company the South Cheshire operations at Crewe and Etruria were transferred to Midland Red North. The Runcorn and Warrington depots were transferred to North Western, and the Macclesfield and Congleton depots were merged into Bee Line Buzz of which more later. The remaining operations at Rock Ferry and Chester were sold to PMT Ltd along with the trading name of 'Crosville' which PMT, now part of First Bus, still uses. The original Crosville Motor Services Company was renamed North British Bus Ltd, and existed for some time but did not trade as a bus company.

Midland Fox was bought from its management team in September 1989, and a minority share holding in the company from Stevensons of Uttoxeter. Bee Line Buzz operations in Manchester had been started up by BET venturing back into bus operation in the UK after selling its companies in 1968. A similar operation was started in Preston. Both were sold to Ribble's management buyout team, who in turn sold Ribble to the Stagecoach Group. As part of an exchange of assets with Stagecoach in the Manchester area Drawlane bought Bee Line Buzz from Stagecoach along with Hulme Hall Road depot in Manchester and added into the company the former Crosville operations at Macclesfield and Congleton. Bee Line had an independent existence within the group until 1993 when its operations were merged into North Western, with Macclesfield depot going to Midland Red North.

Drawlane in Transition

In 1991 Drawlane became a partner in a consortium with several banks setting up a company called Speedtheme Ltd, which offered to buy National Express Holdings from its management team. National Express Holdings as well as the main National Express business owned Crosville Wales Ltd and its Liverpool subsidiary Amberline Ltd, Express Travel in Perth, and Carlton PSV the Neoplan coach dealer in Rotherham. Speedtheme Ltd did not want Crosville Wales and Amberline/Express Travel and these were immediately sold to a company set up by two of the main shareholders of Drawlane, Ray McEnhill and Adam Mills, called Catchdeluxe Ltd. Whilst not part of Drawlane these two companies were under common management.

Ray McEnhill became the Chairman and Chief Executive of National Express Group and as this group prepared for its floatation on the Stock Exchange Ray McEnhill and Adam Mills severed their involvement with Drawlane. The London and Country business called Speedlink Airport Services was sold by Drawlane to National Express at this time, though Drawlane retained the Green Line Travel Company.

There was in effect a management buyout of Drawlane in the autumn of 1992 to coincide with the successful floatation of National Express and shortly thereafter Drawlane was renamed British Bus plc. (British Bus Ltd had been a dormant subsidiary of National Express Holdings, originally set up by NBC to market the Britexpress card overseas). Shortly before this Crosville Wales had become part of the Drawlane Group as had Express Travel. Express Travel was the combined businesses of Amberline and Express Travel.

British Bus grows

There were throughout this period various smaller acquisitions by the group companies but these are dealt with in the short histories of these companies that follow. More significant acquisitions in 1993 were Southend Transport and Colchester Transport both former municipal operations. Southend had found itself fighting a bus war with Thamesway, the Badgerline subsidiary and weakened by this extended competition found itself offered for sale by its owners. A similar story applied at Colchester where Eastern National had put the municipally owned company under pressure. After acquisition the two companies were put under common management and the supervision of London and Country, a programme of rationalisation put both back onto a firm footing, though down sized.

1993 also saw North Western acquire Liverline of Liverpool, by then a 51 vehicle company, which it was to run as a separate subsidiary until 1997, North Western had also by this time absorbed the bus operations of Amberline. There was also a sale of Tellings Golden Miller back to its original owners, Tellings had been taken over by Midland Fox and come into the group, at the time of its sale it had bases both in Surrey and Cardiff. In the latter location Tellings had become the joint operator of the Trawscambria service with Crosville Cymru! That role has by 1997 passed to Rhondda Bus in which British Bus had a share holding for a while.

At the end of 1993 British Bus became the preferred bidder for the purchase of GM Buses North, however the position was overturned by the vendors and new bids invited. The outcome of this exercise was a winning bid from a employee based team which was eventually completed in the spring of 1994.

Further expansion was to be funded by expanding the capital base of the group through investment by two merchant banks who took a share of the increased equity in a new parent company British Bus Group, though operational control remained with British Bus plc.

During 1994 ownership of both East Lancs and Express Travel were transferred out of the group, though they were still associated companies. East Lancs in particular was still a preferred supplier to the group for bus bodies. The National Greenway programme was coming to an end at this point, the programme saw the stripping down and re-engineering of Leyland National shells with new Gardner or Volvo engines and gearbox and new body panels mounted on the shell framework. The stripping down and mechanical overhaul work was carried out at London and Country's Reigate garage, though later some of this work was carried out by Blackburn Transport closer to East Lancs. East Lancs then did the body work with customer options as to the front design. Notable numbers were carried out for both Group companies and others. Large orders for new Dennis Darts were by then possible and made inroads into the Leyland National fleets.

Luton, Derby ,and Clydeside

In July 1994 British Bus acquired Luton and District Transport from its employees, by this time it also included the former London Country Bus North West and the Stevenage operations of Sovereign Bus. This meant that a sizeable part of the former London Country company was now in common ownership. Luton and District had also assisted other employee buyouts such as Derby City Transport where as a result it had a 25% share holding, and Clydeside 2000 plc, where there was a 19% share holding. A third company, Lincoln City Transport had not met with success and the employees had agreed to a sale to Yorkshire Traction owned Lincolnshire Road Car Ltd before the British Bus take-over. In both companies the shareholders voted to accept offers from British Bus for the balance of the shares and they became fully owned members of the British Bus group.

At the same time there were discussions about the acquisition of Stevensons of Uttoxeter. Stevensons had grown dramatically after deregulation and operated well away from its traditional area, a strong expansion in the West Midlands was initially successful. however West Midlands Travel responded to the competition and through its Your Bus acquisition started up operations in Burton on Trent which was by then the heartland of Stevensons. A long struggle looked in prospect and a sale to British Bus was agreed. There was a scaling down of operations in the West Midlands and surplus vehicles were distributed around the group. After this process was complete the geographically separated Macclesfield depot of Midland Red North was transferred to Stevensons control in January 1995.

Proudmutual and Caldaire Holdings

The summer of 1994 was a busy time as the Proudmutual group was acquired. Proudmutual had been the management buyout vehicle for the management team of Northumbria Motor Services to buy their business from NBC, it also had acquired some smaller businesses in the North East including Moordale. Proudmutual had also bought Kentish Bus, the former London Country South East from NBC in March 1988. There was considerable success in the London Transport tendering process and further LT work was added when the LT contracts of Boro'line were purchased in February 1992. The Proudmutual acquisition thus gave British Bus a very strong position in LT tendering when the activities of London and Country and the LDT group were taken into account. It also brought another part of the former London and Country into common ownership.

The privatisation of the London Transport Bus companies brought no success for British Bus, but as we have seen earlier the Cowie Group was successful in acquiring two of the subsidiaries.

In March of 1995 the Caldaire group was acquired. Caldaire was the buyout vehicle with which the management of West Riding Group had purchased their business from NBC in January 1987, in the December of that year they also bought United Auto from NBC. However a demerger later on saw the United business being separated off again into North East Bus. The long established independent South Yorkshire Road Transport was acquired and formed one of the trading identities of the Caldaire Group, the others being, West Riding, Yorkshire Woollen, and Selby and District. After acquisition the group of companies was renamed Yorkshire Bus Group by British Bus.

In April 1995 what turned out to be the last major acquisition by British Bus was made. Maidstone and District had been one of the earliest of NBC sales in late 1986 , it purchased New Enterprise of Tonbridge in 1988, and the remaining vehicles and the premises of Maidstone Boro'line in 1992. The head office of the company was moved to Maidstone and the company was put under common management with Kentish Bus and Londonlinks as the Invictaway Group under British Bus ownership.

Floatation or Trade Sale?

Throughout 1995 preparations for floatation had been underway with the appointment of advisors, however in the summer of 1995 these plans were thrown off course by reports of alleged irregularities involving support from the Bank of Boston for British Bus at an earlier point in the group's history. The timing of these allegations made postponing of the floatation a necessary move. The alternative route for shareholders and the investing banks to realise their investment was a trade sale of the group. There were discussions with various interested parties.

The group was in the meantime looking to expand its interests into other modes of transport as the opportunities in the bus industry were becoming scarce due to the growth of the major players. The subsequent sales of the two former GM Buses companies by their employee owners and that of Strathclyde Buses were opportunities for growth, but British Bus was not successful.

British Bus had become a partner in the Eurotrans consortium which had been selected as the preferred bidder for the South Leeds Supertram Project which was being promoted by West Yorkshire PTE. This was a PFI project where bidders were fighting for the concession to Design, Build, Operate, and Maintain the tramway for a period of thirty years. The Eurotrans consortium included big construction companies such as Taylor Woodrow, Morrison Construction, and Christiani and Neilsen, the tram supplier was Vevey Technologies of Switzerland, now part of the Bombardier Group. The intention is that Arriva Yorkshire would set up a tram operating subsidiary to operate the tramway for the concession life on behalf of Eurotrans. The project is presently stalled waiting for UK Government funding commitment, though remains a key part of West Yorkshire PTE's public transport plans. Other similar activities included involvement in a bidding consortium for the Croydon Tramlink project, and the Manchester Metrolink Concession again as Eurotrans.

British Bus was also active in the process of Franchising of the Train Operating Companies by OPRAF though none of these bids were successful, however the exposure to the process paid off in arranging through ticketing deals with the successful bidders later on.

In June 1996 the Cowie Group made an offer to acquire British Bus, though not East Lancs or Express Travel which had been owned outside the group for some time. There was an Monopolies and Mergers Commission investigation into the take-over in view of the concentration of operation in London and the South East in the combined business. However in due course this investigation made no recommendation about disinvestment recognising the considerable presence of the other groups in the area. The acquisition by Cowie was completed in August 1996

Developments since 1996

The enlarged Cowie group became the second largest bus operating group in the UK, ahead of Stagecoach and behind First Bus. The position was consolidated by the acquisition of North East Bus also in August 1996. This was the United Auto, and Teeside Motor Services which after the separation from the Caldaire group had been sold to West Midlands Travel. West Midlands Travel itself had then merged with the National Express Group and it was from this source that North East Bus had been bought, as had County Bus earlier.

The Hughes-DAF bus and coach dealership, acquired earlier in Cowie's growth became responsible for the ordering of new vehicles and an immediate influx of ex-stock vehicles helped the fleet replacement programme of some fleets.

In 1996 British Bus formed a consortium with Cegelec-AEG and Adtranz to bid for the Merseyside Rapid Transit project being promoted by Merseytravel the PTE serving Merseyside. Adtranz withdrew when the technology selection favoured an electronically guided trolleybus rather than a tramway solution. The consortium, Transform, was selected in 1997 as the development partner with Merseytravel to develop the project and to obtain the Transport and Works Act Powers and to obtain both the Private Sector and Public Sector funding for the project. Here too the intention is that the local subsidiary Arriva North West will operate the system on behalf of the consortium for the proposed twenty year concession period. The vehicles proposed are a virtually 100% low floor articulated trolley bus with an auxiliary diesel generator set allowing mobility away from the overhead cables, the final drive will be electric traction motors. The external styling will be more like a tram than a bus. They will be the most sophisticated buses in the UK on entering service at the turn of the century. Cegelec AEG has now become part of Alstom one of the largest rolling stock and electrical equipment supply groups in the world. An interesting historical note is that when NBC created North Western Road Car, now Arriva North West, in the mid 1980's it renamed The Mexborough and Swinton Traction Company a statutory company dormant since 1969, but notably a trolley bus operating subsidiary of BET which had abandoned its trolley buses in March 1961.

Unibus into Arriva Dansk

1997 also saw the acquisition of the first overseas subsidiary in Denmark. Unibus with its Head Office in Hvidovre in the southern suburbs of Copenhagen is a operator of 212 vehicles, employing some 375 employees. Founded in 1985 Unibus has grown by winning tendered bus operation for the Transport Authority for Copenhagen - HT. Unibus was the biggest coach operator in Copenhagen until in 1995 the coaching business was sold to Lyngby Turistfart. Unibus vehicles are painted in a livery of depending upon which contracts they are operating, for example yellow in Copenhagen, and carry the company fleet name on the cove panels or on the side. 40 vehicles are operated on demand responsive services for the disabled and elderly in the Copenhagen area. Eight vehicles are operated on the Copenhagen Airport service. Other operations are in Jutland around Silkeborg, and Falster- one of the islands to the south of Zealand, near Nykobing.

The former British Bus headquarters at Salisbury which dated back to Drawlane days was wound down and closed at the end of 1996, with the group administration being moved to Sunderland. The present Head Office of the Bus Division of the group is to be found at Leicester sharing the Head Office of Arriva Fox County in the Pickerings premises which also now accommodates a depot of Arriva Fox County.

There follows now a brief history of each of the trading companies in the group except those which have been covered in the narrative above. This will cover the smaller acquisitions and developments which the reader will find reflected in the fleet lists which follow.

Clydeside Buses Ltd into Arriva Scotland West Ltd

Clydeside Buses and its predecessors, has been serving its core area of Renfrewshire and Inverclyde since 1928. Prior to 1985 the operation had formed the northern section of Western Scottish part of the Scottish Bus Group (SBG). In preparation for the deregulation of local bus services Clydeside Scottish assumed the responsibility for the Glasgow, Renfrewshire and Inverclyde operations of Western Scottish in 1985. Over the next 6 years there were a complex series of reorganisations between Clydeside and Western, until in 1991 Clydeside became the last SBG subsidiary to be privatised when it was purchased by its employees with assistance from Luton and District Transport Group, emerging as Clydeside 2000 plc.

After 1986 there were numerous competitors in the core area and trading proved extremely difficult. When the LDT group sold to British Bus there was an offer put to the shareholders of Clydeside which was accepted and Clydeside joined British Bus. There was immediate effort to update the fleet against a background of tightening up of enforcement generally in the area. Some of the competitive battles had led to the Traffic Commissioner taking steps to control the number of departures and waiting times in certain town centres.

The development of services has seen Flagship Routes introduced to raise quality levels. Additionally opportunity has been taken to acquire various smaller operators in the area. Ashton Coaches of Greenock, and a significant share in Dart Buses of Paisley. operations from the Greenock base were restyled as GMS-Greenock Motor Services with a separate livery. Also in 1997 McGills Bus Service Ltd of Barrhead was acquired by the group and at present has been kept as a separate entity from Clydeside Buses. Clydeside also acquired Bridge Coaches of Paisley, being fully absorbed into Clydeside.

The Arriva serving Scotland branding will cover all operations including those of GMS and McGills with route branding applied appropriately. The Glasgow Airlink Service will remain in a special livery. May 1999 should see the delivery of 6 Super Low Floor vehicles with LPG power to upgrade the Airport Service.

Crosville Cymru into Arriva Cymru

Crosville Wales Ltd was until August 1986 the Welsh and Shropshire operations of Crosville Motor Services Ltd based in Chester. In 1986 it was resolved that the Crosville company was too large to be offered for privatisation as a whole. Therefore the then dormant Devon General Omnibus and Touring Company Ltd was revived by NBC in order to take over the assets and business of Crosville in Wales to be renamed Crosville Wales. The management team of Crosville Wales purchased the company from NBC in December 1987.

In January 1989 the company was bought by National Express Holdings Ltd, in July of that year it purchased a subsidiary company called Amberline based at Speke in Liverpool and added a bus operation to the mainly National Express coach contracts operated.

In July 1991 the National Express group was purchased by a consortium of banks led by Drawlane as explained above. Ultimately this led to Crosville Wales becoming a full member of the Drawlane Group shortly before its transformation into British Bus plc. In January 1992 the Oswestry depot and its outstation at Abermule had been sold to Midland Red North.

Crosville Wales has taken advantage of second hand vehicles from other group companies and other operators, its fleets of Leyland Lynxes and National 2's being so acquired, whilst at the same time buying further new Mercedes minibuses. New full size vehicles have also started to appear.

In 1995 some of the services, but no vehicles, of Alpine Travel were acquired leading to an operation of certain services as Alpine Bus in a red and white livery. This was superseded by a Shoreline livery of Blue, White and Yellow, which will be phased out and replaced by route branding.

All operations are branded 'Arriva serving Wales/gwansanaethu Cymru', these include the two acquisitions in 1998.

The first was Devaway of Broughton Mills Road, Bretton, Chester. This brought a mixed fleet of VRT's, Nationals, and more Lynxes. An additional operation added to Chester depot is the Wrexham Road Park and Ride service, this will be operated by 4 LPG powered low floor buses in a special livery when delivered in March 1999, until then three Dennis Darts have been diverted from Arriva North East. The second acquisition was Purple Motors of Bethesda, which has now become an outstation of Bangor depot. Further low floor buses are expected in 1999 to provide the Arriva share of a Quality Partnership Corridor on Deeside jointly provided with First Crosville.

Kentish Bus part of Arriva Southern Counties

Though shown as a separate fleet Kentish Bus was part of the Invictaway group of companies. Its size reduced by the transfer of operations at Battersea, the Routemasters, to South London. The operations at Cambridge Heath were transferred to Leaside.

Kentish Bus started its existence as London Country South East on the division of London Country Bus Services in 1986. It had its Head Office at Northfleet and in April 1987 was relaunched as Kentish Bus and Coach Ltd with a new livery.

In March 1988 Kentish Bus was sold to Proudmutual on privatisation. There was considerable expansion into the LT tender market with new buses being added many with North East originating registration indexes. In February 1992 there was further expansion in this area when Kentish acquired the LT tendered work of the troubled Maidstone Boro'line operation, some 57 vehicles, many of which are still current.

After the acquisition of the Proudmutual group by British Bus in 1994 Kentish Bus and Londonlinks were jointly managed from Northfleet, however on the acquisition of Maidstone and District the management was relocated to Maidstone, Armstrong Road under the Invictaway grouping. The balance of the operation continued to be controlled from Maidstone after the reallocation of the two London depots to South London and Leaside.

Kentish Bus was notable in the 1990's for winning the best bus route competition organised by the London Transport Passengers Committee.

The Arriva identity has been applied as 'Arriva serving Kent Thameside' to the operations at Dartford and Northfleet.

London and Country into Arriva Surrey and West Sussex

London and Country Ltd was formerly London Country South West Ltd ,one of the four parts that London Country Bus Services Ltd was divided into in advance of the privatisation of NBC. The former head office of LCBS at Reigate became that of L&C. The company was bought by Drawlane as outlined above in February 1988, though the properties were to be leased having been sold separately. The company was relaunched with a new livery and trading name in April 1989.

London and Country was successful in winning LT tenders and this led to the addition of new vehicles and the high profile opening of an impressive new garage at Beddington Farm in Croydon.

In 1990 the Woking , Guildford, and Cranleigh operations of the former Alder Valley were purchased, and whilst kept as a separate company- Guildford and West Surrey, were put under the same management as L & C. Also in 1990 a separate company was established called Horsham Buses for operations in the Horsham area.

Spare capacity at the Reigate garage allowed the development of the National Greenway concept in conjunction with East Lancs and many vehicles were dealt with at Reigate. Briefly L & C had two subsidiaries in Dorset, Stanbridge and Crichel and Oakfield Travel, both of these were later sold to Damory Coaches. Another subsidiary until recently sold to its management was Linkline Coaches of Harlesden in London which specialised in coaching and corporate work.

1993 saw the acquisition of Southend Transport and Colchester Transport with many L & C influences, but these have now been transferred to the supervision of County Bus which is closer.

The Croydon based operations and other LT tender operations at Walworth had been transferred into a new company called Londonlinks. This was in 1995 put under common management as Kentish Bus and Maidstone and District as part of the Invictaway Group, however the reallocation of responsibilities in the enlarged group saw Londonlinks return to L&C control.

A consequence of the property sales was the vacation of Reigate garage and its replacement by a facility at Merstham, this left the Head Office remote from operation and in 1997 this closed and the functions moved to other premises including Crawley garage.

The three companies were renamed as Arriva Croydon and North Surrey, Arriva West Sussex, and Arriva Guildford and West Surrey, however the trading identity is 'Arriva serving Surrey and West Sussex. In August 1998 the Countryliner coaching operation was sold to its manager.

In 1999 the fleet will be augmented by two further SLF Dennis Darts for the expansion of the Guildford Park and Ride service for which there is a special livery. Many of the existing double deck fleet will be replaced by refurbished Metrobuses from the Arriva London fleets.

Maidstone and District becomes Arriva Southern Counties

This is the original Maidstone and District Motor Services Ltd founded in 1911, though in NBC days it did share common management with East Kent from 1972 to 1983. In 1983 the Hastings and Rye area services were hived off as Hastings and District.

Maidstone and District was one of the first NBC companies to be privatised being bought by its management team in November 1986. In 1988 New Enterprise of Tonbridge was purchased and until recently kept as a separate entity. In June 1992 the remaining operations of Maidstone Boro'line and the premises at Armstrong Road were purchased.

In April 1995 the company was sold to British Bus, that November the hitherto Head Office at Chatham was closed and control moved to the former Maidstone Boro'line premises at Maidstone under the Invictaway banner.

Under British Bus/Cowie control the group acquired a number of additional operators including Mercury Passenger Services of Hoo, Wealden Beeline of Five Oak Green, and the Grey Green (Medway) bus operations. In May of 1997 the Green Line operations at Northfleet and Gravesend were sold to the Pullman Group (London Coaches). In the first part of 1997 103 new vehicles were introduced into Kentish Bus and Maidstone and District, an investment of £8.3m.

The Arriva branding has seen three identities introduced, 'Arriva serving the Medway Towns', 'Arriva serving Kent and East Sussex' , and 'Arriva serving Maidstone'. Exceptions to the standard livery are Route 151 branding, and the Maidstone Park and Ride services.

Midland Red North & Stevensons becomes Arriva Midlands North

Midland Red North Ltd was founded in 1981 when the Midland Red company was divided into four operating parts by NBC. The company traded with local network names for a considerable time such as Chaserider, these were based upon the networks generated from the Viable Network Project later carried out across NBC as Market Analysis Project (MAP).

The company was sold to Drawlane in January 1988 after a false start as described earlier. In 1989 it took over the Crewe and Etruria depots of fellow Drawlane subsidiary Crosville Motor Services Ltd. In 1992 Midland Red North purchased the Oswestry and Abermule operations of Crosville Wales Ltd then an associated company. In 1993 with the dispersion of the Bee Line Buzz Company the Macclesfield depot of that company which had traded as C-Line was taken over, having been part of Crosville for some time in earlier years.

Stevensons of Uttoxeter commenced services in that part of Staffordshire in 1926, and continued as a small but successful family owned business. During the 1980's, and particularly after deregulation, significant growth occurred. In 1985 a controlling interest was acquired in the East

Staffordshire Borough Council's bus operations in Burton-on-Trent. in 1987 the Swadlincote depot of Midland Fox was purchased from NBC.

Growth in the West Midlands and the acquisition of a number of small companies including Crystal Coaches in Burslem and Viking Tours and Travel saw the company become a major independent operator in the early 1990's.

In April 1994, however, West Midlands Travel through its Your Bus subsidiary decided to retaliate in the Burton area against the significant level of operation Stevensons then had in the West Midlands area , this led to the sale of the company to British Bus in August 1994. There followed a significant scaling down of Stevensons operations in the West Midlands.

Macclesfield depot was transferred into Stevensons in January 1995 from Midland Red North. From April 1995, Midland Red and Stevensons have been jointly managed and the closure of the Stevensons Head Office at Spath with the provision of central administration services from the Cannock head office became effective in 1996. A common livery was established between the two fleets though the Stevensons fleet name was retained on vehicles allocated to Stevensons depots. Viking coaches retained a separate two shades of grey livery.

The application of Arriva livery and branding sees the trading identity 'Arriva serving the North Midlands applied to all buses. There are 13 buses carrying the Shrewsbury Park and Ride livery of blue and yellow, two dual purpose vehicles are branded, one each for the X5 Telford to Shrewsbury and the X38 Derby to Burton..

In May 1998 the Shifnal depot of Timeline was acquired with 19 vehicles. The bus operations of Matthews Handybus in the Newcastle under Lyme area were acquired in February 1998, but no buses were involved. In August of the same year the local bus operations of Williamsons of Knockin Heath were taken over and four vehicles came with the work.

1999 will see many SLF Dennis Darts arrive, current plans are for 1 SPD, 12 8.5m variants, and 38 10.6m variants.

Midland Fox turns into Arriva Fox County Ltd

Midland Red East Ltd was formed in 1981 to take over the Leicestershire operations of Midland Red. In 1984 the company name was changed to Midland Fox Ltd , and there was a major relaunch of the company with a new livery and fox logo. There was also the launch of a new minibus network in Leicester under the Fox Cub brand.

In 1987 the company was bought from NBC by its management with the help of the directors of Stevensons of Uttoxeter who also separately bought the Swadlincote depot.

Several smaller operators were taken over, these have included Wreake Valley of Thurmaston, Fairtax of Melton Mowbray, Astill & Jordan of Ratby, Shelton Orsborn of Wollaston, Blands of Stamford, and Loughborough Coach and Bus.

In 1989 Midland Fox was acquired by Drawlane. In 1990 Midland Fox acquired Tellings Golden Miller in Byfleet which in turn acquired the Coach Travel Centre in Cardiff amongst others. Tellings bus operations eventually became part of London and Country, whilst Tellings was sold back to its management in 1994 before expansion into bus operation in Cardiff.

In 1994 Pickerings Transport was purchased by British Bus. Pickerings build lorry bodies at their extensive site at Thurmaston, and also offered body repair and painting services which sees many group vehicles appearing there.

In September 1994 Midland Fox launched a new taxi service in Leicester marketed as Fox Cabs. 1996 saw a launch of high quality services under the Urban Fox brand in a striking new blue livery.

Derby City Transport Ltd was the long established municipally owned bus company. In August 1989 it was sold to its employees who were assisted by Luton and District Transport. Luton and District took a 25% share holding in the business. There was a competitive interlude in Derby where Midland Red North started operations, but this ended with Derby buying out the competition in February 1990. Derby also assisted in the employee purchase of Lincoln City Transport taking a share of that company, this was realised when Lincoln was sold to the Yorkshire Traction group.

In 1990 "75" Taxis started as a division of Derby City Transport building up a fleet of London style taxis.

In 1994 after the acquisition of Luton and District by British Bus, the shareholders in Derby decided to accept an offer from British Bus for the rest of the share capital of the company. After a period of autonomy the business was relaunched under the City Rider brand name and a yellow red and blue livery. In January 1996 Derby City Transport was incorporated into the Midland Fox group.

In September 1996 the Head Office of Midland Fox moved to the Pickerings of Thurmaston premises along with a depot facility. It was later joined by the British Bus head office, now Arriva Passenger Services Ltd.

The Arriva branding has vehicles carrying the 'Arriva serving the Fox County', or 'Arriva serving Derby' identities as appropriate. The taxi businesses remain under their previous brands. Special liveries include 4 vehicles in Quick Silver Shuttle for Leicester Park and Ride, Airport Car Park Shuttle and Airport Rail Link 3 vehicles in a blue livery for East Midland Airport, 2 vehicles in a Corby to Kettering Rail Link for Midland Main Line, and Marks and Spencer Shuttle 2 vehicles in a green livery. One vehicle is cosponsored by Trent, Virgin, Central Trains and Midland Main Line, a very unique livery.

Northumbria Motor Services Ltd into Arriva Northumbria

In 1986 the operations of United Auto were split into two parts in preparation for privatisation. The dormant Southern National Omnibus Company Ltd was renamed Northumbria and took over operations in September 1986 with a new head office in Jesmond.

In October 1987 Northumbria was acquired from NBC by its management using Proudmutual as a holding company, that holding company also acquired Kentish Bus in March 1988. Other acquisitions included Moordale Coaches, and Hunters.

In 1994 the Proudmutual group was acquired by British Bus, at the same time Moordale Coaches was sold back to former directors.

In the Arriva era two trading identities are used 'Arriva serving Northumbria' and 'Arriva serving the North East' are used. This reflects a process of merging the management control of the two North East subsidiaries a process that will continue into 1999. There has been significant investment in low floor vehicles with the latest batch of 15 low floor DAF SB220's going into Newcastle.

North Western Road Car Company Ltd becomes Arriva North West

Ribble Motor Services was another NBC company that was to be divided in preparation for privatisation. The dormant Mexborough and Swinton Traction Company was renamed as above to take over the Merseyside, West Lancashire, and Wigan operations of Ribble in September 1986. The head office of the new company was at Bootle in Liverpool.

The company was acquired by Drawlane in March 1988. In 1989 the Runcorn and Warrington depots of Crosville were acquired. Expansion saw North Western open a depot in Altrincham, though eventually rationalisation saw the operations assumed by the Bee Line Buzz Company during its independent existence as a Drawlane subsidiary.

In 1993 Bee Line was put under the same management as North Western, also in 1993 Liverline of Bootle was acquired with 51 vehicles. Both have been maintained as separate identities. Also acquired in 1993 were the bus operations of Express Travel which were still branded as Amberline, this identity was not maintained.

The head office of the company was moved to Aintree depot, though a subsequent move saw the depot sold and redeveloped leaving the head office building free standing.

1995 was a busy year with two operations in Wigan area acquired, Little White Bus, and Wigan Bus Company. Also acquired in 1995 was Arrowline Travel based in Knutsford, but trading as Star Line, this brought luxury coaches on Airport related work as well as a modern fleet of mini and midi buses. The Star Line operations have since been relocated to Wythenshaw, and the coaching operations sold to Selwyns.

Increase in activity in the Warrington area saw a new depot being established at Haydock to supplement existing facilities. The collapse of a Cheshire operator Lofty's of Mickle Trafford saw further growth in the mid Cheshire area taking vehicles as far south as Whitchurch.

1997 has seen the acquisition by the group of the residue of South Lancs Transport following that operators withdrawal from Chester, the business being under the supervision of North Western. Quality and low floor initiatives are being developed with both Merseytravel and GMPTE, and as explained earlier there is involvement in the development of the Merseyside Rapid Transit project. Considerable investment has seen many new buses, with low floor buses being introduced on the Skyline service based on Manchester International Airport, and on the Liverpool to St Helens route.

In 1998 some bus operations of Timeline in the North West were purchased along with some vehicles, though the majority went to First Group. Arriva North West manages the bus and coach facilities at the new Trafford Centre on behalf of the owners of this striking shopping centre.

In 1999 Arriva North West are set to become the operator of the SMART bus services put out to tender by Merseytravel, the 11 substantive low floor vehicles for the contract are due in May 1999.

The Arriva branding sees one identity used, 'Arriva serving the North West'.

The Shires becomes Arriva the Shires Ltd

In 1986 United Counties Omnibus Company Ltd was divided into three parts, the southernmost of these was Luton and District Transport Ltd which took over operations in Aylesbury , Hitchin, and Luton. The new head office of the company was in Luton.

In August 1987 Luton and District became the first employee owned bus operator in the UK when its employees bought it from NBC. In the period from January 1988 to October 1990, LDT expanded the size and the area of its operations by a number of strategic acquisitions. The assets and business of Red Rover Omnibus Ltd, operating bus services from a depot in Aylesbury, were acquired in January 1988. In June 1988 Milton Keynes Coaches was acquired, and in May 1990 two thirds of the bus services operated in the Stevenage area by Sovereign Bus Ltd.

In October 1990 LDT acquired London Country North West Ltd. LCNW operated a vehicle fleet of a similar size to LDT from a head office and depot in Watford and other depots in Hemel Hempstead, High Wycombe, Amersham, and Slough

LDT assisted in the employee buyouts of two other companies and acquired a share holding in both, Derby City Transport in 1989, and Clydeside 2000 plc in 1991.

In July 1994 LDT became part of British Bus . In October 1994 the bus operations of Stuart Palmer Travel based in Dunstable was taken over, followed in May 1995 by Buffalo Travel of Flitwick and Motts Travel of Aylesbury in July 1995.

April 1995 saw the launch of a brand new blue and yellow company livery with local trading names. The legal name was changed to LDT Ltd in May and the corporate operating name became The Shires.

In late 1997 Lucketts Garages (Watford) Ltd was acquired. in addition to local bus services in Watford there are substantial dial-a-ride operations and a commercial workshop.

1998 saw the acquisition of Lutonian Buses in March, since that time there has been a ruling that the business should be sold under Competition regulations, however this is to be challenged by the Group.

The Arriva branding sees vehicles carrying 'Arriva serving the Shires', except at Garston garage which carries 'Arriva serving Watford'. Management responsibility for Arriva Southend ('Arriva serving Southend'), Arriva Colchester ('Arriva serving Colchester'), and Arriva East Herts & Essex ('Arriva serving East Herts and Essex') now falls to Arriva the Shires Ltd. 1999 will see the 321 route converted to LPG vehicles with some 7 new DAF's due.

United,Tees and District,and Teeside Motor Services Ltd becomes Arriva North East

United Automobile Services Ltd was another NBC subsidiary which was to be divided up in preparation for privatisation. Here in 1986 the northern part of the operating area was hived off into a new company called Northumbria. United continued to trade south of the Tyne with its head office in Darlington. the operations in Scarborough and Pickering were transferred into a subsidiary of East Yorkshire Motor Services.

In December 1987 United was bought from NBC by Caldaire Holdings the management buyout vehicle of the West Riding management team. In 1989 the National Express coaching activities of United were sold off to a joint venture company Durham Travel Services, set up by two ex-United managers with National Express Ltd.

In 1990 United was split into two parts, the Durham and North Yorkshire section continuing to trade as United, the section in Cleveland trading as Tees and District. At this time the associated businesses of Trimdon Motor Services and Teeside Motor Services were acquired , with the Trimdon business being absorbed into United and the Teeside business continuing.

In the summer of 1992 there was a demerger of the Caldaire Group with the North East operations passing to the Westcourt Group, with Caldaire North East becoming North East Bus.

In 1994 a new head office and engineering works in Morton Road, Darlington allowed the vacation of the Grange Road site for redevelopment. Also in 1994 the Westcourt Group sold to West Midlands Travel in the November, this led to North East Bus being part of the National Express Group following the merger with that group in 1995.

Eden Bus Services of Bishop Auckland was acquired in October 1995.

National Express Group sold North East Bus to the Cowie Group on the last day of July 1996, later in October the Ripon depot operations were sold to Harrogate and District Travel.

Yorkshire Bus Group to Arriva Yorkshire

The West Riding Automobile Company and Yorkshire Woollen District Transport were put under common management by NBC. Therefore when privatisation happened in January 1987 the management team bought both companies. Selby and District was a trading title turned into a separate company by the new owners' Caldaire Holding company. Whilst Caldaire became involved in the North East the core business in West Yorkshire changed very little with there being steady investment in fleet replacement and upgrade.

There was involvement in the splitting up of National Travel East leaving a residue of operations on National Express contracts, and also competitive operations in Sheffield that led to corresponding competition in Wakefield.

One acquisition was the South Yorkshire Road Transport Company of Pontefract which was maintained as a separate trading identity. In March 1995 Caldaire Group was acquired by British Bus.

The single deck fleet is particularly modern with a batch of thirty Dennis Dart SLF's delivered in 1997 for Dewsbury displacing the last of the Leyland National 2's to other group companies. The double deck fleet is composed entirely Olympians and the oldest of these are now being cascaded to other group companies.

The Arriva identities used are 'Arriva serving Yorkshire' and 'Arriva serving Selby' seeing a merging together of the West Riding and Yorkshire identities for the first time. 1999 will see the delivery of 18 DAF Optare Spectra Double decks, the chassis sourced from Arriva Bus and Coach at Cleckheaton and the bodies from Crossgates in Leeds, unfortunately Eindhoven is not yet in Yorkshire! Arriva Yorkshire is also partnering with First Leeds in the next extension to the East Leeds Guided Bus Corridor along the A64 York Road, this initiative sees both operators together contributing nearly half the scheme cost of around £9.9m with the other half coming from a partnership of Leeds City Council and West Yorkshire PTE. The opening of the scheme during 2000 will see Arriva supplying new vehicles fitted with guide wheels.

Arriva behind the scenes

The new group identity has seen common elements appearing such as group standards for publicity material, group ticket designs, new uniforms for staff, and local editions of a staff newspaper for the Passenger Services companies. NVQ training schemes for drivers and engineers have made the news in all local areas. The purchasing muscle of the group has led to the adoption of low sulphur 'clean' diesel in most companies, the vehicle purchases have led to cascading of vehicles between companies. A standard vehicle specification has been developed that together with the livery will assist in relocation of vehicles. There will still be vehicles in the former liveries for some time though the stated investment plans for the next two years will see around 500 new vehicles a year.

ARRIVA SCOTLAND WEST

Arriva Scotland West Ltd, The Gatehouse, Porterfield Road, Renfrew, PA4 8JB

ARRIVA serving west Scotland

197	H708UNW	Optare MetroRider MR09	Optare		B23F	1991	Yorkshire Bus (WR), 1997
198	H705UNW	Optare MetroRider MR09	Optare		B23F	1991	Yorkshire Bus (WR), 1997
199	H709UNW	Optare MetroRider MR09	Optare		B23F	1991	Yorkshire Bus (WR), 1997
200	H711UNW	Optare MetroRider MR09	Optare		B23F	1991	Yorkshire Bus (WR), 1997

201-208		Optare MetroRider MR17	Optare		B29F	1996	
201	N201NHS	**203**	N203NHS	**205**	N205NHS	**207** N207NHS	**208** N208NHS
202	N202NHS	**204**	N204NHS	**206**	N206NHS		

209-216		Optare MetroRider MR09	Optare		B23F	1991	Yorkshire Bus (WR), 1997
209	H706UNW	**211**	H713UNW	**213**	H702UNW	**215** H701UNW	**216** H710UNW
210	H712UNW	**212**	H704UNW	**214**	H703UNW		

217-227		Optare MetroRider MR17	Optare		B29F	1996	
217	P217SGB	**219**	P219SGB	**221**	P221SGB	**224** P224SGB	**226** P226SGB
218	P218SGB	**220**	P220SGB	**223**	P223SGB	**225** P225SGB	**227** P227SGB

228	M883DDS	Mercedes-Benz 811D	WS Wessex II	B33F	1994	Ashton Group, Greenock, 1997
229	M95EGE	Mercedes-Benz 709D	WS Wessex II	B33F	1995	Ashton Group, Greenock, 1997
230	M799EUS	Mercedes-Benz 811D	WS Wessex II	B33F	1995	Ashton Group, Greenock, 1997

The availability of Mercedes-Benz' uprated van range for PCV applications allows convertors to design their coachwork. Alexander's offering, the ALX100, replaces their Sprinter model. Scotland West's 341, R341KGG, shows off the design.
Murdoch Currie

Scotland West has become a last stronghold for L608Ds within the Arriva group gathering further examples from The Shires and Cymru in 1998. An earlier arrival from Midland Red North in British Bus days was 235, D205SKD which was new to North Western. *Phillip Stephenson*

231	D168VRP	Mercedes-Benz L608D	Alexander AM	B20F	1986	Crosville Cymru, 1996
232	D85VCC	Mercedes-Benz L608D	Reeve Burgess	B20F	1986	Crosville Cymru, 1998
233	D442UHC	Mercedes-Benz L608D	Alexander AM	B20F	1986	Cymru, 1998
234	D204SKD	Mercedes-Benz L608D	Reeve Burgess	BC19F	1986	Midland, 1995
235	D205SKD	Mercedes-Benz L608D	Reeve Burgess	BC19F	1986	Midland, 1995
236	D188VRP	Mercedes-Benz L608D	Alexander AM	B20F	1986	Cymru, 1998
237	K95RGA	Mercedes-Benz 709D	Dormobile Routemaker	B29F	1993	Bridge Coaches, Paisley, 1997
238	K96RGA	Mercedes-Benz 709D	Dormobile Routemaker	B29F	1993	Bridge Coaches, Paisley, 1997

239-243

		Mercedes-Benz 811D	WS Wessex II	B33F	1995	Ashton Group, Greenock, 1997
239	M278FNS	240	M277FNS	241	M276FNS	242	M422GUS	243	N991KUS

244	N253PGD	Mercedes-Benz 811D	UVG CitiStar	B33F	1996	
245	N808PDS	Mercedes-Benz 811D	Marshall C16	B33F	1996	Ashton Group, Greenock, 1997
246	N806PDS	Mercedes-Benz 811D	Marshall C16	B33F	1996	Ashton Group, Greenock, 1997
247	F760VNH	Mercedes-Benz 609D	Wadham Stringer Wessex	BC21F	1989	Cowan and Hamilton, Johnstone, 1995
248	H901GNC	Mercedes-Benz 609D	Made-to-Measure	BC24F	1991	Inverclyde, Port Glasgow, 1993
249	N807PDS	Mercedes-Benz 811D	Marshall C16	B33F	1996	Ashton Group, Greenock, 1997
250	J218HDS	Mercedes-Benz 709D	Carlyle	B29F	1992	Ashton Group, Greenock, 1997
251	L51LSG	Mercedes-Benz 709D	Plaxton Beaver	B25F	1993	
252	L52LSG	Mercedes-Benz 709D	Plaxton Beaver	B25F	1993	
253	L53LSG	Mercedes-Benz 709D	Plaxton Beaver	B25F	1993	
254	L54LSG	Mercedes-Benz 709D	Plaxton Beaver	B25F	1993	

255-265

		Mercedes-Benz 711D	Plaxton Beaver	B25F	1994		
255	L860LFS	258	L863LFS	260	L865LFS	262	L867LFS	264	L869LFS
256	L861LFS	259	L864LFS	261	L866LFS	263	L868LFS	265	L870LFS
257	L862LFS								

266	N809PDS	Mercedes-Benz 811D	Marshall C16	B33F	1996	Ashton Group, Greenock, 1997
267	N81PUS	Mercedes-Benz 811D	Marshall C16	B33F	1996	Ashton Group, Greenock, 1997
268	N82PUS	Mercedes-Benz 811D	Marshall C16	B33F	1996	Ashton Group, Greenock, 1997
269	N26KYS	Mercedes-Benz 811D	Plaxton Beaver	B33F	1995	Ashton Group, Greenock, 1997
270	N27KYS	Mercedes-Benz 811D	Plaxton Beaver	B33F	1995	Ashton Group, Greenock, 1997
271	P932YSB	Mercedes-Benz 811D	Mellor	B33F	1997	Ashton Group, Greenock, 1997
272	P936YSB	Mercedes-Benz 811D	Mellor	B33F	1997	Ashton Group, Greenock, 1997
273	P937YSB	Mercedes-Benz 811D	Mellor	B33F	1997	Ashton Group, Greenock, 1997
274	P491TGA	Mercedes-Benz 711D	UVG CitiStar	B29F	1996	Ashton Group, Greenock, 1997
275	P490TGA	Mercedes-Benz 711D	UVG CitiStar	B29F	1996	Ashton Group, Greenock, 1997
276	P492TGA	Mercedes-Benz 711D	UVG CitiStar	B29F	1996	Ashton Group, Greenock, 1997
277	P527UGA	Mercedes-Benz 711D	Marshall C19	B29F	1996	Ashton Group, Greenock, 1997
278	P526UGA	Mercedes-Benz 711D	Marshall C19	B29F	1996	Ashton Group, Greenock, 1997

279-283		Mercedes-Benz 709D	TBP	B29F	1995	Ashton Group, Greenock, 1997
279	M791EUS	280	M792EUS	281	M793EUS	282	M794EUS	283	M423GUS

284	N752LUS	Mercedes-Benz 709D	UVG CitiStar	B29F	1996	Ashton Group, Greenock, 1997
285	N753LUS	Mercedes-Benz 709D	UVG CitiStar	B29F	1996	Ashton Group, Greenock, 1997

286-296		Mercedes-Benz 709D	Marshall C19	B29F	1996	Ashton Group, Greenock, 1997
286	N754LUS	289	N256PGD	291	N258PGD	293	N802PDS	295	N804PDS
287	N228MUS	290	N257PGD	292	N801PDS	294	N803PDS	296	N805PDS
288	N254PGD								

297	P930YSB	Mercedes-Benz 709D	Plaxton Beaver	B29F	1997	Ashton Group, Greenock, 1997
298	P931YSB	Mercedes-Benz 709D	Plaxton Beaver	B29F	1997	Ashton Group, Greenock, 1997
299	P529UGA	Mercedes-Benz 709D	Plaxton Beaver	B29F	1997	Ashton Group, Greenock, 1997
300	P528UGA	Mercedes-Benz 709D	Plaxton Beaver	B29F	1997	Ashton Group, Greenock, 1997
301	L263VSU	Mercedes-Benz 709D	Dormobile Routemaker	B29F	1994	Ashton Group, Greenock, 1997
302	M880DDS	Mercedes-Benz 709D	WS Wessex II	B29F	1994	Ashton Group, Greenock, 1997
303	M878DDS	Mercedes-Benz 709D	WS Wessex II	B29F	1994	Ashton Group, Greenock, 1997
304	N941MGG	Mercedes-Benz 709D	Marshall C19	B29F	1995	Ashton Group, Greenock, 1997
305	N942MGG	Mercedes-Benz 709D	Marshall C19	B29F	1995	Ashton Group, Greenock, 1997
306	L970VGE	Mercedes-Benz 709D	WS Wessex II	B29F	1994	Ashton Group, Greenock, 1997
307	H183CNS	Mercedes-Benz 609D	Made-to-Measure	B26F	1991	Ashton Group, Greenock, 1997
308	H185CNS	Mercedes-Benz 609D	Made-to-Measure	B26F	1991	Ashton Group, Greenock, 1997
309	H675AGD	Mercedes-Benz 609D	Rapier	BC24F	1991	Ashton Group, Greenock, 1997
310	D202SKD	Mercedes-Benz L608D	Reeve Burgess	BC19F	1986	Midland, 1995
311	D25KKP	Mercedes-Benz L608D	Rootes	B20F	1986	Maidstone & District, 1997
312	L705AGA	Mercedes-Benz 709D	WS Wessex II	B29F	1994	
313	C707JMB	Mercedes-Benz L608D	Reeve Burgess	B20F	1986	Midland, 1995
314	C514MDS	Mercedes-Benz L608D	Reeve Burgess	B20F	1986	Midland, 1995
315	K91RGA	Mercedes-Benz 709D	Dormobile Routemaker	B25F	1993	Rowe, Muirkirk, 1995
316	K92RGA	Mercedes-Benz 709D	Dormobile Routemaker	B25F	1993	Rowe, Muirkirk, 1995
317	K945SGG	Mercedes-Benz 709D	Dormobile Routemaker	B29F	1993	
318	LAZ5962	Mercedes-Benz L608D	Rootes	B20F	1986	The Shires, 1998
319	HIL8438	Mercedes-Benz L608D	Rootes	B20F	1986	The Shires, 1998
320	D36KKP	Mercedes-Benz L608D	Rootes	B20F	1986	The Shires, 1998
321	C206EKJ	Mercedes-Benz L608D	Rootes	B20F	1986	The Shires, 1998
322	HIL8439	Mercedes-Benz L608D	Rootes	B20F	1986	The Shires, 1998
323	D206SKD	Mercedes-Benz L608D	Reeve Burgess	BC19F	1986	The Shires, 1998
324	E324WYS	Renault-Dodge S56	Alexander AM	B25F	1987	Western Scottish, 1991
325	G32OHS	Mercedes-Benz 811D	Alexander AM	B33F	1989	Westside, Gourock, 1996
326	G902MNS	Mercedes-Benz 811D	Reeve Burgess Beaver	B33F	1989	Stevensons, 1995
327	D438UHC	Mercedes-Benz L608D	Alexander AM	B20F	1986	Crosville Cymru, 1998
328	D433UHC	Mercedes-Benz L608D	Alexander AM	B20F	1986	Crosville Cymru, 1998
329	R129GNW	Mercedes-Benz O814 Vario	Alexander ALX100	B27F	1988	
330	R130GNW	Mercedes-Benz O814 Vario	Alexander ALX100	B27F	1988	
331	LAZ5785	Mercedes-Benz L608D	Alexander AM	B20F	1985	The Shires, 1998
332	E332WYS	Renault-Dodge S56	Alexander AM	B25F	1987	Western Scottish, 1991
333	LAZ5929	Mercedes-Benz L608D	Rootes	B20F	1986	The Shires, 1998
335	D98VCC	Mercedes-Benz L608D	Reeve Burgess	B20F	1986	Cymru, 1998
336	LAZ5964	Mercedes-Benz L608D	Reeve Burgess	B20F	1986	The Shires, 1998
337	D170VRP	Mercedes-Benz L608D	Alexander AM	B20F	1986	Crosville Cymru, 1998
338	D959UDY	Mercedes-Benz L608D	Reeve Burgess	B20F	1986	Cymru, 1998
339	E339WYS	Renault-Dodge S56	Alexander AM	B25F	1987	Western Scottish, 1991
340	R110GNW	Mercedes-Benz O814 Vario	Plaxton Beaver 2	B27F	1998	

341	R341KGG	Mercedes-Benz O814 Vario	Alexander ALX100	B27F	1998		
342	R112GNW	Mercedes-Benz O814 Vario	Plaxton Beaver 2	B33F	1998		
343	R113GNW	Mercedes-Benz O814 Vario	Plaxton Beaver 2	B33F	1998		
344	R344KGG	Mercedes-Benz O814 Vario	Alexander ALX100	B27F	1998		
345	D174VRP	Mercedes-Benz L608D	Alexander AM	B20F	1986	Cymru, 1998	
346	D171VRP	Mercedes-Benz L608D	Alexander AM	B20F	1986	Cymru, 1998	
353w	E353WYS	Renault-Dodge S56	Alexander AM	B25F	1987	Western Scottish, 1991	
355w	E355WYS	Renault-Dodge S56	Alexander AM	B25F	1987	Western Scottish, 1991	
366	G196NWY	Renault-Dodge S56	Reeve Burgess Beaver	B23F	1990	Rider (York), 1992	
401	M65FDS	Dennis Dart 9.8SDL3054	Plaxton Pointer	B41F	1995		
402	M67FDS	Dennis Dart 9.8SDL3054	Plaxton Pointer	B41F	1995		
501	L588JSG	Scania L113CRL	Northern Counties Paladin	N51F	1994	Scania demonstrator, 1995	
502	M102RMS	Scania L113CRL	Northern Counties Paladin	N51F	1995		
503	M103RMS	Scania L113CRL	Northern Counties Paladin	N51F	1995		
504	M104RMS	Scania L113CRL	Alexander Strider	N51F	1995		
505	M105RMS	Scania L113CRL	Alexander Strider	N51F	1995		
506	M106RMS	Scania L113CRL	Alexander Strider	N51F	1995		
507	M107RMS	Scania L113CRL	Alexander Strider	N51F	1995		

508-513   Scania N113CRL   East Lancashire European   N45F*   1995   *509 is N51F

508	M108RMS	509	M109RMS	510	M110RMS	512	M112RMS	513	M113RMS

514-521   Scania L113CRL   East Lancashire European   N51F   1995

514	M114RMS	516	M116RMS	518	M118RMS	520	M120RMS	521	M121RMS
515	M115RMS	517	M117RMS	519	M119RMS				

525	L25LSX	Scania N113CRL	East Lancashire European	N51F	1993	Scania demonstrator, 1995

635-659   Leyland Leopard PSU3D/4R   Alexander AY   B53F   1978   Western Scottish, 1991

635	TSJ35S	638	TSJ38S	652	TSJ52S	654	TSJ54S	659	TSJ59S
636	TSJ36S	647	TSJ47S						

699-767   Leyland Leopard PSU3E/4R   Alexander AY   B53F   1979-80 Western Scottish, 1991

699	BSJ899T	725	BSJ925T	756	GCS56V	766	WDS234V	767	WDS241V
716	BSJ916T								

Opposite:- **The livery of McGills of Barrahead is illustrated in this view of Leyland Lynx H733HWK taken in Paisley. During the 1998 fleet rationalisation the Lynx from Scotland West were dispersed, and this example is now operating with Cymru. The lower picture shows one of the arrivals, a Wright-bodied Dennis Dart which latterly operated for The Shires. It is also seen in Paisley.** *M E Lyons/Murdoch Currie*

Clydeside's need for a quick input of new vehicles led to the sourcing of some ex-stock Scania low-floor saloons with Northern Counties and Alexander bodies. These were followed by East Lancashire-bodied examples from a British Bus order. One of the first Scanias to receive Arriva colours was 506, M106RMS, with Alexander's now discontinued Strider bodywork.
Tony Wilson

Scotland West is becoming a 'Dart' company having transferred several Volvo B6s to The Shires in exchange. New Dart SLF variants are still arriving. However, one of a batch of ten from the pre-Arriva days in 1997, number 807, P807DBS displayed Flagship Renfrew logo when photographed. *Tony Wilson*

769	TSU642W	Leyland Leopard PSU3G/4R	Alexander AYS	B53F	1981	East Midland, 1993
770	KKG109W	Leyland National 2 NL116AL11/1R		B52F	1981	Edmunds, Rassau, 1986
771	WDS199V	Leyland National 2 NL116L11/1R		B49F	1980	Midland Fox, 1994
772	BHS206X	Leyland National 2 NL116AL11/1R		B52F	1981	
773	BHS207X	Leyland National 2 NL116AL11/1R		B52F	1981	
774	C263FGG	Leyland National 2 NL116HLXCT/1R		B52F	1986	
775	C264FGG	Leyland National 2 NL116HLXCT/1R		B52F	1986	
776	UGE388W	Leyland National 2 NL116AL11/1R		B52F	1981	
777	UGE389W	Leyland National 2 NL116AL11/1R		B52F	1981	
779	B724AGD	Leyland National 2 NL116TL11/1R		B52F	1984	
780	B725AGD	Leyland National 2 NL116HLXCT/1R		B52F	1985	
782	MIL7619	Leyland National 11351/1R (DAF)		B50F	1974	North West, 1999
784	MIL7618	Leyland National 11351/1R (DAF)		B50F	1974	North West, 1999
794	YCS91T	Leyland Leopard PSU3E/4R	Alexander AY	B53F	1978	Western Scottish, 1991

801-805

Dennis Dart SLF   Plaxton Pointer   N35F   1996

801	P801RWU	802	P802RWU	803	P803RWU	804	P804RWU	805	P805RWU

806-815

Dennis Dart SLF   Alexander ALX200   N40F   1997

806	P806DBS	808	P808DBS	810	P810DBS	812	P812DBS	814	P814DBS
807	P807DBS	809	P809DBS	811	P811DBS	813	P813DBS	815	P815DBS

816-840

Dennis Dart SLF   Plaxton Pointer   N40F   1997

816	P816GMS	821	P821GMS	826	P826KES	831	P831KES	836	P836KES
817	P817GMS	822	P822GMS	827	P827KES	832	P832KES	837	P837KES
818	P818GMS	823	P823GMS	828	P828KES	833	P833KES	838	P838KES
819	P819GMS	824	P824GMS	829	P829KES	834	P834KES	839	P839KES
820	P820GMS	825	P825KES	830	P830KES	835	P835KES	840	P840KES

841	N439GHG	Dennis Dart	Northern Counties Paladin	B39F	1995
842	N440GHG	Dennis Dart	Northern Counties Paladin	B39F	1995
843	N473MUS	Dennis Dart	Northern Counties Paladin	B39F	1995
844	N474MUS	Dennis Dart	Northern Counties Paladin	B39F	1995

Alexander's redesigned bodywork for minibus applications, replacing the Dash, is the ALX200. Here Scotland West's 850, R384JYS is one of a batch of five delivered early in 1998. It wears dedicated livery for the *Glasgow Airport Link* service. *Tony Wilson*

| 845 | K946SGG | Dennis Dart 9SDL3011 | Plaxton Pointer | B35F | 1993 | |
| 846 | K947SGG | Dennis Dart 9SDL3011 | Plaxton Pointer | B35F | 1993 | |

| **847-851** | | Dennis Dart SLF | Alexander ALX200 | N40F | 1998 | |

| 847 | R381JYS | **848** | R382JYS | **849** | R383JYS | **850** | R384JYS | **851** | R385JYS |

852	M248SPP	Dennis Dart 9.8SDL3054	Wright Handy-bus	B40F	1994	The Shires, 1998
853	M250SPP	Dennis Dart 9.8SDL3054	Wright Handy-bus	B40F	1994	The Shires, 1998
854	H242MUK	Dennis Dart 9.8SDL3004	Carlyle Dartline	B40F	1991	The Shires, 1998
855	M251SPP	Dennis Dart 9.8SDL3054	Wright Handy-bus	B40F	1994	The Shires, 1998
856	M249SPP	Dennis Dart 9.8SDL3054	Wright Handy-bus	B40F	1994	The Shires, 1998
	H244MUK	Dennis Dart 9.8SDL3004	Carlyle Dartline	B40F	1991	The Shires, 1998
	M247SPP	Dennis Dart 9.8SDL3054	Wright Handy-bus	B40F	1994	The Shires, 1998

| **880-884** | | Volvo Citybus B10M-50 | East Lancashire | B45/34F | 1990 | London South, 1998 |

| 880 | H668GPF | **881** | H681GPF | **882** | H675GPF | **883** | H676GPF | **884** | H677GPF |

886	CWR511Y	Leyland Olympian ONLXB/1R	Eastern Coach Works	B45/33F	1982	Yorkshire, 1998
887	A567NWX	Leyland Olympian ONLXB/1R	Eastern Coach Works	B45/32F	1984	Yorkshire, 1998
888	CWR515Y	Leyland Olympian ONLXB/1R	Eastern Coach Works	B45/33F	1982	Yorkshire (South), 1998
889	CWR519Y	Leyland Olympian ONLXB/1R	Eastern Coach Works	B45/33F	1982	Yorkshire (South), 1998
890	C450BKM	Leyland Olympian ONTL11/2R	Eastern Coach Works	C45/28F	1985	Northumbria, 1996
891	C451BKM	Leyland Olympian ONTL11/2R	Eastern Coach Works	C45/28F	1985	Northumbria, 1996
892	C452GKE	Leyland Olympian ONTL11/2RHSp	Eastern Coach Works	C45/28F	1986	Yorkshire (Selby & District), 1997
893	C214UPD	Leyland Olympian ONTL11/2RSp	Eastern Coach Works	C45/28F	1985	Northumbria, 1996
894	C454GKE	Leyland Olympian ONTL11/2RHSp	Eastern Coach Works	B45/28F	1986	Northumbria, 1996
895	HSB948Y	Leyland Olympian ONTL11/2R	Eastern Coach Works	B45/28F	1983	Maidstone & District, 1996
896	C453GKE	Leyland Olympian ONTL11/2RHSp	Eastern Coach Works	B45/28F	1986	Yorkshire (Selby & District), 1997
897	CWR518Y	Leyland Olympian ONLXB/1R	Eastern Coach Works	B45/33F	1982	Yorkshire (South), 1998
898	GKE442Y	Leyland Olympian ONTL11/2R	Eastern Coach Works	B45/28F	1983	Maidstone & District, 1996
899	C449BKM	Leyland Olympian ONTL11/2R(Cummins) ECW		C45/28F	1985	Northumbria, 1996
901	TPD130X	Leyland Olympian ONTL11/1R	Roe	B43/29F	1982	Kentish Bus, 1997
902	A147FPG	Leyland Olympian ONTL11/1R	Roe	B43/29F	1984	Kentish Bus, 1997
903	TPD116X	Leyland Olympian ONTL11/1R	Roe	B43/29F	1982	Kentish Bus, 1997
904	CWR514Y	Leyland Olympian ONLXB/1R	Eastern Coach Works	B45/33F	1982	Yorkshire, 1998
905	WSU475	Leyland Olympian ONTL11/2R	Eastern Coach Works	B45/26F	1985	Maidstone & District, 1996

906	HSB949Y	Leyland Olympian ONTL11/2R	Eastern Coach Works	BC45/28F	1983	Maidstone & District, 1996
907	WSU476	Leyland Olympian ONTL11/2R	Eastern Coach Works	B45/26F	1985	Maidstone & District, 1996
908	WDS220V	Leyland Fleetline FE30AGR	Alexander AD	B44/31F	1980	Western Scottish, 1991
909	XRR50S	Leyland Fleetline FE30AGR	Northern Counties	B43/29F	1978	City Rider (Derby), 1996
910	CUL143V	Leyland Titan TNLXB2RRSp	Park Royal	B44/26F	1980	Londonlinks, 1996
911	CUL152V	Leyland Titan TNLXB2RRSp	Park Royal	B44/26F	1980	Londonlinks, 1996
912	KYV408X	Leyland Titan TNLXB2RR	Leyland	B44/26F	1982	Londonlinks, 1996
913	WYV60T	Leyland Titan TNLXB2RRSp	Park Royal	B44/26F	1979	Londonlinks, 1996
914	CUL88V	Leyland Titan TNLXB2RRSp	Park Royal	B44/31F	1979	Londonlinks, 1997
915	CUL94V	Leyland Titan TNLXB2RRSp	Park Royal	B44/26F	1980	Londonlinks, 1996
916	CUL95V	Leyland Titan TNLXB2RRSp	Park Royal	B44/26F	1979	London North , 1998
917	GYE543W	MCW Metrobus DR101/14	MCW	B43/28D	1981	London North, 1998
918	GYE604W	MCW Metrobus DR101/14	MCW	B43/28D	1981	London North, 1998
w	MEF822W	Bristol VRT/SL3/6LXB	Eastern Coach Works	B43/31F	1978	North East, 1999
w	MEF823W	Bristol VRT/SL3/6LXB	Eastern Coach Works	B43/31F	1978	North East, 1999
w	CWU326T	Bristol VRT/SL3/6LXB	Eastern Coach Works	B43/31F	1978	North East, 1999
1001	N750LUS	Mercedes-Benz OH1416	Wright Urbanranger	B47F	1995	

Ancilliary vehicles:

450	TPD106X	Leyland Olympian ONTL11/1R	Roe	B43/29F	1982	Kentish Bus, 1997
451	PUS226P	Leyland Leopard PSU3E/4R	Alexander AYS	B53F	1976	
453	MGR659P	Bristol LH6L	Eastern Coach Works	B43F	1975	Northumbria, 1997

Previous Registrations:

C514MDS	C708JMB		LAZ5964	D652CVN		
HIL8438	C212EKJ		WDS199V	BVP822V, VLT204		
HIL8439	C214EKJ		WDS220V	HSD83V		
HSB948Y	GKE443Y, YSU865		WDS234V	GCS66V		
HSB949Y	GKE444Y, YSU866		WDS241V	GCS67V		
L588JSG	94D28205		WSU475	B446WKE		
LAZ5785	C203PCD		WSU476	B447WKE		
LAZ5962	C211EKJ	MIL7618	TOE522N		MIL7619	TOE508N

Named vehicles: *228 Coastline Cruiser; 229 Coastline Classic; 279 Coastline Cutter; 281 Coastline Connect; 283 Coastline Coaster*

Allocations:

Barrhead (Muriel Street) - McGill's

Renault-Dodge	370							
Mercedes-Benz	248	310	311	312	313	314	315	316
	317	331	336	346				
Leopard	635	636	639					
National	770	771	772	773	774	775	776	777
	779	780						
Dart	841	842	843	844	845	846	852	
Olympian	886	887	888	889	894	897	904	905
Fleetline/Titan	908	910	911	912	913	914	915	

Those who follow the minutiae of detail will recognise Volvo Citybus 880, H668GPF as one of many vehicles to have spent its initial years in the south. Having passed through various operations within the group it has now settled in the relative peace of Renfrewshire.
Billy Nicol

Cumbernauld (Glencryan Avenue)

Mercedes-Benz	329	330	340	341	342	343	344

Greenock (Pottery Street, Inchgreen)

Mercedes-Benz	228	229	230	234	239	240	241	242
	244	245	246	249	266	267	268	269
	270	271	272	273	274	275	276	277
	278	279	280	281	282	283	284	285
	286	287	288	289	290	291	292	293
	294	295	296	297	298	299	300	301
	302	303	304	305	306	307	308	309
	319	320	335					
Dart	804	805						
Metrobus	917	918						

Inchinnan (Greenock Road)

MetroRider	201	202	203	204	205	206	207	208
	217	218	219	220	221	223	224	225
	226	227						
Mercedes-Benz	74	76	94	95	99	100	231	235
	236	237	238	244	247	250	251	252
	253	254	255	256	257	258	259	260
	261	262	263	264	265	318	321	322
	325	326	328	330	338	340	344	345
Renault-Dodge	324	328	332	338	339	345	353	355
Scania	501	502	503	504	505	506	507	508
	509	510	512	513	514	515	516	517
	518	519	520	521	525			
Leopard	652	654	659	766	767			
	769							
Dart	830	833	834	835	836	837	838	839
	840	854						
Fleetline	909							
Volvo Citybus	880	882	883	884				
Olympian	889	901	902					
Titan	916							

Johnstone (Cochranemill Road)

MetroRider	197	198	199	200	209	210	211	212
	213	214	215	216				
Mercedes-Benz	232	233	327	333	335	337	346	
Renault-Dodge	363	366						
Volvo B6	441	442	443	444				
Leopard	647	699	716	725	756	794		
Dart	401	402	801	802	803	806	807	808
	809	810	811	812	813	814	815	816
	817	818	819	820	821	822	823	824
	825	826	827	828	829	831	832	840
	847	848	849	850	851	852	853	855
	856							
Mercedes-Benz OH	1001							
Olympian	890	891	892	893	895	896	898	899
	903	906	907					
Volvo Citybus	881							

ARRIVA NORTH EAST

Arriva North East Ltd, Arriva Northumbria Ltd, Eden Bus Services Ltd,

Arriva Durham County Ltd, Arriva Tees & District Ltd, Arriva Teesside Ltd,

Arriva House, Admiral Way, Sunderland, SR3 3XP

ARRIVA serving Northumbria
ARRIVA serving the North East

131	K131FKW	Bova FHD12.290	Bova Futura	C44FT	1992	
132	K132FKW	Bova FHD12.290	Bova Futura	C44FT	1992	
133	L33NMS	Bova FHD12.340	Bova Futura	C44FT	1993	
134	NMS700	Bova FHD12.290	Bova Futura	C44FT	1990	Boyden, Castle Donington, 1991
135	J20NMS	Bova FHD12.290	Bova Futura	C44FT	1992	
136	WSV570	Bova FHD12.340	Bova Futura	C44FT	1994	
137	WSV571	Bova FHD12.340	Bova Futura	C44FT	1994	
138	WSV572	Bova FHD12.340	Bova Futura	C44FT	1994	
139	WLT859	Bova FHD12.290	Bova Futura	C46FT	1993	
140	M122UUB	Bova FHD12.340	Bova Futura	C46FT	1994	
191	NGR685P	Bristol LH6L	Eastern Coach Works	B43F	1976	United, 1986
192w	VDV125S	Bristol LH6L	Eastern Coach Works	BC37F	1978	Moor-Dale, 1994
193	LPT701T	Bristol LH6L	Eastern Coach Works	B43F	1979	United, 1986
194	LPT707T	Bristol LH6L	Eastern Coach Works	B43F	1979	United, 1986
195	MUP712T	Bristol LH6L	Eastern Coach Works	B43F	1979	United, 1986
196	AFB593V	Bristol LH6L	Eastern Coach Works	B43F	1980	United, 1986
202	XSV689	Leyland Tiger TRCTL11/3RH	Duple 320	C53F	1986	Kentish Bus, 1997
203	WSV565	Leyland Leopard PSU3E/4RT	Duple 320(1987)	C55F	1977	United, 1986
205	WSV567	Leyland Leopard PSU3E/4RT	Duple 320(1987)	C55F	1977	United, 1986
214	XSV691	Leyland Tiger TRCTL11/3ARZA	Plaxton Paramount 3200 III	C53F	1988	Maidstone & District, 1998
215	YSU870	Leyland Tiger TRCTL11/3ARZ	Plaxton Paramount 3500 III	C53F	1988	Maidstone & District, 1998
216	YSU871	Leyland Tiger TRCTL11/3ARZ	Plaxton Paramount 3500 III	C53F	1988	Maidstone & District, 1998
217	F188HKK	Leyland Tiger TRCL10/3ARZA	Duple 340	C53F	1989	Maidstone & District, 1998
218	F189HKK	Leyland Tiger TRCL10/3ARZA	Duple 340	C53F	1989	Maidstone & District, 1998
219	TSU636	Leyland Tiger TRCTL11/3R	Duple Laser	C53F	1983	Maidstone & District, 1997
220	869SVX	Leyland Tiger TRCTL11/3R	Duple Laser	C53F	1983	Maidstone & District, 1997
221	YOT607	Leyland Tiger TRCTL11/3R	Duple Laser	C53F	1983	Maidstone & District, 1997
222	VAY879	Leyland Tiger TRCTL11/3R	Duple Laser	C53F	1983	Maidstone & District, 1997
239	SND296X	Leyland Leopard PSU5D/4R	Plaxton Supreme V	C53F	1981	Kentish Bus, 1991
242	B262KPF	Leyland Tiger TRCTL11/2RH	Plaxton Paramount 3200 IIE	C51F	1985	Kentish Bus, 1992
243	B265KPF	Leyland Tiger TRCTL11/2RH	Plaxton Paramount 3200 IIE	C51F	1985	Kentish Bus, 1992
244	B273KPF	Leyland Tiger TRCTL11/2RH	Plaxton Paramount 3200 IIE	C51F	1985	Kentish Bus, 1992
245	B279KPF	Leyland Tiger TRCTL11/3RH	Plaxton Paramount 3200 IIE	C51F	1985	Kentish Bus, 1992
246w	B276KPF	Leyland Tiger TRCTL11/3RH	Plaxton Paramount 3200 IIE	C51F	1985	Kentish Bus, 1992
247	B277KPF	Leyland Tiger TRCTL11/3RH	Plaxton Paramount 3200 IIE	C51F	1985	Kentish Bus, 1992
248	B284KPF	Leyland Tiger TRCTL11/3RH	Plaxton Paramount 3200 IIE	C53F	1985	The Shires, 1996
249	YSU896	Leyland Tiger TRCTL11/2R	Plaxton Paramount 3200 E	C53F	1984	Maidstone & District, 1998
250	EDZ215	Leyland Tiger TRCTL11/2R	Plaxton Paramount 3200 E	C53F	1983	Hunters, 1994

In bright summer sunshine 251, G251SRG gleams proudly as it shows-off corporate livery aided by the circular motif and strapline, "*Arriva serving Northumbria*". The subsidiary is fortunate in being able to retain a local identity, which includes the former fleetname.
Malcolm King

251-267		DAF SB220LC550		Optare Delta		BC48F	1989-90		
251	G251SRG	255	G255UVK	258	G258UVK	261	H261CFT	264	H264CFT
252	G252SRG	256	G256UVK	259	H259CFT	262	H262CFT	266	H266CFT
253	G253SRG	257	G257UVK	260	H598CNL	263	H263CFT	267	H267CFT
254	G254SRG								

268	F701ECC	DAF SB220LC550	Optare Delta	BC48F	1989	Crosville Cymru, 1997
269	F702ECC	DAF SB220LC550	Optare Delta	BC48F	1989	Crosville Cymru, 1997

271-280		Scania L113CRL		East Lancashire European		NC45F	1996		
271	P271VRG	273	P273VRG	275	P275VRG	277	P277VRG	279	P279VRG
272	P272VRG	274	P274VRG	276	P276VRG	278	P278VRG	280	P814VTY

281-290		Scania L113CRL		East Lancashire European		NC45F	1995		
281	N281NCN	283	N283NCN	285	N285NCN	287	N287NCN	289	N289NCN
282	N282NCN	284	N284NCN	286	N286NCN	288	N288NCN	290	N290NCN

291	R291KRG	DAF DE33WSSB3000	Plaxton Prima	C51F	1997
292	R292KRG	DAF DE33WSSB3000	Plaxton Prima	C51F	1997
293	R293KRG	DAF DE33WSSB3000	Plaxton Prima	C51F	1997
294	R294KRG	DAF DE33WSSB3000	Plaxton Prima	C51F	1997

301	C263XEF	Leyland Olympian ONLXB/1R	Eastern Coach Works	BC42/30F	1986	United, 1986
302	C264XEF	Leyland Olympian ONLXB/1R	Eastern Coach Works	BC42/30F	1986	United, 1986

303-312		Leyland Olympian ONCL10/2RZ	Alexander RH			BC43/33F	1988		
303	F303JTY	305	F305JTY	307	F307JTY	309	F309JTY	311	F311JTY
304	F304JTY	306	F306JTY	308	F308JTY	310	F310JTY	312	F312JTY

At one stroke almost the whole allocation at the Blyth depot of the former *Northumbria* operation was transformed, following the introduction of a large number of new vehicles. These appeared in the shape of both double and single-deckers. Representing the former is one of the East Lancs Cityzen bodied Scania N113s. Fleet number 385, N385OTY, heads into the centre of Newcastle just south of Gosforth Park on one of the few sunny days during August 1998. The angular and slanting livery shows up here against the vegetation behind the vehicle. *Tony Wilson*

313	C616ANW	Leyland Olympian ONLXB/1R(TL11) Eastern Coach Works	BC42/30F	1985	West Riding, 1993
314	C617ANW	Leyland Olympian ONLXB/1R(TL11) Eastern Coach Works	BC42/30F	1985	West Riding, 1993
315	C613ANW	Leyland Olympian ONLXB/1R(TL11) Eastern Coach Works	BC42/30F	1985	West Riding, 1993
316	C614ANW	Leyland Olympian ONLXB/1R(TL11) Eastern Coach Works	BC42/30F	1985	West Riding, 1993
317	EEH901Y	Leyland Olympian ONLXB/1R Eastern Coach Works	BC41/32F	1983	Kentish Bus, 1990
318	EEH908Y	Leyland Olympian ONLXB/1R Eastern Coach Works	BC41/32F	1983	Kentish Bus, 1990
319	SPY205X	Leyland Olympian ONLXB/1R Eastern Coach Works	BC41/32F	1982	United, 1986
320	SPY210X	Leyland Olympian ONLXB/1R Eastern Coach Works	BC41/32F	1982	United, 1986
321	WDC212Y	Leyland Olympian ONLXB/1R Eastern Coach Works	BC41/32F	1982	United, 1986
322	SPY204X	Leyland Olympian ONLXB/1R Eastern Coach Works	BC41/32F	1982	United, 1986

370-377
Volvo Olympian YN2RC18Z4   Northern Counties Palatine II BC45/27F 1994

| 370 | M370FTY | 372 | M372FTY | 374 | M374FTY | 376 | M376FTY | 377 | M377FTY |
| 371 | M371FTY | 373 | M373FTY | 375 | M375FTY | | | | |

381-393
Scania N113DRB   East Lancashire Cityzen   BC43/31F 1996

381	N381OTY	384	N384OTY	387	N387OTY	390	N390OTY	392	N392OTY
382	N382OTY	385	N385OTY	388	N388OTY	391	N391OTY	393	N393OTY
383	N383OTY	386	N386OTY	389	N389OTY				

Opposite, top:- **The cream and turquoise livery gradually became evident during mid-1998 with some of the existing fleet of DAF Deltas being so repainted. Pictured shortly after receiving the new colours is 252, G252SRG. Interestingly, the Northumbria fleet is the recipient of other Deltas from within the group, two from Cymru having joined during 1997.** *Malcolm King*
Opposite, bottom:- **Route 685, between Newcastle and Carlisle is a joint operation between Arriva Northumbria and Stagecoach Cumberland with each partner providing vehicles dedicated for the service. Pictured here is 292, R292KRG, one of four Plaxton Prima coaches in the fleet based on DAF chassis.** *Phillip Stephenson*

401-405

Leyland Olympian ONLXB/1R   Eastern Coach Works   B44/32F   1982   United, 1986

401	SPY201X	402	SPY202X	403	SPY203X	404	WDC211Y	405	WDC213Y

406	C259UAJ	Leyland Olympian ONLXB/1R	Eastern Coach Works	B45/32F	1985	United, 1986
407	C260UAJ	Leyland Olympian ONLXB/1R	Eastern Coach Works	B45/32F	1985	United, 1986
408	C261UAJ	Leyland Olympian ONLXB/1R	Eastern Coach Works	B45/32F	1985	United, 1986
409	C262UAJ	Leyland Olympian ONLXB/1R	Eastern Coach Works	B45/32F	1985	United, 1986

410-420

Volvo Olympian   Northern Counties Palatine II   B43/29F   1997

410	P410CCU	413	P413CCU	415	P415CCU	417	P417CCU	419	P419CCU
411	P411CCU	414	P414CCU	416	P416CCU	418	P418CCU	420	P420CCU
412	P412CCU								

421-429

Volvo Olympian YN2RV16Z4   East Lancashire   B44/30F   1994   Southern Counties (C&NS) 1998

421	M685HPF	423	M687HPF	425	M689HPF	427	M691HPF	429	M693HPF
422	M686HPF	424	M688HPF	426	M690HPF	428	M692HPF		

504	OCU809R	Leyland Fleetline FE30AGR	Alexander AL	B44/29F	1977	Busways, 1994
505	OCU810R	Leyland Fleetline FE30AGR	Alexander AL	B44/29F	1977	Busways, 1994
506	OCU812R	Leyland Fleetline FE30AGR	Alexander AL	B44/29F	1977	Busways, 1994
527	BPT919S	Bristol VRT/SL3/6LXB	Eastern Coach Works	B43/31F	1977	United, 1986
530w	BPT923S	Bristol VRT/SL3/6LXB	Eastern Coach Works	B43/31F	1977	United, 1986

536-553

Bristol VRT/SL3/6LXB   Eastern Coach Works   B43/31F   1978-79 United, 1986

536	CPT734S	541	CPT739S	544w	DUP747S	547	HUP757T	549w	HUP759T
538	CPT736S	543	DUP745S	546	DUP753S	548	HUP758T	553	OBR769T
540	CPT738S								

558-572

Bristol VRT/SL3/6LXB   Eastern Coach Works   B43/31F   1980   United, 1986

558	SGR777V	563	SGR784V	566	SGR789V	570	SGR795V	572	SGR797V
562	SGR783V	565	SGR788V						

576-584

Bristol VRT/SL3/6LXB   Eastern Coach Works   B43/31F   1980   United, 1986; 577 rebodied 1980

576	XPT802V	580	APT810W	581w	APT811W	583	APT816W	584w	APT817W
577w	XPT803V								

590	PAJ827X	Bristol VRT/SL3/6LXB	Eastern Coach Works	B43/31F	1981
591	PAJ829X	Bristol VRT/SL3/6LXB	Eastern Coach Works	B43/31F	1981

592-597

Daimler Fleetline CRG6LXB   Northern Counties   B43/32F   1976-77 GM Buses, 1987

592	PRJ486R	594	PRJ489R	595	PRJ490R	596	PRJ492R	597	PRJ494R
593	PRJ488R								

598	OBN505R	Leyland Fleetline FE30AGR	Northern Counties	B43/34F	1977	GM Buses, 1987
599	PTD639S	Leyland Fleetline FE30AGR	Northern Counties	B43/34F	1977	GM Buses, 1987

601-607

MCW Metrobus DR101/14   MCW   H43/28D   1981-82 London North, 1998; * 601 is DR101/12

601	BYX210V	603	KYV643X	605	KYV698X	606	KYV730X	607	KYV790X
602	KYO624X	604	KYV646X						

798	L532EHD	DAF SB220LC550	Ikarus CitiBus	B48F	1994	North Western (Starline), 1997
799	L533EHD	DAF SB220LC550	Ikarus CitiBus	B48F	1994	North Western (Starline), 1997

801-827

MCW MetroRider MF150/27*   MCW   BC25F*   1987   *801/3-6 are MF150/21
*804 is B23F; 813/5 are B21F

801	E801BTN	810	E810BTN	815	E815BTN	819	E819BTN	824w	E824BTN
803	E803BTN	812	E812BTN	816	E816BTN	820	E820BTN	825	E825BTN
804	E804BTN	813	E813BTN	817	E817BTN	822w	E822BTN	826	E826BTN
805w	E805BTN	814	E814BTN	818	E818BTN	823	E823BTN	827	E827BTN
806	E806BTN								

828	E676DCU	MCW MetroRider MF150/63	MCW	BC21F	1987	Rochester & Marshall, 1994

The Bristol VR with ECW bodywork is a fast disappearing model. With its pedigree stretching as far back as the pre-*National Bus Company* days, the vehicle was the mainstay of many companies throughout the seventies and eighties. Thus in company with a rapidly decreasing number of its sisters during 1998, 541,CPT739S here could be regularly found involved in the important transportation of children and older students. A glimpse at the blind configuration will indicate that while the bus runs a schoolday route, the service is open to others who might wish to avail themselves of the operation. *Malcolm King*

820-845

MCW MetroRider MF150/27   MCW   BC25F*   1987   *845 is B23F

829	E829BTN	832	E832BTN	834	E834BTN	840	E840BTN	844	E844BTN
831	E831BTN	833	E833BTN	836	E836BTN	841	E841BTN	845	E845BTN

846	H840UUA	Optare MetroRider	Optare	B25F	1990	Lancaster, 1993
847	J363BNW	Optare MetroRider	Optare	B23F	1991	Lancaster, 1993
850	J366BNW	Optare MetroRider	Optare	B29F	1992	Lancaster, 1993

851-858

Optare MetroRider   Optare   BC28F*   1992-93   *855-8 are BC29F

851	K851RBB	853	K853RBB	855	L855WRG	857	L857WRG	858	L858WRG
852	K852RBB	854	K854RBB	856	L856WRG				

859-871

Optare MetroRider   Optare   BC29F   1995

859	M859KCU	862	M862KCU	865	M865KCU	868	M868KCU	870	M870KCU
860	M860KCU	863	M863KCU	866	M866KCU	869	M869KCU	871	M871KCU
861	M861KCU	864	M864KCU	867	M867KCU				

872-876

Optare MetroRider   Optare   B31F   1995

872	M872LBB	873	M873LBB	874	M874LBB	875	M875LBB	876	M876LBB

877-896

Optare MetroRider   Optare   B31F   1996

877	N877RTN	881	N881RTN	885	N885RTN	889	N889RTN	893	P893XCU
878	N878RTN	882	N882RTN	886	N886RTN	890	N890RTN	894	P894XCU
879	N879RTN	883	N883RTN	887	N887RTN	891	N891RTN	895	P895XCU
880	N880RTN	884	N884RTN	888	N192RVK	892	P892XCU	896	P896XCU

Complimenting the Scania double-deckers allocated to the Blyth depot, a batch of single-deckers were acquired at the same time. Based on the L113CRL chassis and running units, East Lancashire placed thereon their *European* bodywork. With high-back seating, the vehicles regularly ply their trade on the network of routes north of Newcastle. Number 276, P276VRG, is seen heading citywards on the 300 group of routes during 1998, still bearing the former *Northumbria* livery. *Malcolm King*

897-901

		Optare MetroRider		Optare		B31F	1997		
897	P56XTN		898	P57XTN	899	P58XTN	900	P59XTN	901	P61XTN

902-923

		Optare MetroRider MR15		Optare		B31F	1997-98		
902	P902DRG	907	R907JNL	912	R912JNL	916	R916JNL	920	R920JNL
903	P903DRG	908	R908JNL	913	R913JNL	917	R917JNL	921	R921JNL
904	P904DRG	909	R909JNL	914	R914JNL	918	R918JNL	922	R922JNL
905	P905JNL	910	R910JNL	915	R915JNL	919	R919JNL	923	R923JNL
906	P906JNL	911	R251JNL						

965	G174YRE	Mercedes-Benz 811D	Carlyle		B33F	1990	Stevensons, 1994
966	G175DRF	Mercedes-Benz 811D	LHE Commuter		B33F	1990	Stevensons, 1994

1232	C75UHN	Leyland Tiger TRCTL11/2RP	Duple Dominant	B55F	1985	Trimdon, 1990
1234	H278LEF	Leyland Tiger TRCL10/3ARZA	Alexander Q	B55F	1990	
1235	H279LEF	Leyland Tiger TRCL10/3ARZA	Alexander Q	B55F	1990	

1301	A516EVN	Leyland Tiger TRCTL11/2R	Plaxton Paramount 3200 E	C47F	1983	
1302	A517EVN	Leyland Tiger TRCTL11/2R	Plaxton Paramount 3200 E	C47F	1983	
1305	B266KPF	Leyland Tiger TRCTL11/2R	Plaxton Paramount 3200 IIE	C53F	1985	Green, Kirkintilloch, 1990

1306-1315

		Leyland Tiger TRCTL11/2RP	Plaxton Paramount 3200 III	C53F*	1987	*1309/12 are C47F	
1306	E266KEF	1308	E268KEF	1310	E270KEF	1312	E272KEF	1314	E274KEF
1307	E267KEF	1309	E269KEF	1311	E271KEF	1313	E273KEF	1315	E275KEF

1324w	C39CWT	Leyland Tiger TRCTL11/2RH	Plaxton Paramount 3200 IIE	C53F	1986	West Riding, 1991
1327	NLG35Y	Leyland Tiger TRCTL11/2R	Plaxton Paramount 3200 E	C51F	1983	Careline, Coventry, 1992
1328	LHO992Y	Leyland Tiger TRCTL11/2R	Plaxton Paramount 3200 E	C53F	1983	Tillingbourne, 1992
1331w	C38CWT	Leyland Tiger TRCTL11/2RH	Plaxton Paramount 3200 IIE	C53F	1986	West Riding, 1992

1333	A117EPA	Leyland Tiger TRCTL11/2R	Plaxton Paramount 3200 E	C53F	1983	London & Country, 1992
1334w	A119EPA	Leyland Tiger TRCTL11/2R	Plaxton Paramount 3200 E	C53F	1983	London & Country, 1992
1336w	A122EPA	Leyland Tiger TRCTL11/2R	Plaxton Paramount 3200 E	C53F	1983	London & Country, 1992
1339w	RMO202Y	Leyland Tiger TRCTL11/2R	Plaxton Paramount 3200 E	C53F	1983	Pulham, Bourton, 1993
1340	RMO204Y	Leyland Tiger TRCTL11/2R	Plaxton Paramount 3200 E	C53F	1983	Pulham, Bourton, 1993

1342-1346

		Leyland Tiger TRCTL11/2RH	Plaxton Paramount 3200 IIE	C53F*	1986	West Riding, 1993

*1344/6 are C49F

1342	C42CWT	1343	C43CWT	1344	C34CWT	1345	C35CWT	1346	C41CWT

1401	C131HJN	Leyland Tiger TRCTL11/3RH	Plaxton Paramount 3200 IIE	C53F	1986	Eastern National, 1989
1402	C132HJN	Leyland Tiger TRCTL11/3RH	Plaxton Paramount 3200 IIE	C53F	1986	Eastern National, 1989
1403	C133HJN	Leyland Tiger TRCTL11/3RH	Plaxton Paramount 3200 IIE	C53F	1986	Eastern National, 1989
1404	B112GRR	Leyland Tiger TRCTL11/3RH	Plaxton Paramount 3200 II	C51F	1985	Trent, 1991
1405	B113GRR	Leyland Tiger TRCTL11/3RH	Plaxton Paramount 3200 II	C51F	1985	Trent, 1991
1406	A949KAJ	Leyland Tiger TRCTL11/3R	Plaxton Paramount 3200 E	C57F	1983	Vanguard, Bedworth, 1991
1410	B110GRR	Leyland Tiger TRCTL11/3RH	Plaxton Paramount 3200 II	C51F	1985	Trent, 1991
1412	B907RVF	Leyland Tiger TRCTL11/3RH	Plaxton Paramount 3200 IIE	C53F	1985	Ambassador Travel, 1991
1415	B111GRR	Leyland Tiger TRCTL11/3RH	Plaxton Paramount 3200 II	C51F	1985	Trent, 1991
1416	B114GRR	Leyland Tiger TRCTL11/3RH	Plaxton Paramount 3200 II	C51F	1985	Trent, 1991
1417	B115GRR	Leyland Tiger TRCTL11/3RH	Plaxton Paramount 3200 II	C51F	1985	Trent, 1991
1418w	B908RVF	Leyland Tiger TRCTL11/3RH	Plaxton Paramount 3200 IIE	C53F	1985	Ambassador Travel, 1991
1419w	A146EPA	Leyland Tiger TRCTL11/3R	Plaxton Paramount 3200 E	CB57F	1984	Luton & District, 1992
1420w	B283KPF	Leyland Tiger TRCTL11/3RH	Plaxton Paramount 3200 IIE	C53F	1985	Luton & District, 1992
1423	B281KPF	Leyland Tiger TRCTL11/3RH	Plaxton Paramount 3200 IIE	C53F	1985	Luton & District, 1992
1426w	A909LWU	Leyland Tiger TRCTL11/3R	Plaxton Paramount 3200 E	CB57F	1983	Scutt, Owston Ferry, 1993
1431	YLX281	Leyland Tiger TRCTL11/3R	Duple Laser	C50F	1983	Maidstone & District, 1997
1432	445YMU	Leyland Tiger TRCTL11/3R	Duple Laser	C50F	1983	Maidstone & District, 1997
1433	681CXM	Leyland Tiger TRCTL11/3R	Duple Laser	C50F	1983	Maidstone & District, 1997
1434	648WHK	Leyland Tiger TRCTL11/3R	Duple Laser	C53F	1983	Maidstone & District, 1997

1501	J661UHN	MAN 11.190 HOCLR	Optare Vecta	B42F	1991	
1502	J620UHN	MAN 11.190 HOCLR	Optare Vecta	B42F	1991	

1503-1543

		MAN 11.190 HOCLR	Optare Vecta	B42F	1993	*1509-13 are BC42F

1503	K503BHN	1512	K512BHN	1520	L520FHN	1528	L528FHN	1536	L536FHN
1504	K504BHN	1513	K513BHN	1521	L521FHN	1529	L529FHN	1537	L537FHN
1505	K505BHN	1514	K514BHN	1522	L522FHN	1530	L530FHN	1538	L538FHN
1506	K506BHN	1515	K515BHN	1523	L523FHN	1531	L531FHN	1539	L539FHN
1507	K507BHN	1516	K516BHN	1524	L524FHN	1532	L532FHN	1540	L540FHN
1508	K508BHN	1517	K517BHN	1525	L525FHN	1533	L533FHN	1541	L541FHN
1509	K509BHN	1518	K518BHN	1526	L526FHN	1534	L534FHN	1542	L542FHN
1510	K510BHN	1519	L519FHN	1527	L527FHN	1535	L535FHN	1543	L543FHN
1511	K511BHN								

1544-1551

		MAN 11.190 HOCLR	Optare Vecta	B42F	1993-94	

1544	L544GHN	1546	L546GHN	1548	L548GHN	1550	L550GHN	1551	L551GHN
1545	L545GHN	1547	L547GHN	1549	L549GHN				

1552	M501AJC	MAN 11.190 HOCLR	Optare Vecta	B42F	1995	Cymru, 1998
1553	M502AJC	MAN 11.190 HOCLR	Optare Vecta	B42F	1995	Cymru, 1999
1554	M503AJC	MAN 11.190 HOCLR	Optare Vecta	B42F	1995	Cymru, 1999
1555	M504AJC	MAN 11.190 HOCLR	Optare Vecta	B42F	1995	Cymru, 1999

1601-1643

		Dennis Dart SLF	Plaxton Pointer 2	N39F	1997-98	

1601	R601MHN	1610	S610KHN	1619	S619KHN	1628	S628KHN	1636	S636KHN
1602	R602MHN	1611	S611KHN	1620	S620KHN	1629	S629KHN	1637	S637KHN
1603	R603MHN	1612	S612KHN	1621	S621KHN	1630	S630KHN	1638	S638KHN
1604	R604MHN	1613	S613KHN	1622	S622KHN	1631	S631KHN	1639	S639KHN
1605	R605MHN	1614	S614KHN	1623	S623KHN	1632	S632KHN	1640	S640KHN
1606	R606MHN	1615	S615KHN	1624	S624KHN	1633	S633KHN	1641	S641KHN
1607	R607MHN	1616	S616KHN	1625	S625KHN	1634	S634KHN	1642	S642KHN
1608	S608KHN	1617	S617KHN	1626	S626KHN	1635	S635KHN	1643	S643KHN
1609	S609KHN	1618	S618KHN	1627	S627KHN				

1701	T	Dennis Dart SLF	Plaxton Pointer MPD	N29F	1999	
1702	T	Dennis Dart SLF	Plaxton Pointer MPD	N29F	1999	

The 1989 Duple 340 bodywork on Leyland Tiger 217, F188HKK,was given a makeover during 1998 upon transfer from sister subsidiary, *Maidstone & District*. The move from the south eastern sees the vehicle swiftly transport customers on one of the express routes into the city centre of Newcastle through the northern suburbs near Gosforth. *Tony Wilson*

2448	D648CVN	Mercedes-Benz L608D	Reeve Burgess	B20F	1986	
2451	D651CVN	Mercedes-Benz L608D	Reeve Burgess	B20F	1986	
2453	D653CVN	Mercedes-Benz L608D	Reeve Burgess	B20F	1986	
2466	D466EAJ	Mercedes-Benz L608D	Reeve Burgess	B20F	1987	
2473	D473EAJ	Mercedes-Benz L608D	Reeve Burgess	B20F	1987	
2479	D479EAJ	Mercedes-Benz L608D	Reeve Burgess	B20F	1987	

2601-2605 Optare MetroRider MR33 — Optare — B25F — 1994

2601	L601FHN	2602	L602FHN	2603	L603FHN	2604	L604FHN	2605	L605FHN

2606-2645 Optare MetroRider MR35 — Optare — B25F — 1996-97

2606	P606FHN	2614	P614FHN	2622	P622FHN	2630	P630FHN	2638	P638FHN
2607	P607FHN	2615	P615FHN	2623	P623FHN	2631	P631FHN	2639	P639FHN
2608	P608FHN	2616	P616FHN	2624	P624FHN	2632	P632FHN	2640	P640FHN
2609	P609FHN	2617	P617FHN	2625	P625FHN	2633	P633FHN	2641	P641FHN
2610	P610FHN	2618	P618FHN	2626	P626FHN	2634	P634FHN	2642	P642FHN
2611	P611FHN	2619	P619FHN	2627	P627FHN	2635	P635FHN	2643	P643FHN
2612	P612FHN	2620	P620FHN	2628	P628FHN	2636	P636FHN	2644	P644FHN
2613	P613FHN	2621	P621FHN	2629	P629FHN	2637	P637FHN	2645	P645FHN

2701-2725 Optare MetroRider MR15 — Optare — B31F — 1997-98

2701	R701MHN	2706	R706MHN	2711	R711MHN	2716	R716MHN	2721	R721MHN
2702	R702MHN	2707	R707MHN	2712	R712MHN	2717	R717MHN	2722	R722MHN
2703	R703MHN	2708	R708MHN	2713	R713MHN	2718	R718MHN	2723	R723MHN
2704	R704MHN	2709	R709MHN	2714	R714MHN	2719	R719MHN	2724	R724MHN
2705	R705MHN	2710	R710MHN	2715	R715MHN	2720	R720MHN	2725	R725MHN

3001-3025 — Mercedes-Benz 0405 — Optare Prisma — B49F — 1995

3001	M301SAJ	3006	N806XHN	3011	N511XVN	3016	N516XVN	3021	N521XVN
3002	M302SAJ	3007	N807XHN	3012	N512XVN	3017	N517XVN	3022	N522XVN
3003	M303SAJ	3008	N808XHN	3013	N513XVN	3018	N518XVN	3023	N523XVN
3004	M304SAJ	3009	N809XHN	3014	N514XVN	3019	N519XVN	3024	N524XVN
3005	M305SAJ	3010	N810XHN	3015	N515XVN	3020	N520XVN	3025	N525XVN

3130-3142 — Leyland National 2 NL116HLXCT/1R — B49F — 1983-84

3130	A130FDC	3134	A134FDC	3136	A136FDC	3138	A138FDC	3142	A142FDC
3131	A131FDC	3135	A135FDC	3137	A137FDC	3140	A140FDC		

No.	Reg	Type	Body	Seat	Year	History
3143	RHG882X	Leyland National 2 NL116AL11/1R (6HLXCT)		B52F	1982	
3147	ARN895Y	Leyland National 2 NL116AHLXB/1R		B52F	1983	Shearings, 1991
3148	ARN896Y	Leyland National 2 NL116AHLXB/1R		B52F	1983	Shearings, 1991
3149w	ARN897Y	Leyland National 2 NL116AHLXB/1R		B52F	1983	Shearings, 1991
3150	ARN898Y	Leyland National 2 NL116AHLXB/1R		B52F	1983	Shearings, 1991
3152	A542PCW	Leyland National 2 NL116AHLXCT/1R		B49F	1984	Blackpool, 1991
3153	A543PCW	Leyland National 2 NL116AHLXCT/1R		B49F	1984	Blackpool, 1991
3505	SIB6705	Leyland 10351B/1R (6HLXB)	East Lancs Greenway(1992)	B41F	1978	Kentish Bus, 1998
3506	SIB6706	Leyland NL106AL11/1R(6HLXB)	East Lancs Greenway(1992)	B41F	1981	Kentish Bus, 1998
3507	SIB6707	Leyland NL106AL11/1R(6HLXB)	East Lancs Greenway(1992)	B41F	1981	Kentish Bus, 1998
3508	SIB6708	Leyland NL106AL11/1R(6HLXB)	East Lancs Greenway(1992)	B41F	1982	Kentish Bus, 1998
3509	SIB1279	Leyland 10351B/1R	East Lancs Greenway(1992)	B41F	1979	Kentish Bus, 1998
3510	SIB1280	Leyland 10351B/1R	East Lancs Greenway(1992)	B41F	1979	Kentish Bus, 1998
3511	SIB1281	Leyland 10351B/1R	East Lancs Greenway(1992)	B41F	1979	Kentish Bus, 1998
3512	SIB1282	Leyland 10351B/1R	East Lancs Greenway(1992)	B41F	1978	Kentish Bus, 1998
3513	SIB1283	Leyland 10351B/1R	East Lancs Greenway(1992)	B41F	1979	Kentish Bus, 1998
3514	SIB1284	Leyland 10351B/1R	East Lancs Greenway(1992)	B41F	1978	Kentish Bus, 1998
3515	SIB1285	Leyland 10351B/1R	East Lancs Greenway(1992)	B41F	1979	Kentish Bus, 1998
3516	SIB1286	Leyland 10351B/1R	East Lancs Greenway(1992)	B41F	1979	Kentish Bus, 1998
3517	SIB1287	Leyland 10351B/1R	East Lancs Greenway(1992)	B41F	1979	Kentish Bus, 1998
3518	SIB1288	Leyland 10351B/1R	East Lancs Greenway(1992)	B41F	1979	Kentish Bus, 1998
3519	PDZ6261	Leyland 1035A1/1R	East Lancs Greenway(1994)	B41F	1977	Kentish Bus, 1998
3520	PDZ6262	Leyland 1035A1/1R	East Lancs Greenway(1994)	B41F	1977	Kentish Bus, 1998
3521	SIB6715	Leyland 1051/1R/0402(6HLXB)	East Lancs Greenway(1993)	B41F	1973	Kentish Bus, 1998
3522	SIB6716	Leyland 1051/1R/0402(6HLXB)	East Lancs Greenway(1993)	B41F	1974	Kentish Bus, 1998
3523	SIB6710	Leyland NL106L11/1R	East Lancs Greenway(1992)	B41F	1981	Southern Counties (K&S), 1998
3524	SIB6712	Leyland 10351A/1R	East Lancs Greenway(1992)	B41F	1979	Southern Counties (K&S), 1998
3744	WAO399Y	Leyland National 2 NL116HLXB/1R		B52F	1983	Shearings, 1991
3745	WAO395Y	Leyland National 2 NL116HLXB/1R		B52F	1983	Shearings, 1991
3747	WRA224Y	Leyland National 2 NL116AHLXB/1R		B52F	1983	Trent, 1991
3748	WRA225Y	Leyland National 2 NL116AHLXB/1R		B52F	1983	Trent, 1991
3749	RRA219X	Leyland National 2 NL116AHLXB/1R		B52F	1981	Trent, 1991

During 1993 five Leyland Olympian double-deckers were acquired by the then *United Automobile* Services, sporting 74-seater Alexander RH bodywork. Incorporated now into *Arriva serving the North East*, 272, L272FVN here has received the livery of its new owners.
Les Peters

3751	DOC31V	Leyland National 2 NL116L11/1R			B50F	1980	West Midlands Travel, 1995
3756	VBG89V	Leyland National 2 NL116L11/2R(6HLXB)			B49F	1980	North West, 1999
3757	FCA10X	Leyland National 2 NL116AL11/2R(6HLXB)			B52F	1982	North West, 1999
3758	CCY819V	Leyland National 2 NL116L11/1R(6HLXB)			BC49F	1980	Yorkshire Bus (WR), 1997
3759	HED204V	Leyland National 2 NL116AL11/1R(6HLXB)			B49F	1980	Yorkshire Bus (WR), 1997
3760	HED205V	Leyland National 2 NL116AL11/1R(6HLXB)			B49F	1980	Yorkshire Bus (WR), 1997
3761	VBG93V	Leyland National 2 NL116AL11/1R(6HLXB)			B49F	1980	Yorkshire Bus (WR), 1997
3762	XWA72X	Leyland National 2 NL116L11/1R(6HLXB)			B49F	1982	Yorkshire Bus (WR), 1997
3763	XWA73X	Leyland National 2 NL116L11/1R(6HLXB)			B49F	1982	Yorkshire Bus (WR), 1997
3764	XWA74X	Leyland National 2 NL116L11/1R(6HLXB)			B49F	1982	Yorkshire Bus (WR), 1997
3765	XWA75X	Leyland National 2 NL116L11/1R(6HLXB)			B49F	1982	Yorkshire Bus (WR), 1997
3766	EWT206Y	Leyland National 2 NL116HLXB/1R			B49F	1982	Yorkshire Bus (WR), 1997
3767	EWT208Y	Leyland National 2 NL116HLXB/1R			B49F	1983	Yorkshire Bus (WR), 1997
3768	EWT210Y	Leyland National 2 NL116HLXB/1R			B49F	1983	Yorkshire Bus (WR), 1997
3769	BPR48Y	Leyland National 2 NL116HLXB/1R			B49F	1983	Yorkshire Bus (WR), 1997
3770	BPR49Y	Leyland National 2 NL116HLXB/1R			B49F	1983	Yorkshire Bus (WR), 1997
3771	NTU11Y	Leyland National 2 NL116HLXB/2R			B52F	1983	North West (Bee Line), 1999
3772	NTU12Y	Leyland National 2 NL116HLXB/2R			B52F	1983	North West, 1999
3773	NTU13Y	Leyland National 2 NL116HLXB/2R			B52F	1983	North West, 1999

4001-4005 DAF SB220LC550 Optare Delta B51F 1990

4001	G209HCP	4002	G210HCP	4003	G211HCP	4004	G212HCP	4005	G214HCP

4006	J866UPY	DAF SB200LC550	Optare Delta	B49F	1992
4007	J867UPY	DAF SB200LC550	Optare Delta	B49F	1992

4008-4022 DAF SB220LC550 Optare Delta B49F 1993

4008	K408BHN	4011	K411BHN	4014	K414BHN	4017	K417BHN	4020	L420FHN
4009	K409BHN	4012	K412BHN	4015	K415BHN	4018	L418FHN	4021	L421FHN
4010	K410BHN	4013	K413BHN	4016	K416BHN	4019	L419FHN	4022	L422FHN

4023-4058 DAF DE02GSSB220 Plaxton Prestige N45F 1998

4023	R423RPY	4031	R431RPY	4038	R438RPY	4045	S345KHN	4052	S352KHN
4024	R424RPY	4032	R432RPY	4039	R439RPY	4046	S346KHN	4053	S353KHN
4025	R425RPY	4033	R433RPY	4040	R440RPY	4047	S347KHN	4054	S354KHN
4026	R426RPY	4034	R434RPY	4041	S341KHN	4048	S348KHN	4055	S355KHN
4027	R427RPY	4035	R435RPY	4042	S342KHN	4049	S349KHN	4056	S356KHN
4028	R428RPY	4036	R436RPY	4043	S343KHN	4050	S350KHN	4057	S357KHN
4029	R429RPY	4037	R437RPY	4044	S344KHN	4051	S351KHN	4058	S358KHN
4030	R430RPY								

4059	R701KCU	DAF DE02SB220GS	Northern Counties Paladin	B39F	1997

4060-4073 DAF DE02GSSB220 Plaxton Prestige N41F 1998

4060	S702KFT	4063	S705KFT	4066	S708KFT	4069	S711KFT	4072	S714KRG
4061	S703KFT	4064	S706KFT	4067	S709KFT	4070	S712KRG	4073	S715KRG
4062	S704KFT	4065	S707KFT	4068	S710KFT	4071	S713KRG		

5001-5005 Leyland Lynx LX2R11C15Z4S Leyland Lynx B49F 1990

5001	G508EAJ	5002	G509EAJ	5003	G510EAJ	5004	G511EAJ	5005	G512EAJ

5006-5018 Leyland Lynx LX2R11C15Z4S Leyland Lynx 2 B49F 1991

5006	H31PAJ	5009	H253PAJ	5012	J652UHN	5016	J656UHN	5018	J658UHN
5007	H32PAJ	5011	J651UHN	5013	J653UHN	5017	J657UHN		

Opposite, top:- **Progress on applying the new Arriva colours has been most notable in the North East fleet where a combination of new buses and transfers into the area have seen a swift increase in vehicles liveried in the scheme. Most of the MetroRiders now sport the style including 2611, P611FHN, pictured in Stockton.** *Phillip Stephenson*
Opposite, bottom:- **1998 saw the displacement of early Leyland Nationals from the North East fleet with Greenway versions displaced from Kentish Bus. Photographed while heading for Netherfields is 3517, SIB1287. The vehicles were repainted into the corporate style on transfer.** *Phillip Stephenson*

The 1999 Arriva Bus Handbook

7202-7238 Leyland Olympian ONLXB/1R   Eastern Coach Works   B45/32F*   1982-84 7202-4/10 ex West Riding, 1993
*7233/4 are BC42/28F; 7206/14 are B44/32F

7202	XWY477X	7208	SPY208X	7216	WDC216Y	7226	AEF226Y	7235	A235GHN
7203	XWY478X	7209w	SPY209X	7217	WDC217Y	7227	AEF227Y	7236	A236GHN
7204	XWY479X	7210	CWR505Y	7218	WDC218Y	7228	AEF228Y	7237	A237GHN
7206	SPY206X	7214	WDC214Y	7223	AEF223Y	7233	A233GHN	7238	A238GHN
7207	SPY207X	7215	WDC215Y	7225	AEF225Y	7234	A234GHN		

7239	A563KWY	Leyland Olympian ONLXB/1R	Eastern Coach Works	BC42/28F	1983	West Riding, 1994

7240-7247 Leyland Olympian ONLXB/1R   Eastern Coach Works   B45/32F   1984-85 KentishBus , 1998
7245-7 Southern Counties(KT), 1998

7240	A240GHN	7242	A242GHN	7244	A244GHN	7246	B246NVN	7247	B247NVN
7241	A241GHN	7243	A243GHN	7245w	B245NVN				

7250	B45NDX	Leyland Olympian ONLXB/1RV	East Lancashire	B40/33F	1985	Stevensons, 1993
7251	B251NVN	Leyland Olympian ONLXB/1R	Eastern Coach Works	B45/32F	1985	
7252	B252PHN	Leyland Olympian ONLXB/1R	Eastern Coach Works	B45/32F	1985	
7253	B253PHN	Leyland Olympian ONLXB/1R	Eastern Coach Works	B45/32F	1985	
7255	B255RAJ	Leyland Olympian ONLXB/1R	Eastern Coach Works	B45/32F	1985	
7256	B256RAJ	Leyland Olympian ONLXB/1R	Eastern Coach Works	B45/32F	1985	
7258	B598SWX	Leyland Olympian ONLXB/1R	Eastern Coach Works	BC40/31F	1984	West Riding, 1994
7263	E963PME	Leyland Olympian ONLXB/1R	Optare	B47/29F	1988	London Cityrama, 1992
7265w	C265XEF	Leyland Olympian ONLXB/1R	Eastern Coach Works	BC42/30F	1986	
7266	C266XEF	Leyland Olympian ONLXB/1R	Eastern Coach Works	BC42/30F	1986	
7267	C267XEF	Leyland Olympian ONLXB/1R	Eastern Coach Works	BC42/30F	1986	
7268	C268XEF	Leyland Olympian ONLXB/1R	Eastern Coach Works	BC42/30F	1986	

7271-7275 Leyland Olympian ON2R50C13Z4   Alexander RH   B45/29F   1993

7271	L271FVN	7272	L272FVN	7273	L273FVN	7274	L274FVN	7275	L275FVN

7276	G21HHG	Leyland Olympian ONCL10/1RZ	Leyland	B47/31F	1989	Atlas Bus, 1994

7277-7285 Leyland Olympian ONCL10/1R   Northern Counties   B43/32F   1989   Atlas Bus, 1994

7277	G754UYT	7279	G756UYT	7281	G758UYT	7283	G760UYT	7285	G762UYT
7278w	G755UYT	7280	G757UYT	7282	G759UYT	7284	G761UYT		

7286-7295 Leyland Olympian ONLXB/1R   Roe   B47/29F   1982-83 Metrobus, Orpington, 1997

7286	UWW13X	7288	CUB60Y	7290	CUB63Y	7292	CUB66Y	7294	CUB69Y
7287	UWW14X	7289	CUB61Y	7291	CUB64Y	7293	CUB68Y	7295	CUB71Y

Previous Registrations:-

445YMU	A177MKE	SIB6708	LFR874X
648WHK	A185MKE	SIB6710	DBV844W
681CXM	A178MKE	SIB6712	BYW425V
869SVX	A179MKE	SIB6715	TPD176M
A949KAJ	A672OKX, 7694VC	SIB6716	UPE196M
EDZ215	RMO203Y	TSU636	A183MKE
GSU347	GOL399N	VAY879	A182MKE
J20NMS	J849MCN	WLT859	K121HWF
LHO992Y	AEF992Y, TBC658	WSV565	ABR865S
NMS700	G418WFP	WSV567	ABR867S
PDZ6261	UPB310S	WSV569	RDC736X
PDZ6262	UPB313S	WSV570	E692JUT
SIB1279	BPL484T	WSV571	C160UHN, NMS700
SIB1280	EPD541V	WSV572	B337WFJ
SIB1281	BPL489T	XSV689	C256SPC
SIB1282	YPL439T	XSV691	E91OJT
SIB1283	BPL479T	YLX281	A176MKE
SIB1284	YPL445T	YOT607	A180MKE
SIB1285	BPL480T	YSU870	E186XKO
SIB1286	BPL482T	YSU871	E187XKO
SIB1287	BPL483T	YSU896	A135EPA
SIB1288	EPD522V		
SIB6705	YPF762T		
SIB6706	LFR855X		
SIB6707	JCK850W		

A large batch of MAN single-deck saloons were introduced into the North East during the early 1990s replacing an equally large number of Bristol LH types. These were placed into the incorporated fleets of *United Automobile Services*, *Tees & District* and the *Teesside Motor Services*, all of which were then being operated latterly under the ownership of *West Midlands Travel*. Number 1502, J620UHN in Stockton High Street, was one of the first of this type to receive the new corporate livery. Standing amid market day stalls in 1998, a crew change takes place. *Phillip Stephenson*

A vivid yellow and red livery adorns 1336, A122EPA here along with the former operator's name. Operating an express route between Stockton and Middlesborough, this Leyland Tiger carries a Plaxton Paramount 3200 body, a 1983 design from the Scarborough factory. But the vehicle is not a direct delivery from the East Coast town, having originally provided sterling service on *Green Line* duties with *London Country Bus Services* from 1983 until 1992. *Tony Wilson*

Ancilliary Vehicles:-

86	JUP111T	Leyland Leopard PSU5C/4R	Plaxton Supreme III	RV	1979	
9990	GSU347	Leyland National 11351/1R		B49F	1975	Midland Red North, 1987
9991	UBR110V	Leyland National 2 NL116L11/1R		B49F	1981	United, 1986
9992	WSV569	Leyland National 2 NL116AL11/1R		B49F	1980	United, 1986
9993	LPT703T	Bristol LH6L	Eastern Coach Works	B43F	1983	
9994	WAE192T	Bristol LH6L	Eastern Coach Works	B43F	1979	Provincial, 1994
9995	UGR698R	Bristol VRT/SL3/6LXB	Eastern Coach Works	B43/31F	1976	

Allocations:-

Alnwick (Lisburn Street) - Northumbria

Tiger	219	220	222	242	243	244	248	249
	250							
MetroRider	859	890	891					
Bristol LH	193							
DAF/Delta	251	252	255					
Bristol VR	536	546	547	558				
Olympian	302	313	315	317				

Ashington (Lintonville Terrace) - Northumbria

MetroRider	813	815	846	847	850	852	853	877
	878	893	894	895	896	897	898	899
	908	909	910	911				
Leopard	203	205						
DAF/Delta	253	254	257	258	263	264	266	267
	268	269						
DAF/Ikarus	798	799						
Bristol VR	530	562	565	570	572			
Olympian	308	309	310	311	421	422	424	

Berwick (Tweedmouth Industrial Park) - Northumbria

MetroRider	803	805	806	810	818	819	823	832
	836							
Bristol LH	191	196						
Leopard	221	239						
Tiger	202	245						
Olympian	304	316	318					

Bishop Auckland (Morland Street) - Durham County- The Eden

Outstations - Crook and Fishburn

Mercedes-Benz	2451	2466						
MetroRider	2613	2614	2642	2643	2644	2645	2709	2710
Tiger	1342	1343	1344	1345	1346	1404♣	1410	1415♣
MAN Vecta	1515	1526	1527	1528	1529	1546	1547	1548
	1549	1552	1553					
Dart	1615	1616	1617	1618	1619	1620	1621	1622
	1627	1628	1629	1630	1631	1632	1633	1634
	1635							
Lynx	5003	5004	5005	5006	5007	5008	5009	5010
	5011	5012	5013	5014	5015	5016	5017	5018
Olympian	7214	7240	7241	7242	7243	7244		

Onwards from the middle of 1998, *Arriva serving the North East* began to receive the next generation of single-deck saloons. These, for services based in the Stockton/Middlesborough region of their operating area. With DAF being the chosen chassis it was natural, owing to the close relationship, that Plaxton would be the provider of the bodywork. One of the latest body designs to appear out of the Scarborough factory included the Prestige. And indeed looking prestigious, as it passes along Stockton High Street during August 1998, 4042,S342KHN shows off the neat and clean lines, while wearing the corporate livery.
Les Peters

Blyth (Bridge Street) - Northumbria

MetroRider	812	820	825	826	829	831	833	840
	841	844	845	851	854	855	856	857
	858	860	866	867	868	869	870	871
	881	882	883	884	901	902	903	
Scania L	275	276	277	278	279	280	281	282
	283	285	286	287	288	289	290	
Olympian	301	314	319	320	321	322	401	402
	403	425	426	427	428	429		
Scania N	381	382	383	384	385	386	387	388
	389	390	391	392	393			

Darlington (Feethams) - Durham County

Outstation - Barnard Castle

MetroRider	2610	2629	2630	2631	2640	2641	2701	2702
	2703	2704	2705	2706	2707	2708	2711	2712
	2713	2714	2715	2716	2717	2718	2719	2720
	2721	2722	2723	2724				
Tiger	1234	1235						
MAN/Vecta	1518							
Dart	1601	1602	1603	1604	1605	1606	1607	1608
	1610	1611	1612	1613	1614			
Greenway	3505	3506	3507	3508				
DAF/Prestige	4055	4056	4057	4058				
Olympian	7215	7216	7246	7247	7266	7271	7272	

Durham (Waddington Steet) - Durham County

Mercedes-Benz	2453	2479						
MetroRider	2615	2616	2617	2618	2619	2620	2621	2622
	2623	2624	2625					
National	3130	3131	3134	3135	3136	3137	3138	3140
	3142	3143	3147	3148	3150	3152	3153	3773
DAF/Delta	4016	4017	4018	4019	4020	4021	4022	
Olympian	7207	7208	7217	7218	7227	7228	7250	7251
	7252	7253	7255	7256	7273	7274	7275	

Hexham (Burn Lane)- Northumbria

MetroRider	803	804	814	828	879	880	900	922
	923							
Tiger	247	250						
DAF/Prima	291	292	293	294	295			
Bristol VR	527	553						
Olympian	371	372	373	374	375	376	377	

Loftus (Whitby Road) - Tees & District - The Eden

Outstation at Whitby

MetroRider	2635	2636	2637	2638	2639			
National	3512	3519	3521	3522	3524	3744	3745	3747
	3748	3749	3756	3758	3759	3760		
Tiger	1232	1311	1312	1313	1314	1315	1340	1431♣
	1432♣	1433♣	1434♣					
MAN/Vecta	1509	1510	1511	1512	1513	1534	1535	
DAF/Prestige	4050	4051	4052	4053	4054			

Morpeth (Park Lane) - Northumbria

MetroRider	816	872	873	874	875	876	885	886
	889	892	904	905	906	907	912	913
	914							
Tiger	202	214	215	215	216	217	218	
Bristol LH	193	194	195					
DAF/Delta	256	259	260					
Bristol VR	538	548	563	576				
Olympian	305	306	307					

Newcastle (Jesmond Road) - Northumbria - National Express

MetroRider	861	862	863	864	865	887	888	915
	916	917	918	919	920	921		
Bova	131X	132X	133X	134X	135X	136X	137X	138X
	139X	140X						
DAF/Delta	251	252	254	255	256	258	261	262
Scania L	271	272	273	274	281	282	283	284
DAF/Paladin	4059							
DAF/Prestige	4060	4061	4062	4063	4064	4065	4066	4067
	4068	4069	4070	4071	4072	4073		
Bristol VR	540	541	543	580	583	590	591	
Fleetline	504	505	506	592	593	594	595	596
	597	598	599					
Metrobus	605							
Olympian	303	312	370	403	404	405	406	407
	408	409	410	411	412	413	414	415
	416	417	418	419	420			

Peterlee (Davey Drive) - Durham County

MetroRider	2626	2627	2628				
Dart	1636	1643					
National	3514	3520	3761	3762	3763	3764	3765	3766
	3767	3768	3769	3770				
Tiger	1301	1302	1328	1333	1401	1402	1403	1412
Olympian	7263	7286	7287	7288	7289	7290	7291	7292
	7293	7295						

Redcar (Railway Terrace) - Tees & District - The Eden

Tiger	1327	1405♣	1416♣	1417♣			
National	3518						
MB/Prisma	3003	3004	3005	3006	3007	3008	3009	3010
	3011	3012	3013	3014	3015	3016	3017	3018
	3019	3020	3021	3022	3023	3024	3025	
Olympian	202	203	204	206	210	223	235	236
	237	238	256	258	279	280	281	282
	283	284	285					

Richmond (Station Yard) - Durham County

Outstation - Hawes

MetroRider	2601	2602	2603	2604	2605	2609	2632	2633
	2634							
Tiger	1305	1306	1307	1308	1309	1310	1406	
MAN/Vecta	1530	1531	1532	1533	1551			
Olympian	7267	7268						

Stockton (Boathouse Lane) - Teeside

MetroRider	2606	2607	2608	2611	2612	2725		
Mercedes-Benz	2448							
National	3510	3511	3513	3515	3516	3517	3523	
Tiger	1342	1343	1344	1346	1423			
MAN/Vecta	1501	1502	1503	1504	1505	1506	1507	1508
	1516	1517	1519	1520	1521	1522	1523	1524
	1525	1540	1541	1542	1543	1544	1545	
DAF/Delta	4001	4002	4003	4004	4005	4006	4007	4008
	4009	4010	4011	4012	4013	4014	4015	
DAF/Prestige	4023	4024	4025	4026	4027	4028	4029	4030
	4031	4032	4033	4034	4035	4036	4037	4038
	4039	4040	4041	4042	4043	4044	4045	4046

Another view, albeit from an offside aspect of one of the five Leyland Olympians with Alexander RH bodywork. This compares with a similar vehicle now displaying the corporate image already illustrated. 274,L274FVN appears beneath the viaduct carrying the *GNER* line above the cathedral city of Durham during August 1998.
Tony Wilson

Arriva North East took delivery of fifty Plaxton-bodied DAF SB220 buses during 1998. These were to the later, low-floor version of the model and were divided between the former fleets. However, on fleet amalgamation the Northumbria examples were renumbered into the former United series. Pictured at Stockton is one of the early arrivals with North East, 4027, R427RPY. *Terry Wightman*

Stokesley (North Road) - Tees & District

Tiger	1327							
MAN/Vecta	1536	1537	1538	1539	1550	1551		
MB/Prisma	3001	3002						
Olympian	7225	7226	7233	7234	7239	7276	7277	7278

Withdrawn and unallocated:-

MetroRider	805	822	824					
Mercedes-Benz	965	966	2473					
National	3149	3757	3771	3772				
Bristol LH	192							
MAN/Vecta	1514	1516	1517					
Tiger	246	1324	1331	1334	1336	1339	1418	1419
	1420	1426						
Bristol VR	530	549	581	584				
Metrobuses	601	602	603	604	606	607		
Olympian	7209	7245	7265	7278	7294			

ARRIVA YORKSHIRE

Arriva Yorkshire Ltd; Arriva Yorkshire South Ltd; Arriva Yorkshire North Ltd,

24 Barnsley Road, Wakefield, West Yorkshire, WF1 5JX

Arriva Yorkshire West Ltd, Mill Street East, Dewsbury, West Yorkshire, WF12 9AG

ARRIVA serving Yorkshire

31	P31XUG	DAF DE33WSSB3000		Van Hool Alizée	C44FT	1997			
32	R32JYG	DAF DE33WSSB3000		Van Hool Alizée	C44FT	1998			
51	M51AWW	Scania K113CRB		Van Hool Alizée	C44FT	1995			
52	M52AWW	Scania K113CRB		Van Hool Alizée	C44FT	1995			
53	M53AWW	Scania K113CRB		Van Hool Alizée	C44FT	1995			
54	M54AWW	Scania K113CRB		Van Hool Alizée	C44FT	1995			

170-199		Dennis Dart SLF		Alexander ALX200	B40F	1997			
170	P170VUA	176	P176VUA	182	P182VUA	188	P188VUA	194	P194VUA
171	P171VUA	177	P177VUA	183	P183VUA	189	P189VUA	195	P195VUA
172	P172VUA	178	P178VUA	184	P184VUA	190	P190VUA	196	P196VUA
173	P173VUA	179	P179VUA	185	P185VUA	191	P191VUA	197	P197VUA
174	P174VUA	180	P180VUA	186	P186VUA	192	P192VUA	198	P198VUA
175	P175VUA	181	P181VUA	187	P187VUA	193	P193VUA	199	P199VUA

253	D204FBK	Leyland Lynx LX112TL11ZR1	Leyland Lynx	B51F	1986	Ex Solent Blue Line, 1987

255-264		Leyland Lynx LX1126LXCTFR1S	Leyland Lynx	B49F	1987-88	
255	E255TUB	259	E259TUB	261	E261TUB	263	E263TUB	264	E264TUB
257	E257TUB	260	E260TUB							

During 1997 the first of a batch of thirty Dennis Dart single-deck saloons began to make their presence felt on the streets of West Yorkshire. Bearing the recently revealed body design from Alexanders, they were delivered to the *Yorkshire Woollen District* company. All 39 buses, inlcuding 170, P170VUA, are based at Dewsbury.
Phillip Stephenson

265-314 Leyland Lynx LX112L10ZR1S Leyland Lynx B49F 1988-89

265	E265WUB	275	F275AWW	285	F285AWW	295	F295AWW	305	F305AWW
266	E266WUB	276	F276AWW	286	F286AWW	296	F296AWW	306	F306AWW
267	E267WUB	277	F277AWW	287	F287AWW	297	F297AWW	307	F307AWW
268	E268WUB	278	F278AWW	288	F288AWW	298	F298AWW	308	F308AWW
269	E269WUB	279	F279AWW	289	F289AWW	299	F299AWW	309	F309AWW
270	E270WUB	280	F280AWW	290	F290AWW	300	F300AWW	310	F310AWW
271	E271WUB	281	F281AWW	291	F291AWW	301	F301AWW	311	F311AWW
272	F272AWW	282	F282AWW	292	F292AWW	302	F302AWW	312	F312AWW
273	F273AWW	283	F283AWW	293	F293AWW	303	F303AWW	313	F313AWW
274	F274AWW	284	F284AWW	294	F294AWW	304	F304AWW	314	F314AWW

315	E116UTX	Leyland Lynx LX112L10ZR1R	Leyland Lynx	B51F	1988	Merthyr Tydfil, 1989
316	F117XTX	Leyland Lynx LX112L10ZR1R	Leyland Lynx	B51F	1988	Merthyr Tydfil, 1989
317	F118XTX	Leyland Lynx LX112L10ZR1R	Leyland Lynx	B51F	1988	Merthyr Tydfil, 1989

318-332 Leyland Lynx LX2R11C15Z4S Leyland Lynx B49F 1990

318	G317NNW	321	G321NNW	324	G324NUM	327	G327NUM	330	G330NUM
319	G319NNW	322	G322NNW	325	G110OUG	328	G109OUG	331	G331NUM
320	G324NNW	323	G108OUG	326	G326NUM	329	G329NUM	332	G332NUM

333-337 Leyland Lynx LX2R11C15Z4S Leyland Lynx 2 B49F 1990

333	H338TYG	334	H334TYG	335	H335TYG	336	H336TYG	337	H337TYG

338-347 Leyland Lynx LX2R11C15Z4S Leyland Lynx 2 B49F 1990-91

338	H338UWT	340	H343UWT	342	H342UWT	344	H344UWX	346	H346UWX
339	H339UWT	341	H341UWT	343	H343UWX	345	H345UWX	347	H347UWX

348	G542GAC	Leyland Lynx LX2R11C15Z4R	Leyland Lynx	B49F	1990	Volvo Bus, Warwick, 1991
349	G148CHP	Leyland Lynx LX2R11C15Z4R	Leyland Lynx	B49F	1990	Volvo Bus, Warwick, 1991
350	G149CHP	Leyland Lynx LX2R11C15Z4R	Leyland Lynx	B51F	1990	Volvo Bus, Warwick, 1991
351	G49CVC	Leyland Lynx LX112L10ZR1R	Leyland Lynx	B51F	1990	Volvo Bus, Warwick, 1991

352-382 Leyland Lynx LX2R11C15Z4S* Leyland Lynx 2 B49F 1991 *378 is LX2R11V18Z4S

352	H755WWW	359	H359WWY	365	J365YWX	371	J371YWX	377	J377AWT
353	H756WWW	360	H460WWY	366	J366YWX	372	J372AWT	378	J371AWT
354	H757WWW	361	H393WWY	367	J367YWX	373	J373AWT	379	J379BWU
355	H355WWX	362	J362YWX	368	J368YWX	374	J374AWT	380	J380BWU
356	H356WWX	363	J363YWX	369	J369YWX	375	J375AWT	381	J381BWU
357	H357WWX	364	J364YWX	370	J370YWX	376	J376AWT	382	J382BWU
358	H358WWY								

401-405 Volvo B10B-58 Alexander Strider B51F 1993

401	K401HWW	402	K402HWW	403	K403HWW	404	K404HWW	405	K405HWX

406	L406NUA	Volvo B10B-58	Wright Endeavour	BC49F	1993
407	L407NUA	Volvo B10B-58	Wright Endeavour	BC49F	1993
408	L408NUA	Volvo B10B-58	Wright Endeavour	BC49F	1993
409	L409NUA	Volvo B10B-58	Wright Endeavour	BC49F	1993

410-433 Volvo B10B-58 Alexander Strider B51F 1994

410	M410UNW	415	M415UNW	420	M420UNW	425	M425UNW	430	M430UNW
411	M411UNW	416	M416UNW	421	M421UNW	426	M426UNW	431	M431UNW
412	M412UNW	417	M417UNW	422	M422UNW	427	M427UNW	432	M432UNW
413	M413UNW	418	M418UNW	423	M423UNW	428	M428UNW	433	M433UNW
414	M414UNW	419	M419UNW	424	M424UNW	429	M429UNW		

Opposite, top:- **Sheffield interchange is the location for this picture of Volvo B10B 406, L406NUA which carries route branding for service X33, the White Rose Express. One of four of the type with Wright Endeavour bodywork - the only ones operated by Arriva - they are fitted with high-back seating for their duties.** *Tony Wilson*

Opposite, bottom:- **The 1997 batches of Mercedes-Benz Vario were divided two deliveries with differing seating capacities. The last of the second batch, 799. R799DUB, is seen heading for Castleford where it is based.** *Malcolm King*

With many of its sisters now departing for other companies within the *Arriva* empire, the double-deck Olympian was seeming to become a poor relation within *Arriva serving Yorkshire*. Back in July 1998 though, 578, A578NWX passes through the offset junction near to the bus station in Wakefield, whilst operating on a run to Bradford. Retaining a former livery, a change of ownership is evident by the addition of a sticker in the first window behind the entrance/exit. *Tony Wilson*

440-471

DAF DE02GSSB220 — Alexander ALX300 — N42F — 1998

440	R440GWY	448	R448KWT	454	R454KWT	460	R460KWT	466	S466GUB
441	R441KWT	449	R449KWT	455	R455KWT	461	R461KWT	467	S467GUB
442	R442KWT	450	R450KWT	456	R456KWT	462	S462GUB	468	S468GUB
443	R443KWT	451	R451KWT	457	R457KWT	463	S463GUB	469	S469GUB
445	R445KWT	452	R452KWT	458	R458KWT	464	S464GUB	470	S470GUB
446	R446KWT	453	R453KWT	459	R459KWT	465	S465GUB	471	S471GUB
447	R447KWT						

472-491

DAF DE02GSSB220 — Alexander ALX300 — N42F — 1998

472	S472ANW	476	S476ANW	480	S480ANW	484	S484ANW	488	S488ANW
473	S473ANW	477	S477ANW	481	S481ANW	485	S485ANW	489	S489ANW
474	S474ANW	478	S478ANW	482	S482ANW	486	S486ANW	490	S490ANW
475	S475ANW	479	S479ANW	483	S483ANW	487	S487ANW	491	S491ANW

517-552

Leyland Olympian ONLXB/1R — Eastern Coach Works — B45/33F — 1982-83

517	CWR517Y	528	EWX528Y	534	EWX534Y	539	EWW539Y	547	EWW547Y
520	CWR520Y	529	EWX529Y	535	EWX535Y	541	EWW541Y	548	EWW548Y
521	CWR521Y	530	EWX530Y	536	EWX536Y	542	EWW542Y	552	EWW552Y
524	CWR524Y	532	EWX532Y	537	EWX537Y	545	EWW545Y		

562-612

Leyland Olympian ONLXB/1R — Eastern Coach Works — B45/32F* — 1983-85 *seating varies

562	A562KWY	574	A574NWX	584	A584NWX	593	B593SWX	603	B603UUM
564	A564KWY	575	A575NWX	585	A585NWX	594	B594SWX	604	B604UUM
565	A565NWX	577	A577NWX	586	A586NWX	595	B595SWX	606	B606UUM
566	A566NWX	578	A578NWX	587	A587NWX	596	B596SWX	607	B607UUM
568	A568NWX	579	A579NWX	588	A588NWX	597	B597SWX	608	B608UUM
569	A569NWX	580	A580NWX	589	A589NWX	599	B599SWX	609	B609UUM
570	A570NWX	581	A581NWX	590	A590NWX	600	B600UUM	610	C610ANW
571	A571NWX	582	A583NWX	591	B593SWX	601	B601UUM	611	C611ANW
572	A572NWX	583	A584NWX	592	B593SWX	602	B602UUM	612	C612ANW
573	A573NWX						

Few Northern Counties bodied vehicles operate with Arriva in the West Yorkshire area. However, a small batch of four was inherited with the acquisition of the South Yorkshire Transport company based in Pontefract. With the original livery of dark blue and white now history, 613, E205TUB now wears an alternative livery of corporate cream and aquamarine, while pausing in Pontefract bus station.
Phillip Stephenson

613	E205TUB	Leyland Olympian ONTL11/1RH	Northern Counties	B43/28F	1988	South Yorkshire, Pontefract, 1995	
614	TWY7	Leyland Olympian ONCL10/1RZ	Northern Counties	B43/28F	1988	South Yorkshire, Pontefract, 1995	
615	H106RWT	Leyland Olympian ON2R50C13Z4	Northern Counties	B43/28F	1990	South Yorkshire, Pontefract, 1995	
616	H108RWT	Leyland Olympian ON2R50C13Z4	Northern Counties	B43/28F	1990	South Yorkshire, Pontefract, 1995	
621	N621KUA	Volvo Olympian YN2RV18Z4	Northern Counties Palatine II	B43/30F	1996		
622	N622KUA	Volvo Olympian YN2RV18Z4	Northern Counties Palatine II	B43/30F	1996		
623	N623KUA	Volvo Olympian YN2RV18Z4	Northern Counties Palatine II	B43/30F	1996		
707	H707UNW	Optare MetroRider MR09	Optare	B23F	1991		

714-725   Optare MetroRider MR05   Optare   B31F   1992-93

714	J714CUM	716	J716CUM	717	J717CUM	720	J720CUM	725	K725HUG

730-745   Optare MetroRider MR15   Optare   B31F   1993-94

730	L730MWW	734	L734MWW	737	L737PUA	740	L740PUA	743	M743UUA
731	L731MWW	735	L735PUA	738	L738PUA	741	L741PUA	744	M744UUA
732	L732MWW	736	L736PUA	739	L739PUA	742	M742UUA	745	M745UUA
733	L733MWW								

746-750   Optare MetroRider MR15   Optare   B31F   1995

746	M746WWX	747	M247WWX	748	M748WWX	749	M749WWR	750	M750WWR

751	M751WWR	Optare MetroRider MR31	Optare	B25F	1995
752	M752WWR	Optare MetroRider MR31	Optare	B25F	1995
753	M753WWR	Optare MetroRider MR31	Optare	B25F	1995
754	N754LWW	Optare MetroRider MR15	Optare	B31F	1996
755	N755LWW	Optare MetroRider MR15	Optare	B31F	1996
756	N756LWW	Optare MetroRider MR15	Optare	B31F	1996
757	N757LWW	Optare MetroRider MR15	Optare	B31F	1996

The Corn Exchange junction in Leeds City Centre provides both the observer and the photographer with ample opportunity to while away many hours. Even with the introduction of traffic restrictions during 1998, buses continue to pass through the junction in droves. The variety includes *Arriva*-owned buses such as 432, M432UNW a 1994 built Volvo B10B with a 51-seater Alexander Strider body, which was one of the first of its type repainted into the corporate livery. *Les Peters*

758-770

									Mercedes-Benz Vario O810		Plaxton Beaver 2		B27F		1997

758	R758DUB	761	R761DUB	764	R764DUB	767	R767DUB	769	R769DUB
759	R758DUB	762	R762DUB	765	R765DUB	768	R768DUB	770	R770DUB
760	R760DUB	763	R763DUB	766	R766DUB				

771-778

Mercedes-Benz 811D — Plaxton Beaver — B31F — 1994

771	L771RWW	773	L773RWW	775	L775RWW	777	L779RWW	778	L778RWW
772	L772RWW	774	L774RWW	776	L776RWW				

779-784

Mercedes-Benz 811D — Plaxton Beaver — B31F* — 1995 — *779 is B27F

779	N779EUA	781	N781EUA	782	N782EUA	783	N783EUA	784	N784EUA
780	N780EUA								

785-799

Mercedes-Benz Vario O810 — Plaxton Beaver 2 — B31F — 1997

785	R785DUB	789	R789DUB	792	R792DUB	795	R795DUB	798	R798DUB
787	R787DUB	790	R790DUB	793	R793DUB	796	R796DUB	799	R799DUB
788	R788DUB	791	R791DUB	794	R794DUB	797	R797DUB		

801-830

Dennis Lance 11SDA3107 — Alexander Strider — B47F — 1993

801	K801HWW	807	L807NNW	813	L813NNW	819	L819NWY	825	L825NWY
802	K802HWW	808	L808NNW	814	L814NNW	820	L820NWY	826	L826NYG
803	K803HWW	809	L809NNW	815	L815NWY	821	L821NWY	827	L827NYG
804	K804HWW	810	L810NNW	816	L816NWY	822	L822NWY	828	L828NYG
805	K805HWX	811	L811NNW	817	L817NWY	823	L823NWY	829	L829NYG
806	L806NNW	812	L812NNW	818	L818NWY	824	L824NWY	830	L830NYG

Representing the midibus in Yorkshire is this Optare MetroRider. The centre of Wakefield is host to 740, L740PUA as this wide bodied version passes through in the former *West Riding* green and cream livery. The MetroRider was originally a product of MCW at Washwood Heath in the West Midlands. Production subsequently passed to Optare who are based in Leeds. *Tony Wilson*

Ancilliary vehicles

252	C920FMP	Leyland Lynx LX1126LXCTFR1	Leyland Lynx	B16F	1986	Leyland Bus, 1987
255	E255TUB	Leyland Lynx LX1126LXCTFR1	Leyland Lynx	B51F	1986	Leyland Bus, 1987
990	C103UHO	Leyland National 2 NL116HLXCT/1R		B16F	1985	Ex Stevensons, Uttoxeter, 1989
995	C104UHO	Leyland National 2 NL116HLXCT/1R		B16F	1985	Ex Stevensons, Uttoxeter, 1989

Previous Registrations:

TWY7   From new

Allocations:-

Castleford (Wheldon Road) - Yorkshire

Mercedes-Benz	758	785	787	788	789	790	791	792
	793	794	795	796	797	798	799	
Lynx	267	269	276	289	290	293	294	299
	301	329	330	331	332	333	334	335
	336	337	338	339	340	341	342	343
	344	345	346	347	352	353	354	355
	356	357	360	366	367	368	369	370
	371	372	373	374				
Olympian	528	529	537	539	541	572	573	595
	596	597						

Dewsbury (Mill Street East) - Yorkshire West - ✈(Flightlink).

Coach	31✈	32✈	51✈	52✈	53✈	54✈		
Mercedes-Benz	771	772	773	774	775	776	777	778
	779	780	781	782	783	784		

Dart	170	171	172	173	174	175	176	177
	178	179	180	181	182	183	184	185
	186	187	188	189	190	191	192	193
	194	195	196	197	198	199		
Lynx	279	291	295	296	303	304	328	350
	351							
DAF/ALX 300	448	449	450	451	452	453	454	455
	456	457	458	459	460	461		

Heckmondwike (Beck Lane) - Yorkshire West

Volvo B10B	401	402	403	404	405	410	411	412
	413	414	415					
Lance	801	802	803	804	805	806	807	808
	809	810	811	812	813	814	815	816
	817	818	819	820	821	822	823	824
	825	826	827	828	829	830		
Olympian	521	524	536	545	547	548	562	564
	565	568	569	570	571	585	586	587
	588	589	600	601	602			

Pontefract (Northgate) - Yorkshire South

MetroRider	707	745	749	750	754	755	756	757
Lynx	265	268	280	281	284	315	316	317
	318	319	320	321	322	323	324	325
	326	327						
Olympian	566	613	614	615	616			

Selby (Cowie Drive, Ousegate) - Yorkshire North

Mercedes-Benz	759	760	761	762	768			
DAF	441	442	443	444	445	446	447	
Olympian	520	534	535	542	552	575	590	591
	592	593	594	603	607	621	622	623

Wakefield (Belle Isle, Barnsley Road) - Yorkshire

MetroRider	714	716	717	720	725	730	731	732
	733	734	735	736	737	738	739	740
	741	742	743	744	746	747	748	751
	752	753						
Mercedes-Benz	763	764	765	766	767	769	770	
Lynx	266	270	271	272	273	274	275	277
	278	282	283	285	286	287	288	292
	297	298	300	302	305	306	307	308
	309	310	311	312	312	313	314	348
	349	358	359	361	362	363	364	365
	375	376	377	378	379	380	381	382
Volvo B10B	416	417	418	419	420	421	422	423
	424	425	426	427	428	429	430	431
	432	433						
DAF/ALX300	440	462	463	464	465	466	467	468
	469	470	471	472	473	474	475	476
	477	478	479	480	481	482	483	484
	485	486	487	488	489	490	491	
Olympian	517	530	532	574	577	578	579	580
	581	582	583	584	604	606	608	609
	610	611	612					

Withdrawn and unallocated

Lynx	253	257	259	260	261	263	264

ARRIVA NORTH WEST

Arriva North West Ltd, 73 Ormskirk Road, Aintree, Liverpool, L9 5AE

Arriva Manchester Ltd, Hulme Hall Road, Manchester, M15 4LY

Arriva Merseyside Ltd, 73 Ormskirk Road, Aintree, Liverpool, L9 5AE

50	J78MHF			Mercedes-Benz 709D		Wright NimBus	B29F	1992	Amberline, 1993	
51	J734MFY			Mercedes-Benz 709D		Wright NimBus	B29F	1992	Amberline, 1993	
52	J735MFY			Mercedes-Benz 709D		Wright NimBus	B29F	1992	Amberline, 1993	

53-67				Mercedes-Benz 709D		Alexander Sprint	B25F	1994		
53	L153UEM	56	L156UEM	59	M59WKA	62	M62WKA	65	M65WKA
54	L154UEM	57	M157WWM	60	M160WTJ	63	M63WKA	66	M166WTJ
55	L155UEM	58u	M158WWM	61	M61WKA	64	M64WKA	67	M67WKA

| 69 | L647DNA | | | Mercedes-Benz 709D | | Plaxton Beaver | B23F | 1994 | Star Line, 1995 | |

70-95				Mercedes-Benz 811D		Carlyle	B33F	1989-90		
70	G100TND	76w	G106TND	79	G109TND	88	G118TND	94w	G124TJA
72w	G102TND	77	G107TND	80	G110TND	89	G119TND	95	G125TJA
74	G104TND	78	G108TND	86	G116TND	93	G123TND		

97	J292NNB			Mercedes-Benz 709D		Carlyle	B29F	1991	Star Line, 1995	
98	J293NNB			Mercedes-Benz 709D		Carlyle	B29F	1991	Star Line, 1995	
99	H129CDB			Mercedes-Benz 811D		LHE Commuter	B31F	1990	Ex C-Line, 1993	
100	H130CDB			Mercedes-Benz 811D		LHE Commuter	B31F	1990	Ex C-Line, 1992	

All minibus services that are operated by Arriva North West are undertaken by Mercedes-Benz products, with the 709D now the earliest model remaining. Pictured in Wigan is 182, P182GND from near-by Haydock depot carrying a Plaxton Beaver body.
Les Peters

101-105 — Mercedes-Benz 709D — Alexander Sprint — BC23F — 1994

101	M101WKA	102	M102WKA	103	M103WKA	104	M104WKA	105	M105WKA

107	L646DNA	Mercedes-Benz 709D	Dormobile Routemaker	B27F	1994	Star Line, 1995
108	L648DNA	Mercedes-Benz 709D	Marshall C19	B29F	1994	Star Line, 1995
109	L649DNA	Mercedes-Benz 709D	Marshall C19	B29F	1994	Star Line, 1995
119	J4SLT	Mercedes-Benz 709D	Plaxton Beaver	B23F	1992	South Lancashire, 1997

120-129 — Mercedes-Benz 709D — Alexander Sprint — B29F — 1995

120	M120YCM	122	M122YCM	125	M125YCM	127	M127YCM	129	M129YCM
121	M121YCM	124	M124YCM	126	M126YCM	128	M128YCM		

130-134 — Mercedes-Benz 709D — Reeve Burgess Beaver — B27F — 1992 Star Line, 1995

130	J296NNB	131	J297NNB	132	J298NNB	133	J299NNB	134	K876UDB

135-142 — Mercedes-Benz 709D — Plaxton Beaver — B27F* — 1993-94 Star Line, 1995
*139 is B29F

135	K878UDB	137	K882UDB	139	K887UDB	141	L642DNA	142	L643DNA
136	K879UDB	138	K884UDB	140	L641DNA				

143-149 — Mercedes-Benz 709D — Alexander Sprint — B27F — 1994-95 Star Line, 1995

143	M363KVR	145	M365KVR	147	M367KVR	148	M368KVR	149	M369KVR
144	M364KVR	146	M366KVR						

150	J3SLT	Mercedes-Benz 709D	Plaxton Beaver	B29F	1997	South Lancashire, 1997
151	L151FRJ	Mercedes-Benz 709D	Alexander Sprint	B23F	1993	Timeline, Leigh, 1998
152	L152FRJ	Mercedes-Benz 709D	Alexander Sprint	B23F	1993	Timeline, Leigh, 1998
153	L153FRJ	Mercedes-Benz 709D	Alexander Sprint	B23F	1993	Timeline, Leigh, 1998
154	L154FRJ	Mercedes-Benz 709D	Alexander Sprint	B23F	1993	Timeline, Leigh, 1998

158-163 — Mercedes-Benz 709D — Alexander Sprint — B23F — 1996 Timeline, Leigh, 1998

158	P178FNF	160	P180FNF	161	P181FNF	162	P182FNF	163	P183FNF
159	P179FNF								

166	M166LNC	Mercedes-Benz 709D	Alexander Sprint	B23F	1994	Timeline, Leigh, 1998
167	M167LNC	Mercedes-Benz 709D	Alexander Sprint	B23F	1994	Timeline, Leigh, 1998
168	M156LNC	Mercedes-Benz 709D	Alexander Sprint	B23F	1994	Timeline, Leigh, 1998
169	M157LNC	Mercedes-Benz 709D	Alexander Sprint	B23F	1994	Timeline, Leigh, 1998
170	J10SLT	Mercedes-Benz 811D	Reeve Burgess Beaver	B31F	1991	South Lancashire, 1997
171	K1SLT	Mercedes-Benz 811D	Plaxton Beaver	B31F	1993	South Lancashire, 1997
172	K2SLT	Mercedes-Benz 811D	Plaxton Beaver	B31F	1993	South Lancashire, 1997
173	K3SLT	Mercedes-Benz 811D	Plaxton Beaver	B31F	1992	South Lancashire, 1997

175-184 — Mercedes-Benz 811D — Plaxton Beaver — B31F — 1996

175	N175DWM	177	N177DWM	179	N179DWM	181	P181GND	183	P183GND
176	N176DWM	178	N178DWM	180	P180GND	182	P182GND	184	P184GND

191	K457EVC	Mercedes-Benz 811D	Wright NimBus	B31F	1993	Little White Buses, 1995
192	K787VNR	Mercedes-Benz 811D	Dormobile Routemaker	B33F	1993	Little White Buses, 1995
193	L193DBC	Mercedes-Benz 811D	Marshall C16	B31F	1994	Little White Buses, 1995
194	L529XNR	Mercedes-Benz 811D	Dormobile Routemaker	B31F	1993	Little White Buses, 1995
195	M689FJF	Mercedes-Benz 811D	Marshall C16	B31F	1994	Little White Buses, 1995
196	M615XLG	Mercedes-Benz 811D	Marshall C16	B31F	1994	Little White Buses, 1995
197	M998XRF	Mercedes-Benz 811D	Marshall C16	B31F	1995	Little White Buses, 1995
198	G113PGT	Mercedes-Benz 811D	Alexander Sprint	B28F	199	South Lancashire, 1997

Scania L113 chassis were again the choice for North Western's 1997 delivery of single-deck buses, though the body order for this batch was placed with Northern Counties, after earlier products were sourced from East Lancashire and Wrights. Though pictured in Manchester with Bee Line names, the vehicle is currently allocated to Liverpool for North West duties. *Tony Wilson*

200-210

Leyland National 10351A/2R · B44F · 1979-80 Parfitt's, 1995

200	BYW359V	202	BYW379V	204	BYW406V	206	BYW413V	209	BYW432V
201	BYW367V	203	BYW402V	205	BYW412V	208	BYW430V	210	BYW437V

211	MIL5581	Leyland National 10351A/1R(Volvo)	B41F	1976	London & Country, 1989

215-253

Leyland National 11351A/1R · B49F · 1976-78 Ribble, 1986

215w	SCK688P	219	SCK693P	229w	UHG724R	241w	ACW764R	251w	CBV792S
218w	SCK692P								

284w	NTU15Y	Leyland National 2 NL116HLXB/2R	B52F	1983	Crosville, 1989
286w	VBG92V	Leyland National 2 NL116L11/2R(6HLXB)	B49F	1980	Cymru, 1998
287w	VBG94V	Leyland National 2 NL116L11/2R(6HLXB)	B49F	1980	Cymru, 1998
294w	KNV514P	Leyland National 11351/1R	B49F	1976	Midland Fox, 1994
331w	NPK242P	Leyland National 10351A/1R	B41F	1976	London & Country, 1989
332w	NPK245P	Leyland National 10351A/1R	B41F	1976	London & Country, 1989
340	UPB335S	Leyland National 10351A/1R	B41F	1977	London & Country, 1989

356-370

Leyland National 11351A/1R (6HLX) · B49F · 1977-79 Crosville, 1990

356w	CFM350S	364	GMB380T	370	KMA400T
361	EMB367S				

East Lancashire-bodied vehicles were purchased in large numbers when the bodybuilder was associated to British Bus. Pictured in Manchester is Dennis Falcon 382, G382EKA, one of eight purchased in 1990. Similar vehicles were delivered to Midland Red North and London & Country, though those from the latter have now been transferred back to Arriva North West. The North West operation comprises the former North Western, Bee Line and Liverline licences which have been re-named as shown in the section heading. In common with other areas the new name identity only takes place on repainting and old fleet names remain displayed, although only the new names are shown here. *Tony Wilson*

381-388

		Dennis Falcon SDA421		East Lancashire EL2000		B48F	1990		
381	G381EKA	383	G383EKA	385	G385EKA	387	G387EKA	388	G388EKA
382	G382EKA	384	G384EKA	386	G386EKA				

389	A50LHG	Dennis Falcon H SDA413	East Lancashire	BC43F	1984	South Lancashire, 1997	
390	B51XFV	Dennis Falcon H SDA413	East Lancashire	BC40F	1985	South Lancashire, 1997	
392	G302DPA	Dennis Falcon HC SDA421	East Lancashire EL2000	B48F	1990	Southern Counties (C&NS), 1998	
393	G303DPA	Dennis Falcon HC SDA421	East Lancashire EL2000	B48F	1990	Southern Counties (C&NS), 1998	
394	G304DPA	Dennis Falcon HC SDA421	East Lancashire EL2000	B48F	1990	Southern Counties (C&NS), 1998	
395	G305DPA	Dennis Falcon HC SDA421	East Lancashire EL2000	B48F	1990	Southern Counties (C&NS), 1998	

400-409

		Leyland National 11351/1R (DAF)				B50F	1974	West Midlands Travel, 1995-96	
400	MIL5580	403	MIL5573	405	MIL5575	408	MIL6678	409	MIL6679
402	MIL5582	404	MIL5574	406	MIL6676				

Opposite, top:- **The Dennis Dart made a large impact on the North Western fleet when new with the type dominating Liverpool services and fifty-four currently based at the former Ribble depot. Pictured near Lime Street rail station is Plaxton-bodied 1178, M178YKA.** *Les Peters*
Opposite, bottom:- **The last of a batch of thirty-four Wright-bodied Scania single-deck buses is 1034, N134DWM, pictured here passing through Wigan on service 660 to Warrington sporting the new livery. Its home depot at Haydock houses much of the Scania fleet, and initially was entirely so equipped.** *Tony Wilson*

410-424   Leyland National 11351/1R (DAF)   B50F   1974-75 West Midlands Travel, 1996

410	MIL6680	413	MIL7613	417	MIL7617	421	MIL7621	423	MIL7623
411	MIL6681	414	MIL7614	420	MIL7620	422	MIL7622	424	MIL7624
412	MIL7612	416	MIL7616						

425-436   Leyland National 11351A/1R (DAF)   B50F   1977-79 West Midlands Travel, 1996

425	OOX801R	428	OOX805R	431	OOX810R	433	OOX813R	435w	TVP837S
426	OOX802R	429	OOX807R	432	OOX811R	434	OOX818R	436	AOL11T
427	OOX803R	430	OOX809R						

437	XYS596S	Leyland National 2 NL116L11/1R(DAF)	B52F	1980	McGills, 1997

450-460   Leyland National 2 NL116L11/1R(DAF)   B50F   1980 West Midlands Travel, 1996
460 North East, 1998

450	DOC20V	453	DOC36V	455	DOC43V	457	DOC47V	459	DOC22V
451	DOC30V	454	DOC38V	456	DOC45V	458	DOC21V	460	DOC33V
452	DOC32V								

600-625   Leyland Olympian ONLXB/1R   Eastern Coach Works   B45/32F   1983-85 Ribble, 1986

600	DBV133Y	605	A141MRN	610	B149TRN	615	B155TRN	622	B966WRN
601	DBV135Y	606w	A144OFR	611	B150TRN	618	B962WRN	623	B967WRN
602	DBV136Y	607	A146OFR	612	B151TRN	619	B963WRN	624	B968WRN
603	A139MRN	608	A147OFR	613	B153TRN	620	B964WRN	625	B969WRN
604	A140MRN	609	B148TRN	614	B154TRN	621	B965WRN		

630-635   Dennis Dominator DDA1026   East Lancashire   B43/25F   1989

630	F630BKD	632	F632BKD	633	F633BKD	634	F634BKD	635	F635BKD

646	G661DTJ	Volvo Citybus B10M-50	East Lancashire	B49/39F	1990	Southern Counties (C&NS), 1998
647	G647EKA	Volvo Citybus B10M-50	East Lancashire	B49/39F	1990	Southern Counties (C&NS), 1998
650	G650EKA	Volvo Citybus B10M-50	East Lancashire	B49/39F	1990	
651	G651EKA	Volvo Citybus B10M-50	East Lancashire	B49/39F	1990	
652	G652EKA	Volvo Citybus B10M-50	East Lancashire	B49/39F	1990	
653	G653EKA	Volvo Citybus B10M-50	East Lancashire	B49/39F	1990	

654-662   Leyland Olympian ONLXB/1R   Eastern Coach Works   B45/32F   1983-84 Crosville, 1989

654	PFM126Y	656	PFM129Y	658	A140SMA	660	A149UDM	662	A153UDM
655	PFM128Y	657	A139SMA	659	A141SMA	661	A151UDM		

667	GFM110X	Leyland Olympian ONLXB/1R	Eastern Coach Works	B45/32F	1982	Crosville, 1989
668	A142SMA	Leyland Olympian ONLXB/1R	Eastern Coach Works	B45/32F	1983	Crosville, 1989
669	A148UDM	Leyland Olympian ONLXB/1R	Eastern Coach Works	B45/32F	1983	Crosville, 1989

671-680   Scania N113DRB   Northern Counties   B47/33F   1990-91 Liverline, 1993

671	G34HKY	673	G36HKY	675	G38HKY	677	G714LKW	679	H804RWJ
672	G35HKY	674	G37HKY	676	G711LKW	678	H803RWJ	680	H805RWJ

690-699   Volvo Citybus B10M-50   East Lancashire   B45/34F   1991 London South, 1998

690	H660GPF	692	H662GPF	695	H665GPF	697	H667GPF	699	H679GPF
691	H661GPF								

778-788   Volvo B10M-50 Citybus   Alexander Q   B55F   1992 Timeline, Leigh, 1998

778	H78DVM	785	H85DVM	786	H86DVM	787	H87DVM	788	H588DVM
779	H79DVM								

848	D154THG	Leyland Tiger TRBTL11/2RP	East Lancashire	B55F	1986	South Lancashire, 1997
849	49XBF	Leyland Tiger TRBTL11/2RP	Plaxton Derwent 2	B54F	1988	South Lancashire, 1997
855	TSU646	Leyland Tiger TRCTL11/3R	Plaxton Paramount 3200 E	C53F	1983	Maidstone & District, 1997

Volvo Citybus 650, G650EKA is seen at the Wigan terminus of route 385 for which the vehicle carries route branding. Four of the type remained in north west England while the remainder of the batch moved south. However, this last year has seen the return of two from Surrey. *Richard Godfrey*

Acquired from South Lancashire, 849, 49XBF is a Leyland Tiger with Plaxton Derwent bodywork and based at Winsford depot in Cheshire. This unit replaced the Northwich depot that has since been redeveloped. *Les Peters*

1001-1005   Scania L113CRL   Wright Axcess-ultralow   N42F   1996

1001	N101YVU	1002	M2SLT	1003	N103YVU	1004	N104YVU	1005	N105YVU

1006-1034   Scania L113CRL   Wright Axcess-ultralow   N43F   1996

1006	N106DWM	1012	N112DWM	1018	N118DWM	1024	N124DWM	1030	N130DWM
1007	N107DWM	1013	N113DWM	1019	N119DWM	1025	N125DWM	1031	N131DWM
1008	N108DWM	1014	N114DWM	1020	N120DWM	1026	N126DWM	1032	N132DWM
1009	N109DWM	1015	N115DWM	1021	N121DWM	1027	N127DWM	1033	N133DWM
1010	N110DWM	1016	N116DWM	1022	N122DWM	1028	N128DWM	1034	N134DWM
1011	N211DWM	1017	N117DWM	1023	N123DWM	1029	N129DWM		

1035-1040   Scania L113CRL   East Lancashire Flyte   N47F   1996

1035	P135GND	1037	P137GND	1038	P138GND	1039	P139GND	1040	P140GND
1036	P136GND								

1041-1061   Scania L113CRL   Northern Counties Paladin   N42F   1997

1041	P41MVU	1046	P46MVU	1050	P250NBA	1054	R54XVM	1058	P58MVU
1042	P42MVU	1047	R47XVM	1051	R51XVM	1055	R255WRJ	1059	R59XVM
1043	P43MVU	1048	R48XVM	1052	P52MVU	1056	P56MVU	1060	P260NBA
1044	P244NBA	1049	P49MVU	1053	P53MVU	1057	R57XVM	1061	P61MVU
1045	P45MVU								

1150	L150SBG	Dennis Dart 9SDL3034	East Lancashire	B32F	1993
1151	L151SBG	Dennis Dart 9SDL3034	East Lancashire	B32F	1993
1152	L152SBG	Dennis Dart 9SDL3034	East Lancashire	B32F	1993
1153	L153UKB	Dennis Dart 9SDL3034	Plaxton Pointer	B20F	1994
1154	L154UKB	Dennis Dart 9SDL3034	Plaxton Pointer	B20F	1994
1155	L155UKB	Dennis Dart 9SDL3034	Plaxton Pointer	B20F	1994
1156	L156UKB	Dennis Dart 9SDL3034	Plaxton Pointer	B20F	1994

1157-1170   Dennis Dart 9.8SDL3040*   East Lancashire   B40F   1994-95 1170 is 9.8SDL3054

1157	M157WKA	1160	M160WKA	1163	M163WKA	1166	M166WKA	1169	M169WKA
1158	M158WKA	1161	M161WKA	1164	M164WKA	1167	M167WKA	1170	M170WKA
1159	M159WKA	1162	M162WKA	1165	M165WKA	1168	M168WKA		

1171-1187   Dennis Dart 9.8SDL3040   Plaxton Pointer   B40F   1995

1171	M171YKA	1175	M175YKA	1179	M179YKA	1182	M182YKA	1185	M185YKA
1172	M172YKA	1176	M176YKA	1180	M180YKA	1183	M183YKA	1186	M186YKA
1173	M173YKA	1177	M177YKA	1181	M181YKA	1184	M184YKA	1187	M187YKA
1174	M174YKA	1178	M178YKA						

1188-1199   Dennis Dart 9.8SDL3054   Plaxton Pointer   B40F   1995

1188	M188YKA	1191	M191YKA	1194	M194YKA	1196	M196YKA	1198	M198YKA
1189	M189YKA	1192	M192YKA	1195	M195YKA	1197	M197YKA	1199	M199YKA
1190	M190YKA	1193	M193YKA						

1200	P452BPH	Dennis Lance 11SDA	Northern Counties	B49F	1997	On loan from Plaxton

1201-1210   Dennis Lance 11SDA3113   Plaxton Verde   B49F   1995

1201	M201YKA	1203	M203YKA	1205	M205YKA	1207	M207YKA	1209	M209YKA
1202	M202YKA	1204	M204YKA	1206	M206YKA	1208	M208YKA	1210	M210YKA

1211	M211YKD	Dennis Dart 9.8SDL3040	Plaxton Pointer	B40F	1995
1212	M212YKD	Dennis Dart 9.8SDL3040	Plaxton Pointer	B40F	1995
1213	M213YKD	Dennis Dart 9.8SDL3040	Plaxton Pointer	B40F	1995
1214	M214YKD	Dennis Dart 9.8SDL3054	Plaxton Pointer	B40F	1995
1215	M215YKD	Dennis Dart 9.8SDL3054	Plaxton Pointer	B40F	1995
1216	M216YKD	Dennis Dart 9.8SDL3054	Plaxton Pointer	B40F	1995

1217-1264 — Dennis Dart 9.8SDL3054 — East Lancashire — B40F — 1995

1217	M217AKB	1227	M227AKB	1237	N237CKA	1247	N247CKA	1256	N256CKA
1218	M218AKB	1228	M228AKB	1238	N238CKA	1248	N248CKA	1257	N257CKA
1219	M219AKB	1229	M229AKB	1239	N239CKA	1249	N249CKA	1258	N258CKA
1220	M220AKB	1230	M230AKB	1240	N240CKA	1250	N250CKA	1259	N259CKA
1221	M221AKB	1231	M231AKB	1241	N241CKA	1251	N251CKA	1260	N260CKA
1222	M322AKB	1232	M232AKB	1242	N242CKA	1252	N252CKA	1261	N261CKA
1223	M223AKB	1233	N233CKA	1243	N243CKA	1253	N253CKA	1262	N262CKA
1224	M224AKB	1234	N234CKA	1244	N244CKA	1254	N254CKA	1263	N263CKA
1225	M225AKB	1235	N235CKA	1245	N245CKA	1255	N255CKA	1264	N264CKA
1226	M226AKB	1236	N236CKA	1246	N246CKA				

1265	K877UDB	Dennis Dart 9.8SDL3017	Plaxton Pointer	B40F	1992	Star Line, 1995
1266	M370KVR	Dennis Dart 9.8SDL3035	Northern Counties Paladin	B40F	1994	Star Line, 1995
1267	M371KVR	Dennis Dart 9.8SDL3035	Northern Counties Paladin	B40F	1994	Star Line, 1995
1268	M372KVR	Dennis Dart 9.8SDL3035	Northern Counties Paladin	B40F	1995	Star Line, 1995
1269	M841RCP	Dennis Dart 9.8SDL3054	Northern Counties Paladin	B39F	1995	Wigan Bus Company, 1995
1270	M842RCP	Dennis Dart 9.8SDL3054	Northern Counties Paladin	B39F	1995	Wigan Bus Company, 1995
1271	M843RCP	Dennis Dart 9.8SDL3054	Northern Counties Paladin	B39F	1995	Wigan Bus Company, 1995
1273	K73SRG	Dennis Dart 9.8SDL3017	Plaxton Pointer	B43F	1993	Northumbria (Hunters), 1997
1274	K74SRG	Dennis Dart 9.8SDL3017	Plaxton Pointer	B43F	1993	Northumbria (Hunters), 1997
1275	K75SRG	Dennis Dart 9.8SDL3017	Plaxton Pointer	B43F	1993	Northumbria (Hunters), 1997
1276	J6SLT	Dennis Dart 9.8SDL3040	Plaxton Pointer	B40F	1996	South Lancashire, 1997
1277	J7SLT	Dennis Dart 9.8SDL3040	Plaxton Pointer	B38F	1996	South Lancashire, 1997
1278	J8SLT	Dennis Dart 9.8SDL3017	Plaxton Pointer	B38F	1992	South Lancashire, 1997
1279	J9SLT	Dennis Dart 9.8SDL3017	Plaxton Pointer	B38F	1992	South Lancashire, 1997
1280	L11SLT	Dennis Dart 9.8SDL3025	Plaxton Pointer	B38F	1993	South Lancashire, 1997
1281	L1SLT	Dennis Dart 9SDL3011	Plaxton Pointer	B35F	1993	South Lancashire, 1997
1282	L2SLT	Dennis Dart 9SDL3011	Plaxton Pointer	B35F	1993	South Lancashire, 1997
1285	M5SLT	Dennis Dart 9.8SDL3040	Plaxton Pointer	B40F	1994	South Lancashire, 1997

1290-1299 — Dennis Lance 11SDA3113 — Plaxton Verde — B49F — 1994 — Clydeside, 1996

1290	M930EYS	1292	M932EYS	1294	M934EYS	1296	M936EYS	1298	M928EYS
1291	M931EYS	1293	M933EYS	1295	M935EYS	1297	M927EYS	1299	M929EYS

1300	P3SLT	Dennis Dart	Plaxton Pointer	B40F	1996	South Lancashire, 1997

1301-1313 — Dennis Dart SLF — Aleaxander ALX200 — N40F — 1998

1301	R301CVU	1304	R304CVU	1307	R307CVU	1310	R310CVU	1312	R312CVU
1302	R302CVU	1305	R305CVU	1308	R308CVU	1311	R311CVU	1313	R313CVU
1303	R303CVU	1306	R606FBU	1309	R309CVU				

Heritage fleet:-

918	AJA118	Bristol L5G	Burlingham (1950)	B35R	1938	preservation, 1994

Ancilliary vehicles:-

857	G644EVN	CVE Omni	CVE	B15FL	1990	Greater Manchester PTE, 1994
916t	VDB916	Leyland Leopard PSU3/3RT	Alexander Highlander	CB49F	1962	preservation, 1994
938t	WSU442S	Leyland Leopard PSU3/3R	Alexander AYS	B53F	1977	Clydeside, 1996
941t	HFM186N	Leyland National 11351/1R		BC48F	1975	Crosville, 1989
950t	WSU450S	Leyland Leopard PSU3/3R	Alexander AYS	B53F	1977	Clydeside, 1996
952t	WSU441S	Leyland Leopard PSU3/3R	Alexander AYS	B53F	1977	Clydeside, 1996
1912	YFM1M	Freight Rover Sherpa	Carlyle	Van	1987	
1914	GGR406N	Leyland Leopard PSU3	Plaxton/UAS	RV	1974	
1918	AJA142B	Leyland Leopard PSU3/3RT	Alexander AY/CMS	RV	1964	
1960w	D409NNA	Renault-Dodge S46	Northern Counties	B22F	1987	Ribble, 1989
1961w	D431NNA	Renault-Dodge S46	Northern Counties	B22F	1987	Ribble, 1989
1962w	D445NNA	Renault-Dodge S46	Northern Counties	B22F	1987	Ribble, 1989

1973-1983 — Mercedes-Benz 609D — Reeve Burgess — B20F — 1987 — Southern Counties, 1998

1973	E63UKL	1976w	E52UKL	1978	E57UKL	1980	E53UKL	1982	E55UKL
1974	E64UKL	1977	E47UKL	1979	E44UKL	1981	E54UKL	1983	E56UKL
1975	E65XKE								

Previous Registrations

49XBF	F603CET, A19RBL, F603CET	MIL6679	TOE498N
J4SLT	J61MHF	MIL6680	TOE499N
K3SLT	K445EDT, 30938 (GBG), K455EDT	MIL6681	TOE492N
M2SLT	N102YVU	MIL7612	TOE495N
M5SLT	M20CLA	MIL7613	TOE496N
MIL5573	TOE487N	MIL7614	TOE505N
MIL5574	TOE488N	MIL7615	TOE510N
MIL5575	TOE489N	MIL7616	TOE511N
MIL5580	ROK468N	MIL7617	TOE513N
MIL5581	LPB209P	MIL7620	TOE512N
MIL5582	TOE486N	MIL7621	TOE523N
MIL6676	TOE490N	MIL7622	ROK469M
MIL6677	TOE491N	MIL7623	ROK470M
MIL6678	TOE497N	MIL7624	GOK618N

Allocations:-

Haydock (Yew Tree Trading Estate, Kilbuck Lane)

Mercedes-Benz	150	171	175	176	177	178	179	180
	181	182	183	184				
Scania L	1006	1007	1008	1009	1010	1011	1012	1013
	1014	1015	1016	1017	1018	1019	1020	1021
	1022	1023	1024	1025	1026	1027	1028	1029
	1030	1031	1032	1033	1034			

Liverpool (Hawthorne Road, Bootle)

Mercedes-Benz	97	98	133	134	135	136	137	138
	139							
Dart	1150	1151	1152	1171	1173	1176	1178	1179
	1222	1223	1224	1225	1226	1227	1228	1229
	1230	1231	1232	1233	1234	1235	1236	1237
	1238	1239	1240	1241	1242	1243	1244	1245
	1246	1247	1248	1249	1250	1251	1252	1253
	1254	1255	1256	1257	1258	1259	1260	1261
	1262	1263	1264	1266	1267	1268	1269	1270
	1271							
National	256	340	421	422	424	425	426	427
	428	429	430	431	432	433	434	435
	436	437						
Lance	1293	1294	1295	1296	1297	1298	1299	
Scania L	1001	1002	1003	1004	1005	1041	1042	1043
	1044	1045	1046	1047	1048	1049		
Scania N	671	672	673	674	675	676	677	678
	679	680						

Manchester (Hulme Hall Road)

Mercedes-Benz	70	77	79	80	108	154	158	159
	160	161	166	167	168	168		
National	400	402	403	404	405	406	408	409
	410	414						
Falcon	381	382	383	384	385	386	387	388
	389	390						
Dominator	630	633	634					
Citybus	690	697						
Olympian	601	602	604	605	607	608	609	610
	611	613	614	615	618	619	620	621
	622	623	625	658	659	660	661	662
	668	669						

All six of the East Lancashire-bodied Scania L113s are allocated to Skelmersdale. Representing the type is 1037, P137GND pictured in Wigan. For several months while engineering were based in Hulme Hall Road, index marks from the Manchester local office were used, though recent deliveries have again been obtained from Liverpool. *Richard Godfrey*

In the period when Greater Manchester South was management owned, the Bee Line operation increased significantly its presence in the Wythenshawe/Altrincham area. Service 19A links Altrincham interchange with Manchester International Airport. Seen on the service is 1312, R312CVU. *Cliff Beeton*

Runcorn (Beechwood)

Mercedes-Benz	121	122	125	127	129			
National	286	287	411	412	413	416	417	418
	419	420	450	451	452	453	454	455
	456	457	458	459	460			
Dart	1157	1158	1159	1160	1161	1162	1163	1164
	1165	1166	1167	1168	1169	1170	1217	1218
	1219	1220	1221					
Lance	1201	1202	1203	1204	1205	1206	1207	1208
	1209	1210	1290	1291	1292			

Skelmersdale (Neverstich Road)

Mercedes-Benz	52	59	66	67	126	128	170	172
	173	191	192	193	194	195	196	197
	198							
Dart	1193	1215	1273	1274	1275	1276	1277	1278
	1279	1280	1281	1282	1285	1300		
National	200	201	206	208	209			
Scania L	1035	1036	1037	1038	1039	1040	1050	1051
	1052	1053	1054	1055	1056	1057	1058	1059
	1060	1061						
Dominator	632	635	646	647				
Citybus	650	651	652	653				

Warrington (Athlone Road)

Mercedes-Benz	51	61	64	65	107	109	123	130
	131	132						
Dart	1172	1174	1175	1177	1180	1181	1182	1183
	1184	1186	1188	1189	1190	1191	1192	1194
	1195	1196	1197	1198	1199	1212	1213	1214
	1216							
Volvo B10M	778	779	785	786	787	788		

Winsford (Winsford Industrial Estate)

Mercedes-Benz	50	53	54	55	56	57	58	62
	63	69	101	102	103	104	105	119
Dart	1301							
Tiger	848	849	855					
National	202	204	205	210	211	361	364	373
Olympian	600	603	624	654	655	656	657	667

Wythenshawe (Grebba Road)

Mercedes-Benz	60	78	86	88	89	93	120	124
	140	141	142	143	144	145	146	147
	148	149	151	152	153	162	163	
Dart	1185	1187	1211	1265	1302	1303	1304	1305
	1306	1307	1308	1309	1310	1311	1312	1313
Falcon	392	393	394	395				

Unallocated -

Mercedes-Benz	72	74	75	76	94	95	99	100
	413	419						
Leopard	854							
National	203	219	215	218	229	241	251	271
	280	281	282	283	284	294	331	332
	356	370	372	423				
Dart	1153	1154	1155	1156				
Lance	1200	1960	1961	1962	1982	1983		
Olympian	606	612	630	646	647			
Citybus	691	692						

ARRIVA CYMRU

Arriva Cymru Ltd, Imperial Buildings, Glan-y-Mor Road,
Llandudno Junction, LL31 9RU

ARRIVA gwasanaethu Cymru
/serving Wales

Single deck vehicles:

SDD24	N24FWU	DAF SB220LC550	Northern Counties Paladin	B49F	1995	West Coast Motors, Campbeltown, 1996
SDD25	N25FWU	DAF SB220LC550	Northern Counties Paladin	B49F	1995	West Coast Motors, Campbeltown, 1996
SLC27	K27EWC	Leyland Lynx LX2R11C15Z4R	Leyland Lynx 2	B49F	1992	Colchester, 1994
SLG28	H28MJN	Leyland Lynx LX2R11G15Z4R	Leyland Lynx	B49F	1991	Colchester, 1994
SLG29	H29MJN	Leyland Lynx LX2R11G15Z4R	Leyland Lynx	B49F	1991	Colchester, 1994
SLC30	H130LPU	Leyland Lynx LX2R11C15Z4R	Leyland Lynx 2	B49F	1990	Colchester, 1994
SLL31	D31RWC	Leyland Lynx LX112TL11FR1	Leyland Lynx	B49F	1986	Colchester, 1994
SLL32	D32RWC	Leyland Lynx LX112TL11FR1	Leyland Lynx	B49F	1986	Colchester, 1994

SLC33-37

		Leyland Lynx LX112L10ZR1	Leyland Lynx	B49F	1988-89 Colchester, 1994

33	E33EVW	34	E34EVW	35	E35EVW	36	E36EVW	37	E37EVW

SLC38	G38YHJ	Leyland Lynx LX2R11C15Z4R	Leyland Lynx	B49F	1989	Colchester, 1994
SLC39	G39YHJ	Leyland Lynx LX2R11C15Z4R	Leyland Lynx	B49F	1989	Colchester, 1994
SLC40	G40YHJ	Leyland Lynx LX2R11C15Z4R	Leyland Lynx	B49F	1989	Colchester, 1994
SDD47	M847RCP	DAF SB220LC550	Northern Counties Paladin	B49F	1995	Citybus, Southampton, 1996
SDD49	M849RCP	DAF SB220LC550	Northern Counties Paladin	B49F	1995	Citybus, Southampton, 1996
SNL49	C49OCM	Leyland National 2 NL116TL11/1R		B52F	1985	Devaway, Bretton, 1998
SLC49	E49WEM	Leyland Lynx LX112L10ZR1R	Leyland Lynx	B49F	1988	Devaway, Bretton, 1998
CTL63	C63JTU	Leyland Tiger TRCTL11/3RH	Duple 340	C49FT	1986	Crosville, 1986

SLC66-70

		Leyland Lynx LX112L10ZR1R	Leyland Lynx	B49F	1989	Chesterfield, 1995

66	F66FKW	67	F67FKW	68	F68FKW	69	F69FKW	70	F70FKW

1998 was a significant year for Arriva Cymru. The last National series 1 and B variants left the fleet after dominating it for so many years. They were largely replaced by National 2s and Lynx from Yorkshire such as SNG213 (EWX213Y) seen here. However, withdrawal of the first National 2s, including this one, commenced at the end on 1998.
Les Peters

CTC68	IIL9168	Leyland Tiger TRCL10/3ARZM	Plaxton Paramount 3200 III	C53F	1989	Maidstone & District, 1997
CTC69	IIL9169	Leyland Tiger TRCL10/3ARZM	Plaxton Paramount 3200 III	C53F	1989	Maidstone & District, 1997
SLC73	H733HWK	Leyland Lynx LX2R11C15Z4R	Leyland Lynx 2	B51F	1990	Clydeside (McGills), 1997
SNG76	XUA76X	Leyland National 2 NL116AL11/1R(6HLXB)		B49F	1982	Yorkshire Bus (WR), 1997
SNL131	B131SED	Leyland National 2 NL116L11/1R		B52F	1985	Devaway, Bretton, 1998
SNL132	B132SED	Leyland National 2 NL116L11/1R		B49F	1985	Devaway, Bretton, 1998
SNL206	LRB206W	Leyland National 2 NL116L11/1R		B52F	1980	Yorkshire Bus (YB), 1996

SNG207-215

	Leyland National 2 NL116HLXB/1R		B49F	1982-83 Yorkshire Bus (WR) 213-5(SY), 1996-97

207	EWT207Y	211w	EWX211Y	212	EWX212Y	214	EWX214Y	215	EWX215Y
209	EWT209Y								

SLC254	H254PAJ	Leyland Lynx LX2R11C15Z4S	Leyland Lynx 2	B49F	1991	North East (Durham County), 1999
SLG254	E254TUB	Leyland Lynx LX1126LXCTFRR	Leyland Lynx	B50F	1987	Yorkshire , 1998
SLG256	E256TUB	Leyland Lynx LX1126LXCTFR1S	Leyland Lynx	B49F	1987	Yorkshire , 1998
SLG258	E258TUB	Leyland Lynx LX1126LXCTFR1S	Leyland Lynx	B49F	1987	Yorkshire , 1998
SLG262	E262TUB	Leyland Lynx LX1126LXCTFR1S	Leyland Lynx	B49F	1988	Yorkshire , 1998
SLG299	E299OMG	Leyland Lynx LX112TL11ZR1S	Leyland Lynx	B49F	1988	Atlas Bus, 1994
SSC302	F302MNK	Leyland Swift LBM6T/2RA	Wadham Stringer Vanguard II	B35F	1989	The Shires, 1997
SSC303	F303MNK	Leyland Swift LBM6T/2RA	Wadham Stringer Vanguard II	B35F	1989	The Shires, 1997

SLG311-316

	Leyland Lynx LX2R11G15Z4S	Leyland Lynx	B49F	1990	Southern Counties (C&NS), 1998

311	G311DPA	313	G313DPA	314	G314DPA	315	G315DPA	316	G316DPA
312	G312DPA								

SLG328	E328OMG	Leyland Lynx LX112TL11ZR1S	Leyland Lynx	B49F	1988	Atlas Bus, 1994
SLC334	H34PAJ	Leyland Lynx LX2R11C15Z4S	Leyland Lynx 2	B49F	1991	North East (Durham County), 1999
SLC340	G34VME	Leyland Lynx LX2R11C15Z4S	Leyland Lynx	B49F	1989	Southern Counties (C&NS), 1998
SLC350	G35VME	Leyland Lynx LX2R11C15Z4S	Leyland Lynx	B49F	1989	Southern Counties (C&NS), 1998
SBB389	GEY389Y	Bedford YNT	Duple Dominant IV	C53F	1982	Purple, Bethesda, 1998
CVV395	MEY395	Volvo B10M-61	Plaxton Paramount 3500 II	C53F	1986	Purple, Bethesda, 1998
LDC521	R521UCC	Dennis Dart SLF	Plaxton Pointer	N39F	1997	
LDC522	R522UCC	Dennis Dart SLF	Plaxton Pointer	N39F	1997	
CTL554	JEY554Y	Leyland Tiger TRCTL11/3R	Plaxton Paramount 3500	C49F	1983	Purple, Bethesda, 1998
SDC558	S558MCC	Dennis Dart SLF	Alexander ALX200	N40F	1998	
SDC559	S559MCC	Dennis Dart SLF	Alexander ALX200	N40F	1998	
CVV592	HIL7592	Volvo B10M-61	Duple 340	C51FT	1988	Moor-Dale, 1994
CVV593	HIL7593	Volvo B10M-61	Duple 340	C51FT	1988	Moor-Dale, 1994
LDC623	S623KHN	Dennis Dart SLF	Plaxton Pointer 2	N40F	1998	on loan from North East
LDC624	S624KHN	Dennis Dart SLF	Plaxton Pointer 2	N40F	1998	on loan from North East
LDC625	S625KHN	Dennis Dart SLF	Plaxton Pointer 2	N40F	1998	on loan from North East
LDC626	S626KHN	Dennis Dart SLF	Plaxton Pointer 2	N40F	1998	on loan from North East
SLL641	E641VFY	Leyland Lynx LX112TL11ZR1R	Leyland Lynx	B51F	1987	Devaway, Bretton, 1998
SLC642	E642VFY	Leyland Lynx LX112L10ZR1R	Leyland Lynx	B51F	1988	Devaway, Bretton, 1998
SLC654	J654UHN	Leyland Lynx LX2R11C15Z4S	Leyland Lynx 2	B49F	1991	North East (Durham County), 1998
SLC655	J655UHN	Leyland Lynx LX2R11C15Z4S	Leyland Lynx 2	B49F	1991	North East (Durham County), 1999
SLC677	E677DCU	Leyland Lynx LX112L10ZR1R	Leyland Lynx	B51F	1987	Northumbria, 1997
SLC678	E678DCU	Leyland Lynx LX112L10ZR1R	Leyland Lynx	B51F	1987	Northumbria, 1997
SLL711	D711SKB	Leyland Lynx LX563TL11FR1	Leyland Lynx	B51F	1986	Devaway, Bretton, 1998
SBB812	TNR812X	Bedford YMQ	Duple Dominant IV	C45F	1981	Purple, Bethesda, 1998
CTL819	NEY819	Leyland Tiger TRCTL11/3RZ	Plaxton Paramount 3200 II	C49F	1987	Purple, Bethesda, 1998
SNL824	SNS824W	Leyland National 2 NL116L11/1R		B49F	1980	Yorkshire Bus (SY), 1996
CDD944	M944LYR	DAF SB3000WS601	Van Hool Alizée	C49FT	1995	London North East, 1998
CDD945	M945LYR	DAF SB3000WS601	Van Hool Alizée	C49FT	1995	London North East, 1998
SLC967	E967PME	Leyland Lynx LX112TL11ZR1R(L10)	Leyland Lynx	B49F	1988	Atlas Bus, 1994
SLC968	E968PME	Leyland Lynx LX112TL11ZR1R(L10)	Leyland Lynx	B49F	1988	Atlas Bus, 1994

Opposite, top:- **Crosville Cymru have a higher proportion of buses sporting the new livery than any other consequent on the fleet having changed considerably in recent months. Latterly with Chesterfield Transport, SLC69, F69FKW is seen in Caernarfon. Visible is the luggage area behind the driver, here being used for a buggy.** *Tony Wilson*
Opposite, bottom:- **An all-Mercedes minibus fleet was injected with several Optare MetroRiders for Aberystwyth during 1998. Pictured at the Penmon terminus of route 57 is another recent arrival, MMM811, R811YJC, one of a large batch of Vario models delivered in 1998.** *Tony Wilson*

Minibuses:

MMM43	D443UHC	Mercedes-Benz L608D	Reeve Burgess	B20F	1986	Hastings & District, 1987
MMM89	D89VCC	Mercedes-Benz L608D	Reeve Burgess	B20F	1986	
MMM117	M943UDT	Mercedes-Benz 709D	Plaxton Beaver	B25F	1995	Mercedes-Benz demonstrator, 1996
MMM118	P688KCC	Mercedes-Benz 709D	Plaxton Beaver	B27F	1997	
MMM119	P658KEY	Mercedes-Benz 711D	Plaxton Beaver	B27F	1997	

MMM210-228

Mercedes-Benz 709D — Robin Hood — BC25F* — 1988-89 *212/5/7 are B25F; 219/21 are B27F

210	F210DCC	214	F214DCC	218	F218DCC	222	F222DCC	226	F426EJC
211	F211DCC	215	F215DCC	219	F219DCC	223	F223DCC	227	F427EJC
212	F212DCC	216	F216DCC	220	F220DCC	224	F424EJC	228	F428EJC
213	F213DCC	217	F217DCC	221	F221DCC	225	F425EJC		

MMM229-240

Mercedes-Benz 709D — Robin Hood — BC25F* — 1989 *232/7/8 are B25F; 229/33/5 are B27F

229	G229FJC	233	G233FJC	235	G235FJC	237	G237FJC	239	G239FJC
230	G230FJC	234	G234FJC	236	G236FJC	238	G238FJC	240	G240FJC
232	G232FJC								

MMM241	G241GCC	Mercedes-Benz 709D	Phoenix	BC25F	1989	
MMM242	G242GCC	Mercedes-Benz 709D	Phoenix	BC25F	1989	
MMM243	G243GCC	Mercedes-Benz 709D	Phoenix	BC25F	1989	
MMM260	G160YRE	Mercedes-Benz 709D	LHE Commuter	B29F	1989	Stevensons, 1994
MMM261	G161YRE	Mercedes-Benz 709D	LHE Commuter	B29F	1989	Stevensons, 1994
MMM262	G162YRE	Mercedes-Benz 709D	LHE Commuter	B29F	1989	Stevensons, 1994
MMM263	G163YRE	Mercedes-Benz 709D	LHE Commuter	B29F	1989	Stevensons, 1994
MMM335	L35OKV	Mercedes-Benz 811D	Wright NimBus	B33F	1993	
MMM336	L36OKV	Mercedes-Benz 811D	Wright NimBus	B33F	1993	
MMM337	L37OKV	Mercedes-Benz 811D	Wright NimBus	B33F	1993	
MMM338	L38OKV	Mercedes-Benz 811D	Wright NimBus	B33F	1993	

MMM351-377

Mercedes-Benz 709D — Reeve Burgess Beaver — BC25F — 1989

351	G151FJC	370	G170FJC	372	G172FJC	374	G174FJC	376	G176FJC
352	G152FJC	371	G171FJC	373	G173FJC	375	G175FJC	377	G177FJC
369	G169FJC								

MMM385	M385KVR	Mercedes-Benz 709D	Alexander Sprint	B27F	1995	North Western (Bee Line), 1996
MMM394	M394KVR	Mercedes-Benz 709D	Alexander Sprint	B27F	1995	North Western (Bee Line), 1996
MMM411	M411BEY	Mercedes-Benz 811D	Alexander Sprint	B33F	1995	
MMM412	M412BEY	Mercedes-Benz 811D	Alexander Sprint	B33F	1995	
MMM413	M413BEY	Mercedes-Benz 811D	Alexander Sprint	B33F	1995	
MMM455	M455HPG	Mercedes-Benz 709D	Alexander Sprint	B25F	1994	Southern Counties (G&WS), 1998
MMM456	M456HPG	Mercedes-Benz 709D	Alexander Sprint	B25F	1994	Southern Counties (G&WS), 1998
MMM457	M457HPG	Mercedes-Benz 709D	Alexander Sprint	B23F	1994	Southern Counties (G&WS), 1998
MMM607	H407BVR	Mercedes-Benz 609D	Reeve Burgess Beaver	B20F	1990	North Western, 1997
MMM638	L638DNA	Mercedes-Benz 709D	Alexander Sprint	B27F	1994	AA, Ayr, 1996

MMM643-660

Mercedes-Benz 609D — Reeve Burgess — B20F — 1987 — Maidstone & District, 1997

643	E43UKL	648	E48UKL	650	E50UKL	659	E59UKL	660	E60UKL
645	E45UKL	649	E49UKL	651	E51UKL				

MMM666	F66BKK	Mercedes-Benz 609D	Reeve Burgess	B20F	1988	Southern Counties (K&S), 1998
MMM676	G76PKR	Mercedes-Benz 609D	Reeve Burgess	B20F	1988	Southern Counties (K&S), 1998
MMM680	E980NMK	Mercedes-Benz 709D	Reeve Burgess	B20F	1988	Maidstone & District, 1997
MMM687	G87SKR	Mercedes-Benz 609D	Reeve Burgess	B20F	1990	Maidstone & District, 1997
MMM701	F701KMA	Mercedes-Benz 709D	Reeve Burgess Beaver	B27F	1989	Midland, 1995
MMM702	F702KMA	Mercedes-Benz 709D	Reeve Burgess Beaver	B27F	1989	Midland, 1995
MMM704	F704KMA	Mercedes-Benz 709D	Reeve Burgess Beaver	B27F	1989	Midland, 1995
MMM711	M711YJC	Mercedes-Benz 709D	Marshall C19	B25F	1994	
MMM712	M712YJC	Mercedes-Benz 709D	Marshall C19	B25F	1994	
MMM713	M713YJC	Mercedes-Benz 709D	Marshall C19	B25F	1994	
MMM714	M714YJC	Mercedes-Benz 709D	Marshall C19	B25F	1994	
MMM715	L715WCC	Mercedes-Benz 709D	Marshall C19	B27F	1993	
MMM716	L716WCC	Mercedes-Benz 709D	Marshall C19	B27F	1993	
MMM717	L717WCC	Mercedes-Benz 709D	Marshall C19	B27F	1993	
MMM718	N718DJC	Mercedes-Benz 811D	Alexander Sprint	B31F	1995	
MMM719	N719DJC	Mercedes-Benz 811D	Alexander Sprint	B31F	1995	
MMM721	L421CPB	Mercedes-Benz 709D	Dormobile Routemaker	B25F*	1993	London & County (G&WS), 1997

Among the first Cymru buses into corporate livery were a pair of Leyland Swifts acquired from W&H Motors in Horley for lightly loaded services out of Aberystwyth here SSC303 (F303MNK) awaits departure from the new bus station in the town.
Laurie Rufus

Cymru's MMM796 (N996CCC) carries Sprint bodywork assembled at Alexander's Belfast plant. The independence of the former Potters Coachbuilders is now much reduced to the assembly of pre-manufactured parts to Falkirk design, and until recently, a separate numbering series was maintained.
Laurie Rufus

Arriva Cymru still maintain a fleet of open-top vehicles for summer services between Talacre and Abergele (Pensarn) serving the seaside towns of Prestatyn and Rhyl. With large numbers of caravan sites along the route it attracts good custom. OVG467, WTU467W, will probably outlast the seventeen remaining close-top VRs in the Cymru fleet.
Malcolm King

MMM738	L438FPA	Mercedes-Benz 709D	Plaxton Beaver	B23F	1994	Southern Counties(G&WS), 1998
MMM739	L439FPA	Mercedes-Benz 709D	Plaxton Beaver	B23F	1994	Southern Counties(G&WS), 1998
MMM749	H149NOJ	Mercedes-Benz 709D	Carlyle	B29F	1991	Kentish Bus, 1997
MMM755	K155CRE	Mercedes-Benz 709D	Dormobile Routemaker	B27F	1993	London & Country (HB), 1997
MMM756	K156BRF	Mercedes-Benz 709D	Dormobile Routemaker	B27F	1993	London & Country (HB), 1997
MMM757	K157BRF	Mercedes-Benz 709D	Dormobile Routemaker	B27F	1993	London & Country (HB), 1997
MMM758	M458JPA	Mercedes-Benz 709D	Alexander Sprint	B23F	1994	Southern Counties(G&WS), 1998
MMM768	N468SPA	Mercedes-Benz 709D	Alexander Sprint	B27F	1995	Southern Counties(G&WS), 1998
MMM770	N470SPA	Mercedes-Benz 709D	Alexander Sprint	B27F	1995	Southern Counties(G&WS), 1998
MMM771	N671TPF	Mercedes-Benz 709D	Plaxton Beaver	B23F	1995	Southern Counties(G&WS), 1998

MMM793-797   Mercedes-Benz 709D   Alexander Sprint   B27F   1995

793	N993CCC	794	N994CCC	795	N995CCC	796	N996CCC	797	N997CCC

MMM801-819   Mercedes-Benz Vario O814   Plaxton Beaver 2   B27F   1998

801	R801YJC	805	R805YJC	810	R810YJC	814	R814YJC	817	R817YJC
802	R802YJC	807	R807YJC	811	R811YJC	815	R815YJC	818	R818YJC
803	R803YJC	808	R808YJC	812	R812YJC	816	R816YJC	819	R819YJC
804	R804YJC	809	R809YJC	813	R813YJC				

MMM820	G120TJA	Mercedes-Benz 811D	Carlyle	B31F	1990	London & Country (GWS), 1997
MMM821	R821YJC	Mercedes-Benz Vario O814	Plaxton Beaver 2	B27F	1998	
MMM822	S822MCC	Mercedes-Benz Vario O814	Plaxton Beaver 2	B27F	1998	
MMM823	S823MCC	Mercedes-Benz Vario O814	Plaxton Beaver 2	B27F	1998	
MMM824	S824MCC	Mercedes-Benz Vario O814	Plaxton Beaver 2	BC29F	1998	
MMM825	S825MCC	Mercedes-Benz Vario O814	Plaxton Beaver 2	BC29F	1998	
MMM886	R486UCC	Mercedes-Benz Vario O814	Plaxton Beaver 2	B27F	1997	
MMM887	R487UCC	Mercedes-Benz Vario O814	Plaxton Beaver 2	B27F	1997	

MMC915-928   Optare MetroRider MR05   Optare   B31F   1992   Yorkshire, 1998

915	J715CUM	921	J721CUM	923	K723HUG	926	K726HUG	928	K728HUG
918	J718CUM	922	J722CUM	924	K724HUG	927	K727HUG	929	K729HUG
919	J719CUM								

MMM981	K981KGY	Mercedes-Benz 709D	Dormobile Routemaker	B29F	1993	Kentish Bus, 1997
MMM982	K982KGY	Mercedes-Benz 709D	Dormobile Routemaker	B29F	1993	Kentish Bus, 1997
MMM983	K983KGY	Mercedes-Benz 709D	Dormobile Routemaker	B29F	1993	Kentish Bus, 1997
MMM996	N996KUS	Mercedes-Benz 709D	UVG Citistar	B29F	1995	Redline, Penwortham, 1996

Double Deck Vehicles:

DOL103	A103OUG	Leyland Olympian ONTL11/1R	Northern Counties	B43/28F	1984	Yorkshire Bus (WR), 1997
DOL104	A104OUG	Leyland Olympian ONTL11/1R	Northern Counties	B43/28F	1984	Yorkshire Bus (SY), 1997
DOL119	TPD119X	Leyland Olympian ONTL11/1R	Roe	B43/29F	1982	Londonlinks, 1997
DOL122	TPD122X	Leyland Olympian ONTL11/1R	Roe	B43/29F	1982	Londonlinks, 1997
DOL126	TPD126X	Leyland Olympian ONTL11/1R	Roe	B43/29F	1982	Londonlinks, 1997
DOG186	B186BLG	Leyland Olympian ONLXB/1R	Eastern Coach Works	B45/32F	1984	Yorkshire, 1998
ODL190	JTD390P	Daimler Fleetline CRL6-33	Northern Counties	O49/29F	1975	Southend, 1993
DOG191	B191BLG	Leyland Olympian ONLXB/1R	Eastern Coach Works	B45/32F	1985	Crosville, 1986
DOG192	B192BLG	Leyland Olympian ONLXB/1R	Eastern Coach Works	B45/32F	1985	Crosville, 1986
DOG193	B193BLG	Leyland Olympian ONLXB/1R	Eastern Coach Works	B45/32F	1985	Crosville, 1986
DOG194	B194BLG	Leyland Olympian ONLXB/1R	Eastern Coach Works	B45/32F	1985	Crosville, 1986
ODL195	JTD395P	Daimler Fleetline CRL6-33	Northern Counties	O49/29F	1976	Southend, 1993
DOG196	B196BLG	Leyland Olympian ONLXB/1R	Eastern Coach Works	B45/32F	1985	Crosville, 1986
DOG208	C208GTU	Leyland Olympian ONLXB/1R	Eastern Coach Works	B45/32F	1985	Crosville, 1986
EOG209	C209GTU	Leyland Olympian ONLXB/1R	Eastern Coach Works	BC42/29F	1985	Crosville, 1986
EOG210	C210GTU	Leyland Olympian ONLXB/1R	Eastern Coach Works	BC42/29F	1985	Crosville, 1986
EOG211	C211GTU	Leyland Olympian ONLXB/1R	Eastern Coach Works	BC42/29F	1985	Crosville, 1986
EOG212	C212GTU	Leyland Olympian ONLXB/1R	Eastern Coach Works	BC42/29F	1985	Crosville, 1986

DOG220-232   Leyland Olympian ONLXB/1R   Eastern Coach Works   B45/32F*   1983   Kentish Bus, 1995
*220 is B44/32F

220	WDC220Y	222	AEF222Y	229	AEF229Y	230	CEF230Y	232	CEF232Y
221	AEF221Y	224	AEF224Y						

Seven Northern Counties-bodied Volvo Olympians joined the fleet in 1998. Pictured at the Chester end of Route 1, DVV235, R235AEY, illustrates the route branding carried for this group of services. Production of the last Palatine buses took place in February 1999, the double-deck production at the the re-named Plaxton Wigan factory being the President low-floor double-deck bus. Interestingly the last Palatine II models were completed some weeks earlier. *Malcolm King*

DVV233-239

Volvo Olympian   Northen Counties Palatine I   B45/32F   1998

233	R233AEY	**235**	R235AEY	**237**	R237AEY	**238**	R238AEY	**239**	R239AEY
234	R234AEY	**236**	R236AEY						

DOG258	C258UAJ	Leyland Olympian ONLXB/1R	Eastern Coach Works	B45/32F	1985	Kentish Bus, 1995
DOL401	YWX401X	Leyland Olympian ONTL11/1R	Northern Counties	B43/28F	1982	Yorkshire Bus (SY), 1996
DOL402	YWX402X	Leyland Olympian ONTL11/1R	Northern Counties	B43/28F	1982	Yorkshire Bus (SY), 1996
DOG413	B513LFP	Leyland Olympian ONLXB/1R	Eastern Coach Works	B45/32F	1984	Fox County, 1998
OVL429	RLG429V	Bristol VRT/SL3/501	Eastern Coach Works	O43/27F	1980	Crosville, 1991

DVG447-478

Bristol VRT/SL3/6LXB   Eastern Coach Works   B43/31F*   1980-81 Crosville, 1986
*467/78 are O43/31F (prefix OVG) and ex Midland 1994

447	UDM447V	**459**	VCA459W	**467**	WTU467W	**468**	WTU468W	**478**	WTU478W

DVG500-534

Bristol VRT/SL3/6LXB   Eastern Coach Works   B43/31F*   1981 Crosville, 1986
*512/9/28 are O43/31F (prefix OVG); 519/20 are ex Midland, 1994

500	YMB500W	**512**	YMB512W	**518**	YMB518W	**524**	BMA524W	**530**	DCA530X
501	YMB501W	**516**	YMB516W	**519**	YMB519W	**527**	BMA527W	**532**	DCA532X
503	YMB503W	**517**	YMB517W	**522**	BMA522W	**528**	DCA528X	**533**	DCA533X
510	YMB510W								

DOG506	CWR506Y	Leyland Olympian ONLXB/1R	Eastern Coach Works	B45/32F	1982	Yorkshire Bus (SY), 1997
DOG507	CWR507Y	Leyland Olympian ONLXB/1R	Eastern Coach Works	B45/32F	1982	Yorkshire Bus (WR), 1997
DOG508	CWR508Y	Leyland Olympian ONLXB/1R	Eastern Coach Works	B45/32F	1982	Yorkshire (South), 1998
DOG509	CWR509Y	Leyland Olympian ONLXB/1R	Eastern Coach Works	B45/32F	1982	Yorkshire Bus (SY), 1997
DOG510	CWR510Y	Leyland Olympian ONLXB/1R	Eastern Coach Works	B45/32F	1982	Yorkshire (South), 1998
DOG512	CWR512Y	Leyland Olympian ONLXB/1R	Eastern Coach Works	B45/32F	1983	Yorkshire (North), 1998
DOG513	CWR513Y	Leyland Olympian ONLXB/1R	Eastern Coach Works	B45/32F	1982	Yorkshire Bus (SY), 1997
DOG522	CWR522Y	Leyland Olympian ONLXB/1R	Eastern Coach Works	B45/32F	1983	Yorkshire Bus (WR), 1997
DOG523	CWR523Y	Leyland Olympian ONLXB/1R	Eastern Coach Works	B45/32F	1983	Yorkshire Bus (WR), 1997
DOG527	CWR527Y	Leyland Olympian ONLXB/1R	Eastern Coach Works	B45/32F	1983	Yorkshire Bus (YB), 1997
DOG531	EWX531Y	Leyland Olympian ONLXB/1R	Eastern Coach Works	B45/32F	1983	Yorkshire, 1998

DOG576	A576NWX	Leyland Olympian ONLXB/1R	Eastern Coach Works	B45/32F	1984	Yorkshire, 1998
OVG961	YCU961T	Bristol VRT/SL3/6LXB	Eastern Coach Works	O43/31F	1979	Northumbria, 1994

Ancilliary:

G144	AJA144B	Leyland Leopard PSU3/3RT	Alexander Y	RV	1964	Midland, 1993
G581	HFM581D	Bristol MW6G	Eastern Coach Works	RV	1966	Crosville, 1986
REC3	C221EKJ	Mercedes-Benz L608D	Rootes	RV	1986	Maidstone & District, 1997
REC4	D28KKP	Mercedes-Benz L608D	Rootes	RV	1986	Maidstone & District, 1997
REC5	C220EKJ	Mercedes-Benz L608D	Rootes	RV	1986	Maidstone & District, 1997
REC6	TXA114K	Leyland Leopard PSU3/3R	Alexander Y	RV	1972	Clydeside (McGills), 1997
TB1	JTL804V	Bedford YLQ	Plaxton Supreme IV Exp	C45F	1979	Lewis, Llanrhystyd, 1995
TB3	REU323S	Bristol LH6L	Eastern Coach Works	B43F	1978	NE Bus (Tees), 1997
TB4	MUP713T	Bristol LH6L	Eastern Coach Works	B43F	1979	NE Bus (Tees), 1997

Previous Registrations:

EJC447X	LFT93X, HIL2147	IIL9169	F710ENE
HIL2148	TUP572V	JEY554Y	UTN956Y, HCC852
HIL7592	E179FFT	MEY395	C120DWR
HIL7593	E180FFT	NEY819	D900STU
IIL9168	F714ENE	YCU961T	OBR774T, WSV571

Allocations:-

Aberystwyth (Park Avenue)

Outstations - Llanrhystud, New Quay and Tregaron

Mercedes-Benz	MMM210	MMM455	MMM456	MMM457	MMM758	MMM796	MMM797	MMM812
	MMM813							
Swift	SSC302	SSC303		National	SNG76	SNG84	SNL727	
Lynx	SLG311	SLG312	SLC340	SLC350				
Coach	CVV592	CDD945						
VR	DVG447	DVG501	DVG516	DVG518	DVG524	DVG532	DVG533	
Olympian	DOL119	DOL122	DOL126					

Bangor (Beach Road)

Outstations - Amlwch, Caernarfon and Holyhead

Mercedes-Benz	MMM215	MMM217	MMM238	MMM239	MMM240	MMM241	MMM243	MMM260
	MMM261	MMM262	MMM263	MMM335	MMM336	MMM338	MMM411	MMM412
	MMM413	MMM808	MMM809	MMM810	MMM811			
Dart	SDC558	SDC559						
Coach	CVV593	CDD944						
Lynx	SLG28	SLG29	SLC37	SLC66	SLC68	SLC69	SLC70	
Olympian	DOL103	DOL104	DOL402	DOG 413	DOG506	DOG508	DOG512	DOG513
	DOG527							

DOL122, TPD122X, is one of three Roe-bodied Olympians to join the Cymru fleet in 1997 from the Londonlinks operation. The vehicle was one of the last to receive Crosville green colours and is seen prepared for school duties.
Laurie Rufos

Bethesda (Castle Garage)

Bedford	SBB389	SBB812		
Coach	CTL63	CVV395	CTL554	CTL819
Lynx	SLG254	SLG256	SLG262	

Chester (Broughton Mills Road, Bretton)

Mercedes-Benx	MMM212	MMM702	MMM704	MMM819	MMM821	MMM824	MMM825
Dart	LDC623	LDC624	LDC625	LDC626			
DAF/NC	SDD24						
National	SNL49	SNG211	SNL824				
Lynx	SLC36	SLC49	SLC73	SLC641	SLC642	SLC677	SLL711
Olympian	DOG220	DOG221	DOG222	DOG224	DOG229	DOG230	DOG523

Dolgellau (Arran Road)

Mercedes-Benz	MMM211	MMM216	MMM701	MMM715	MMM716	MMM717	MMM749	MMM771
	MMM820							
MetroRider	MMC922	MMC923						
Coach	CTC68	CTC69						
National	SNL206							
Lynx	SLC30	SLC38	SLC39	SLC40				
Bristol VR	DVG503	DVG517	DVG530					
Olympian	DOG510							

Llandudno Junction (Glan-y-mor Road)

Outstation - Llanrwst

Mercedes-Benz	MMM117	MMM118	MMM119	MMM214	MMM385	MMM394	MMM638	MMM643
	MMM645	MMM648	MMM649	MMM650	MMM651	MMM659	MMM666	MMM676
	MMM680	MMM687	MMM714	MMM718	MMM719	MMM721	MMM755	MMM756
	MMM757	MMM886	MMM887					
MetroRider	MMC918	MMC919	MMC921					
Lynx	SLC33	SLC34	SLC67	SLG258	SLG299	SLG315	SLG328	
National	SNG207	SNG209	SNG212	SNG214	SNG215			
VR	DVG459	DVG468	DVG500					

Mold (Ponterwyl)

Mercedes-Benz	MMM236	MMM237	MMM351	MMM352	MMM823	MMM981	MMM982	MMM983
National	SNL131	SNL132						
Lynx	SLC35							
DAF	SDD24	SDD25	SDD47	SDD49				
Olympian	DOG186	DOG191	DOG192	DOG193	DOG194	DOG196	DOG232	DOG522

Pwllheli (West End Garage)

Mercedes-Benz	MMM213	MMM337
Dart	LDC521	LDC522
Olympian	DOG507	DOG509

Arriva Cymru acquired the Devaway operation during 1998 bringing into the fleet several ex-Halton vehicles including Leyland National 2 C49OCM. This became the third '49' in the fleet and is seen in Chester working service 2 to Mold. *Malcolm King*

Rhyl (Ffynnongroew Road)

Outstation - Denbigh

Mercedes-Benz	MMM369	MMM370	MMM371	MMM372	MMM373	MMM374	MMM375	MMM376
	MMM377	MMM660	MMM711	MMM712	MMM713	MMM738	MMM739	MMM793
	MMM801	MMM802	MMM803	MMM804	MMM805	MMM807	MMM822	MMM996
National	SNL820							
Lynx	SLL31	SLL32	SLG313	SLG314	SLG316	SLC334	SLC654	SLC967
	SLC968							
Bristol VR Closed-top	DVG510	DVG522	DVG527					
Open-top	ODL190	ODL195	OVL429	OVG467	OVG478	OVG512	OVG519	OVG528
	OVG961							
Olympian	EOG209	EOG210	EOG211	EOG212	DOG531	DOG576		

Wrexham (Berse Road, Caego)

Mercedes-Benz	MMM43	MMM89	MMM218	MMM219	MMM220	MMM221	MMM222	MMM223
	MMM224	MMM225	MMM226	MMM227	MMM228	MMM229	MMM230	MMM232
	MMM233	MMM234	MMM235	MMM242	MMM768	MMM770	MMM794	MMM795
	MMM814	MMM815	MMM816	MMM817	MMM818			
MetroRider	MMC915	MMC924	MMC926	MMC927	MMC928	MMC929		
Lynx	SLC27	SLC678						
Olympian	DOG208	DVV233	DVV234	DVV235	DVV236	DVV237	DVV238	DVV239
	DOG258	DOL401						

Unallocated

Mercedes-Benz	MMM607							

ARRIVA MIDLANDS GROUP

Arriva Fox County Ltd, POBox 613, Leicester, LE4 8ZN

Arriva Derby Ltd, Ascot Drive, Derby, DE24 8ND

Arriva Midlands North Ltd, Delta Way, Longford Road, Cannock, Staffordshire   WS11 3XB

Arriva Cheshire East Ltd, Delta Way, Longford Road, Cannock, Staffordshire   WS11 3XB

ARRIVA serving the north Midlands

3	565LON	Volvo B10M-61	Plaxton Paramount 3200 II	C57F	1985	Blue Bus Services, 1995
4	614WEH	Volvo B58-61	Plaxton P 3200 II (1986)	C53F	1976	Coliseum, Southampton, 1985
7	HIL3652	Volvo B10M-61	Duple 340	C55F	1987	Crosville Cymru, 1995
10	803HOM	Volvo B10M-61	Plaxton Paramount 3200 III	C53F	1987	Blue Bus Services, 1995
12	AAL303A	Leyland Leopard PSU5D/4R (TL11) Plaxton P3200 III (1987)		C53F	1980	Rhondda, 1992
13	AAL404A	Leyland Leopard PSU5D/4R (TL11) Plaxton P3200 III (1987)		C53F	1980	Rhondda, 1992
21	YSU953	Volvo B10M-60	Van Hool Alizée	C53F	1989	
23	123TKM	Volvo B58-56	Plaxton Supreme IV	C53F	1979	Blue Bus Services, 1995
24	124YTW	Volvo B58-61	Plaxton Supreme IV	C53F	1980	G M Buses, 1986
25	422AKN	Volvo B10M-60	Plaxton Paramount 3200 III	C53F	1989	
26	XOR841	Volvo B10M-61	Van Hool Alizée	C53F	1983	Sealandair, West Bromwich, 1991
27	TOU962	Volvo B10M-61	Van Hool Alizée	C53F	1983	Sealandair, West Bromwich, 1991
29	YSU954	Volvo B10M-60	Van Hool Alizée	C49F	1990	

51-61		Mercedes-Benz Vario O810	Alexander ALX100	B27F	1997

51	P51HOJ	54	P54HOJ	56	P56HOJ	58	P58HOJ	60	P260HOJ
52	P52HOJ	55	P255HOJ	57	P57HOJ	59	P59HOJ	61	P61HOJ
53	P53HOJ								

Much publicised service route 49 is sponsored by doctors in south Telford to convey patients to the Princess Royal Hospital. The savings on missed appointments are estimated to be more than the cost of the service. Pictured after receiving its new colours is 369, N169WNF.
Bill Potter

Congleton in Cheshire is the location of this picture of North Midlands 167, G167YRE, one of a dozen Mercedes-Benz operated by the company with LHE bodywork which, along with Robin Hood, Phoenix and ECC is one of entrepreneur Robbie Hood's former ventures. *Tony Wilson*

121w	C823SDY	Mercedes-Benz L608D	Alexander	B20F	1986	East Midland, 1993
122	C78WRE	Mercedes-Benz L608D	PMT Hanbridge	BC19F	1986	
123	C802SDY	Mercedes-Benz L608D	Alexander	B20F	1986	East Midland, 1993
124	F68BKK	Mercedes-Benz 609D	Reeve Burgess Beaver	BC19F	1988	Southern Counties (K&S), 1998
125	F188REH	Mercedes-Benz 609D	PMT	B21F	1988	
126	D176LNA	Mercedes-Benz 609D	Dixon Lomas	B27F	1988	Marriott, Clayworth, 1988
127	F77ERJ	Mercedes-Benz 609D	Reeve Burgess Beaver	B25F	1988	Star Line, Knutsford, 1991
129	D135NUS	Mercedes-Benz L608D	Alexander	B21F	1986	Kelvin Central, 1992
131w	D534FAE	Mercedes-Benz L608D	Dormobile	B20F	1986	Frontline, 1996
133	F187REH	Mercedes-Benz 609D	Whittaker Europa	B20F	1988	
134	D538FAE	Mercedes-Benz L608D	Dormobile	B20F	1986	Frontline, 1996
135w	C218EKJ	Mercedes-Benz L608D	Rootes	B20F	1986	Maidstone & District, 1997
136	K136ARE	Mercedes-Benz 709D	Wright NimBus	B29F	1992	
137	K137ARE	Mercedes-Benz 709D	Wright NimBus	B29F	1992	
138	K403VPK	Mercedes-Benz 709D	Dormobile Routemaker	B25FL	1992	Southern Counties (G&WS), 1998
139	K404VPK	Mercedes-Benz 709D	Dormobile Routemaker	B25FL	1992	Southern Counties (G&WS), 1998
140	F190RRF	Mercedes-Benz 709D	Robin Hood	B29F	1988	
141	F191SRF	Mercedes-Benz 709D	Robin Hood	B29F	1989	
142	F192VFA	Mercedes-Benz 709D	Robin Hood	B29F	1989	
143	J143SRF	Mercedes-Benz 709D	Wright NimBus	B29F	1992	
146	F189RRF	Mercedes-Benz 709D	Robin Hood	B29F	1988	
147	K947BRE	Mercedes-Benz 709D	Dormobile Routemaker	B29F	1993	
148	J208SRF	Mercedes-Benz 709D	Wright NimBus	B27F	1992	
149	J209SRF	Mercedes-Benz 709D	Wright NimBus	B27F	1992	
150	K150BRF	Mercedes-Benz 709D	Wright NimBus	B27F	1992	

152	G183DRF	Mercedes-Benz 709D	LHE Commuter	B29F	1990	
153	F703KFM	Mercedes-Benz 709D	Reeve Burgess Beaver	B25F	1989	C-Line, 1992
154	E564YBU	Mercedes-Benz 709D	Reeve Burgess Beaver	B25F	1988	Star Line, Knutsford, 1990
155	F705KFM	Mercedes-Benz 709D	Reeve Burgess Beaver	B25F	1989	C-Line, 1992
156	F186PRE	Mercedes-Benz 709D	Reeve Burgess Beaver	B25F	1988	
157	G184DRF	Mercedes-Benz 709D	LHE Commuter	B29F	1990	
158	F326PPO	Mercedes-Benz 709D	Robin Hood	B29F	1989	Robin Hood demonstrator, 1989
159	H880NFS	Mercedes-Benz 709D	PMT Ami	B29F	1991	Gold Circle, Airdrie, 1994
160	F700LCA	Mercedes-Benz 709D	Reeve Burgess Beaver	B23F	1989	C-Line, 1992
161	H801SKY	Mercedes-Benz 709D	Reeve Burgess Beaver	B25F	1990	North East (Northumbria), 1998
162	H802SKY	Mercedes-Benz 709D	Reeve Burgess Beaver	B25F	1990	North East (Northumbria), 1998

164-173

Mercedes-Benz 709D LHE Commuter B29F 1990

| 164 | G164YRE | 166 | G166YRE | 168 | G168YRE | 170 | G170YRE | 172 | G172YRE |
| 165 | G165YRE | 167 | G167YRE | 169 | G169YRE | 171 | G171YRE | 173 | G173YRE |

| 175 | F185PRE | Mercedes-Benz 709D | Robin Hood | B29F | 1988 | |
| 178 | E478NSC | Mercedes Benz 709D | Alexander Sprint | BC25F | 1988 | Oakley Buses, 1994 |

185-191

Ford Transit VE6 Dormobile B18F 1990-91

| 185 | H185DHA | 187 | H187EHA | 188 | H188EHA | 189 | H189EHA | 191 | H191EHA |
| 186 | H186EHA | | | | | | | | |

218	H708LOL	Freight Rover Sherpa	Carlyle Citybus 2	B20F	1991	
219	H709LOL	Freight Rover Sherpa	Carlyle Citybus 2	B20F	1991	
221	H731LOL	Freight Rover Sherpa	Carlyle Citybus 2	B20F	1991	
222	H729LOL	Freight Rover Sherpa	Carlyle Citybus 2	B20F	1991	
229	L229HRF	Mercedes-Benz 709D	Dormobile Routemaker	B27F	1993	
230	L230HRF	Mercedes-Benz 709D	Dormobile Routemaker	B27F	1993	
252	L232HRF	Mercedes-Benz 709D	Dormobile Routemaker	B27F	1993	
253	L253NFA	Mercedes-Benz 709D	Wadham Stringer Wessex II	B29F	1994	
254	L254NFA	Mercedes-Benz 709D	Wadham Stringer Wessex II	B29F	1994	
255	L255NFA	Mercedes-Benz 709D	Wadham Stringer Wessex II	B29F	1994	
256	L226JFA	Mercedes-Benz 709D	Dormobile Routemaker	B29F	1993	
274	F44XVP	Iveco Daily 40.06	Carlyle Dailybus 2	B21F	1989	Carlyle demonstrator, 1989
285	F485EJC	Iveco Daily 49.10	Carlyle Dailybus 2	BC25F	1989	Crosville Cymru, 1991
286	F486EJC	Iveco Daily 49.10	Carlyle Dailybus 2	BC25F	1989	Crosville Cymru, 1991

301-328

Iveco Daily 49-10 Carlyle Dailybus B23F 1989-90

301	F601EHA	306	F606EHA	311	F611EHA	316	F616EHA	325	F625EHA
302	F602EHA	307	F607EHA	312	F612EHA	319	F619EHA	326	F626EHA
303	F603EHA	308	F608EHA	313	F613EHA	320	F620EHA	327	G327PHA
304	F604EHA	309	F609EHA	315	F615EHA	322	F622EHA	328	G328PHA
305	F605EHA	310	F610EHA						

330-338

Renault-Dodge S56 Northern Counties B23F 1990-91

| 330 | H330DHA | 332 | H332DHA | 334 | H334DHA | 336 | H336DHA | 338w | H338DHA |
| 331 | H331DHA | 333w | H433DHA | 335 | H335DHA | 337 | H337DHA | | |

| 346w | E96WCM | Renault-Dodge S56 | Northern Counties | B23F | 1988 | North Western, 1991 |
| 349w | E99WCM | Renault-Dodge S56 | Northern Counties | B23F | 1988 | North Western, 1991 |

355-370

Mercedes-Benz 709D Alexander Sprint B23F 1994-95 Timeline, Leigh, 1998

| 355 | N171WNF | 362 | M162LNC | 364 | M164LNC | 368 | N168LNF | 370 | N170LNF |
| 356 | N172WNF | 363 | M163LNC | 365 | M165LNC | 369 | N169LNF | | |

371-381

Mercedes-Benz 709D Alexander Sprint B29F* 1995-96 *376-81 are B27F

371	M371EFD	374	M374EFD	376	M376EFD	378	M378EFD	380	M380EFD
372	M372EFD	375	M375EFD	377	M377EFD	379	M379EFD	381	M381EFD
373	M373EFD								

382-401   Mercedes-Benz 709D   Alexander Sprint   B25F   1996

382	P382FEA	386	P386FEA	390	P390FEA	394	P394FEA	398	P398FEA
383	P383FEA	387	P387FEA	391	P391FEA	395	P395FEA	399	P399FEA
384	P384FEA	388	P388FEA	392	P392FEA	396	P396FEA	401	P401FEA
385	P385FEA	389	P389FEA	393	P393FEA	397	P397FEA		

402	K142BFA	Mercedes-Benz 811D	Dormobile Routemaker	B31F	1993	
403	F822GDT	Mercedes-Benz 811D	Reeve Burgess Beaver	BC25F	1989	Gordons, Rotherham, 1993
404	IDZ8561	Mercedes-Benz 811D	Wright NimBus	B26F	1990	Wright demonstrator, 1992
405	F985EDS	Mercedes Benz 811D	Alexander Sprint	BC33F	1988	Rhondda, 1994
406	H176JVT	Mercedes-Benz 811D	Wright NimBus	B29F	1990	
407	H177JVT	Mercedes-Benz 811D	Wright NimBus	B29F	1990	
410	G807FJX	Mercedes-Benz 811D	PMT Ami	B33F	1990	Abbeyways, Halifax, 1993
411	G111TND	Mercedes-Benz 811D	Carlyle	B31F	1989	C-Line, 1991
413	G901MNS	Mercedes-Benz 811D	Reeve Burgess Beaver	B33F	1989	Edinburgh Transport, 1994

414-428   Mercedes-Benz 811D   Carlyle   B33F   1989-90   C-Line, 1991-92
                                                                   414 ex Bee Line Buzz, 1993

414	G114TND	417	G117TND	422	G122TJA	427	G127TJA
415	G115TND	421	G121TJA	426	G126TJA	428	G128TJA

430	F836BCW	Mercedes-Benz 811D	Reeve Burgess Beaver	B33F	1989	Northumbria, 1998

431-436   Mercedes-Benz 811D   LHE Commuter   B31F   1990   C-Line, 1992

431	H131CDB	433	H133CDB	434	H134CDB	435	H135CDB	436	H136CDB
432	H132CDB						

438	K138BRF	Mercedes-Benz 811D	Dormobile Routemaker	B31F	1993	
439	K139BRF	Mercedes-Benz 811D	Dormobile Routemaker	B31F	1993	
440	K140BFA	Mercedes-Benz 811D	Dormobile Routemaker	B31F	1993	
441	K141BFA	Mercedes-Benz 811D	Dormobile Routemaker	B31F	1993	
442	H112DDS	Mercedes-Benz 811D	Carlyle	B33F	1990	Harte Coaches, Greenock, 1995
447	G897TGG	Mercedes-Benz 811D	Reeve Burgess Beaver	B33F	1990	Stevensons, 1995
448	904AXY	Mercedes-Benz 811D	Alexander AM	BC33F	1988	Happy Days, Woodseaves, 1991
449	G399FSF	Mercedes-Benz 811D	PMT Ami	B33F	1990	Stevensons, 1994
450	G900TJA	Mercedes-Benz 811D	Mellor	B32F	1990	Stevensons, 1994

451-461   Mercedes-Benz 811D   Marshall C16   B31F   1995

451	M451EDH	454	M454EDH	456	M456EDH	458	M458EDH	460	M460EDH
452	M452EDH	455	M455EDH	457	M457EDH	459	M459EDH	461	M461EDH
453	M453EDH								

463-472   Mercedes-Benz 811D   Alexander Sprint   B31F   1995

463	N463EHA	465	N465EHA	467	N467EHA	469	N469EHA	471	N471EHA
464	N464EHA	466	N466EHA	468	N468EHA	470	N470EHA	472	N472EHA

481-498   Mercedes-Benz 814D   Wright NimBus   B31F*   1991   *481/2/97/8 are B33F

481	H201LRF	483	J203REH	486	J206REH	495	J205REH	497	H197JVT
482	H202LRF	484	J204REH	487	J207REH	496	H196JVT	498	H198JVT

499	H199KEH	Mercedes-Benz 814D	Phoenix	BC31F	1990	
501	H501GHA	Dennis Dart 8.5SDL3003	East Lancashire EL2000	B35F	1991	

502-523   Dennis Dart 9SDL3034   East Lancashire EL2000   B33F   1994

502	L502BNX	507	L507BNX	512	L512BNX	516	L516BNX	520	L620BNX
503	L503BNX	508	L508BNX	513	L513BNX	517	L517BNX	521	L521BNX
504	L504BNX	509	L509BNX	514	L514BNX	518	L618BNX	522	L522BNX
505	L605BNX	510	L510BNX	515	L515BNX	519	L519BNX	523	L523BNX
506	L506BNX	511	L511BNX						

524	J556GTP	Dennis Dart 9SDL3002	Wadham Stringer Portsdown	B35F	1991	Irwell Valley, Boothstown, 1992
525	H192JNF	Dennis Dart 9SDL3002	Wadham Stringer Portsdown	B35F	1990	Jim Stones, Glazebury, 1993
541	G141GOL	Dennis Dart 9SDL3002	Duple Dartline	B39F	1990	Arrowline, Knutsford, 1992
551	H851NOC	Dennis Dart 9.8SDL3004	Carlyle Dartline	B43F	1991	Thanet Bus, Ramsgate, 1992
580	JOX480P	Leyland National 11351/1R		B49F	1976	

In recent years several batches of Dennis Darts have been delivered to North Midlands, the initial batches being bodied by East Lancashire. More recent arrivals have featured Plaxton bodywork like 1329, R329TJW, pictured here with Network Stafford lettering. Strict rules for route branding have been applied by Arriva's marketing people and these specify the colours and letter fonts to be used. Interestingly, the word 'Arriva' is a specifically arranged design and is not part of a font set. *Les Peters*

647-767					Leyland National 11351A/1R			B49F	1977-80 Midland Red, 1981, 647 MRE 1982
647	PUK647R	698	TOF698S	705	TOF705S	763	BVP763V	767	BVP767V
685	TOF685S	702	TOF702S	719	TOF719S	765	BVP765V		

790	L300SBS	Dennis Dart 9.8SDL3035	Plaxton Pointer	B40F	1994
791	L301NFA	Dennis Dart 9.8SDL3035	Plaxton Pointer	B40F	1994
792	L302NFA	Dennis Dart 9.8SDL3035	Plaxton Pointer	B40F	1994
793	L303NFA	Dennis Dart 9.8SDL3035	Plaxton Pointer	B40F	1994
794	L304NFA	Dennis Dart 9.8SDL3035	Plaxton Pointer	B40F	1994
795	L305NFA	Dennis Dart 9.8SDL3035	Plaxton Pointer	B40F	1994
799	J328VAW	Dennis Dart 9.8SDL3004	Carlyle Dartline	B40F	1991	Williamsons, Shrewsbury, 1998
800	J327VAW	Dennis Dart 9.8SDL3004	Carlyle Dartline	B40F	1991	Williamsons, Shrewsbury, 1998
801	J701NHA	Dennis Dart 9.8SDL3004	East Lancashire EL2000	B40F	1991
802	M802MOJ	Dennis Dart 9.8SDL3040	Marshall C37	B40F	1994
803	M803MOJ	Dennis Dart 9.8SDL3040	Marshall C37	B40F	1994
804w	M804MOJ	Dennis Dart 9.8SDL3054	Marshall C37	B40F	1994
805	M805MOJ	Dennis Dart 9.8SDL3054	Marshall C37	B40F	1994
806	N806EHA	Dennis Dart 9.8SDL3054	East Lancashire	B40F	1995
807	N807EHA	Dennis Dart 9.8SDL3054	East Lancashire	B40F	1995
808	N808EHA	Dennis Dart 9.8SDL3054	East Lancashire	B40F	1995
826	DOC26V	Leyland National 2 NL116L11/1R		B50F	1980	West Midlands Travel, 1996
829	DOC29V	Leyland National 2 NL116L11/1R		B50F	1980	West Midlands Travel, 1996
837	DOC37V	Leyland National 2 NL116L11/1R		B50F	1980	West Midlands Travel, 1996

859	TPE159S	Leyland National 11351A/1R (6HLXB)		B49F	1978	Alder Valley, 1990
863	TPE163S	Leyland National 11351A/1R (6HLXB)		B49F	1978	Alder Valley, 1990
866	TPE166S	Leyland National 11351A/1R (6HLXB)		B49F	1978	Alder Valley, 1990
872	GMB372T	Leyland National 11351A/1R (6HLXB)		B49F	1978	C-Line, 1992
873	GMB373T	Leyland National 11351A/1R (6HLXB)		B49F	1978	Crosville, 1989
875	LFR875X	Leyland National 2 NL106L11/1R East Lancs Greenway (1995)	B41F	1981	North Western, 1995
876	GMB376T	Leyland National 11351A/1R (6HLXB)		B49F	1978	Crosville, 1989
878	GMB378T	Leyland National 11351A/1R (6HLXB)		B49F	1979	Crosville, 1989
883	GMB383T	Leyland National 11351A/1R (6HLXB)		B49F	1978	C-Line, 1992
890	GMB390T	Leyland National 11351A/1R (6HLXB)		B49F	1978	Crosville, 1989
891	KMA401T	Leyland National 11351A/1R (6HLXB)		B49F	1979	C-Line, 1992
892	KMA402T	Leyland National 11351A/1R (6HLXB)		B49F	1979	C-Line, 1992
901	TOF701S	Leyland National 11351A/1R		B49F	1978	
904	TOF704S	Leyland National 11351A/1R		B49F	1978	
917	JOX517P	Leyland National 11351A/1R (Volvo)		B49F	1976	
937	PUK637R	Leyland National 11351A/1R East Lancs Greenway (1994)	B49F	1977	Midland Red, 1981
939	PUK639R	Leyland National 11351A/1R (Cummins)		B49F	1977	
952	PUK652R	Leyland National 11351A/1R East Lancs Greenway (1994)	B49F	1977	Midland Red East, 1983

973-984

		Volvo Citybus B10M-50	Alexander Q	B55F	1991	Ex Timeline, Leigh, 1998

973	H73DVM	975	H575DVM	977	H577DVM	981	H81DVM	983	H83DVM
974	H74DVM	976	H76DVM	980	H580DVM	982	H82DVM	984	H84DVM

1006	HXI3006	Leyland Lynx LX5636LXCTFR	Alexander N	B53F	1985	Citybus, Belfast, 1992
1007	HXI3007	Leyland Lynx LX5636LXBFR	Alexander N	B49F	1986	Citybus, Belfast, 1992
1008	HXI3008	Leyland Lynx LX5636LXBFR	Alexander N	B53F	1986	Citybus, Belfast, 1992
1009	HXI3009	Leyland Lynx LX5636LXBFR	Alexander N	B49F	1986	Citybus, Belfast, 1992
1010	HXI3010	Leyland Lynx LX563TL11FR	Alexander N	B49F	1986	Citybus, Belfast, 1992
1011	HXI3011	Leyland Lynx LX563TL11FR	Alexander N	B53F	1986	Citybus, Belfast, 1992
1012	HXI3012	Leyland Lynx LX563TL11FR	Alexander N	B53F	1986	Citybus, Belfast, 1992
1013	H408YMA	Leyland Lynx LX2R11C15Z4R	Leyland Lynx	B51F	1990	The Wright Company, Wrexham, 1994
1014	F258GWJ	Leyland Lynx LX112L10ZR1R	Leyland Lynx	B51F	1989	The Wright Company, Wrexham, 1993
1015	E72KBF	Leyland Lynx LX112L10ZR1	Leyland Lynx	B51F	1988	
1016	D401MHS	Leyland Lynx LX5636LXCTFR1	Leyland Lynx	B47F	1986	Kelvin Central, 1991
1017	F61PRE	Leyland Lynx LX112L10ZR1R	Leyland Lynx	B48F	1989	

1100	L100SBS	Mercedes-Benz 0405	Wright Cityranger	B51F	1993	
1102	L102MEH	MAN 11.190 HOCLR	Optare Vecta	B42F	1994	
1103	K140RYS	MAN 11.190 HOCLR	Optare Vecta	B37F	1993	Express Travel, Perth, 1994
1104	UOI772	MAN 11.190 HOCLR	Optare Vecta	B40F	1993	Express Travel, Perth, 1994
1106	G785PWL	DAF SB220LC550	Optare Delta	B49F	1989	Edinburgh Transport, 1994
1107	F792DWT	DAF SB220LC550	Optare Delta	B49F	1989	Edinburgh Transport, 1994
1108	P315FAW	Optare L1150	Optare Excel	N40F	1997	Williamsons, Shrewsbury, 1998
1109	P316FAW	Optare L1150	Optare Excel	N40F	1997	Williamsons, Shrewsbury, 1998
1131	J31SFA	Leyland Swift ST2R44C97A4	Wright Handybus	B39F	1992	
1132	J32SFA	Leyland Swift ST2R44C97A4	Wright Handybus	B39F	1992	
1133	H313WUA	Leyland Swift ST2R44C97A4	Reeve Burgess Harrier	BC39F	1991	Pennine, Gargrave, 1992
1134	J34SRF	Leyland Swift ST2R44C97A4	Wright Handybus	B39F	1992	
1135	H314WUA	Leyland Swift ST2R44C97A4	Reeve Burgess Harrier	BC39F	1991	Pennine, Gargrave, 1992
1136	J36SRF	Leyland Swift ST2R44C97A4	Wright Handybus	B39F	1992	
1137	G616WGS	Leyland Swift LBM6T/2RA	Reeve Burgess Harrier	B39F	1989	Chambers, Stevenage, 1992
1138	F907PFH	Leyland Swift LBM6T/2RA	G C Smith Whippet	B36F	1988	Gloucestershire CC, 1993
1139	G727RGA	Leyland Swift LBM6T/2RA	Reeve Burgess Harrier	B39F	1990	Kelvin Central, 1993
1140	H166MFA	Leyland Swift ST2R44C97A4	Wadham Stringer Vanguard II	B39F	1991	
1141	F956XCK	Leyland Swift LBM6N/2RAO	Wadham Stringer Vanguard II	B39F	1989	Jim Stones, Glazebury, 1991
1142	F155DKU	Leyland Swift LBM6T/2RA	Reeve Burgess Harrier	B41F	1989	K-Line, Kirkburton, 1993
1143	J169REH	Leyland Swift ST2R44C97A4	Wadham Stringer Vanguard II	B39F	1991	
1144	J162REH	Leyland Swift ST2R44C97A4	Wadham Stringer Vanguard II	B39F	1991	
1145	G98VMM	Leyland Swift LBM6T/2RA	Wadham Stringer Vanguard II	B39F	1989	Green, Kirkintilloch, 1991
1146	E990NMK	Leyland Swift LBM6T/2RS	Wadham Stringer Vanguard II	B37F	1988	Armchair, Brentford, 1993
1147	E992NMK	Leyland Swift LBM6T/2RS	Wadham Stringer Vanguard II	B37F	1988	Armchair, Brentford, 1993
1148	E993NMK	Leyland Swift LBM6T/2RS	Wadham Stringer Vanguard II	B37F	1988	Armchair, Brentford, 1993

Opposite, top:- **Arriva acquired the Timeline operations south of Manchester in 1998. Some of the south Manchester operations passed to North West, the Shifnal base in Shropshire transferred to North Midlands, and with Wellington and Bridgnorth form the three depots that provide services to Telford. Pictured on service 12 to Madeley is Volvo Citybus 983, H83DVM.** *Bill Potter*

Opposite, bottom:- **The alternative to the Dart for single-deck purchases have been Scania full-size saloons with a batch of the L113 low-floor variety arriving in 1998. These carry Plaxton Prestige bodies represented here by Burton-on-Trent based 1415, R415TJW.** *Tony Wilson*

Telford has gained several Dennis Falcons dispersed from Oswestry following the Arrival of new Darts for that part of Shropshire. Pictured in Ironbridge is 1216, K216UHA. *Bill Potter*

1201-1210
Dennis Falcon HC SDA421 · East Lancashire EL2000 · B48F · 1990 · London & Country, 1991

1201	G301DPA	1207	G307DPA	1208	G308DPA	1209	G309DPA	1210	G310DPA
1206	G306DPA								

1211-1219
Dennis Falcon HC SDA423 · East Lancashire EL2000 · B48F · 1992-93

1211	K211UHA	1213	K213UHA	1215	K215UHA	1217	K217UHA	1219	K219UHA
1212	K212UHA	1214	K214UHA	1216	K216UHA	1218	K218UHA		

1301-1305
Dennis Dart SLF · Plaxton Pointer · N37F · 1996 · *1301 is B43F

1301	N301ENX	1302	N302ENX	1303	N303ENX	1304	N304ENX	1305	N305ENX

1306-1310
Dennis Dart SLF · Plaxton Pointer · NC37F · 1996

1306	P306FEA	1307	P307FEA	1308	P308FEA	1309	P309FEA	1310	P310FEA

1311-1315
Dennis Dart SLF · East Lancashire Spryte · N41F · 1996

1311	P311FEA	1312	P312FEA	1313	P313FEA	1314	P314FEA	1315	P315FEA

1316-1327
Dennis Dart SLF · Plaxton Pointer · NC39F · 1997

1316	P316FEA	1319	P319HOJ	1322	P322HOJ	1324	P324HOJ	1326	P326HOJ
1317	P317FEA	1320	P320HOJ	1323	P323HOJ	1325	P325HOJ	1327	P327HOJ
1318	P318FEA	1321	P321HOJ						

1329-1344
Dennis Dart SLF · Plaxton Pointer 2 · NC39F · 1997-98

1329	R329TJW	1332	R332TJW	1336	R336TJW	1339	R339TJW	1342	R342TJW
1330	R330TJW	1334	R334TJW	1337	R337TJW	1340	R340TJW	1343	R343TJW
1331	R331TJW	1335	R335TJW	1338	R338TJW	1341	R341TJW	1344	R344TJW

1345-1353 — Dennis Dart SPD 10.6m, Plaxton Pointer 2, NC44F, 1999

1345	S345YOG	1347	S347YOG	1349	S349YOG	1351	S351YOG	1353	S353YOG
1346	S346YOG	1348	S348YOG	1350	S350YOG	1352	S352YOG		

1354	S354YOG	Dennis Dart SLF 8.8m	Plaxton Pointer 2	NC--F	1999
1355	S355YOG	Dennis Dart SLF 8.8m	Plaxton Pointer 2	NC--F	1999
1356	S356YOG	Dennis Dart SLF 8.8m	Plaxton Pointer 2	NC--F	1999
1357	S357YOG	Dennis Dart SLF 8.8m	Plaxton Pointer 2	NC--F	1999

1401	M401EFD	Scania N113CRL	East Lancashire European	B42F	1995	
1402	M402EFD	Scania N113CRL	East Lancashire European	B42F	1995	
1403	M403EFD	Scania N113CRL	East Lancashire European	B42F	1995	
1404	M404EFD	Scania N113CRL	East Lancashire European	B42F	1995	
1407	F170DET	Scania K93CRB	Plaxton Derwent II	B57F	1989	Capital Citybus, 1993
1409	G109YRE	Scania K93CRB	Alexander PS	B51F	1989	
1410	F110SRF	Scania K93CRB	Alexander PS	B51F	1989	
1411	G611CFA	Scania K93CRB	Plaxton Derwent	B57F	1990	North Western (Liverline), 1996
1412	G612CFA	Scania K93CRB	Plaxton Derwent	B57F	1990	North Western (Liverline), 1996
1413	G41HKY	Scania K93CRB	Plaxton Derwent	B57F	1990	North Western (Liverline), 1996
1414	G610CFA	Scania K93CRB	Plaxton Derwent	B57F	1990	North Western (Liverline), 1996

1415-1429 — Scania L113CRL, Plaxton Prestige, N47F, 1998, 1416-25 are NC45F

1415	R415TJW	1418	R418TJW	1421	R421TJW	1424	R424TJW	1427	R427TJW
1416	R416TJW	1419	R419TJW	1422	R422TJW	1425	R425TJW	1428	R428TJW
1417	R417TJW	1420	R420TJW	1423	R423TJW	1426	R426TJW	1429	R429TJW

1500	OKY822X	Leyland Leopard PSU5C/4R	Plaxton Supreme VI Exp	C57F	1982	Frontline, 1996
1508	KUB671V	Leyland Leopard PSU3E/4R	Plaxton Supreme IV Exp	C49F	1980	Frontline, 1996
1514	479BOC	Leyland Leopard PSU3B/4R (TL11) Duple 320 (1987)		C53F	1973	Blue Bus, Rugeley, 1985
1516	B516OEH	Leyland Tiger TRCTL11/3RH	Duple Laser 2	C53F	1985	
1518	A518EVN	Leyland Tiger TRCTL11/2R	Plaxton Paramount 3200 E	CB55F	1983	North East (Teeside), 1998
1522	BPR102Y	Leyland Tiger TRCTL11/3R	Duple Laser	C50F	1983	London & Country, 1991
1604	B604OEH	Leyland Tiger TRCTL11/3RH	Duple Laser 2	C55F	1984	
1606	B606OEH	Leyland Tiger TRCTL11/3RH	Duple Laser 2	C55F	1984	
1607	B607OEH	Leyland Tiger TRCTL11/3RH	Duple Laser 2	C55F	1984	
1612	A152EPA	Leyland Tiger TRCTL11/3R	Plaxton Paramount 3200 E	C53F	1984	The Shires, 1998
1613	A113EPA	Leyland Tiger TRCTL11/2R	Plaxton Paramount 3200 E	C53F	1984	The Shires, 1998
1614	A153EPA	Leyland Tiger TRCTL11/3R	Plaxton Paramount 3200 E	C53F	1984	The Shires, 1998
1615	A215PEV	Leyland Tiger TRCTL11/2R	Duple Dominant IV Express	CB53F	1983	Southdown, 1990
1616	A115EPA	Leyland Tiger TRCTL11/2R	Plaxton Paramount 3200 E	C53F	1984	The Shires, 1996
1618	A118EPA	Leyland Tiger TRCTL11/2RH	Plaxton Paramount 3200 E	C53F	1984	London & Country, 1997
1619	GDZ795	Leyland Tiger TRCTL11/3RH	Duple 320	C53F	1986	Crosville Cymru, 1996
1620	YYJ955	Leyland Tiger TRCTL11/3RH	Duple 320	C53F	1986	Crosville Cymru, 1996
1621	A121EPA	Leyland Tiger TRCTL11/2R	Plaxton Paramount 3200 E	C53F	1983	London & Country, 1997
1628	A101EPA	Leyland Tiger TRCTL11/2RH	Plaxton Paramount 3200 E	C53F	1983	The Shires, 1996
1635	A195KKF	Leyland Tiger TRCTL11/2R	Duple Laser	CB49F	1983	North Western, 1995
1636	A136EPA	Leyland Tiger TRCTL11/2RH	Plaxton Paramount 3200 E	C53F	1984	The Shires, 1996
1637	C37CWT	Leyland Tiger TRCTL11/2RH	Plaxton Paramount 3200 IIE	C53F	1986	North East, 1998
1638	C36CWT	Leyland Tiger TRCTL11/2RH	Plaxton Paramount 3200 IIE	C53F	1986	North East, 1998
1639	A139EPA	Leyland Tiger TRCTL11/2R	Plaxton Paramount 3200 E	C53F	1984	C-Line, 1992
1640	C40CWT	Leyland Tiger TRCTL11/2RH	Plaxton Paramount 3200 IIE	C53F	1986	North East, 1998
1642	A39SMA	Leyland Tiger TRCTL11/2R	Duple Laser	C49F	1983	North Western, 1995
1643	A858YOX	Leyland Tiger TRCTL11/3RH	Plaxton Paramount 3200 E	C53F	1983	Frontline, 1996
1645	B145ALG	Leyland Tiger TRCTL11/2RH	Duple Laser 2	C49F	1984	North Western, 1995
1646	488BDN	Leyland Tiger TRCTL11/3R	Duple 320	C53F	1986	Crosville Cymru, 1996
1647	B147ALG	Leyland Tiger TRCTL11/2RH	Duple Laser 2	C49F	1984	North Western, 1995
1650	B150ALG	Leyland Tiger TRCTL11/2RH	Duple Laser 2	C49F	1984	North Western, 1995
1653	A859YOX	Leyland Tiger TRCTL11/3RH	Plaxton Paramount 3200 E	C53F	1983	Frontline, 1996
1654	TDC854X	Leyland Tiger TRCTL11/3R	Duple Dominant IV Express	C53F	1982	Shamrock & Rambler, 1998
1660	A160EPA	Leyland Tiger TRCTL11/3R	Plaxton Paramount 3200 E	C53F	1984	C-Line, 1992
1679	FAZ5279	Leyland Tiger TRCTL11/3R	Plaxton Paramount 3200 E	C53F	1984	Crosville Cymru, 1995
1681	FAZ5181	Leyland Tiger TRCTL11/3R	Plaxton Paramount 3200 E	C53F	1984	Crosville Cymru, 1996
1683	SIB8583	Leyland Tiger TRCTL11/3R	Plaxton Paramount 3200 E	C51F	1984	Crosville Cymru, 1998
1689	SIB7689	Leyland Tiger TRCTL11/3RH	Duple 320	C53F	1986	Crosville Cymru, 1997
1692	SIB9492	Leyland Tiger TRCTL11/3R	Plaxton Paramount 3200 E	C51F	1984	Crosville Cymru, 1997
1693	JSK994	Leyland Tiger TRCTL11/3RH	Berkhof Everest 370	C53F	1986	Crosville Cymru, 1998
1694	FAZ3194	Leyland Tiger TRCTL11/3RH	Duple 320	C53F	1986	Crosville Cymru, 1997
1695	FAZ3195	Leyland Tiger TRCTL11/2RH	Plaxton Paramount 3200 II	C53F	1985	Crosville Cymru, 1995
1698	A898KAH	Leyland Tiger TRCTL11/3RH	Plaxton Paramount 3200 E	C53F	1983	C-Line, 1992

Transferred from the North West's Liverline operation, 1735, E829AWA carries Stevensons colours when pictured in Uttoxeter bus station. The North Midlands fleet comprises those previously known as Stevensons and Midland Red North, though two separate operators licences are required. *Tony Wilson*

1701-1709

	Leyland Tiger TRCTL11/2R			Duple Dominant		B51F		1984	

1701	A701HVT	1703	A703HVT	1705	A705HVT	1707	A707HVT	1709	A709HVT
1702	A702HVT	1704	A704HVT	1706	A706HVT	1708	A708HVT		

1710-1720

	Leyland Tiger TRCTL11/2R			East Lancashire (1989)		B51F*		1982 London & Country, 1989	
								*1710/3/4/8 are BC49F; 1712 is B55F	

1710	TPC101X	1713	TPC103X	1715	WPH125Y	1717	TPC107X	1719	WPH139Y
1711	WPH121Y	1714	TPC104X	1716	WPH126Y	1718	TPC114X	1720	WPH122Y
1712	TPC102X								

1721-1729

	Leyland Tiger TRCTL11/3RH			East Lancashire (1991)		B59F		1984-86 London & Country, 1991	

1721	C141SPB	1723	B103KPF	1725	B105KPF	1728	B108KPF	1729	B109KPF
1722	B102KPF	1724	B104KPF	1726	C262SPC				

1730	YPJ207Y	Leyland Tiger TRCTL11/3R	East Lancashire (1992)	B59F	1982	County, 1991
1733	OOV761X	Leyland Tiger TRCTL11/3R	East Lancashire (1992)	B59F	1982	Tame Valley, Birmingham, 1992
1735	DJN25X	Leyland Tiger TRCTL11/2R	East Lancashire (1992)	B53F	1982	County, 1992
1737	UJN430Y	Leyland Tiger TRCTL11/2R	East Lancashire (1991)	B53F	1982	County, 1991
1738	WPH118Y	Leyland Tiger TRCTL11/2R	East Lancashire (1992)	B53F	1983	County, 1991
1739	E829AWA	Leyland Tiger TRBTL11/2RP	Plaxton Derwent II	B54F	1988	Liverline, 1993
1740	AAX590A	Leyland Tiger TRCTL11/3R	East Lancashire (1993)	B61F	1984	Rhondda, 1992
1742	A42SMA	Leyland Tiger TRCTL11/2R	East Lancashire (1992)	B53F	1984	North Western, 1991
1743	WPH123Y	Leyland Tiger TRCTL11/2R	East Lancashire (1992)	B53F	1983	County, 1991

1745-1752

	Leyland Tiger TRBTL11/3ARZA			Alexander N		B53F		1988 Timeline, 1993-95	

1745	E25UNE	1747	E27UNE	1749	E29UNE	1751	E31UNE	1752	E32UNE
1746	E26UNE	1748	E28UNE	1750	E30UNE				

1753-1772

Leyland Tiger TRBL10/3ARZA | Alexander N | B53F* | 1988-89 Timeline, 1994-95;*1759/60/71/2 are B55F

| 1753 | F33ENF | 1755 | F35ENF | 1759 | F39ENF | 1771 | F51ENF | 1772 | F52ENF |
| 1754 | F34ENF | 1756 | F36ENF | 1760 | F40ENF | | | | |

| 1778 | F278HOD | Leyland Tiger TRBTL11/2RP | Plaxton Derwent 2 | B54F | 1988 | Thames Transit, 1994 |

1801-1806

Dennis Dominator DDA1032* | East Lancashire | B47/29F | 1990 | *1803-6 are DDA1031

| 1801 | G801THA | 1803 | H803AHA | 1804 | H804AHA | 1805 | H805AHA | 1806 | H806AHA |
| 1802 | G802THA | | | | | | | | |

1823	BMA523W	Bristol VRT/SL3/6LXB	Eastern Coach Works	B43/31F	1981	Crosville Cymru, 1991
1831	M831SDA	Scania N113DRB	East Lancashire	BC43/29F	1995	
1832	M832SDA	Scania N113DRB	East Lancashire	BC43/29F	1995	
1833	M833SDA	Scania N113DRB	East Lancashire	BC43/29F	1995	
1834	M834SDA	Scania N113DRB	East Lancashire	B45/33F	1995	
1835	M835SDA	Scania N113DRB	East Lancashire	B45/33F	1995	
1858	VCA458W	Bristol VRT/SL3/6LXB	Eastern Coach Works	B43/31F	1981	Crosville Cymru, 1991
1860	VCA460W	Bristol VRT/SL3/6LXB	Eastern Coach Works	B43/31F	1981	Crosville Cymru, 1991
1870	WTU470W	Bristol VRT/SL3/6LXB	Eastern Coach Works	B43/31F	1981	Crosville Cymru, 1991
1887	AHW206V	Bristol VRT/SL3/6LXB	Eastern Coach Works	B43/27F	1980	Frontline, 1996

1902-1910

Leyland Olympian ONLXB/1R | Eastern Coach Works | B45/32F | 1983

| 1902 | EEH902Y | 1904 | EEH904Y | 1906 | EEH906Y | 1909 | EEH909Y | 1910 | EEH910Y |
| 1903 | EEH903Y | 1905 | EEH905Y | 1907 | EEH907Y | | | | |

1911	B911NBF	Leyland Olympian ONLXB/1R	Eastern Coach Works	BC42/28F	1984	
1912	B912NBF	Leyland Olympian ONLXB/1R	Eastern Coach Works	BC42/28F	1984	
1913	B913NBF	Leyland Olympian ONLXB/1R	Eastern Coach Works	BC42/28F	1984	
1914	B197DTU	Leyland Olympian ONLXB/1R	Eastern Coach Works	B45/32F	1985	Crosville, 1989
1915	B198DTU	Leyland Olympian ONLXB/1R	Eastern Coach Works	B45/32F	1985	Crosville, 1989
1916	G916LHA	Leyland Olympian ON2R50G16ZA	East Lancashire	B45/29F	1989	
1917	G917LHA	Leyland Olympian ON2R50G16ZA	East Lancashire	B45/29F	1989	
1918	G918LHA	Leyland Olympian ON2R50G16ZA	East Lancashire	B45/29F	1989	
1919	G919LHA	Leyland Olympian ON2R50G16ZA	East Lancashire	B45/29F	1989	
1923	B203DTU	Leyland Olympian ONLXB/1R	Eastern Coach Works	BC42/27F	1985	Crosville Cymru, 1990
1924	B204DTU	Leyland Olympian ONLXB/1R	Eastern Coach Works	BC42/27F	1985	Crosville Cymru, 1990
1937	GFM107X	Leyland Olympian ONLXB/1R	Eastern Coach Works	B45/32F	1982	Crosville, 1989
1938	PFM130Y	Leyland Olympian ONLXB/1R	Eastern Coach Works	B45/32F	1983	Crosville, 1989
1950	A150UDM	Leyland Olympian ONLXB/1R	Eastern Coach Works	B45/32F	1983	Stevensons, 1995
1952	A152UDM	Leyland Olympian ONLXB/1R	Eastern Coach Works	B45/32F	1984	Midland, 1994
1954	A154UDM	Leyland Olympian ONLXB/1R	Eastern Coach Works	B45/32F	1984	Crosville, 1989
1955	A155UDM	Leyland Olympian ONLXB/1R	Eastern Coach Works	B45/32F	1984	Crosville, 1989
1972	A172VFM	Leyland Olympian ONLXB/1R	Eastern Coach Works	B45/32F	1984	C-Line, 1992
1996	F96PRE	Leyland Olympian ONCL10/1RZ	Alexander RL	B47/32F	1988	
1997	F97PRE	Leyland Olympian ONCL10/1RZ	Alexander RL	B47/32F	1988	
2005	G505SFT	Leyland Olympian ONCL10/1RZ	Northern Counties Palatine	B47/30F	1989	Bee Line Buzz, 1993
2007	G507SFT	Leyland Olympian ONCL10/1RZ	Northern Counties Palatine	B47/30F	1989	Bee Line Buzz, 1993
2010	G510SFT	Leyland Olympian ONCL10/1RZ	Northern Counties Palatine	B47/30F	1989	Bee Line Buzz, 1993
2011	G511SFT	Leyland Olympian ONCL10/1RZ	Northern Counties Palatine	B47/30F	1989	Bee Line Buzz, 1993
2012	A146FPG	Leyland Olympian ONTL11/1R	Roe	B43/29F	1984	Southern Counties (G&WS), 1998
2013	A148FPG	Leyland Olympian ONTL11/1R	Roe	B43/29F	1984	Southern Counties (G&WS), 1998
2014	A150FPG	Leyland Olympian ONTL11/1R	Roe	B43/29F	1984	Southern Counties (G&WS), 1998
2015	B274LPH	Leyland Olympian ONTL11/1R	Eastern Coach Works	B43/29F	1985	Southern Counties (C&NS), 1998
2016	B275LPH	Leyland Olympian ONTL11/1R	Eastern Coach Works	B43/29F	1985	Southern Counties (G&WS), 1998

2038-2043

Volvo Citybus B10M-50 | East Lancashire | B45/38F | 1990 | London South, 1998

| 2038 | H648GPF | 2040 | H651GPF | 2041 | H656GPF | 2042 | H657GPF | 2043 | H658GPF |
| 2039 | H649GPF | | | | | | | | |

2044	G644BPH	Volvo Citybus B10M-50	Northern Counties Palatine	B45/35F	1989	Bee Line Buzz, 1993
2045	G645BPH	Volvo Citybus B10M-50	Northern Counties Palatine	B45/35F	1989	Bee Line Buzz, 1993
2046	G646BPH	Volvo Citybus B10M-50	Northern Counties Palatine	B45/35F	1989	Bee Line Buzz, 1993
2047	G647BPH	Volvo Citybus B10M-50	Northern Counties Palatine	B45/35F	1989	Bee Line Buzz, 1993

2051-2071

MCW Metrobus DR102/22 | MCW | B43/30F | 1981 | West Midlands Travel, 1990

| 2051 | KJW296W | 2053 | KJW305W | 2055 | KJW310W | 2070 | KJW318W | 2071 | KJW320W |
| 2052 | KJW301W | | | | | | | | |

2075w	UWW515X	MCW Metrobus DR101/15	Alexander RH	B43/32F	1982	Yorkshire Rider, 1987
2076	UWW517X	MCW Metrobus DR101/15	Alexander RH	B43/32F	1982	Yorkshire Rider, 1987
2080	TOJ592S	MCW Metrobus DR101/2	MCW	B43/30F	1977	MCW demonstrator, 1989
2081	F181YDA	MCW Metrobus DR132/12	MCW	H43/30F	1988	MCW demonstrator, 1989

Ancilliary vehicles

AV14	B504PRF	Ford Transit 190D	Dormobile	B6F	1985	publicity vehicle
AV37	C37WBF	Ford Transit 190D	Dormobile	B16F	1986	
RV23	SBF233	Leyland Titan PD2/28	Northern Counties	RV	1962	Midland Red, 1981
RV24	Q124VOE	Leyland Leopard PSU4/4R	Plaxton Panorama	RV	1966	Midland Red, 1981
RV25	Q125VOE	Leyland Leopard PSU4/4R	Plaxton Panorama	RV	1966	Midland Red, 1981
RV26	Q126VOE	Leyland Leopard PSU4/4R	Plaxton Panorama	RV	1966	Midland Red, 1981
TV51	RUJ351R	Ford R1114	Plaxton Supreme III	C49F	1977	Grimsby Cleethorpes, 1991
TV53w	MRO993P	Ford R1114	Plaxton Supreme III	C53F	1977	Grimsby Cleethorpes, 1991
TV55	GSU854T	Leyland Leopard PSU3E/4R	Alexander AT	BC49F	1979	Kelvin Central, 1994
TV81	NGR681P	Bristol LH6L	Eastern Coach Works	B43F	1976	City Rider, 1995
TV	F484EJC	Iveco Daily 49.10	Carlyle Dailybus 2	BC25F	1989	Crosville Cymru, 1991
TV84	SNU384R	Bristol LH6L	Eastern Coach Works	B43F	1976	Northumbria, 1997
TV86	XPT686R	Bristol LH6L	Eastern Coach Works	B43F	1977	Northumbria, 1996
TV93	TOF693S	Leyland National 11351A/1R		B49F	1978	

Previous Registrations:

123TKM	DVO1T, ERC247T	HXI3008	From new
124YTW	DEN247W	HXI3009	From new
422AKN	G25YVT	HXI3010	From new
479BOC	AJA360L	HXI3011	From new
488BDN	C252SPC	HXI3012	From new
565LON	B549BMH, MSU432, B413LRA	IDZ8561	From new
614WEH	LOT777R	JSK994	C153SPB
803HOM	D264HFX	OIB8606	FTD758W
904AXY	F148USX	OOV761X	VSS1X, WLT610, LTS93X
A858YOX	A622ATV, YSU954	Q124VOE	GHA326D
A859YOX	A618ATV, YSU953	Q125VOE	GHA338D
AAL303A	BUH226V	Q126VOE	GHA336D
AAL404A	BUH222V	SIB7689	C251SPC
AAX590A	A217VWO	SIB8583	A142EPA
AVT345S	SOA676S, 488BDN	SIB9492	A149EPA
BOK364T	TWH687T, WYR562	TOU962	MSU573Y
CBF31Y	THM689M	TR6147	NLJ516M
DJN25X	TPC106X, OIB3510	UJN430Y	WPH124Y, FBZ2514
FAZ3194	C250SPC	UOI772	K141RYS
FAZ3195	B269KPF	VOV926S	XRE305S, 422AKN
FAZ5181	A147EPA	WXI3006	From new
FAZ5279	A145EPA	XOR841	MHS665Y
GDZ795	C299SPC	YSU953	G21YVT
HIJ3652	E472BTN	YSU954	G122DRE
HIL7596	E31SBO	YYJ955	C249SPC
HXI3006	From new		
HXI3007	From new		

Allocations

Abermule (Station Yard, Kerry Road)

Tiger	1722	1730	1737	1742

Bridgnorth (Chartwell Business Park)

Mercedes-Benz	414		
Tiger bus	1705	1706	1709

Opposite:- **The Midlands North double-deck fleet is mostly based in Staffordshire with only a small requirement in Shropshire and Cheshire. The latest arrivals have been Volvo Citybuses from South London. Pictured here are former MCW demonstrator 2080, TOJ592S, seen in Burton-upon-Trent shortly after repaint, and 2007, G507SFT, a Leyland Olympian with Northern Counties Palatine bodywork. It was photographed passing Sudbury Hall in Staffordshire.** *Tony Wilson*

Scania L113 chassis were again the choice for North Western's 1997 delivery of single-deck buses, though the body order for this batch was placed with Northern Counties, after earlier products were sourced from East Lancashire and Wrights. Though pictured in Manchester with Bee Line names, the vehicle is currently allocated to Liverpool for North West duties. *Tony Wilson*

200-210

Leyland National 10351A/2R · B44F · 1979-80 Parfitt's, 1995

200	BYW359V	**202**	BYW379V	**204**	BYW406V	**206**	BYW413V	**209**	BYW432V
201	BYW367V	**203**	BYW402V	**205**	BYW412V	**208**	BYW430V	**210**	BYW437V

211	MIL5581	Leyland National 10351A/1R(Volvo)	B41F	1976	London & Country, 1989

215-253

Leyland National 11351A/1R · B49F · 1976-78 Ribble, 1986

215w	SCK688P	**219**	SCK693P	**229**w	UHG724R	**241**w	ACW764R	**251**w	CBV792S
218w	SCK692P								

284w	NTU15Y	Leyland National 2 NL116HLXB/2R	B52F	1983	Crosville, 1989
286w	VBG92V	Leyland National 2 NL116L11/2R(6HLXB)	B49F	1980	Cymru, 1998
287w	VBG94V	Leyland National 2 NL116L11/2R(6HLXB)	B49F	1980	Cymru, 1998
294w	KNV514P	Leyland National 11351/1R	B49F	1976	Midland Fox, 1994
331w	NPK242P	Leyland National 10351A/1R	B41F	1976	London & Country, 1989
332w	NPK245P	Leyland National 10351A/1R	B41F	1976	London & Country, 1989
340	UPB335S	Leyland National 10351A/1R	B41F	1977	London & Country, 1989

356-370

Leyland National 11351A/1R (6HLX) · B49F · 1977-79 Crosville, 1990

356w	CFM350S	**364**	GMB380T	**370**	KMA400T	
361	EMB367S					

Burslem (Nevada Lane)

Mercedes-Benz	148	149	150	152	156	157	161	162
	164	165	167	168	169	403	404	405
	407	413	449	486	497	499		
Swift	1133	1135	1141					

Burton-on-Trent (Wetmore Road)

Mercedes-Benz	230	253	481	482	483			
Dart	790	791	792	793	794	795		
MAN/Vecta	1102	1103	1104					
Leopard	1513							
National	826	829	837					
Tiger	1516	1614	1639	1642	1647	1654	1689	1694
Olympian	1911	1912	1923	1924	2007	2010		
Spectra	1994	1995						
Scania L	1415	1416	1417	1418				
Metrobus	2050	2051	2052	2055	2076	2079	2080	2081
Volvo Citybus	2040	2041	2042	2043				

Cannock (Delta Way)

Mercedes-Benz	136	137	153	155	159	166	175	382
	383	384	385	386	387	388	389	390
	391	411	415	417	442	447	450	496
Sherpa	218	219	222					
Volvo coach	4							
Dart	516	519	522	523	524	525	541	551
Tiger	1713	1740	1749	1752	1753	1754	1756	1760
	1778							
Olympian	1903	1905	1906	1907	1909	1910	1912	1938

Crewe (Bus Station, Delamere Street)

Mercedes-Benz	51	52	53	54	55	56	57	133
	160	394	395	432	433	434	435	436
Renault-Dodge	330	331	334	335	336			
Tiger	1748	1750	1751	1755	1759	1771	1772	
Dominator	1801	1802	1803	1804	1805	1806		
Olympian	1914	1916	1918	1937	1954	1972		

Lichfield (Freeford Bridge, Common Road)

Mercedes-Benz	58	59	60	61	402	406	484	487
Cityranger	1100							
Scania K	1407	1409	1410	1411	1412	1413	1414	
Tiger	1522	1604	1606	1616	1636	1643	1647	1653
	1660	1681	1698					

Macclesfield (Bus station, Sunderland Street)

Mercedes-Benz	121	126	141	142	143	154	156	157
	158	171	252	368	396	397	398	399
	401	441						
National	763							
Lynx	1007	1009	1010	1012				
Swift	1131	1132	1138	1139	1143	1144	1147	1148
Olympian	1902	1904	1911	1913	1915	1924	1950	1952
	1996	1997						

Oswestry (Oswald Road)

Renault-Dodge	337						
Mercedes-Benz	422	431	453				
Dart (from Jan 99)	1347	1348	1349	1350	1351	1352	1353
National	859	873	875	876	878	890	
Falcon	1201	1206	1207	1208	1209	1210	1214	1219
Bristol VR	1823						
Olympian	1917	1919	1955				

Shifnal (Railway Yard)

Mercedes-Benz	364	365	369	370			
Dart	515	806	807	808	1316	1317	
Volvo B10M	973	974	975	976	977	980	981	982
	983	984					

Shrewsbury (Spring Gardens, Ditherington)

Volvo	7	10					
Mercedes-Benz	421	426	428	451	452		
Iveco	301	302	303	304	305	306	308	309
	310	311	312	313	315	316	319	327
	328						
National	580	698	705	765	767	872	883	901
	904	937	939	952			
Tiger	1735						
Excel	1108	1109					
Dart	799	802	803	805	1301	1302	1303	1304
	1305	1306	1307	1308	1309	1310	1318	1338
	1339	1340	1341	1342	1343	1344	1345	1346
Scania N	1401	1402	1403	1404			

Stafford (Dorrington Park Industrial Estate, Common Road)

Mercedes-Benz	123	125	129	138	139	140	362	363
	392	393	410	438	440	454	456	457
	459						
Transit	185	186	187	188	189	191	
Dart	514	517	520	521	1329	1330	1331	1332
	1334	1335	1336	1337			
National	917						
Lynx	1006	1008	1011	1013	1014	1015	1016	1017
Tiger	1710	1711	1712	1715	1716	1717	1721	1725
	1726	1728	1733	1738	1743		

Swadlincote (Midland Road)

Mercedes-Benz	146	147	172	173	254	256	495	498
Swift	1134	1136	1137	1140	1142	1145	1146	
Dart	1321	1322	1323	1324	1325	1326	1327	
Leopard	1508	1510	1514				
Tiger	1618	1723					
Lynx	1006						
Bristol VR	1887						
Metrobus	2051	2052	2071				

Tamworth (Aldergate)

Mercedes-Benz	371	372	373	374	375	376	377	378
	379	380	381	445	458	460	461	462
	481	482						
Renault-Dodge	333(w)	338(w)	346	349				
Dart	1311	1312	1313	1314	1315	1354	1355	1356
	1357							
Scania L	1420	1421	1422	1423	1424	1425	1426	1427
	1428	1429						
Tiger	1607	1683	1692	1714	1745	1747		
Scania N	1831	1832	1833	1834	1835			
Citybus	2038	2039	2044	2045	2046	2047		

Uttoxeter (The Garage, Spath)

Volvo Coach	3	21	23	25	26	27	29	
Mercedes-Benz	126	127	255	448				
Leopard	12	13	1500					
Tiger	1619	1620	1621	1628	1646	1650	1679	1695
	1718	1739	1746					
Olympian	2005	2007	2010	2011	2014			

Wellington (Charlton Street, Telford)

Iveco	274	285	286	322	323	324	325	326
Mercedes-Benz	427	463	464	465	466	467	468	469
	470	471	472					
Dart	501	502	503	504	505	506	507	508
	509	510	511	512	513	518	800	801
	1319	1320						
National	647	685	702	719	863	866	891	892
Falcon	1211	1212	1213	1215	1216	1217	1218	
Tiger	1701	1702	1703	1704	1707	1708	1719	1720
	1724	1729						
Bristol VR	1858	1860	1870					

Unallocated

Loan to Fox County	134						
Minibus	122	131	135				
Dart	804						
Tiger	1518	1612	1613	1637	1638	1640	1641
	2012	2013	2015	2016			

Shrewsbury's low floor Dennis Darts are route-branded for the Harlescott services that terminate in Sundorne Grove. Pictured in the town centre, 1343, R343TJW is one of the batch delivered in 1998.
Les Peters

ARRIVA serving Derby
ARRIVA serving the Fox County

2	FAZ2784	Leyland Tiger TRCTL11/3RH	Plaxton Paramount 3200 IIE	C53F	1986	Crosville Cymru, 1996
4	FIL3452	Leyland Tiger TRCTL11/3RH	Plaxton Paramount 3200 II	C50FT	1985	
9	A125EPA	Leyland Tiger TRCTL11/2R	Plaxton Paramount 3200 E	C53F	1983	London Country NE, 1989
19	109CRC	Leyland Tiger TRCTL11/3R	Plaxton Paramount 3200	C48FT	1983	London & Country, 1990
20	LJI5632	Leyland Tiger TRCTL11/3R	Plaxton Paramount 3200	C48FT	1983	London & Country, 1990
21	111XKT	Leyland Tiger TRCTL11/3R	Plaxton Paramount 3200	C46FT	1983	London & Country, 1990
22	JDE972X	Leyland Tiger TRCTL11/3R	Plaxton Supreme VI Exp	C53F	1982	Hills, Nuneaton, 1991
28	BPR108Y	Leyland Tiger TRCTL11/3R	Duple Laser	C50F	1983	London & Country, 1990
87	LJI8157	DAF MB200DKFL600	Van Hool Alizée	C49FT	1984	Orsborn, Wollaston, 1989
153	662NKR	DAF MB200DKFL615	Plaxton Supreme VI	C57F	1982	Bland, Stamford, 1990
192	C632PAU	DAF MB200DKFL600	Plaxton Paramount 3500	C49F	1985	
211	N211TBC	Volvo B10M-62	Plaxton Expressliner 2	C49FT	1996	
212	N212TBC	Volvo B10M-62	Plaxton Expressliner 2	C49FT	1996	
213	FIL3451	Volvo B10M-60	Van Hool Alizée	C50F	1989	Tellings-Golden Miller, Byfleet, 1992
214	XPA110	Volvo B10M-60	Van Hool Alizée	C52F	1989	Tellings-Golden Miller, Byfleet, 1992
233	GIL6253	Volvo B10M-61	Plaxton Paramount 3200 III	C50F	1987	The Shires, 1997
234	HIL7594	Volvo B10M-61	Plaxton Paramount 3500 III	C53F	1988	The Shires, 1997
235	GIL6949	Volvo B10M-61	Plaxton Paramount 3200 III	C50F	1987	The Shires, 1997
236	F406DUG	Volvo B10M-60	Plaxton Paramount 3200 III	C50F	1989	Wallace Arnold, 1992
237	F407DUG	Volvo B10M-60	Plaxton Paramount 3200 III	C50F	1989	Wallace Arnold, 1992
246	J246MFP	Volvo B10M-60	Plaxton Expressliner	C46FT	1992	Express Travel, Liverpool, 1995
247	J247MFP	Volvo B10M-60	Plaxton Expressliner	C46FT	1992	Express Travel, Liverpool, 1995
785	BVP785V	Leyland Leopard PSU3E/4R	Plaxton Supreme IV	C53F	1980	Midland Red, 1981
2142	JIL2193	Leyland 11351/1R	East Lancs Greenway(1994)	B49F	1974	Southern Counties (C&NS), 1998
2143	JIL2197	Leyland 1151/1R	East Lancs Greenway(1994)	B49F	1973	Southern Counties (C&NS), 1998
2144	JIL2196	Leyland 11351/1R	East Lancs Greenway(1994)	B49F	1975	Southern Counties (C&NS), 1998
2145	JIL2198	Leyland 11351A/1R	East Lancs Greenway(1994)	B49F	1976	Southern Counties (C&NS), 1998
2146	JIL2199	Leyland 11351A/1R	East Lancs Greenway(1994)	B49F	1976	Southern Counties (C&NS), 1998
2147	JIL2190	Leyland 11351/1R	East Lancs Greenway(1994)	B49F	1976	Southern Counties (C&NS), 1998

Foxhound was the name applied to the coaching unit when Midland Fox was formed from Midland Red East in 1981. Pictured in Leicester is Leyland Tiger 20, LJI5632, an example with Plaxton Paramount 3200 bodywork.
Terry Whiteman

2148	JIL5367	Leyland 11351A/1R(Volvo)	East Lancs Greenway(1994)B49F	1977	Southern Counties (C&NS), 1998
2149	SJI5569	Leyland 11351A/1R(Volvo)	East Lancs Greenway(1994)B49F	1977	Southern Counties (C&NS), 1998
2150	SIB1278	Leyland 10351B/1R	East Lancs Greenway(1994)B41F	1979	Southern Counties (C&NS), 1998
2151	SJI5570	Leyland 11351/1R(Volvo)	East Lancs Greenway(1994)B49F	1976	Southern Counties (C&NS), 1998
2152	MSU433	Leyland National 2 NL116L11/1R	B49F	1980	Stevensons, 1997
2153	BVP813V	Leyland National 2 NL116L11/1R	B49F	1980	London & Country, 1997
2154	EON831V	Leyland National 2 NL116L11/1R	B49F	1980	London & Country, 1997
2156	JIL2156	Leyland National 11351/1R	East Lancs Greenway (1994)	B49F	1974	National Welsh, 1989
2157	JIL2157	Leyland National 1151/1R/0402	East Lancs Greenway (1994)	B49F	1973	Kinch, Barrow-on-Soar, 1989
2158	JIL2158	Leyland National 11351A/1R	East Lancs Greenway (1994)	B49F	1977	Midland Red, 1981
2159	JIL2159	Leyland National 11351A/1R	East Lancs Greenway (1994)	B49F	1977	Midland Red, 1981
2160	JIL2160	Leyland National 11351/1R	East Lancs Greenway (1994)	B49F	1975	London & Country, 1994
2161	JIL2161	Leyland National 11351/1R	East Lancs Greenway (1994)	B49F	1974	Kinch, Barrow-on-Soar, 1989
2162	JIL2162	Leyland National 1151/1R/0102	East Lancs Greenway (1994)	B49F	1974	Kinch, Barrow-on-Soar, 1989
2163	JIL2163	Leyland National 11351/1R	East Lancs Greenway (1994)	B49F	1974	National Welsh, 1989
2164	JIL2164	Leyland National 11351A/1R	East Lancs Greenway (1994)	B49F	1978	London & Country, 1994
2165	JIL2165	Leyland National 11351A/1R	East Lancs Greenway (1994)	B49F	1976	London & Country, 1994

2166-2179   Scania L113CRL   East Lancashire European   B51F   1996

2166	N166PUT	2169	N169PUT	2172	N172PUT	2175	N175PUT	2178	N178PUT
2167	N167PUT	2170	N170PUT	2173	N173PUT	2176	N176PUT	2179	N179PUT
2168	N168PUT	2171	N171PUT	2174	N174PUT	2177	N177PUT		

2201-2206   Dennis Dart SLF   Plaxton Pointer   N39F   1997

2201	P201HRY	2203	P203HRY	2204	P204HRY	2205	P205HRY	2206	P206HRY
2202	P202HRY								

2207	S207DTO	Dennis Dart SLF	Plaxton Pointer 2	N39F	1998	
2208	S208DTO	Dennis Dart SLF	Plaxton Pointer 2	N39F	1998	
2453	JHE153W	MCW Metrobus DR104/6	MCW	B46/31F	1981	South Yorkshire's Transport, 1991
2467	JHE167W	MCW Metrobus DR104/6	MCW	B46/31F	1981	South Yorkshire's Transport, 1991
2474	EWF474V	MCW Metrobus DR102/13	MCW	B46/27D	1980	Stevensons, 1988
2477	JHE177W	MCW Metrobus DR104/6	MCW	B46/31F	1981	South Yorkshire's Transport, 1991
2479	JHE179W	MCW Metrobus DR104/6	MCW	B46/31F	1981	South Yorkshire's Transport, 1991
2480	JHE189W	MCW Metrobus DR104/6	MCW	B46/31F	1981	Stevensons, 1994
2482	JHE192W	MCW Metrobus DR104/6	MCW	B46/31F	1981	Stevensons, 1994
2484	EWF484V	MCW Metrobus DR102/13	MCW	B46/27D	1980	Stevensons, 1988
2486	CKS386X	MCW Metrobus DR102/24	Alexander RL	B45/33F	1981	North Western, 1992
25	EPH210V	Leyland Atlantean AN68A/1R	Roe	B43/30F	1979	Kentish Bus, 1998
25	EPH212V	Leyland Atlantean AN68A/1R	Roe	B43/30F	1980	Kentish Bus, 1998
2534	PWE534R	Leyland Fleetline FE30AGR	Alexander AL	B45/29D	1977	South Yorkshire's Transport, 1990
2539	GTO49V	Leyland Fleetline FE30AGR	Northern Counties	B43/29F	1980	
2547	GTO307V	Leyland Fleetline FE30AGR	Northern Counties	B43/30F	1980	

4001	L94HRF	DAF DB250RS200505	Optare Spectra	B48/29F	1993	Midland (Stevensons), 1998
4002	L95HRF	DAF DB250RS200505	Optare Spectra	B48/29F	1993	Midland (Stevensons), 1998
4151	E701XKR	Scania N112DRB	Alexander RH	B47/31F	1988	Kentish Bus, 1996
4152	E702XKR	Scania N112DRB	Alexander RH	B47/31F	1988	Kentish Bus, 1996

4153-4158   Scania N113DRB   Alexander RH   B47/33F   1989   BTS, Borehamwood, 1993

4153	F153DET	4155	F155DET	4156	F156DET	4157	F157DET	4158	F158DET
4154	F154DET								

Opposite:- **Arriva Fox County, and the former Derby operation share a fleet that identified the Derby vehicles using fleet numbers prefixed D; similarly the minibuses carry an M-prefix. Recent changes have seen the introduction of standard four number fleetnumbers into Derby, and the previous practice of indentification will be eliminated in time. Pictured in Leicester are two of the buses from that city. The upper picture shows 2171, N171PUT in the Urban fox blue livery used before the new corporate scheme was introduced. The lower picture shows recently delivered Volvo Olympian 4646, S646KJU. One of the large intake of the type to join the fleet in 1998, it is allocated to the Southgates depot. Six vehicles from this batch work in Derby operation.** *Tony Wilson/Malcolm King*

4159-4178

											Scania N113DRB	East Lancashire	B47/33F	1994-95

4159	M159GRY	4163	M163GRY	4167	M167GRY	4171	M171GRY	4175	M175GRY
4160	M160GRY	4164	M164GRY	4168	M168GRY	4172	M172GRY	4176	M176GRY
4161	M161GRY	4165	M165GRY	4169	M169GRY	4173	M173GRY	4177	M177GRY
4162	M162GRY	4166	M166GRY	4170	M170GRY	4174	M174GRY	4178	M178GRY

4180-4184

Scania N113DRB — East Lancashire — B45/33F — 1995

4180	N160VVO	4181	N161VVO	4182	N162VVO	4183	N163VVO	4184	N164VVO

4320-4334

Volvo Citybus B10M-50 — East Lancashire — B45/35F — 1990-91 London South, 1998

4320	H650GPF	4323	H654GPF	4326	H663GPF	4329	H672GPF	4332	H680GPF
4321	H652GPF	4324	H655GPF	4327	H664GPF	4330	H677GPF	4333	H682GPF
4322	H653GPF	4325	H659GPF	4328	H671GPF	4331	H674GPF	4334	H684GPF

4476	TPD127X	Leyland Olympian ONTL11/1R	Roe	B43/29F	1982	Southern Coutnies (CNS), 1998
4477	TPD129X	Leyland Olympian ONTL11/1R	Roe	B43/29F	1982	Southern Counties (CNS), 1998
4478	D80UTF	Leyland Olympian ONLXCT/1RH	Eastern Coach Works	C39/27F	1986	Reading, 1994
4480	C42HHJ	Leyland Olympian ONLXCT/1RH	Eastern Coach Works	B47/31F	1985	Colchester, 1994
4481	D44RWC	Leyland Olympian ONLXCT/1RH	Eastern Coach Works	B47/31F	1986	Colchester, 1994
4486	ACM706X	Leyland Olympian ONT11/1R	Eastern Coach Works	B46/31F	1981	Merseybus, 1993
4487	ACM707X	Leyland Olympian ONT11/1R	Eastern Coach Works	B46/31F	1981	Merseybus, 1993
4488w	ACM710X	Leyland Olympian ONT11/1R	Eastern Coach Works	B46/31F	1981	Merseybus, 1993
4489	ACM711X	Leyland Olympian ONT11/1R	Eastern Coach Works	B46/31F	1981	Merseybus, 1993
4491	MTU117Y	Leyland Olympian ONLXB/1R	Eastern Coach Works	B45/32F	1983	Crosville Cymru, 1989
4492	MTU118Y	Leyland Olympian ONLXB/1R	Eastern Coach Works	B45/32F	1983	Crosville Cymru, 1989
4493	MTU119Y	Leyland Olympian ONLXB/1R	Eastern Coach Works	B45/32F	1983	Crosville Cymru, 1989
4494	MTU121Y	Leyland Olympian ONLXB/1R	Eastern Coach Works	B45/32F	1983	Crosville Cymru, 1989

4501-4514

Leyland Olympian ONLXB/1R — Eastern Coach Works — B45/32F — 1983-84

4501	A501EJF	4504	A504EJF	4508	A508EJF	4510	A510EJF	4512	B512LFP
4502	A502EJF	4505	A505EJF	4509	A509EJF	4511	A511EJF	4514	B514LFP
4503	A503EJF	4507	A507EJF						

4516	A132SMA	Leyland Olympian ONLXB/1R	Eastern Coach Works	B45/32F	1983	Crosville Cymru, 1989
4517	A133SMA	Leyland Olympian ONLXB/1R	Eastern Coach Works	B45/32F	1983	Crosville Cymru, 1989
4518	A134SMA	Leyland Olympian ONLXB/1R	Eastern Coach Works	B45/32F	1983	Crosville Cymru, 1989
4519	A135SMA	Leyland Olympian ONLXB/1R	Eastern Coach Works	B45/32F	1983	Crosville Cymru, 1989

4521-4525

Leyland Olympian ONCL10/1RZ — Alexander RL — B45/30F — 1989

4521	G521WJF	4522	G522WJF	4523	G523WJF	4524	G524WJF	4525	G525WJF

4527	B187BLG	Leyland Olympian ONLXB/1RZ	Eastern Coach Works	B45/32F	1984	Crosville Cymru, 1990
4528	B190BLG	Leyland Olympian ONLXB/1RZ	Eastern Coach Works	B45/32F	1984	Crosville Cymru, 1990

4529-4533

Leyland Olympian ONCL10/1RZ — Northern Counties — B47/30F — 1989 Kentish Bus, 1992

4529	G506SFT	4530	G508SFT	4531	G509SFT	4532	G512SFT	4533	G513SFT

4601-4613

Volvo Olympian YN2RV18Z4 — Northern Counties Palatine — B47/29F — 1996

4601	P601CAY	4604	P604CAY	4607	P607CAY	4610	P610CAY	4612	P612CAY
4602	P602CAY	4605	P605CAY	4608	P608CAY	4611	P611CAY	4613	P613CAY
4603	P603CAY	4606	P606CAY	4609	P609CAY				

Opposite, top:- **The final livery applied to City Rider, the former name of Arriva Derby, was based on a yellow scheme using blue and red relief. As a reminder of the scheme, East Lancashire-bodied Scania D029, N429XRC is seen entering the bus station. In practice only part of the official fleet number is seen on the vehicles.** *Tony Wilson*

Opposite, bottom:- **Two Alexander-bodied Dennis Darts joined the Derby fleet in 1998 to undertake *PRIDE PARK & ride* duties, for which they carry appropriate names on the corporate livery. Pictured in Corporation Street is D045, R45VJF. Interesting typography is the use of capital letters for PRIDE and PARK while a lower case style is used for the ride in recognition of the destination Pride Park, home to Derby County FC.** *Tony Wilson*

4614-4643 — Volvo Olympian — Northern Counties Palatine — B47/29F — 1998

4614	R614MNU	4620	R620MNU	4626	R626MNU	4632	R632MNU	4638	R638MNU
4615	R615MNU	4621	R621MNU	4627	R627MNU	4633	R633MNU	4639	R639MNU
4616	R616MNU	4622	R622MNU	4628	R628MNU	4634	R634MNU	4640	R640MNU
4617	R617MNU	4623	R623MNU	4629	R629MNU	4635	R635MNU	4641	R641MNU
4618	R618MNU	4624	R624MNU	4630	R630MNU	4636	R636MNU	4642	R642MNU
4619	R619MNU	4625	R625MNU	4631	R631MNU	4637	R637MNU	4643	R643MNU

4644-4653 — Volvo Olympian — Northern Counties Palatine — B47/29F — 1998

4644	S644KJU	4646	S646KJU	4648	S648KJU	4650	S650KJU	4652	S652KJU
4645	S645KJU	4647	S647KJU	4649	S649KJU	4651	S651KJU	4653	S653KJU

C001-C020 — Carbodies Taxi FX4 — Carbodies Fairway Driver — M5 — 1994

C001	M901DHP	C005	M905DHP	C009	M909DHP	C013	M913DHP	C017	M917DHP
C002	M890DHP	C006	M906DHP	C010	M910DHP	C014	M914DHP	C018	M918DHP
C003	M903DHP	C007	M907DHP	C011	M911DHP	C015	M915DHP	C019	M919DHP
C004	M904DHP	C008	M908DHP	C012	M912DHP	C016	M916DHP	C020	M920DHP

C022	P95HOF	Carbodies Taxi FX4	Carbodies	M5	1996
C023	P96HOF	Carbodies Taxi FX4	Carbodies	M5	1996
C024	P58LOE	Carbodies Taxi FX4	Carbodies	M5	1997
C025	P29LOE	Carbodies Taxi FX4	Carbodies	M5	1996
C026	P57LOE	Carbodies Taxi FX4	Carbodies	M5	1997

D021-D026 — Scania K92CRB — Alexander PS — B51F — 1988

D021	E21ECH	D023	E23ECH	D024	E24ECH	D025	E25ECH	D026	E26ECH

D027	F27JRC	Scania K93CRB	Alexander PS	B51F	1989
D028	F28JRC	Scania K93CRB	Alexander PS	B51F	1989

D029-D033 — Scania L113CRL — East Lancashire European — N51F — 1996

D029	N429XRC	D030	N430XRC	D031	N431XRC	D032	N432XRC	D033	N433XRC

D034-D038 — Dennis Dart 9.8SDL3040 — East Lancashire EL2000 — B40F — 1994

D034	L34PNN	D035	L35PNN	D036	L36PNN	D037	L37PNN	D038	L38PNN

D045	R45VJF	Dennis Dart SLF	Alexander ALX200	N40F	1997
D046	R46VJF	Dennis Dart SLF	Alexander ALX200	N40F	1997
D048	GTO48V	Leyland Fleetline FE30AGR	Northern Counties	B43/29F	1980

D072-D081 — Mercedes-Benz 709D — Alexander Sprint — B27F — 1996

D072	N472XRC	D074	N474XRC	D076	N476XRC	D078	N478XRC	D080	N480XRC
D073	N473XRC	D075	N475XRC	D077	N477XRC	D079	N479XRC	D081	N481XRC

D082-D092 — Mercedes-Benz 709D — Plaxton Beaver — B27F — 1996

D082	P482CAL	D084	P484CAL	D086	P486CAL	D088	P488CAL	D091	P491CAL
D083	P483CAL	D085	P485CAL	D087	P487CAL	D090	P490CAL	D092	P492CAL

D114	SRC114X	Ailsa B55-10	Northern Counties	B38/35F	1982
D118	TCH118X	Ailsa B55-10	Northern Counties	B38/35F	1982
D120	TCH120X	Ailsa B55-10	Northern Counties	B38/35F	1982
D121	TCH121X	Ailsa B55-10	Northern Counties	B38/35F	1982
D126	YAU126Y	Volvo Citybus B10M-50	Marshall	B45/33F	1983
D127	YAU127Y	Volvo Citybus B10M-50	Marshall	B45/33F	1983
D128	YAU128Y	Volvo Citybus B10M-50	Marshall	B43/33F	1983

The 1999 Arriva Bus Handbook

D129-D133 — Volvo Citybus B10M-50 — East Lancashire — B45/31F — 1984

D129	A129DTO	D130	A130DTO	D131	A131DTO	D132	A132DTO	D133	A133DTO

D134-D143 — Volvo Citybus B10M-50 — Marshall — B45/33F — 1984

D134	B134GAU	D136	B136GAU	D138	B138GAU	D140	B140GAU	D142	B142GAU
D135	B135GAU	D137	B137GAU	D139	B139GAU	D141	B141GAU	D143	B143GAU

D144-D153 — Volvo Citybus B10M-50 — Northern Counties — B42/33F — 1986/88

D144	C144NRR	D146	C146NRR	D148	C148NRR	D150	E150BTO	D152	E152BTO
D145	C145NRR	D147	C147NRR	D149	E149BTO	D151	E151BTO	D153	E153BTO

D165-D169 — Volvo Olympian YN2RV18Z4 — Northern Counties Palatine I — B47/30F — 1996

D165	N165XVO	D166	N166XVO	D167	P167BTV	D168	P168BTV	D169	P169BTV

D301-D315 — Leyland Fleetline FE30AGR — Northern Counties — B43/30F — 1978-81

D301	GTO301V	D305	GTO305V	D310	MTV310W	D312	MTV312W	D314	MTV314W
D302	GTO302V	D306	GTO306V	D311	MTV311W	D313	MTV313W	D315	MTV315W
D304	GTO304V	D309	MTV309W						

M101-M126 — Mercedes-Benz Vario O810 — Alexander ALX100 — B29F — 1997

M101	P101HCH	M106	P106HCH	M112	P112HCH	M117	P117HCH	M122	P122HCH
M102	P102HCH	M107	P107HCH	M113	P113HCH	M118	P118HCH	M123	P123HCH
M103	P103HCH	M108	P108HCH	M114	P114HCH	M119	P119HCH	M124	P124HCH
M104	P104HCH	M109	P109HCH	M115	P115HCH	M120	P120HCH	M125	P125HCH
M105	P105HCH	M110	P110HCH	M116	P116HCH	M121	P121HCH	M126	P126HCH

M127-M156 — Mercedes-Benz Vario O814 — Plaxton Beaver 2 — B27F — 1998

M127	R127LNR	M136	R136LNR	M145	R145LNR	M154	R154UAL	M163	R163UAL
M128	R128LNR	M137	R137LNR	M146	R146LNR	M155	R155UAL	M164	R164UAL
M129	R129LNR	M138	R138LNR	M147	R147UAL	M156	R156UAL	M165	R165UAL
M130	R130LNR	M139	R139LNR	M148	R148UAL	M157	R157UAL	M166	R166UAL
M131	R131LNR	M140	R140LNR	M149	R149UAL	M158	R158UAL	M167	R167UAL
M132	R132LNR	M141	R141LNR	M150	R150UAL	M159	R159UAL	M168	R168UAL
M133	R133LNR	M142	R142LNR	M151	R151UAL	M160	R160UAL	M169	R169UAL
M134	R134LNR	M143	R143LNR	D52	R152UAL	D61	R161UAL	M170	R170UUT
M135	R135LNR	M144	R144LNR	M153	R153UAL	M162	R162UAL		

M226	F26XVP	Iveco Daily 49.10	Carlyle Dailybus 2	B25F	1988
M227	F27XVP	Iveco Daily 49.10	Carlyle Dailybus 2	B25F	1988
M229	F29XVP	Iveco Daily 49.10	Carlyle Dailybus 2	B25F	1988
M232	G232EOA	Iveco Daily 49.10	Carlyle Dailybus 2	B25F	1989
M236	G236EOA	Iveco Daily 49.10	Carlyle Dailybus 2	B25F	1989
M253w	G83OTU	Iveco Daily 49.10	Carlyle Dailybus	B25F	1989	Bee Line Buzz, 1990
M254w	G84OTU	Iveco Daily 49.10	Carlyle Dailybus	B25F	1989	Bee Line Buzz, 1990
M256w	G86OTU	Iveco Daily 49.10	Carlyle Dailybus	B25F	1989	Bee Line Buzz, 1990
M257w	G87OTU	Iveco Daily 49.10	Carlyle Dailybus	B25F	1989	Bee Line Buzz, 1990
M282	E62UKL	Mercedes-Benz 609D	Reeve Burgess Beaver	B20F	1988	Maidstone & District, 1997
M289	F379UCP	Mercedes-Benz 609D	Reeve Burgess Beaver	B20F	1988	Edinburgh Transport, 1994
M291	D906MVU	Mercedes-Benz 609D	Mercedes	B27F	1987	
M293	D223SKD	Mercedes-Benz L608D	Alexander	B20F	1986	North Western 1992
M294	D224SKD	Mercedes-Benz L608D	Alexander	B20F	1986	North Western 1992
M296	D226SKD	Mercedes-Benz L608D	Alexander	B20F	1986	North Western 1992
M301	F301RUT	Mercedes-Benz 709D	Robin Hood	B26F	1989	
M302	F302RUT	Mercedes-Benz 709D	Robin Hood	B26F	1989	

M303-M322 — Mercedes-Benz 709D — Alexander Sprint — B25F — 1994

M303	L303AUT	M307	L307AUT	M311	L311AUT	M315	L315AUT	M319	L319AUT
M304	L304AUT	M308	L308AUT	M312	L312AUT	M316	L316AUT	M320	L320AUT
M305	L305AUT	M309	L309AUT	M313	L313AUT	M317	L317AUT	M321	L321AUT
M306	L306AUT	M310	L310AUT	M314	L314AUT	M318	L318AUT	M322	L322AUT

Almost seventy Mercedes-Benz Vario minibuses have joined the Fox County fleet during the last year leaving only a few of the L608D model and Iveco Daily products. Pictured in Melton Mowbray is M137, R137LNR, which carries an O814 badge on the radiator rather than the generic O810 motif often found on the higher rated model. *Tony Wilson*

M323	L323AUT	Mercedes-Benz 709D	Leicester Carriage Builders	B25F	1994	
M324	L324AUT	Mercedes-Benz 709D	Leicester Carriage Builders	B25F	1994	
M325	L325AUT	Mercedes-Benz 709D	Leicester Carriage Builders	B25F	1994	
M326	N331OFP	Mercedes-Benz 709D	Leicester Carriage Builders	B25F	1995	Leicester Carriage demonstrator, 1996
M329	L227HRF	Mercedes-Benz 709D	Dormobile Routemaker	B29F	1993	Stevensons, 1994
M330	L228HRF	Mercedes-Benz 709D	Dormobile Routemaker	B29F	1993	Stevensons, 1994
M331	L231HRF	Mercedes-Benz 709D	Dormobile Routemaker	B27F	1993	Stevensons, 1994
M332	G64SNN	Mercedes-Benz 709D	Carlyle	BC29F	1990	Midland Red North, 1995
M333	L233HRF	Mercedes-Benz 709D	Dormobile Routemaker	B27F	1993	Stevensons, 1994
M335	G65SNN	Mercedes-Benz 709D	Carlyle	B29F	1990	Stevensons, 1994
M336	J151WEH	Mercedes-Benz 709D	Dormobile Routemaker	B29F	1992	Stevensons, 1994
M337	K148BRF	Mercedes-Benz 709D	Dormobile Routemaker	B27F	1992	Stevensons, 1994
M338	K158BRF	Mercedes-Benz 709D	Dormobile Routemaker	B27F	1993	Stevensons, 1994
M339	G301RJA	Mercedes-Benz 709D	Reeve Burgess Beaver	B25F	1990	Stevensons, 1994
M341	K131XRE	Mercedes-Benz 709D	Dormobile Routemaker	B29F	1992	Stevensons, 1994
M342	G142GOL	Mercedes-Benz 709D	Carlyle	B29F	1990	Stevensons, 1994
M343	G143GOL	Mercedes-Benz 709D	Carlyle	B29F	1990	Stevensons, 1994

M344-M358   Mercedes-Benz 709D   Alexander Sprint   B27F   1995

M344	N344OBC	M347	N347OBC	M350	N350OBC	M353	N353OBC	M356	N356OBC
M345	N345OBC	M348	N348OBC	M351	N351OBC	M354	N354OBC	M357	N357OBC
M346	N346OBC	M349	N349OBC	M352	N352OBC	M355	N355OBC	M358	N358OBC

M359	P111MML	Mercedes-Benz 709D	Reeve Burgess Beaver	B27F	1996	
M360	P222MML	Mercedes-Benz 709D	Reeve Burgess Beaver	B27F	1996	
M390	K390NGG	Mercedes-Benz 811D	Dormobile Routemaker	BC33F	1992	Irving & McIntyre, Greenock, 1995
M391	J401FNS	Mercedes-Benz 709D	Dormobile Routemaker	B29F	1991	Irving & McIntyre, Greenock, 1995
M402	F272OPX	Mercedes-Benz 811D	Robin Hood	B22F	1988	

T01	J255TJW	Reliant Metrocab		Reliant		M5	1991		

T15-T30		Carbodies Taxi		Carbodies FX4		M5	1990		
T15	H912KUD	T23	J655OWK	T25	J651OWK	T27	J656OWK	T29	J473RDU
T19	H695KKV	T24	J650OWK	T26	J649OWK	T28	J657OWK	T30	J474RDU
T21	H697KKV								

T31	J766SOC	Reliant Metrocab	Reliant	M5	1991
T32	J961TOF	Reliant Metrocab	Reliant	M5	1991
T33	J963TOF	Reliant Metrocab	Reliant	M5	1991

T34-T52		Carbodies Taxi		Carbodies FX4		M5	1992-94		
T34	J248SHP	T38	J917VHP	T42	K745CWK	T46	L143NHP	T50	L149NHP
T35	J249SHP	T39	J918VHP	T43	K746CWK	T47	L145NHP	T51	M651ERW
T36	J658UDU	T40	K741CWK	T44	L132NHP	T48	L146NHP	T52	M652ERW
T37	J659UDU	T41	K742CWK	T45	L133NHP	T49	L148NHP		

T57	M331MRW	Carbodies Taxi	Carbodies Fairway Driver	M5	1994
T58	M332MRW	Carbodies Taxi	Carbodies Fairway Driver	M5	1994

T59-T67		Carbodies Taxi		Carbodies FX		M5	1997		
T59	P36LOE	T61	P28LOE	T65	P94MOX	T66	P95MOX	T67	P96MOX
T60	P37LOE	T62	P29LOE						

T68	R278VOK	Reliant Metrocab	Metrocab	M5	1997
T69	R279VOK	Reliant Metrocab	Metrocab	M5	1997
T70	R288VOK	Reliant Metrocab	Metrocab	M5	1997
T71	R289VOK	Reliant Metrocab	Metrocab	M5	1997

One of the distinctive features of the Fox County business are the two taxi operations. One uses a maroon livery and Foxcabs name while the other, based in Derby uses a traditional black scheme. Pictured outside Derby rail station is T23, J655OWK.
Arriva Fox County

Ancilliary vehicles:-

317t	TVC402W	Leyland Leopard PSU5C/4R	Plaxton Supreme IV	C51F	1981	Hills, Nuneaton, 1991
612t	796UHT	Leyland Leopard PSU5D/5R	Plaxton Supreme IV	C50F	1981	Fen Travel, Syston, 1992
9045	D59TLV	Freight Rover Sherpa	Carlyle	B2F	1987	North Western, 1991
9047	RBC500W	Bedford YMT	Plaxton Supreme IV	C53F	1981	
D350	JDJ350N	Bedford YRT	Plaxton Elite III	C53F	1975	Grayway, Wigan, 1996
D395	SVL830R	Bristol LH6L	Eastern Coach Works	B43F	1977	RoadCar, 1994
M75	C475TAY	Ford Transit 190	Robin Hood	B16F	1985	

Named vehicles: -
D034 *John Barton*; D035 *Peter Varley*

Previous Registrations:

109CRC	A103HNC		JIL2164	XNG760S
111XKT	A102HNC		JIL2165	JOX516P
662NKR	OWA23X		JIL2190	JOX499P
796UHT	NMV612W		JIL2193	RKE520M
FAZ2784	B282KPF		JIL2196	KDW332P
FIL3451	F803TMD		JIL2197	BCD808L
FIL3452	B104LJU		JIL2198	SCK703P
GIL6253	D209LWX		JIL2199	UHG736R
GIL6949	D210LWX		JIL5367	NOE598R
HIL7594	E662UNE		LJI5631	B568NJF
JIL2156	GHB677N		LJI5632	A104HNC, XPA110, A927KFP
JIL2157	NPD142L		LJI8157	B310LUT
JIL2158	PUK649R		MSU433	STW18W
JIL2159	PUK643R		SIB1278	BPL481T
JIL2160	JOX482P		SJI5569	NPJ471R
JIL2161	HWC87N		SJI5570	JOX491P
JIL2162	SEO208M		TVC402W	PWK5W, DJI8467
JIL2163	GHB790N		XPA110	F804TMD

Allocations and liveries

Coalville (Ashby Road)

Mercedes-Benz	M155	M289	M291	M301	M302	M303	M304	M305
	M306	M311	M312	M335	M338	M339	M342	M343
	M348	M349						
National	2144	2145	2146	2147	2148	2149	2150	2152
	2154	2164	2165					
Dart	2205	2206						
Olympian	4501	4502	4503	4512	4527	4614	4615	4620
	4621	4622	4623					

Derby (London Road) - *(The D-prefix is not carried on the vehicles)*

Mercedes-Benz	D52	D61	D72	D73	D74	D75	D76	D77
	D78	D79	D80	D81	D82	D83	D84	D85
	D86	D87	D88	D89	D90	D91	D92	
Dart	D34	D35	D36	D37	D38	D45	D46	
Scania K	D21	D23	D24	D25	D26	D27	D28	
Scania L	D29	D30	D31	D32	D33			
Ailsa	D120	D121						
Fleetline	D301	D304	D306	D309	D310	D311	D312	D313
	D315							
Volvo Citybus	4320	4321	4322	4323	4324	4325	4326	4327
	4328	4329	4330	4331	4332	4333	4334	D126
	D127	D128	D129	D130	D131	D132	D133	D134
	D135	D136	D137	D138	D139	D140	D141	D142
	D143	D144	D145	D146	D147	D148	D149	D150
	D151	D152	D153					
Olympian	4625	4626	4627	4629	4630	4631	4639	4640
	4641	4642	4643	D165	D166	D167	D168	D169

Derby Taxis

Foxcabs   C001-C020/2-4
Derby 75   T01/15/9/21/3-52/7-63/5-71

Hinckley (Jacknell Road, Dodwells Bridge)

Mercedes-Benz	M128	M129	M130	M131	M132	M133	M134	M296
	M310	M326	M329	M344	M390	M391	M402	
Tiger	9	19	22					
Leopard	785							
DAF	153							
National	2151	2156	2157	2158				
Fleetline	2534							
Olympian	4476	4505	4508	4514				

Leicester (St Ives Road) - Foxhound - National Express

Tiger	4							
DAF	87	192						
Volvo	211♥	212♥	213	214	233	234	235	236
	237	246♥	247♥					

Southgates (Peacock Lane, Leicester)

Mercedes-Benz	M101	M102	M103	M104	M105	M106	M147	M148
	M149	M150	M151	M154	M157	M158	M159	M330
	M331	M332	M333	M350	M351	M357	M358	
National	2159	2160	2161	2162	2163			
Scania L	2166	2167	2168	2169	2170	2171	2172	2173
	2174	2175						
Metrobus	2453	2467	2474	2477	2479	2480	2482	2484
	2486							
Scania N	4169	4170	4171	4172	4173	4174	4175	4176
	4177	4178	4180	4181	4182	4183	4184	
Olympian	4644	4645	4646	4647	4648	4649	4650	4651
	4652	4653						

Stamford

Mercedes-Benz	M356			
Tiger	20	21	28	
Fleetline	2547	D048	D302	D314

Thurmaston (Melton Road, Thurmaston, Leicester)

Mercedes-Benz	M107	M108	M109	M110	M112	M113	M114	M115
	M116	M117	M118	M119	M120	M121	M122	M127
	M135	M136	M137	M138	M139	M140	M141	M142
	M143	M144	M145	M146	M156	M162	M163	M164
	M165	M166	M167	M168	M169	M170	M307	M308
	M309	M313	M314	M316	M317	M318	M319	M320
	M321	M322	M323	M324	M325	M336	M337	M341
	M352	M353	M354	M355				
Iveco	M226	M227	M229	M232	M236			
Dart	2201	2202	2203	2204	2207	2208		
National	2153							
Scania L	2176	2177	2178	2179				
Olympian	4489	4504	4507	4509	4511	4518	4519	4616
	4617	4618	4619	4624	4632	4633	4634	4636
	4637	4638						

Photographed in Leicester while operating to Nuneaton is Hinckley's Greenway number 2157, JIL2157. All bar three of the Leyland Nationals operated in the main fleet are Greenway conversions undertaken during the time British Bus plc owned both the company and East Lancashire Coachbuilders. *Tony Wilson*

Wigston (Station Street, South Wigston)

Mercedes	M123	M124	M125	M126	M153	M160	M282	M315
	M345	M346	M347	M359	M360			
National	2142	2143						
DAF/Spectra	4001	4002						
Scania N	4151	4152	4153	4154	4155	4156	4157	4158
	4159	4160	4161	4162	4163	4164	4165	4166
	4167	4168						
Olympian	4478	4480	4481	4486	4487	4491	4492	4493
	4494	4510	4516	4517	4521	4522	4523	4524
	4525	4528	4529	4530	4531	4532	4533	4601
	4602	4603	4604	4605	4606	4607	4608	4609
	4610	4611	4612	4613				

ARRIVA THE SHIRES

Arriva The Shires Ltd, Castle Street, Luton, Bedfordshire, LU1 3AJ

Arriva Watford Ltd, Castle Street, Luton, Bedfordshire, LU1 3AJ

Lutonian Buses Ltd, Castle Street, Luton, Bedfordshire, LU1 3AJ

Arriva East Herts & Essex Ltd, 15th Floor, Terminus House, Terminus Street,

Harlow, Essex, CM20 1YD

Arriva Colchester Ltd, Magdalen Street, Colchester, Essex, CO1 2LD

Arriva Southend Ltd, 87 London Road, Southend-on-Sea, Essex, SS1 1PP

ARRIVA serving The Shires

0365	P865VYT	LDV Convoy	Whitacre	M8L	1996	owned by Essex CC
2020	E990DNK	MCW MetroRider MF150/83	MCW	B23F	1988	London Country NW, 1990
2037	F122TRU	Mercedes-Benz 709D	Reeve Burgess Beaver	B25F	1988	Kentish Bus, 1991
2038	F123TRU	Mercedes-Benz 709D	Reeve Burgess Beaver	B25F	1988	Metrobus, Orpington, 1991
2039	F124TRU	Mercedes-Benz 709D	Reeve Burgess Beaver	B25F	1988	Kentish Bus, 1991
2040	F125TRU	Mercedes-Benz 709D	Reeve Burgess Beaver	B25F	1988	Metrobus, Orpington, 1991
2043	F128TRU	Mercedes-Benz 709D	Reeve Burgess Beaver	B25F	1988	Metrobus, Orpington, 1991
2050	G58BEL	Mercedes-Benz 811D	Wadham Stringer Wessex	BC31F	1989	Buffalo, Flitwick, 1995
2051	F985GKJ	Iveco Daily 49.10	Robin Hood City Nippy	B25F	1990	Buffalo, Flitwick, 1995
2052	MBZ6455	Iveco Daily 49.10	Carlyle Dailybus	B23F	1988	Buffalo, Flitwick, 1995
2054	G360FOP	Mercedes-Benz 709D	Carlyle	B25F	1989	Yellow Bus, Stoke Mandeville, 1995
2055	G896TGG	Mercedes-Benz 811D	Reeve Burgess Beaver	B33F	1990	Stevensons, 1995
2056	H523SWE	Mercedes-Benz 709D	Whittaker Europa	B29F	1990	Rhondda, 1995
2057	H407FGS	Mercedes-Benz 811D	Reeve Burgess Beaver	B31F	1991	Sovereign, 1996
2058	H408FGS	Mercedes-Benz 811D	Reeve Burgess Beaver	B31F	1991	Sovereign, 1996
2059	H406FGS	Mercedes-Benz 811D	Reeve Burgess Beaver	B31F	1990	Sovereign, 1996
2060	H848AUS	Mercedes-Benz 709D	Dormobile Routemaker	B29F	1990	Argyll Bus & Coach, 1992
2061	H641UWE	Mercedes-Benz 811D	Whittaker Europa Enterprise	B31F	1991	Buffalo, Flitwick, 1995
2062	H642UWE	Mercedes-Benz 811D	Whittaker Europa Enterprise	B31F	1991	Buffalo, Flitwick, 1995
2063	H35DGD	Mercedes-Benz 709D	Dormobile Routemaker	B33F	1991	Pathfinder, Newark, 1995
2065	F121TRU	Mercedes-Benz 709D	Reeve Burgess Beaver	B25F	1988	Kentish Bus, 1991
2066	J917HGD	Mercedes-Benz 709D	Dormobile Routemaker	B29F	1991	Argyll Bus & Coach, 1992
2068	H408BVR	Mercedes-Benz 709D	Reeve Burgess Beaver	B25F	1990	Star Line, Knutsford, 1995
2069	H409BVR	Mercedes-Benz 709D	Reeve Burgess Beaver	B25F	1990	Star Line, Knutsford, 1995
2070	J65UNA	Mercedes-Benz 709D	Reeve Burgess Beaver	B25F	1992	South Lancashire, St Helens, 1996
2071	K8BUS	Mercedes-Benz 811D	Wright NimBus	B33F	1993	Patterson, Birmingham, 1995
2072	K578YOJ	Mercedes-Benz 709D	Dormobile Routemaker	B29F	1993	Patterson, Birmingham, 1995
2073	K543OGA	Mercedes-Benz 811D	Dormobile Routemaker	B29F	1992	Pathfinder, Newark, 1995
2074	K579YOJ	Mercedes-Benz 709D	Dormobile Routemaker	B29F	1993	Patterson, Birmingham, 1995

An interesting minibus with Arriva Colchester is H123WFM now numbered 2326 in the Shires fleet which provides vehicles for the Colchester operation. The vehicle was latterly in the Southern Counties fleet, operating for Guildford & West Surrey . *David Heath*

2075-2079

2075-2079	Mercedes-Benz 709D	Made-to-Measure	B24F	1992	Birmingham Omnibus, Tividale, 1995

2075	K25WND	2076	K26WND	2077	K27WND	2078	K28WND	2079	K29WND

2080	K580YOJ	Mercedes-Benz 811D	Wright NimBus	B33F	1993	Patterson, Birmingham, 1995
2081	K31WND	Mercedes-Benz 709D	Made-to-Measure	B24F	1992	Birmingham Omnibus, Tividale, 1995
2082	K32WND	Mercedes-Benz 709D	Made-to-Measure	B24F	1992	Birmingham Omnibus, Tividale, 1995
2083	K203FEH	Mercedes-Benz 709D	Dormobile Routemaker	B27F	1993	Stevensons, 1995
2084	L864BEA	Iveco TurboDaily 59.12	Marshall	B23F	1993	Buffalo, Flitwick, 1994
2085	L863BEA	Iveco TurboDaily 59.12	Marshall	B23F	1993	Buffalo, Flitwick, 1994
2086	L326AUT	Mercedes-Benz 709D	Leicester Carriage Builders	B25F	1994	Midland Fox, 1994
2087	L327AUT	Mercedes-Benz 709D	Leicester Carriage Builders	B25F	1994	Midland Fox, 1994
2088	L328AUT	Mercedes-Benz 709D	Leicester Carriage Builders	B25F	1994	Midland Fox, 1994
2089	K202FEH	Mercedes-Benz 709D	Dormobile Routemaker	B29F	1993	Stevensons, 1995

2090-2094

2090-2094	Iveco TurboDaily 59-12	Marshall C31	B27F	1994

2090	M150RBH	2091	M151RBH	2092	M152RBH	2093	M153RBH	2094	M154RBH

2095	K184GDU	Mercedes-Benz 811D	Wright	B31F	1993	Yellow Bus, Stoke Mandeville, 1995

2096-2100

2096-2100	Iveco TurboDaily 59-12	Marshall C31	B27F	1994

2096	M156RBH	2097	M157RBH	2098	M158RBH	2099	M159RBH	2100	M160RBH

2101	J171GGG	Mercedes-Benz 709D	Dormobile Routemaker	B29F	1991	Yellow Bus, Stoke Mandeville, 1995
2102	L600BUS	Optare MetroRider MR11	Optare	B31F	1995	Lucky Bus, Watford, 1997
2103	L700BUS	Optare MetroRider MR11	Optare	B32F	1996	Lucky Bus, Watford, 1997
2104	L800BUS	Optare MetroRider MR11	Optare	B31F	1996	Lucky Bus, Watford, 1997
2105	M45WUR	Mercedes-Benz 709D	Plaxton Beaver	B27F	1995	
2106	M46WUR	Mercedes-Benz 709D	Plaxton Beaver	B27F	1995	
2107	M47WUR	Mercedes-Benz 709D	Plaxton Beaver	B27F	1995	
2108	M38WUR	Mercedes-Benz 811D	Plaxton Beaver	BC31F	1995	
2109	M39WUR	Mercedes-Benz 811D	Plaxton Beaver	BC31F	1995	

Pictured while working London Transport route U9, *Arriva serving the Shires* 2196, R196DNM is one of three from the 1998 delivery to be based at High Wycombe, all of which have thirty-one seats and the higher-rated Vario O814 engine management system. *Malcolm King*

2110	N906ETM	Mercedes-Benz 709D	Plaxton Beaver	B27F	1995
2111	M41WUR	Mercedes-Benz 811D	Plaxton Beaver	BC31F	1995
2112	M42WUR	Mercedes-Benz 811D	Plaxton Beaver	BC31F	1995
2113	M43WUR	Mercedes-Benz 709D	Plaxton Beaver	B27F	1995
2114	N918ETM	Mercedes-Benz 709D	Plaxton Beaver	B27F	1995
2115	N919ETM	Mercedes-Benz 709D	Plaxton Beaver	BC27F	1995

2116-2137

Mercedes-Benz 709D   Plaxton Beaver   B27F*   1995   *2116 is BC27F

2116	N186EMJ	2121	N191EMJ	2126	N196EMJ	2130	N910ETM	2134	N914ETM
2117	N187EMJ	2122	N192EMJ	2127	N907ETM	2131	N911ETM	2135	N915ETM
2118	N188EMJ	2123	N193EMJ	2128	N908ETM	2132	N912ETM	2136	N916ETM
2119	N189EMJ	2124	N194EMJ	2129	N909ETM	2133	N913ETM	2137	N917ETM
2120	N190EMJ	2125	N195EMJ						

2138-2162

Mercedes-Benz 709D   Plaxton Beaver   B27F   1996

2138	N368JGS	2143	N373JGS	2148	N378JGS	2153	N383JGS	2158	N366JGS
2139	N369JGS	2144	N374JGS	2149	N379JGS	2154	N384JGS	2159	N367JGS
2140	N370JGS	2145	N375JGS	2150	N380JGS	2155	N385JGS	2160	P670PNM
2141	N371JGS	2146	N376JGS	2151	N381JGS	2156	N386JGS	2161	P671PNM
2142	N372JGS	2147	N377JGS	2152	N382JGS	2157	N387JGS	2162	P669PNM

2165	WIB1114	Mercedes-Benz 609D	PMT Hanbridge	BC26F	1987	Checker, Garston, 1997
2166	J465UFS	Mercedes-Benz 609D	Crystals	BC24F	1992	Checker, Garston, 1997
2167	SLU261	Ford Transit VE6	Williams Deansgate	M12	1987	Checker, Garston, 1997
2169	G735PGA	Ford Transit VE6	Williams Deansgate	M14	1989	Checker, Garston, 1997
2170	J964NLL	Ford Transit VE6	Crystals	M13	1992	Checker, Garston, 1997

2171-2195   Mercedes-Benz Vario O810   Plaxton Beaver 2   B27F   1997-98

2171	R171VBM	2176	R176VBM	2181	R181DNM	2186	R186DNM	2191	R191DNM
2172	R172VBM	2177	R177VBM	2182	R182DNM	2187	R187DNM	2192	R192DNM
2173	R173VBM	2178	R178VBM	2183	R183DNM	2188	R188DNM	2193	R193DNM
2174	R174VBM	2179	R179VBM	2184	R184DNM	2189	R189DNM	2194	R194DNM
2175	R175VBM	2180	R180VBM	2185	R185DNM	2190	R190DNM	2195	R195DNM

2196	R196DNM	Mercedes-Benz Vario O814	Plaxton Beaver 2	B31F	1998	
2197	R197DNM	Mercedes-Benz Vario O814	Plaxton Beaver 2	B31F	1998	
2198	R198DNM	Mercedes-Benz Vario O814	Plaxton Beaver 2	B31F	1998	
2199	L429CPC	Mercedes-Benz 709D	Dormobile Routemaker	B27F	1994	Guildford & West Surrey, 1998
2200	L426CPB	Mercedes-Benz 709D	Dormobile Routemaker	B27F	1993	Guildford & West Surrey, 1998
2205	G277HDW	Freight Rover Sherpa	Carlyle Citybus 2	B20F	1990	Lutonian, Luton, 1998
2206	G145GOL	Iveco Daily 49.10	Carlyle Dailybus 2	B25F	1990	Lutonian, Luton, 1998
2207	G146GOL	Iveco Daily 49.10	Carlyle Dailybus 2	B25F	1990	Lutonian, Luton, 1998
2208	G148GOL	Iveco Daily 49.10	Carlyle Dailybus 2	B23F	1990	Lutonian, Luton, 1998
2210	H475KSG	Iveco Daily 49.10	Carlyle Dailybus 2	B23F	1990	Lutonian, Luton, 1998
2213	J37VDW	Iveco Daily 49.10	Carlyle Dailybus 2	B25F	1992	Lutonian, Luton, 1998
2214	N124GNM	Iveco TurboDaily 59.12	Marshall C31	BC29F	1996	Lutonian, Luton, 1998
2215	P860PBH	Iveco TurboDaily 59.12	Marshall C31	B27F	1996	Lutonian, Luton, 1998
2216	P861PBH	Iveco TurboDaily 59.12	Marshall C31	B27F	1996	Lutonian, Luton, 1998
2217	P570TBH	Iveco TurboDaily 59.12	Marshall C31	B27F	1997	Lutonian, Luton, 1998
2218	P571TBH	Iveco TurboDaily 59.12	Marshall C31	B27F	1997	Lutonian, Luton, 1998
2219	P26KOP	Iveco TurboDaily 59.12	Marshall C31	B27F	1997	Lutonian, Luton, 1998
2220	R981PKX	Iveco TurboDaily 59.12	Marshall C31	B27F	1997	Lutonian, Luton, 1998
2221	M239XLV	Iveco TurboDaily 59.12	Marshall C31	B27F	1995	North West, 1998
2222	M240XLV	Iveco TurboDaily 59.12	Marshall C31	B27F	1995	North West, 1998
2230	M290AJC	Iveco TurboDaily 59.12	Marshall C31	B27F	1994	Cymru, 1998
2231	M291AJC	Iveco TurboDaily 59.12	Marshall C31	B27F	1994	Cymru, 1998
2233	M583SSX	Iveco TurboDaily 59-12	Mellor	B29F	1994	Cymru, 1998
2235	N935ETU	Iveco TurboDaily 59-12	Mellor	B25F	1995	Cymru, 1998
2236	N936ETU	Iveco TurboDaily 59-12	Mellor	B25F	1995	Cymru, 1998
2308	F367CHE	MCW MetroRider MF150/110	MCW	B23F	1988	West's, Woodford Green, 1997

2309-2318   Mercedes-Benz 709D   Reeve Burgess Beaver   B23F   1990-92

2309	G924WGS	2311	G926WGS	2313	J933WHJ	2315	J935WHJ	2317	J937WHJ
2310	G925WGS	2312	G932WGS	2314	J934WHJ	2316	J936WHJ	2318	J938WHJ

2319	L613LVX	Mercedes-Benz 811D	Dormobile Routemaker	B31F	1993	
2320	L614LVX	Mercedes-Benz 811D	Dormobile Routemaker	B31F	1993	
2321	L801KNO	Peugeot-Talbot Freeway	TBP	B18FL	1993	
2322	L802KNO	Peugeot-Talbot Freeway	TBP	B18FL	1993	
2323	L803KNO	Peugeot-Talbot Freeway	TBP	B18FL	1993	
2324	L804KNO	Peugeot-Talbot Freeway	TBP	B18FL	1993	
2325	L805OVX	Peugeot-Talbot Freeway	TBP	B18FL	1994	
2326	H123WFM	Mercedes-Benz 814D	North West Coach Sales	BC24F	1991	London & Country (GWS), 1996

2327-2332   Iveco TurboDaily 59.12   Dormobile Routemaker   B25F   1993

2327	K707FNO	2329	K709FNO	2330	K710FNO	2331	K711FNO	2332	**K712FNO**
2328	K708FNO							

2334-2349   Iveco TurboDaily 59.12   Marshall C31   B25F   1994

2334	L724PHK	2339	M719UTW	2341	M721UTW	2346	M726UTW	2348	M728UTW
2337	L717OVX	2340	M720UTW	2345	M725UTW	2347	M727UTW	2349	M729UTW
2338	L718OVX							

2350-2364	Iveco TurboDaily 59.12		Marshall C31		B25F		1995	
2350	M730AOO	**2353**	M733AOO	**2356**	M736AOO	**2359**	N739AVW	**2362**	N742AVW
2351	M731AOO	**2354**	M734AOO	**2357**	M737AOO	**2360**	N740AVW	**2363**	N743ANW
2352	M732AOO	**2355**	M735AOO	**2358**	M738AOO	**2361**	N741AVW	**2364**	N744AVW

2369	P939HVX	Mercedes-Benz 711D	Plaxton Beaver	BC25F	1997

2370-2384
Mercedes-Benz O810 Vario   Plaxton Beaver 2   B27F*   1998   *2373 is BC25F

2370	R940VPU	**2373**	R943VPU	**2376**	R946VPU	**2379**	R949VPU	**2383**	R953VPU
2371	R941VPU	**2374**	R944VPU	**2377**	R947VPU	**2380**	R950VPU	**2384**	R954VPU
2372	R942VPU	**2375**	R945VPU	**2378**	R948VPU	**2382**	R952VPU		

2388	P478DPE	Mercedes-Benz 711D	Plaxton Beaver 2	B27F	1997
2391	P481DPE	Mercedes-Benz 711D	Plaxton Beaver 2	B27F	1997
2392	P482DPE	Mercedes-Benz 711D	Plaxton Beaver 2	B27F	1997

3031	NRP581V	Leyland National 2 NL116L11/1R		B49F	1980	United Counties, 1986
3033	SVV588W	Leyland National 2 NL116L11/1R		B49F	1980	United Counties, 1986

3035-3043
Leyland National 2 NL106AL11/2R   B44F   1981   Parfitt's, Rhymney Bridge, 1995

3035	GUW465W	**3037**	GUW457W	**3039**w	GUW447W	**3041**w	GUW461W	**3043**	GUW475W
3036w	GUW456W	**3038**w	GUW441W	**3040**w	GUW494W	**3042**	GUW462W		

3044	IIL4821	Leyland 10351/1R/SC(6HLX)	East Lancs Greenway (1993)	B41F	1974	Crosville Cymru, 1995
3045	IIL4822	Leyland 10351/1R/SC(6HLX)	East Lancs Greenway (1993)	B41F	1976	Crosville Cymru, 1995
3046	TIB4873	Leyland 10351B/1R(6HLX)	East Lancs Greenway (1993)	B41F	1979	Crosville Cymru, 1995
3048	BAZ6869	Leyland 10351B/1R(6HLX)	East Lancs Greenway (1994)	B41F	1979	Crosville Cymru, 1995
3049	RJI6861	Leyland 10351B/1R(6HLX)	East Lancs Greenway (1994)	B41F	1979	Crosville Cymru, 1995
3050	BTX152T	Leyland 10351A/2R(6HLX)	East Lancs Greenway (1994)	B44F	1979	Parfitts, Rhymney Bridge, 1995
3052	IAZ4037	Leyland National 11351A/1R(Volvo)		B49F	1977	United Counties, 1986
3053	CAZ6852	Leyland 10351B/1R(6HLX)	East Lancs Greenway (1994)	B41F	1978	Crosville Cymru, 1995
3054	TIB7835	Leyland 10351B/1R(6HLX)	East Lancs Greenway (1994)	B41F	1979	Crosville Cymru, 1995
3055	RJI6862	Leyland 10351B/1R(6HLX)	East Lancs Greenway (1994)	B41F	1979	Crosville Cymru, 1995
3056	IIL4823	Leyland 10351B/1R(6HLX)	East Lancs Greenway (1993)	B41F	1978	Crosville Cymru, 1995
3057	TIB4886	Leyland 10351B/1R(6HLX)	East Lancs Greenway (1993)	B41F	1975	Crosville Cymru, 1995
3058	GHB574V	Volvo B58-61	East Lancs EL2000(1994)	B53F	1980	Parfitt's, Rhymney Bridge, 1995
3061	D603ACW	Leyland Lynx LX112L10ZR1R	Leyland Lynx	B51F	1987	Sovereign, 1990
3062	E970NMK	Leyland Lynx LX112TL11ZR1S	Leyland Lynx	B49F	1987	Sovereign, 1990
3063	E420EBH	Leyland Lynx LX112TL11ZR1R	Leyland Lynx	B51F	1988	Sovereign, 1996
3064	E969PME	Leyland Lynx LX112L10ZR1R	Leyland Lynx	B49F	1988	Atlas Bus, Harlesden, 1994
3065	E965PME	Leyland Lynx LX112TL11ZR1R	Leyland Lynx	B49F	1988	Yellow Bus, Stoke Mandeville, 1995
3066	E966PME	Leyland Lynx LX112TL11ZR1R	Leyland Lynx	B49F	1988	Yellow Bus, Stoke Mandeville, 1995
3067	H407ERO	Leyland Lynx LX2R11C15Z4S	Leyland Lynx	BC45F	1990	
3068	H408ERO	Leyland Lynx LX2R11C15Z4S	Leyland Lynx	BC45F	1990	
3069	H409ERO	Leyland Lynx LX2R11C15Z4S	Leyland Lynx	BC45F	1990	
3070	H410ERO	Leyland Lynx LX2R11C15Z4S	Leyland Lynx	BC45F	1990	

3071-3075
Leyland Lynx LX112L10ZR1R   Leyland Lynx   B51F   1989

3071	F401PUR	**3072**	F402PUR	**3073**	F403PUR	**3074**	F404PUR	**3075**	F400PUR

3076	E970PME	Leyland Lynx LX112L10ZR1R	Leyland Lynx	B49F	1988	Atlas Bus, Harlesden, 1994
3077	NIB8459	Volvo B10M-61	East Lancs EL2000(1991)	B55F	1988	Buffalo, Flitwick, 1995
3078	F314RMH	Volvo B10M-56	Plaxton Derwent II	B54F	1988	Buffalo, Flitwick, 1995
3079	F151KGS	Volvo B10M-56	Plaxton Derwent II	B54F	1988	Buffalo, Flitwick, 1995
3080	F152KGS	Volvo B10M-56	Plaxton Derwent II	B54F	1988	Buffalo, Flitwick, 1995
3081	F153KGS	Volvo B10M-56	Plaxton Derwent II	B54F	1988	Buffalo, Flitwick, 1995
3087	G97VMM	Leyland Swift LBM6T/2RS	Wadham Stringer Vanguard II	B39F	1989	London Country NW, 199
3089	L133HVS	Volvo B10B-58	Alexander Strider	B51F	1993	Buffalo, Flitwick, 1995

No fewer than 256 Leyland Lynx are currently operated by Arriva companies, some 12% of the whole model production. One of the early examples is now in the Shires fleet as number 3065, E965PME. The vehicle was new to Pan Atlas for one of their London services. Now allocated to Watford it is seen leaving Watford Junction rail station for Luton Airport. *Tony Wilson*

3091-3098

Dennis Dart 9.8SDL3004 — Carlyle Dartline — B40F — 1991 — London Country NW, 1991

3091	H922LOX	3093	H925LOX	3094	H926LOX	3096	H243MUK	3098	H245MUK
3092	H923LOX							

3099	K447XPA	Dennis Dart 9.8SDL3017	Plaxton Pointer	B40F	1992	Buffalo, Flitwick, 1995
3100	K448XPA	Dennis Dart 9.8SDL3017	Plaxton Pointer	B40F	1992	Buffalo, Flitwick, 1995
3101	L100BUS	Dennis Dart 9.8SDL3035	Plaxton Pointer	B39F	1994	Lucky Bus, Watford, 1997
3102	L200BUS	Dennis Dart 9.8SDL3035	Plaxton Pointer	B39F	1994	Lucky Bus, Watford, 1997
3103	L300BUS	Dennis Dart 9SDL3031	Marshall C36	B34F	1994	Lucky Bus, Watford, 1997
3104	L400BUS	Dennis Dart 9SDL3031	Marshall C36	B34F	1994	Lucky Bus, Watford, 1997

3105-3136

Volvo B6-9.9M — Northern Counties Paladin — N40F — 1994

3105	L305HPP	3112	L312HPP	3119	M719OMJ	3125	M725OMJ	3131	M711OMJ
3106	L306HPP	3113	L313HPP	3120	M720OMJ	3126	M726OMJ	3132	M712OMJ
3107	L307HPP	3114	L314HPP	3121	M721OMJ	3127	M727OMJ	3133	M713OMJ
3108	L308HPP	3115	L315HPP	3122	M722OMJ	3128	M728OMJ	3134	M714OMJ
3109	L309HPP	3116	L316HPP	3123	M723OMJ	3129	M729OMJ	3135	M715OMJ
3110	L310HPP	3117	M717OMJ	3124	M724OMJ	3130	M710OMJ	3136	M716OMJ
3111	L311HPP	3118	M718OMJ					

3137	L43MEH	Volvo B6-9.9M	Plaxton Pointer	B40F	1994	Stevensons, 1994
3138	L922LJO	Volvo B6-9.9M	Northern Counties Paladin	B40F	1994	Yellow Bus, Stoke Mandeville, 1995
3139	L923LJO	Volvo B6-9.9M	Northern Counties Paladin	B40F	1994	Yellow Bus, Stoke Mandeville, 1995

3143-3149

Scania L113CRL — East Lancashire European — N51F — 1995

3143	N693EUR	3145	N695EUR	3147	N697EUR	3148	N698EUR	3149	N699EUR
3144	N694EUR	3146	N696EUR					

An early arrival at Showbus in September 1998, where Arriva displayed many vehicles in the new livery, was 3418, P418HVX newly allocated to Southend. The Shires fleet encompases the vehicles from several operations which were renumbered into a common series during that autumn. The vehicle is a Dennis Dart with Wright Crusader bodywork. *Phillip Stephenson*

3151-3166

Scania L113CRL · East Lancashire European · NC47F · 1995

3151	N701EUR	3155	N705EUR	3158	N708EUR	3161	N711EUR	3164	N714EUR
3152	N702EUR	3156	N706EUR	3159	N709EUR	3162	N712EUR	3165	N715EUR
3153	N703EUR	3157	N707EUR	3160	N710EUR	3163	N713EUR	3166	N716EUR
3154	N704EUR								

3167	N28KGS	Scania L113CRL	East Lancashire European	N51F	1996
3168	N29KGS	Scania L113CRL	East Lancashire European	N51F	1996
3169	N31KGS	Scania L113CRL	East Lancashire European	N51F	1996
3170	N32KGS	Scania L113CRL	East Lancashire European	N51F	1996
3171	P671OPP	Dennis Dart SLF	East Lancashire Flyte	N41F	1996
3172	P672OPP	Dennis Dart SLF	East Lancashire Flyte	N41F	1996
3173	P673OPP	Dennis Dart SLF	East Lancashire Flyte	N41F	1996
3174	P674OPP	Dennis Dart SLF	East Lancashire Flyte	N41F	1996

3175-3190

Dennis Dart SLF · Plaxton Pointer · N39F* · 1997 · *3175-8 are N41F

3175	P175SRO	3179	P179SRO	3182	P182SRO	3185	P185SRO	3188	P188SRO
3176	P176SRO	3180	P180SRO	3183	P183SRO	3186	P186SRO	3189	P189SRO
3177	P177SRO	3181	P181SRO	3184	P184SRO	3187	P187SRO	3190	P190SRO
3178	P178SRO								

3191-3205

Scania L113CRL · Northern Counties Paladin · N51F* · 1997 · *3196-9,3201-5 are NC47F

3191	R191RBM	3194	R194RBM	3197	R197RBM	3201	R201RBM	3204	R204RBM
3192	R192RBM	3195	R195RBM	3198	R198RBM	3202	R202RBM	3205	R205RBM
3193	R193RBM	3196	R196RBM	3199	R199RBM	3203	R203RBM		

3206-3215

Dennis Dart SLF · Plaxton Pointer · N31F · 1997-98

3206	R206GMJ	3208	R208GMJ	3210	R210GMJ	3212	R212GMJ	3214	R214GMJ
3207	R207GMJ	3209	R209GMJ	3211	R211GMJ	3213	R213GMJ	3215	R215GMJ

3241-3247

Volvo B6-9.9 — Alexander Dash — B40F — 1993 — Scotland West, 1998

3241	M841DDS	3243	M843DDS	3245	M845DDS	3246	M846DDS	3247	M847DDS
3242	M842DDS	3244	M844DDS						

Fleet	Reg	Chassis	Body	Seat	Year	History
3304	JIL2194	Leyland 11351A/1R(6HLXB)	East Lancs Greenway(1994)	B49F	1977	London & Country, 1996
3305	JIL2195	Leyland 11351/1R(6HLXB)	East Lancs Greenway(1994)	B49F	1975	London & Country, 1996
3307	NIW6507	Leyland 1151/1R/2402(6HLXB)	East Lancs Greenway(1993)	B49F	1974	London & Country, 1996
3308	NIW6508	Leyland 11351/1R(6HLXB)	East Lancs Greenway(1993)	B49F	1974	London & Country, 1996
3309	NIW6509	Leyland 11351A/1R(6HLXB)	East Lancs Greenway(1993)	B49F	1977	London & Country, 1996
3310	NIW6510	Leyland NL116AL11/2R(6HLXB)	East Lancs Greenway(1993)	B49F	1982	London & Country, 1996
3311	NIW6511	Leyland 11351/1R(6HLXB)	East Lancs Greenway(1993)	B49F	1978	London & Country, 1996
3312	NIW6512	Leyland NL116AL11/2R(6HLXB)	East Lancs Greenway(1993)	B49F	1982	London & Country, 1996

3315-3321

Volvo B10M-61 — East Lancashire(1992) — B49F — 1984-85 Grey Green, 1997

3315	A855UYM	3317	B857XYR	3319	B859XYR	3320	B860XYR	3321	B861XYR
3316	A856UYM	3318	B858XYR						

Fleet	Reg	Chassis	Body	Seat	Year	History
3324	E564BNK	Volvo B10M-56	Plaxton Derwent II	B54F	1988	Sampsons, Hoddesdon, 1989
3325	E565BNK	Volvo B10M-56	Plaxton Derwent II	B54F	1988	Sampsons, Hoddesdon, 1989
3328	G621YMG	DAF SB220LC550	Optare Delta	B47F	1989	West's, Woodford Green, 1997
3329	K760JVX	DAF SB220LC550	Optare Delta	B49F	1992	West's, Woodford Green, 1997
3331	F61SMC	Leyland Tiger TRBTL11/2RP	Duple 300	B55F	1988	Sovereign, 1989
3332	F62SMC	Leyland Tiger TRBTL11/2RP	Duple 300	B55F	1988	Sovereign, 1989
3333	F63SMC	Leyland Tiger TRBTL11/2RP	Duple 300	B55F	1988	Sovereign, 1989
3335	H350PNO	Leyland Swift LBM6T/2RS	Wadham Stringer Vanguard	B39F	1991	West's, Woodford Green, 1997
3338	E888KYW	Leyland Lynx LX1126LXCTZR1S	Leyland Lynx	B47F	1987	Grey Green, 1996
3339	E889KYW	Leyland Lynx LX1126LXCTZR1S	Leyland Lynx	B47F	1987	Grey Green, 1996

3341-3348

Leyland Lynx LX2R11C15Z4S — Leyland Lynx — B49F — 1990

3341	H251GEV	3343	H253GEV	3345	H255GEV	3347	H257GEV	3348	H258GEV
3342	H252GEV	3344	H254GEV	3346	H256GEV				

Fleet	Reg	Chassis	Body	Seat	Year
3349	J316XVX	Dennis Dart 9SDL3011	Wright Handybus	B35F	1992
3350	J317XVX	Dennis Dart 9SDL3011	Wright Handybus	B35F	1992
3351	J401XVX	Dennis Dart 9.8SDL3012	Wright Handybus	B40F	1992
3352	J402XVX	Dennis Dart 9.8SDL3012	Wright Handybus	B40F	1992
3353	J403XVX	Dennis Dart 9.8SDL3012	Wright Handybus	B40F	1992
3354	J404XVX	Dennis Dart 9.8SDL3012	Wright Handybus	B40F	1992

3355-3364

Dennis Dart 9.8SDL3017 — Plaxton Pointer — B40F — 1993

3355	K405FHJ	3357	K407FHJ	3359	K409FHJ	3361	K411FHJ	3363	K413FHJ
3356	K406FHJ	3358	K408FHJ	3360	K410FHJ	3362	K412FHJ	3364	K414FHJ

Fleet	Reg	Chassis	Body	Seat	Year	History
3365	L415NHJ	Dennis Dart 9.8SDL3025	Wright Handybus	B40F	1994	
3366	J64BJN	Dennis Dart 9SDL3012	Wright Handybus	BC40F	1992	West's, Woodford Green, 1997
3367	J65BJN	Dennis Dart 9SDL3011	Wright Handybus	B35F	1992	West's, Woodford Green, 1997

3368-3373

Dennis Dart 9SDL3011 — Plaxton Pointer — B35F — 1992

3368	K318CVX	3370	K320CVX	3371	K321CVX	3372	K322CVX	3373	K323CVX
3369	K319CVX							

Fleet	Reg	Chassis	Body	Seat	Year	History
3374	K761JVX	Dennis Dart 9SDL3017	Wright Handybus	B40F	1992	West's, Woodford Green, 1997
3375	K762JVX	Dennis Dart 9SDL3017	Wright Handybus	B40F	1992	West's, Woodford Green, 1997
3376	M266VPU	Dennis Lance SLF	Wright Pathfinder	N40F	1994	
3377	M267VPU	Dennis Lance SLF	Wright Pathfinder	N40F	1994	
3378	M268VPU	Dennis Lance SLF	Wright Pathfinder	N40F	1994	
3379	M269VPU	Dennis Lance SLF	Wright Pathfinder	N40F	1994	
3381	M761JPA	Dennis Lance SLF 11SDA3201	Wright Pathfinder	N39F	1995	
3382	M762JPA	Dennis Lance SLF 11SDA3201	Wright Pathfinder	N39F	1995	
3383	M763JPA	Dennis Lance SLF 11SDA3201	Wright Pathfinder	N39F	1995	
3384	M764JPA	Dennis Lance SLF 11SDA3201	Wright Pathfinder	N39F	1995	
3385	M951LYR	Dennis Dart 9.8SDL3040	Plaxton Pointer	B40F	1995	Grey Green, 1996

Opposite:- Two former liveries used by vehicles in the Shires fleet are seen here. The upper picture shows one of the early lowfloor buses, Dennis Lance 3373, M763JPA, seen here with its former Southend number LSL003. The vehicle is seen in the bus station and carries the bright blue used by Southend. The lower view is of 3435, R205VPU, one of nine DAF DE02's with Plaxton Prestige bodywork dedicated to Green Line service 724, the Green Line name being owned by Arriva. The vehicle is pictured at London Heathrow. *Tony Wilson*

The 1999 Arriva Bus Handbook

Bova coaches feature in the Arriva Northumbria, London (Leeside Travel), Touring BV and The Shires fleets. The sole example here is 4344, HDZ8354 which originated with West Midlands Travel Central fleet and arrived through County which was for a short while a member of that group. *Malcolm King*

3386-3397 — Dennis Dart SLF — Plaxton Pointer — N39F — 1997

3386	P256FPK	3389	P259FPK	3392	P262FPK	3394	P264FPK	3396	P266FPK
3387	P257FPK	3390	P260FPK	3393	P263FPK	3395	P265FPK	3397	P267FPK
3388	P258FPK	3391	P261FPK						

3404-3414 — Dennis Dart — Plaxton Pointer — B34F — 1996

3404	P324HVX	3407	P327HVX	3409	P329HVX	3411	P331HVX	3413	P833HVX
3405	P325HVX	3408	P328HVX	3410	P330HVX	3412	P332HVX	3414	P334HVX
3406	P326HVX								

3416	R416HVX	Dennis Dart SLF	Wright Crusader	N41F	1998
3417	R417HVX	Dennis Dart SLF	Wright Crusader	N41F	1998
3418	R418HVX	Dennis Dart SLF	Wright Crusader	N41F	1998

3419-3431 — Dennis Dart SLF — Plaxton Pointer — N42F — 1996

3419	P419HVX	3422	P422HVX	3425	P425HVX	3428	P428HVX	3430	P430HVX
3420	P420HVX	3423	P423HVX	3426	P426HVX	3429	P429HVX	3431	P431HVX
3421	P421HVX	3424	P424HVX	3427	P427HVX					

3435	R165GNW	Dennis Dart SLF	Wright Crusader	N36F	1997
3439	R169GNW	Dennis Dart SLF	Wright Crusader	N36F	1997
3440	R170GNW	Dennis Dart SLF	Wright Crusader	N36F	1997

3441-3449 — DAF DE02GSSB220 — Plaxton Prestige — NC37F — 1997

3441	R201VPU	3443	R203VPU	3445	R205VPU	3447	R207VPU	3449	R209VPU
3442	R202VPU	3444	R204VPU	3446	R206VPU	3448	R208VPU		

3899	GFR799W	Leyland National 116690/1R		B52F	1979	Surrey & West Sussex, 1998
4002	A152EPA	Leyland Tiger TRCTL11/3R	Plaxton Paramount 3200 E	C57F	1984	London Country NW, 1990
4007	A157EPA	Leyland Tiger TRCTL11/3R	Plaxton Paramount 3200 E	C57F	1984	London Country NW, 1990
4008	A143EPA	Leyland Tiger TRCTL11/2RH	Plaxton Paramount 3200 E	C51F	1984	London Country NW, 1990

4009	FIL4919	Volvo B10M-61	Duple 320	C49FT	1987	Lucky Bus, Watford, 1997
4015	HIL7595	Volvo B10M-61	Plaxton Paramount 3500 III	C53F	1988	Moor-Dale, 1994
4016	SIB4846	Leyland Tiger TRCTL11/3ARZA	Plaxton Paramount 3200 III	C53F	1988	London Country NW, 1990
4020	SIB7480	Leyland Tiger TRCTL11/3ARZA	Plaxton Paramount 3200 III	C53F	1988	London Country NW, 1990
4021	E881YKY	Leyland Tiger TRCTL11/3ARZ	Plaxton Paramount 3200 III	C53F	1988	
4022	E882YKY	Leyland Tiger TRCTL11/3ARZ	Plaxton Paramount 3200 III	C53F	1988	
4023	E323OMG	Leyland Tiger TRCTL11/3ARZA	Plaxton Paramount 3200 III	C53F	1988	London Country NW, 1990
4025	SIB8529	Leyland Tiger TRCTL11/3ARZA	Plaxton Paramount 3500 III	C53FT	1988	London Country NW, 1990
4026	SIB7481	Leyland Tiger TRCTL11/3ARZA	Plaxton Paramount 3500 III	C51FT	1988	London Country NW, 1990
4027	HIL7597	Volvo B10M-61	Plaxton Paramount 3500 III	C53F	1988	Moor-Dale, 1994
4028	MIL2350	Dennis Javelin 12SDA1919	Duple 320	C57F	1990	Lucky Bus, Watford, 1997
4034	H198AOD	Volvo B10M-60	Plaxton Expressliner	C46FT	1996	Trathens, Plymouth, 1996
4035	H199AOD	Volvo B10M-60	Plaxton Expressliner	C46FT	1996	Trathens, Plymouth, 1996
4036	L500BUS	Iveco Country Rider 48-10-21	WS Coachbuilders Vanguard	BC47F	1995	Lucky Bus, Watford, 1997
4037	P100LOW	Dennis Javelin	UVG Unistar	C55FTL	1996	Lucky Bus, Watford, 1997
4038	ADZ4731	Volvo B10M-56	Plaxton Viewmaster IV Exp	C51F	1982	The Shires, 1997
4039	WIB1113	Volvo B10M-61	Plaxton Paramount 3200 II	C53F	1985	Checker, Garston, 1997
4040	YIB2396	Volvo B10M-61	Plaxton Paramount 3200 II	C53F	1986	Checker, Garston, 1997
4043w	YIB2397	Leyland Tiger TRCTL11/3RZ	Duple 320	C57F	1987	Checker, Garston, 1997
4046	TIB5906	Leyland Tiger TRCTL11/3RH	Duple 320	C51F	1986	Kentish Bus, 1997

4047-4056
	DAF DE33WSSB3000	Plaxton Premiere 320	C53F	1997	

4047	R447SKX	4049	R449SKX	4051	R451SKX	4053	R453SKX	4055	R455SKX
4048	R448SKX	4050	R450SKX	4052	R452SKX	4054	R454SKX	4056	R456SKX

4057-4061
	DAF SB3000WS601	Van Hool Alizée HE	C49FT	1994-95	London North East, 1998

4057	M947LYR	4058	M946LYR	4059	M942LYR	4060	M948LYR	4061	M949LYR

4302	OHE274X	Leyland Tiger TRCTL11/3R	Duple Dominant IV	C53F	1982	West Riding, 1987
4303	OHE280X	Leyland Tiger TRCTL11/3R	Duple Dominant IV	C53F	1982	West Riding, 1987
4304	A124EPA	Leyland Tiger TRCTL11/2R	Plaxton Paramount 3200 E	C51F	1984	Kentish Bus, 1990
4305	BAZ7384	Leyland Tiger TRCTL11/3RH	Plaxton Paramount 3500 II	C49FT	1985	Guildford & West Surrey, 1992
4306	A246SVW	Leyland Tiger TRCTL11/3RP	Duple Caribbean	C57F	1984	
4307	A247SVW	Leyland Tiger TRCTL11/3RP	Duple Caribbean	C57F	1984	
4308	A248SVW	Leyland Tiger TRCTL11/3RP	Duple Caribbean	C57F	1984	
4309	A249SVW	Leyland Tiger TRCTL11/3RP	Duple Caribbean	C57F	1984	
4310	A250SVW	Leyland Tiger TRCTL11/3RP	Duple Caribbean	C57F	1984	
4311	A141EPA	Leyland Tiger TRCTL11/2R	Plaxton Paramount 3200 E	C51F	1984	London & Country, 1990
4312	B100XTW	Leyland Tiger TRCTL11/3RP	Duple Caribbean	C57F	1984	
4313	B83SWX	Leyland Tiger TRCTL11/3RH	Plaxton Paramount 3200 IIE	C53F	1985	Yorkshire Voyager, 1990
4314	B84SWX	Leyland Tiger TRCTL11/3RH	Plaxton Paramount 3200 IIE	C53F	1985	Yorkshire Voyager, 1990
4315	B85SWX	Leyland Tiger TRCTL11/3RH	Plaxton Paramount 3200 IIE	C53F	1985	Yorkshire Voyager, 1991
4318	C255SPC	Leyland Tiger TRCTL11/3RH	Duple 320	C53F	1986	
4320	C265SPC	Leyland Tiger TRCTL11/3RH	Duple 320	C53F	1986	
4322	F572UPB	Volvo B10M-60	Plaxton Paramount 3200 III	C53F	1989	Express Travel, 1995
4323	F523UVW	Volvo B10M-60	Plaxton Paramount 3200 III	C53F	1989	Express Travel, 1995
4325	F425UVW	Volvo B10M-60	Plaxton Paramount 3200 III	C53F	1989	Express Travel, 1995
4327	F467UVW	Volvo B10M-60	Plaxton Paramount 3200 III	C53F	1989	Express Travel, 1995
4330	H372PHK	Volvo B10M-60	Plaxton Paramount 3500 III	C53F	1991	Express Travel, 1995
4331	H566MPD	Volvo B10M-60	Plaxton Paramount 3500 III	C53F	1991	Express Travel, 1995
4332	H567MPD	Volvo B10M-60	Plaxton Paramount 3500 III	C53F	1991	Express Travel, 1995
4333	H845AHS	Volvo B10M-60	Plaxton Paramount 3500 III	C53F	1991	Express Travel, 1995
4335	J56GCX	DAF SB220LC550	Ikarus CitiBus	B48F	1992	South London, 1997
4336	J926CYL	DAF SB220LC550	Ikarus CitiBus	B48F	1992	Grey Green, 1997
4337	J927CYL	DAF SB220LC550	Ikarus CitiBus	B48F	1992	Grey Green, 1997
4339	K124TCP	DAF SB220LC550	Ikarus CitiBus	B48F	1992	Cowie South London, 1997
4344	HDZ8354	Bova FHD12.280	Bova Futura	C49FT	1986	WMT (Smiths), 1995

5000	BKE847T	Bristol VRT/SL3/6LXB	Eastern Coach Works	B43/31F	1979	Maidstone & District, 1997	
5013	LBD837P	Bristol VRT/SL3/6LX	Eastern Coach Works	B43/31F	1975	United Counties, 1986	

5025-5030

		Bristol VRT/SL3/6LXB	Eastern Coach Works	B43/31F	1978-80 United Counties, 1986		
5025	CBD897T	5026	CBD899T	5028w	ONH928V	5029	ONH929V	5030	CBD904T

5032	SNV932W	Bristol VRT/SL3/6LXB	Eastern Coach Works	B43/31F	1980	United Counties, 1986
5033	SNV933W	Bristol VRT/SL3/6LXB	Eastern Coach Works	B43/31F	1980	United Counties, 1986
5034	SNV934W	Bristol VRT/SL3/6LXB	Eastern Coach Works	B43/31F	1980	United Counties, 1986
5035	ONH925V	Bristol VRT/SL3/6LXB	Eastern Coach Works	B43/31F	1980	United Counties, 1986
5036	UDM448V	Bristol VRT/SL3/6LXB	Eastern Coach Works	B43/31F	1980	Crosville Cymru, 1995
5038	SNV938W	Bristol VRT/SL3/6LXB	Eastern Coach Works	B43/31F	1980	United Counties, 1986

5046-5052

		Bristol VRT/SL3/6LXB	Eastern Coach Works	B43/31F	1981	United Counties, 1986
5046	URP946W	5047	URP947W	5049	VVV956W	5050	VVV960W	5052	VVV957W

5053-5060

		Leyland Olympian ONLXB/1R	Eastern Coach Works	B45/32F	1981-82 United Counties, 1986
5053	ARP613X	5055	ARP615X	5057	ARP617X	5059	ARP619X	5060	ARP620X
5054	ARP614X	5056	ARP616X	5058	ARP618X				

5061	MUH287X	Leyland Olympian ONLXB/1R	Eastern Coach Works	B45/32F	1982	Rhondda, 1994
5062	ARP612X	Leyland Olympian ONLXB/1R	Eastern Coach Works	B45/32F	1981	United Counties, 1986
5063	MUH290X	Leyland Olympian ONLXB/1R	Eastern Coach Works	B45/32F	1982	Rhondda, 1995
5064	MUH284X	Leyland Olympian ONLXB/1R	Eastern Coach Works	B45/32F	1982	Rhondda, 1994
5065	BPF135Y	Leyland Olympian ONTL11/1R	Roe	B43/29F	1983	Sovereign, 1990
5066	BPF136Y	Leyland Olympian ONTL11/1R	Roe	B43/29F	1983	Sovereign, 1990
5067	IAZ2314	Leyland Olympian ONLXB/1R	Eastern Coach Works	B45/32F	1982	Rhondda, 1995
5068	A141DPE	Leyland Olympian ONTL11/1R	Roe	B43/29F	1983	Sovereign, 1990
5069	A149FPG	Leyland Olympian ONTL11/1R	Roe	B43/29F	1984	London Country NW, 1990
5070	A143DPE	Leyland Olympian ONTL11/1R	Roe	B43/29F	1983	Sovereign, 1990

5071-5075

		Leyland Olympian ONTL11/1R	Roe	B43/29F	1984	London Country NW, 1990
5071	A151FPG	5072	A152FPG	5073	A153FPG	5074	A154FPG	5075	A155FPG

5076	B262LPH	Leyland Olympian ONTL11/1R	Eastern Coach Works	B43/29F	1985	Sovereign, 1990
5077	B273LPH	Leyland Olympian ONTL11/1R	Eastern Coach Works	B43/29F	1985	London Country NW, 1990
5078	A698EAU	Leyland Olympian ONTL11/1R	Northern Counties	B47/33D	1984	Buffalo, Flitwick, 1995
5079	A699EAU	Leyland Olympian ONTL11/1R	Northern Counties	B47/33D	1984	Buffalo, Flitwick, 1995
5080	B270LPH	Leyland Olympian ONTL11/1R	Eastern Coach Works	B43/29F	1985	London Country NW, 1990
5081	B271LPH	Leyland Olympian ONTL11/1R	Eastern Coach Works	B43/29F	1985	London Country NW, 1990
5082	B272LPH	Leyland Olympian ONTL11/1R	Eastern Coach Works	B43/29F	1985	London Country NW, 1990

5083-5094

		Leyland Olympian ONCL10/1RZ	Alexander RL	B47/32F*	1988	*5086/91 are BC47/29F
5083	F633LMJ	5086	F636LMJ	5089	F639LMJ	5091	F641LMJ	5093	F643LMJ
5084	F634LMJ	5087	F637LMJ	5090	F640LMJ	5092	F642LMJ	5094	F644LMJ
5085	F635LMJ	5088	F638LMJ						

5095-5107

		Leyland Olympian ON2R50C13Z4	Alexander RL	B47/32F*	1989-90	*5104 is BC47/29F
						5099-5103 are B47/34F
5095	G645UPP	5098	G648UPP	5101	G651UPP	5104	G654UPP	5106	G656UPP
5096	G646UPP	5099	G649UPP	5102	G652UPP	5105	G655UPP	5107	G657UPP
5097	G647UPP	5100	G650UPP	5103	G653UPP				

5108	F506OYW	Leyland Olympian ONTL11/1RH	Northern Counties	B47/30F	1988	Yellow Bus, Stoke Mandeville, 1995
5109	G129YEV	Leyland Olympian ONCL10/2RZ	Northern Counties	B49/34F	1989	London Country NW, 1990
5110	G130YEV	Leyland Olympian ONCL10/2RZ	Northern Counties	B49/34F	1989	London Country NW, 1990

Opposite: **The Shires double-deck fleet is represented here by two vehicles from Essex-based operations. The upper picture shows an Olympian with Southend arriving there from Rhondda. Pictured in Southend while carrying fleet number 281, is 5381, MUH281X. The lower picture features one of the recent arrivals at Colchester. EYE336V is one of the growing number of MCW Metrobuses cascaded to the provinces from London duties. Carrying 336 when seen, the vehicle is 5366, EYE336V in the renumbered series.**
Tony Wilson/Malcolm King

5111-5125 Leyland Olympian ONCL10/1RZ Leyland — B47/31F — 1989-90 London Country NW, 1990

5111	G281UMJ	5114	G284UMJ	5117	G287UMJ	5120	G290UMJ	5123	G293UMJ

5111	G281UMJ	5114	G284UMJ	5117	G287UMJ	5120	G290UMJ	5123	G293UMJ
5112	G282UMJ	5115	G285UMJ	5118	G288UMJ	5121	G291UMJ	5124	G294UMJ
5113	G283UMJ	5116	G286UMJ	5119	G289UMJ	5122	G292UMJ	5125	G295UMJ

5126	H196GRO	Leyland Olympian ON2R50C13Z4 Leyland	B47/29F	1991	
5127	H197GRO	Leyland Olympian ON2R50C13Z4 Leyland	B47/29F	1991	
5128	H198GRO	Leyland Olympian ON2R50C13Z4 Leyland	B47/29F	1991	
5129	H199GRO	Leyland Olympian ON2R50C13Z4 Leyland	B47/29F	1991	
5130	F747XCS	Leyland Olympian ONCL10/1RZ Alexander RL	B47/32F	1989	A1 Service (McMenemy), 1995
5132	H202GRO	Leyland Olympian ON2R50C13Z4 Leyland	B47/29F	1991	
5133	H203GRO	Leyland Olympian ON2R50C13Z4 Leyland	B47/29F	1991	
5134	G131YWC	Leyland Olympian ONCL10/2RZ Northern Counties	B49/33F	1989	Ensign, Purfleet, 1991
5135	G132YWC	Leyland Olympian ONCL10/2RZ Northern Counties	B49/33F	1989	London Country NW, 1990

5136-5145 Volvo Olympian YN2RV18Z4 Northern Counties Palatine B47/30F 1996

5136	N36JPP	5138	N38JPP	5140	N46JPP	5142	N42JPP	5144	N35JPP
5137	N37JPP	5139	N39JPP	5141	N41JPP	5143	N43JPP	5145	N45JPP

5146-5161 Volvo Olympian Northern Counties Palatine BC39/29F 1998

5146	S146KNK	5149	S149KNK	5152	S152KNK	5156	S156KNK	5159	S159KNK
5147	S147KNK	5150	S150KNK	5153	S153KNK	5157	S157KNK	5160	S160KNK
5148	S148KNK	5151	S151KNK	5154	S154KNK	5158	S158KNK	5161	S161KNK

5162-5170 Leyland Olympian ONTLXB/1R Eastern Coach Works B45/32F 1982-85 Yorkshire, 1998 *5170 is BC40/31F

5162	EWX533Y	5164	EWW550Y	5166	CWR516Y	5168	EWW551Y	5170	B605UUM
5163	EWW543Y	5165	544WRA	5167	EWW546Y				

5301	JHK495N	Leyland Atlantean AN68/1R	Eastern Coach Works	O43/31F	1975
5302	JTD392P	Daimler Fleetline CRL6-33	Northern Counties	B49/31D	1975

5308-5320 Leyland Atlantean AN68A/1R Eastern Coach Works B43/31F 1977-80

5308	YNO78S	5312	YNO82S	5315	MEV85V	5317	MEV87V	5319	RVW89W
5310	YNO80S	5313	MEV83V	5316	MEV86V	5318	RVW88W	5320	RVW90W
5311	YNO81S	5314	MEV84V						

5321-5342 Leyland Fleetline FE33ALR Northern Counties B49/31D 1979-81 *5333/5/7/8/42 are B49/33F

5321	XTE221V	5326	XTE226V	5331	MRJ231W	5335	MRJ235W	5339	MRJ239W
5322	XTE222V	5327	XTE227V	5332	MRJ232W	5336	MRJ236W	5340	MRJ240W
5323	XTE223V	5328	XTE228V	5333	MRJ233W	5337	MRJ237W	5341	MRJ241W
5324	XTE224V	5329	XTE229V	5334	MRJ234W	5338	MRJ238W	5342	MRJ242W
5325	XTE225V	5330	XTE230V						

5343	Q553MEV	Daimler Fleetline CRL6-33	Northern Counties(1985)	B49/31D	1972	
5344	Q554MEV	Daimler Fleetline CRL6-33	Northern Counties(1984)	B49/31D	1972	
5345	Q475MEV	Daimler Fleetline CRL6-33	Northern Counties(1984)	B49/31D	1972	
5346	Q476MEV	Daimler Fleetline CRL6-33	Northern Counties(1984)	B49/31D	1972	
5347	Q552MEV	Daimler Fleetline CRL6-33	Northern Counties(1985)	B49/31D	1972	
5349	GYE491W	MCW Metrobus DR101/12	MCW	B43/28F	1980	London North, 1998
5351	GBU1V	MCW Metrobus DR101/6	MCW	B43/30F	1979	Cowie Leaside, 1997
5353	GYE493W	MCW Metrobus DR101/12	MCW	B43/28F	1980	London North, 1998
5354	GBU4V	MCW Metrobus DR101/6	MCW	B43/30F	1979	Cowie Leaside, 1997
5355	GBU5V	MCW Metrobus DR101/6	MCW	B43/30F	1979	Cowie Leaside, 1997
5356	DTG366V	MCW Metrobus DR102/15	MCW	B46/31F	1980	Grey Green, 1997
5357	DTG367V	MCW Metrobus DR102/15	MCW	B46/31F	1980	Grey Green, 1997
5358	GBU8V	MCW Metrobus DR101/6	MCW	B43/30F	1979	Cowie Leaside, 1997
5359	GBU9V	MCW Metrobus DR101/6	MCW	B43/30F	1979	Cowie Leaside, 1997
5360	BYX220V	MCW Metrobus DR101/12	MCW	B43/28D	1979	Cowie Leaside, 1998
5361	BYX301V	MCW Metrobus DR101/12	MCW	B43/28F	1980	Leaside, 1997
5362	BYX232V	MCW Metrobus DR101/12	MCW	B43/28D	1980	London South, 1998
5	BYX233V	MCW Metrobus DR101/12	MCW	B43/28D	1980	London South, 1999
5	BYX240V	MCW Metrobus DR101/12	MCW	B43/28D	1980	London South, 1999
5366	EYE336V	MCW Metrobus DR101/12	MCW	B43/28F	1980	Leaside, 1997
5368	BYX208V	MCW Metrobus DR101/12	MCW	B43/28D	1980	London South, 1998
5369	BYX299V	MCW Metrobus DR101/12	MCW	B43/28D	1979	London North, 1998
5371	TPD101X	Leyland Olympian ONTL11/1R	Roe	B43/29F	1982	
5372	TPD102X	Leyland Olympian ONTL11/1R	Roe	B43/29F	1982	

5373	MUH283X	Leyland Olympian ONLXB/1R	Eastern Coach Works	B45/32F	1982	Rhondda, 1992
5375	MUH285X	Leyland Olympian ONLXB/1R	Eastern Coach Works	B45/32F	1982	Rhondda, 1992
5376	MUH286X	Leyland Olympian ONLXB/1R	Eastern Coach Works	B45/32F	1982	Rhondda, 1992
5377	TPD107X	Leyland Olympian ONTL11/1R	Roe	B43/29F	1982	
5378	TPD117X	Leyland Olympian ONTL11/1R	Roe	B43/29F	1982	
5379	TPD109X	Leyland Olympian ONTL11/1R	Roe	B43/29F	1982	
5380	TPD110X	Leyland Olympian ONTL11/1R	Roe	B43/29F	1982	
5381	MUH281X	Leyland Olympian ONLXB/1R	Eastern Coach Works	B45/32F	1982	Rhondda, 1992
5382	TPD115X	Leyland Olympian ONTL11/1R	Roe	B43/29F	1982	
5383	TPD123X	Leyland Olympian ONTL11/1R	Roe	B43/29F	1982	
5384	A110FDL	Leyland Olympian ONLXB/1R	Eastern Coach Works	BC41/23F	1984	Southern Vectis, 1991
5385	B183BLG	Leyland Olympian ONLXB/1R	Eastern Coach Works	B45/32F	1984	Crosville Cymru, 1990
5386	B184BLG	Leyland Olympian ONLXB/1R	Eastern Coach Works	B45/32F	1984	Crosville Cymru, 1990
5387	B185BLG	Leyland Olympian ONLXB/1R	Eastern Coach Works	B45/32F	1984	Crosville Cymru, 1991
5388	B189BLG	Leyland Olympian ONLXB/1R	Eastern Coach Works	B45/32F	1984	Crosville Cymru, 1991
5389	C41HHJ	Leyland Olympian ONLXCT/1RH	Eastern Coach Works	B47/31F	1985	
5390	D43RWC	Leyland Olympian ONLXCT/1RH	Eastern Coach Works	B47/31F	1985	

| 5392-5396 | | Leyland Olympian ONLXB/1RZ | Alexander RL | | B47/32F | 1988 | London & Country (GWS), 1996 |
| 5392 | F572SMG | 5393 | F573SMG | 5394 | F574SMG | 5395 | F575SMG | 5396 | F576SMG |

5397	F245MTW	Leyland Olympian ONCL10/1RZ	Leyland	BC43/29F	1988	
5398	F246MTW	Leyland Olympian ONCL10/1RZ	Leyland	BC43/29F	1988	Southend, 1996
5399	F579SMG	Leyland Olympian ONLXB/1RZ	Alexander RL	B47/32F	1988	London & Country (GWS), 1996
5402	H262GEV	Leyland Olympian ON2R50G13Z4	Leyland	B47/31F	1990	
5403	H263GEV	Leyland Olympian ON2R50G13Z4	Leyland	B47/31F	1990	
5404	H264GEV	Leyland Olympian ON2R50G13Z4	Leyland	BC43/29F	1990	
5405	H265GEV	Leyland Olympian ON2R50G13Z4	Leyland	BC43/29F	1990	
5407	H47MJN	Leyland Olympian ON2R50C13Z4	Leyland	BC43/29F	1991	Southend, 1996
5408	H48MJN	Leyland Olympian ON2R50C13Z4	Leyland	B47/31F	1991	
5409	H49MJN	Leyland Olympian ON2R50C13Z4	Leyland	B47/31F	1991	

| 5415-5419 | | Volvo Olympian YN2RV18Z4 | Northern Counties Palatine | B47/32F* | 1996 | *5418/9 are BC43/30F |
| 5415 | N705TPK | 5416 | N706TPK | 5417 | N707TPK | 5418 | N708TPK | 5419 | N709TPK |

5825	YNW401S	Bristol VRT/SL3/6LXB	Eastern Coach Works	B43/31F	1980	Southern Counties (K&S), 1999
5840	BKE840T	Bristol VRT/SL3/6LXB	Eastern Coach Works	B43/31F	1980	Southern Counties (K&S), 1999
5866	FKM866V	Bristol VRT/SL3/6LXB	Eastern Coach Works	B43/31F	1979	Maidstone & District, 1997
5874w	FKM874V	Bristol VRT/SL3/6LXB	Eastern Coach Works	B43/31F	1979	Maidstone & District, 1997

Heritage fleet:-

1151	CJN434C	Leyland Titan PD3/6	Massey	H38/32R	1965	preservation
1174	KTF594	AEC Regent III	Park Royal	O--/22R	1949	Brentwood Coaches, 1991
1175	KPJ248W	Leyland Atlantean AN68B/1R	Roe	H43/30F	1980	Luton & District, 1993
1178	FEV178	Leyland Titan TD5	Eastern Coach Works (1949)	L28/27R	1937	preservation, 1987

Ancilliary fleet:

1007	F266CEY	Iveco Daily 49.10	Robin Hood City Nippy	B21F	1988	Crosville Cymru, 1994
1132	C202EKJ	Mercedes-Benz L608D	Rootes	B20F	1986	Midlands North, 1998
1133	D23KKP	Mercedes-Benz L608D	Rootes	B20F	1986	Midlands North, 1998
1148t	DDX741T	Bedford YLQ	Plaxton Supreme III	C45F	1978	Davian, Enfield, 1991
1149t	SGS497W	Bedford YMT	Plaxton Supreme IV	C53F	1981	Davian, Enfield, 1991
1153t	OJN357P	Bedford YRQ	Duple Dominant	C32F	1976	Welwyn & Hatfield, 1990
1203t	RDS83W	Volvo B58-56	Duple Dominant	B53F	1980	Buffalo, Flitwick, 1990
1204t	RDS84W	Volvo B58-56	Duple Dominant	B53F	1980	Buffalo, Flitwick, 1990
1205t	NJF204W	Bedford YMQ	Plaxton Supreme IV	C45F	1980	Lee & District, 1990
2037	F122TRU	Mercedes-Benz 709D	Reeve Burgess Beaver	B25F	1988	Kentish Bus, 1991
2163t	D208SKD	Mercedes-Benz L608D	Reeve Burgess	B20F	1986	London & Country (GWS), 1997
2164t	D210SKD	Mercedes-Benz L608D	Reeve Burgess	B20F	1986	London & Country (GWS), 1997
2303	F713CWJ	MCW MetroRider MF150/110	MCW	B23F	1988	West's, Woodford Green, 1997
2304	F714CWJ	MCW MetroRider MF150/110	MCW	B23F	1988	West's, Woodford Green, 1997
2305	F715CWJ	MCW MetroRider MF150/110	MCW	B23F	1988	West's, Woodford Green, 1997
2306	F718CWJ	MCW MetroRider MF150/110	MCW	B23F	1988	West's, Woodford Green, 1997
2307	F719CWJ	MCW MetroRider MF150/110	MCW	B23F	1988	West's, Woodford Green, 1997

Previous Registrations:

544WRA	EWX544Y	K761JVX	K2BUS
A110FDL	A701DDL, WDL748	K762JVX	J12BUS
ADZ4731	KNP3X	L500BUS	M289CUR
BAZ6869	JTU577T	MBZ6455	E295VOM, 7178KP
BAZ7384	C210PPE	MIL2350	G171BLH
BTX152T	AYR329T, NIW4810	NIB8459	E637NEL
CAZ6852	HMA561T	NIW6507	NEL863M
F425UVW	F449PSL, NXI9004	NIW6508	GUA821N
F467UVW	F450PSL, NXI9005	NIW6509	TEL491R
F523UVW	F451PSL, NXI9006	NIW6510	FCA8X
F572UPB	F452PSL, NXI9007	NIW6511	LPR938P
FIL4919	D614FSL, D448FSP	NIW6512	FCA6X
G621YMG	G259EHD, A10BUS	Q475MEV	GHJ377L
GHB574V	EYH802V, NIW2309	Q476MEV	GHJ374L
H231KBH	CMN414C	Q552MEV	GHJ379L
H350PNO	H550AMT, A19BUS, H20BUS	Q553MEV	GHJ375L
H372PHK	H844AHS, NXI9003	Q554MEV	GHJ376L
H566MPD	H843AHS, NXI9002	RJI6861	HMA569T
H567MPD	H842AHS, NXI9001	RJI6862	MCA677T
HDZ8354	C904JOF, 245DOC, C566LOG	SIB4846	E321OMG
HIL7595	E663UNE	SIB7480	E325OMG
HIL7597	E660UNE	SIB7481	E326OMG
IAZ2314	MUH288X	SIB8529	E324OMG
IAZ4037	VRP532S	SLU261	WET880, D969MDB
IIL4821	XPD299N	TIB4873	MCA671T
IIL4822	LPB180P	TIB4886	HPF322N
IIL4823	GMB659T	TIB5906	C264SPC
J64BJN	J9BUS	TIB7835	JTU594T
J65BJN	J6BUS	WIB1113	B504CGP
J65UNA	J59MHF, J6SLT	WIB1114	E428YDM
J964NLL	J413UUK	YIB2396	C510LGH
JIL2194	CBV779S	YIB2397	D296RKW
JIL2195	JOX477P		
K760JVX	K5BUS		

Now numbered 5416, Volvo Olympian N706TPK is seen in Southend in that operation's pre-Arriva livery. The low-height Northern Counties Palatine body is one of a batch of five delivered in 1996. *Gerry Mead*

Allocations

Aylesbury (Smeaton Close, Brunel Park) - Aylesbury & The Vale

Outstation - Leighton Buzzard

Mercedes-Benz	2068	2069	2073	2083	2089	2095	2101	2105
	2106	2107	2113	2116	2117	2118	2119	2143
	2145							
National	3044	3045	3048	3049	3054			
Lynx	3067							
Scania	3163	3164	3165	3166	3203	3204	3205	
Olympian	5053	5054	5055	5056	5057	5058	5059	5060
	5061	5062	5063	5064	5078	5079	5083	5085
	5088	5097	5099	5100	5101	5102	5103	5104
	5156	5157	5158	5159	5160	5161		

Colchester (Magdalen Street) - Colchester

Mercedes-Benz	2326							
Tiger	4302	4303	4305	4310				
Bova	4344							
Dart	3419	3420	3422	3430				
National	3303	3304	3305	3307	3308	3309	3310	3311
	3312							
Volvo B10M	3315	3316	3317	3318	3319	3320	3321	
Atlantean	5301	5308	5310	5311	5312	5313	5314	
	5315	5316	5317	5318	5319	5320		
Metrobus	5360	5361	5366	5369				
Olympian	5389	5390	5397	5398	5407	5408	5409	

Dunstable (Tavistock Street) - Luton & Dunstable

Mercedes-Benz	2037	2038	2039	2040	2043	2061	2062	2065
	2121	2122	2124	2126				
Dart	3091	3092	3093	3094	3096	3098	3099	
Scania	3143	3167	3169	3170				
Bristol VR	5018	5052						
Olympian	5086	5087	5091	5105	5106	5107	5170	

Grays (Europa Park, London Road) - Thamesside

Iveco	2334	2345	2346	2347	2348	2361	2362	2363
	2364							
Dart	3349	3350	3373	3404	3405	3406	3407	3408
	3409	3410	3411	3412	3413	3414	3421	3423
	3424	3425	3426	3427	3428	3429	3431	
Metrobus	5349	5353	5356	5357	5362	5368		

Harlow (Fourth Avenue) - Townlink

Outstation - Langston Road, Debden

LDV Convoy	0365							
Peugeot-Talbot	2321	2322	2323	2324	2325			
Mercedes-Benz	2309	2310	2311	2312	2313	2314	2315	2316
	2317	2318	2319	2320				
Iveco	2327	2328	2329	2330	2331	2332	2337	2338
	2339	2340	2341	2350	2351	2352	2353	2354
	2355	2356	2357	2358				
Tiger	3331	3332	3333	4320				
Swift	3335							
Dart	3356	3357	3358	3359	3360	3361	3362	3363
	3364	3466	3367	3368	3369	3370	3371	3372
	3374	3375	3385					
Lynx	3338	3339	3341	3342	3343	3344	3345	3346
	3347	3348						
Volvo B10M	3324	3325						
DAF/Delta	3328	3329						

An anomaly of the recent renumbering was the retention in the coach series of five Ikarus-bodied DAF buses used on the former Lea Valley services. Pictured entering Hertford is 4339, J928CYL showing the styling of the model which was imported by the Hughes-DAF (now Arriva Bus and Coach) business, the main dealer for DAF and Ikarus products. *Richard Godfrey*

Lance	3376	3377	3378	3379				
Olympian	5371	5372	5378	5379				

Hemel Hempstead (Whiteleaf Road) - Gade Valley

Mercedes-Benz	2086	2087	2088	2127	2132	2177	2178	2179
	2180	2181	2182	2183	2184	2185	2186	2187
	2188	2189	2190	2191	2192	2193		
Dart	3171	3172	3173	3174				
	3175	3176	3177	3178				
Volvo B6	3241	3242	3243	3244	3245	3246	3247	
Scania	3151	3152	3153	3154	3155	3156	3157	3158
	3159	3160	3161	3162				
Tiger	4002	4016	4020	4023	4025	4026		
Volvo B10M	4034	4035						
DAF/Plaxton	4056							
DAF/Van Hool	4057	4058	4059	4060	4061			
Olympian	5069	5081	5092					

High Wycombe (Lincoln Road, Cressex Industrial Estate) - Chiltern Rover

Outstation - Old Amersham

Mercedes-Benz	2138	2139	2140	2141	2142	2196	2197	2198
National	3031	3033	3043	3046	3050	3053	3055	3056
	3057	3899						
Volvo B6	3110	3115	3116	3126	3127	3138	3139	
Olympian	5066	5067	5068	5070	5071	5075	5076	5108
	5109	5110	5134	5135	5165	5167		

The number of re-bodied vehicles with Arriva is in decline as new low-floor products enter service. In 1992 East Lancashire had re-bodied several mid-life Grey-Green Volvo coaches. Seven of the type are now operated by The Shires represented here by 3320, B860XYR which retained Colchester's cream and maroon scheme when pictured. *Malcolm King*

Hitchin (Fishponds Road) - Hitchin & District

Mercedes-Benz	2055	2056	2060	2063	2071	2080	2108	2109
	2111	2112	2144	2146	2147	2148	2149	2150
	2151	2152	2153	2154	2155	2156	2157	2160
	2161	2162	2176	2194	2195	2199	2200	
Volvo B6	3112	3113	3114	3120	3128	3129		
Volvo B10B	3089							
Scania	3196	3197	3198	3199	3201	3202		

Luton (Castle Street) - Luton & District

Mercedes-Benz	2050	2058	2066	2072	2074	2075	2076	2077
	2078	2079	2081	2082	2120	2123	2125	2158
	2159							
Iveco	2085	2090	2091	2092	2093	2094	2096	2097
	2098	2099	2100					
DAF coach	4047	4048	4049	4050	4051	4052	4053	4054
	4055							
National	3037	3035	3042					
Volvo B10M	3077	3078	3079	3080	3081			
Volvo B6	3117	3118	3119	3121	3122	3123	3124	3125
	3130	3131	3132	3133	3134	3135	3136	3137
Scania	3144	3145	3146	3147	3148	3149	3168	3191
	3192	3193	3194	3195				
Bristol VR	5000	5013	5016	5025	5026	5029	5030	5032
	5033	5034	5035	5036	5038	5046	5047	5049
	5050	5866						
Olympian	5089	5090	5093	5094	5095	5096	5098	5136
	5137	5138	5139	5140	5141	5142	5143	5144
	5145							

Southend (London Road) - Southend

Mercedes-Benz	2383	2384	2388	2391	2392			
Iveco	2349	2359	2360					
Tiger	4304	4306	4307	4308	4309	4311	4312	4313
	4314	4315						
Volvo B10M	4322	4323	4325	4327	4330	4331	4332	4333
Lance	3381	3382	3383	3384				
Dart	3386	3387	3388	3389	3390	3391	3392	3393
	3394	3395	3396	3397	3417	3418		
Fleetline	5302	5321	5322	5323	5324	5325	5326	5327
	5328	5329	5330	5331	5332	5333	5334	5335
	5336	5337	5338	5339	5340	5341	5342	5343
	5344	5345	5346	5347				
Olympian	5373	5375	5376	5381	5384	5385	5386	5387
	5388	5392	5393	5394	5395	5396	5399	5402
	5404	5405	5415	5416	5417	5418	5419	

Stevenage (Norton Green Road) - The Stevenage Line

Mercedes-Benz	2057	2059						
Volvo B6	3105	3106	3107	3108	3109	3111		
Lynx	3061	3062	3063	3064	3070	3071	3074	3076

Ware (Marsh Lane) - Lea Valley

Outstation - Pindar Road, Hoddesdon

Mercedes-Benz	2369	2370	2371	2372	2373	2374	2375	2376
	2377	2378	2379	2380	2382			
Dart	3351	3352	3353	3354	3355	3365	3416	3435
	3439	3440						
DAF/Premiere	3441	3442	3443	3444	3445	3446	3447	3448
	3449							
DAF/Ikarus	4335	4336	4337	4338	4339			
Tiger	4318							
Volvo B10M	4334							
Metrobus	5351	5354	5355	5358	5359			
Olympian	5377	5380	5382	5383				

Watford (St Albans Road, Garston) - Network Watford

Iveco	2230	2231	2235	2236				
Transits	2167	2169	2170	2233				
MetroRider	2102	2103	2104					
Mercedes-Benz	2045	2070	2110	2114	2115	2128	2129	2130
	2133	2134	2135	2136	2137	2165	2166	2171
	2172	2173	2174	2175				
Dart	3100	3101	3102	3103	3104	3179	3180	3181
	3182	3183	3184	3185	3186	3187	3188	3189
	3190	3206	3207	3208	3209	3210	3211	3212
	3213	3214	3215					
National	3052							
Lynx	3065	3066	3068	3069	3072	3073	3075	
Volvo B10M	3058	4009	4015	4027	4039	4040		
Tiger	4007	4008	4021	4022	4043	4046		
Iveco	4036							
Javelin	4028	4037						
Olympian	5065	5072	5073	5074	5077	5080	5082	5084
	5111	5112	5113	5114	5115	5116	5117	5118
	5119	5120	5121	5122	5123	5124	5125	5126
	5127	5128	5129	5130	5132	5133	5146	5147
	5148	5149	5150	5151	5152	5153	5154	

Luton (Sedgewick Road) - Lutonian - (This operation is to be sold during 1999)

Iveco	2051	2052	2084	2206	2207	2208	2210	2213
	2214	2215	2216	2217	2218	2219	2220	2221
Other minibuses	2020	2054	2205					

ARRIVA LONDON

Arriva London North Ltd, 16 Watsons Road, Wood Green, London, N22 4TZ

Arriva London North East Ltd, Rockwood Road, Stamford Hill, London, N16 5TD

Arriva London South Ltd, Croydon Bus Garage, Brighton Road, South Croydon, CR2 6EL

The Original London Sightseeing Tour Ltd, 25 Jews Row, Wandsworth, London, SW18

ARRIVA serving London

104	E104JYV	Volvo Citybus B10M-50	Alexander RV	C41/34F	1987		
105	E105JYV	Volvo Citybus B10M-50	Alexander RV	C41/34F	1987		
107	E107JYV	Scania K92CRB	East Lancashire	B45/31F	1987		

109-114		Scania N112DRB	East Lancashire	B46/29F	1988		
109	E109JYV	111	E111KYN	112	E112KYN	113	E113KYN	114	E114KYN
110	E110JYV								

115-158		Volvo Citybus B10M-55	Alexander RV	B46/29D*	1988-90 *149-54 are B46/33F		
115	F115PHM	128	F128PHM	136	F136PHM	144	F144PHM	152	G152TYT
119	F119PHM	129	F129PHM	137	F137PHM	145	G145TYT	153	G153TYT
120	F120PHM	130	F130PHM	138	F138PHM	146	G146TYT	154	G154TYT
121	F121PHM	131	F131PHM	139	F139PHM	147	G147TYT	155	H155XYU
122	F122PHM	132	F132PHM	140	F140PHM	148	G148TYT	156	H156XYU
125	F125PHM	133	F133PHM	141	F141PHM	149	G149TYT	157	H157XYU
126	F126PHM	134	F134PHM	142	F142PHM	150	G150TYT	158	H158XYU
127	F127PHM	135	F135PHM	143	F143PHM	151	G151TYT		

159	L159GYL	Scania N113DRB	Northern Counties Palatine	B42/25D	1994
160	L160GYL	Scania N113DRB	Northern Counties Palatine	B42/25D	1994
161	L161GYL	Scania N113DRB	Northern Counties Palatine	B42/25D	1994

163-172		Volvo B10M-61	East Lancashire (1992)	B44/30D	1985		
163	B863XYR	165	B865XYR	167	B867XYR	170	B870XYR	172	B872XYR
164	B864XYR	166	B866XYR	168	B868XYR	171	B871XYR		

178	M178LYP	Scania N113DRB	Northern Counties Palatine	B42/25D	1995
179	M179LYP	Scania N113DRB	Northern Counties Palatine	B42/25D	1995
180	M180LYP	Scania N113DRB	Northern Counties Palatine	B42/25D	1995
181	N181OYH	Scania N113DRB	Northern Counties Palatine	B42/25D	1996
182	N182OYH	Scania N113DRB	Northern Counties Palatine	B42/25D	1996
183	N183OYH	Scania N113DRB	Northern Counties Palatine	B42/25D	1996

X01-X10		DAF DB02RSSB250	Alexander ALX 400	N / D	On order for London North East		
X01	S	X03	S	X05	S	X07	S	X09	S
X02	S	X04	S	X06	S	X08	S	X10	S

401-415 — Leyland Olympian ON2R50C13Z4 Northern Counties — B47/30F — 1990

401	H101GEV	404	H104GEV	407	H107GEV	410	H110GEV	414	H114GEV
402	H102GEV	405	H105GEV	408	H108GEV	412	H112GEV	415	H115GEV
403	H103GEV	406	H106GEV	409	H109GEV	413	H113GEV		

721-733 — Volvo Citybus B10M-50 — Alexander RV — B47/29D — 1989

721	F101TML	725	F105TML	727	F107TML	729	F109TML	732	F112TML
723	F103TML	726	F106TML	728	F108TML	730	F110TML	733	F113TML
724	F104TML								

912-925 — Volvo Citybus B10M-55 — East Lancashire EL2000 — B41F — 1990

912w	H912XYT	915w	H915XYT	918w	H918XYT	921w	H921XYT	923w	H923XYT
913w	H913XYT	916w	H916XYT	919w	H919XYT	922w	H922XYT	925w	H925XYT
914w	H914XYT	917w	H917XYT	920w	H920XYT				

934-941 — Dennis Dart 9SDL3024 — Plaxton Pointer — B31F — 1993

934	L934GYL	936	L936GYL	938	L938GYL	940	L940GYL	941	L941GYL
935	L935GYL	937	L937GYL	939	L939GYL				

950	M950LYR	Dennis Dart 9.8SDL3040	Plaxton Pointer	B40F	1995

952-968 — Dennis Dart SLF — Alexander ALX200 — N36F — 1997

952	P952RUL	956	P956RUL	960	P960RUL	963	P963RUL	966	P966RUL
953	P953RUL	957	P957RUL	961	P961RUL	964	P964RUL	967	P967RUL
954	P954RUL	958	P958RUL	962	P962RUL	965	P965RUL	968	P968RUL
955	P955RUL	959	P959RUL						

969-983 — Dennis Dart SLF — Alexander ALX200 — N27D — 1998

969	S169JUA	972	S172JUA	975	S175JUA	978	S178JUA	981	S181JUA
970	S170JUA	973	S173JUA	976	S176JUA	979	S179JUA	982	S182JUA
971	S171JUA	974	S174JUA	977	S177JUA	980	S180JUA	983	S183JUA

BOV595	G545JOG	Bova FHD12.290	Bova Futura	C46FT	1990	East Herts & Essex, 1998
BOV596	JIW3696	Bova FHD12.290	Bova Futura	C47FT	1988	East Herts & Essex, 1998

DBS1-13 — DAF DB250RS505* — Northern Counties Palatine II H47/30F — 1995 — 11-13 are DE02RSSB250

1	N601DWY	4	N604DWY	7	N607DWY	10	N610DWY	12	N612DWY
2	N602DWY	5	N605DWY	8	N608DWY	11	N611DWY	13	N613DWY
3	N603DWY	6	N606DWY	9	N609DWY				

DDL1-18 — Dennis Dart SLF — Plaxton Pointer 2 — N26D — 1998

1	S301JUA	5	S305JUA	9	S309JUA	13	S313JUA	16	S316JUA
2	S302JUA	6	S306JUA	10	S310JUA	14	S314JUA	17	S317JUA
3	S303JUA	7	S307JUA	11	S311JUA	15	S315JUA	18	S318JUA
4	S304JUA	8	S308JUA	12	S312JUA				

DIB1	J929CYL	DAF SB220LC550	Ikarus Citi Bus	B48F	1992	
DIB2	J930CYL	DAF SB220LC550	Ikarus Citi Bus	B48F	1992	
DIB3	J931CYL	DAF SB220LC550	Ikarus Citi Bus	B48F	1992	
DIB4	J413NCP	DAF SB220LC550	Ikarus Citi Bus	B48F	1992	The Birmingham Coach Company, 1997
DIB5	J414NCP	DAF SB220LC550	Ikarus Citi Bus	B48F	1992	The Birmingham Coach Company, 1997
DIL4	P754RWU	DAF DE33WSSB3000	Ikarus Blue Danube 350	C53F	1997	East Herts & Essex, 1998

Opposite:- **To comply with the London Transport requirement that 85% of the vehicle should be in red livery, Arriva's London units use a red version of the Arriva corporate scheme. The upper picture shows Dennis Dart DR28, H128THE operating route G1 through Tooting, while the lower picture shows Northern Counties-bodied Scania N113 number 161, L161GYL performing on London Transport route 24. This latter service was one of the early route tenders to be awarded to a non-LT Buses operator, vis Cowie's Grey-Green.** *Gerry Mead/Tony Wilson*

Associated company, Arriva Bus and Coach are the UK distributor for DAF products. The new low floor chassis from this Netherlands vehicle builder is seen here with Plaxton Prestige bodywork as DLP2, R152GNW. *Colin Lloyd*

DLA1-63

										DAF DE02RSSB250 Alexander ALX400 N45/17D 1998-99

1	R101GNW	14	S214JUA	27	S227JUA	40	S240JUA	52	S252JUA	
2	S202JUA	15	S215JUA	28	S228JUA	41	S241JUA	53	S253JUA	
3	S203JUA	16	S216JUA	29	S229JUA	42	S242JUA	54	S254JUA	
4	S204JUA	17	S217JUA	30	S230JUA	43	S243JUA	55	S255JUA	
5	S205JUA	18	S218JUA	31	S231JUA	44	S244JUA	56	S256JUA	
6	S206JUA	19	S219JUA	32	S232JUA	45	S245JUA	57	S257JUA	
7	S207JUA	20	S220JUA	33	S233JUA	46	S246JUA	58	S258JUA	
8	S208JUA	21	S221JUA	34	S234JUA	47	S247JUA	59	S259JUA	
9	S209JUA	22	S322JUA	35	S235JUA	48	S248JUA	60	S260JUA	
10	S210JUA	23	S223JUA	36	S236JUA	49	S249JUA	61	S261JUA	
11	S211JUA	24	S224JUA	37	S237JUA	50	S250JUA	62	S262JUA	
12	S212JUA	25	S225JUA	38	S238JUA	51	S251JUA	63	S263JUA	
13	S213JUA	26	S226JUA	39	S239JUA					

DLP1	R151GNW	DAF DE02GSSB220	Plaxton Prestige	N32D	1998
DLP2	R152GNW	DAF DE02GSSB220	Plaxton Prestige	N32D	1998
DLP3	R153GNW	DAF DE02GSSB220	Plaxton Prestige	N32D	1998

DP301-313

									Dennis Dart 9SDL3002* Plaxton Pointer B35F 1991 East Herts & Essex, 1998

*302-7/13 are 9SDL3011, 309 rebodied 1992

301	J301WHJ	304	J304WHJ	307	J307WHJ	310	J310WHJ	312	J312WHJ	
302	J302WHJ	305	J305WHJ	308	J308WHJ	311	J311WHJ	313	J313WHJ	
303	J303WHJ	306	J306WHJ	309	J309WHJ					

DPL1	N551LUA	DAF DE33WSSB3000	Plaxton Première 350	C49FT	1996	East Herts & Essex, 1998
DPL2	N552LUA	DAF DE33WSSB3000	Plaxton Première 350	C49FT	1996	East Herts & Essex, 1998
DPL3	P753RWU	DAF DE33WSSB3000	Plaxton Première 350	C53F	1997	East Herts & Essex, 1998

DPP416-431
Dennis Dart SLF   Plaxton Pointer   N36F   1997   East Herts & Essex, 1998

416	R416COO	420	R420COO	423	R423COO	426	R426COO	429	R429COO
417	R417COO	421	R421COO	424	R424COO	427	R427COO	430	R430COO
418	R418COO	422	R422COO	425	R425COO	428	R428COO	431	R431COO
419	R419COO								

DR20-31
Dennis Dart 8.5SDL3003   Plaxton Pointer   B28F   1991   London Buses, 1995

20	H120THE	23	H123THE	26	H126THE	28	H128THE	30	H130THE
21	H621TKU	24	H124THE	27	H127THE	29	H129THE	31	H131THE
22	H122THE	25	H125THE						

DRL38-52
Dennis Dart 9SDL3016   Plaxton Pointer   B34F   1992   London Buses, 1995

38	K538ORH	41	K541ORH	44	K544ORH	47	K547ORH	50	K550ORH
39	K539ORH	42	K542ORH	45	K545ORH	48	K548ORH	51	K551ORH
40	K540ORH	43	K543ORH	46	K546ORH	49	K549ORH	52	K552ORH

DRL147-158
Dennis Dart 9SDL3024   Plaxton Pointer   B34F   1993   London Buses, 1995

147	L247WAG	150	L150WAG	153	L153WAG	155	L155WAG	157	L157WAG
148	L148WAG	151	L151WAG	154	L154WAG	156	L156WAG	158	L158WAG
149	L149WAG	152	L152WAG						

DRL210	N710GUM	Dennis Dart 9SDL3053	Plaxton Pointer	B34F	1995
DRL211	N711GUM	Dennis Dart 9SDL3053	Plaxton Pointer	B34F	1995
DRL212	N712GUM	Dennis Dart 9SDL3053	Plaxton Pointer	B34F	1995

DRL213-218
Dennis Dart   Plaxton Pointer   B34F   1996

| 213 | P913PWW | 215 | P915PWW | 216 | P916PWW | 217 | P917PWW | 218 | P918PWW |
| 214 | P914PWW | | | | | | | | |

DRN115-119
Dennis Dart 9SDL3034   Northern Counties Paladin   B35F   1994   Kentish Bus, 1998

| 115 | L115YVK | 116 | L116YVK | 117 | L117YVK | 118 | L118YVK | 119 | L119YVK |

DT58-70
Dennis Dart 8.5SDL3003   Carlyle Dartline   B28F   1990   London Buses, 1995

58	H458UGO	61	H461UGO	64	H464UGO	67	H467UGO	69	H469UGO
59	H459UGO	62	H462UGO	65	H465UGO	68	H468UGO	70	H470UGO
60	H460UGO	63	H463UGO	66	H466UGO				

DT132	H132MOB	Dennis Dart 8.5SDL3003	Carlyle Dartine	B28F	1991	Metroline, 1997
DT143	H143MOB	Dennis Dart 8.5SDL3003	Carlyle Dartine	B28F	1991	Metroline, 1997
DVH5	G905TYR	DAF MB230LB615	Van Hool Alizée H	C53F	1990	East Herts & Essex, 1998
DVH6	G906TYR	DAF MB230LB615	Van Hool Alizée H	C53F	1990	East Herts & Essex, 1998
DVH7	G907TYR	DAF MB230LB615	Van Hool Alizée H	C49FT	1990	East Herts & Essex, 1998
DVH8	G908TYR	DAF MB230LB615	Van Hool Alizée H	C49FT	1990	East Herts & Essex, 1998
DW314	J314XVX	Dennis Dart 9SDL3011	Wright Handybus	B35F	1992	East Herts & Essex, 1998
DW315	J315XVX	Dennis Dart 9SDL3011	Wright Handybus	B35F	1992	East Herts & Essex, 1998
L1	A101SYE	Leyland Olympian ONTL11/1R	Eastern Coach Works	B47/28D	1984	London Buses, 1994
L2	A102SYE	Leyland Olympian ONLXB/1R	Eastern Coach Works	B47/28D	1984	London Buses, 1994
L3	A103SYE	Leyland Olympian ONLXB/1R	Eastern Coach Works	B47/28D	1984	London Buses, 1994

L4-20
Leyland Olympian ONLXB/1RH   Eastern Coach Works   B42/26D   1986   London Buses, 1994

| 4 | C804BYY | 6 | C806BYY | 13 | VLT13 | 16 | WLT916 | 20 | C820BYY |
| 5 | C805BYY | 8 | WLT807 | 14 | C814BYY | 17 | C817BYY | | |

L31-113
Leyland Olympian ONLXB/1RH   Eastern Coach Works   B42/26D   1986   London Buses, 1994-95

21	C21CHM	32	C32CHM	41	C41CHM	52	C52CHM	66	C66CHM
22	C22CHM	33	330CLT	45	C45CHM	56	C56CHM	78	C78CHM
24	C24CHM	35	C35CHM	46	C46CHM	58	C58CHM	79	C79CHM
25	C25CHM	36	C36CHM	47	VLT47	59	C59CHM	99	C99CHM
26	C26CHM	37	C37CHM	49	C49CHM	63	C63CHM	102	C102CHM
27	VLT27	38	C38CHM	50	C50CHM	65	C65CHM	113	C113CHM
31	C31CHM								

L135-259

Leyland Olympian ONLXB/1RH   Eastern Coach Works   B42/26D*   1986-87 London Buses, 1994-95
*166-71 are BC42/26D

135	D135FYM	166	D166FYM	190	319CLT	214	D214FYM	237	D237FYM
139	D139FYM	167	D167FYM	191	D191FYM	215	815DYE	238	D238FYM
140	D140FYM	168	D168FYM	192	D192FYM	216	D216FYM	239	D239FYM
143	D143FYM	169	D169FYM	193	D193FYM	217	217CLT	240	D240FYM
146	D146FYM	170	7CLT	194	D194FYM	218	D218FYM	241	D241FYM
147	D147FYM	171	D171FYM	195	D195FYM	219	519CLT	242	D242FYM
148	D148FYM	172	WLT372	196	D196FYM	220	D220FYM	243	D243FYM
149	D149FYM	173	VLT173	197	D197FYM	221	D221FYM	244	VLT244
150	D150FYM	174	D174FYM	198	D198FYM	222	D222FYM	245	D245FYM
151	WLT751	175	D175FYM	199	D199FYM	223	D223FYM	246	D246FYM
152	D152FYM	176	D176FYM	200	D200FYM	224	D224FYM	247	D247FYM
153	D153FYM	177	D177FYM	201	D201FYM	225	D225FYM	248	D248FYM
154	WLT554	178	D178FYM	202	D202FYM	226	D226FYM	249	D249FYM
155	D155FYM	179	D179FYM	203	D203FYM	227	D227FYM	250	D250FYM
156	656DYE	180	480CLT	204	D204FYM	228	D228FYM	251	D251FYM
157	D157FYM	181	D181FYM	205	D205FYM	229	D229FYM	252	D252FYM
158	D158FYM	182	D182FYM	206	D206FYM	230	D230FYM	253	D253FYM
159	D159FYM	183	D183FYM	207	D207FYM	231	D231FYM	254	D254FYM
160	D160FYM	184	D184FYM	208	D208FYM	232	D232FYM	255	D255FYM
161	D161FYM	185	D185FYM	209	D209FYM	233	D233FYM	256	D256FYM
162	D162FYM	186	D186FYM	210	D210FYM	234	D234FYM	257	D257FYM
163	D163FYM	187	D187FYM	211	D211FYM	235	D235FYM	258	D258FYM
164	D164FYM	188	D188FYM	212	D212FYM	236	D236FYM	259	D259FYM
165	D165FYM	189	D189FYM	213	D213FYM				

L315-354

Leyland Olympian ON2R50C13Z4   Alexander RH   B43/25D   1992   London Buses, 1994

315	J315BSH	323	J323BSH	331	J331BSH	339	J339BSH	347	J347BSH
316	J316BSH	324	J324BSH	332	J332BSH	340	J340BSH	348	J348BSH
317	J317BSH	325	J325BSH	333	J433BSH	341	J341BSH	349	J349BSH
318	J318BSH	326	J326BSH	334	J334BSH	342	J342BSH	350	J350BSH
319	J319BSH	327	J327BSH	335	J335BSH	343	J343BSH	351	J351BSH
320	J320BSH	328	J328BSH	336	J336BSH	344	J344BSH	352	J352BSH
321	J321BSH	329	J329BSH	337	J337BSH	345	J345BSH	353	J353BSH
322	J322BSH	330	J330BSH	338	J338BSH	346	J346BSH	354	VLT32

L514-L525

Leyland Olympian ON2R50C13Z4* Northern Counties   B47/27D   1990 Kentish Bus, 1998
*514 is type ONCL10/1RZA

514	G514VBB	517	G523VBB	520	G520VBB	522	G522VBB	524	G524VBB
515	G515VBB	518	G524VBB	521	G521VBB	523	G523VBB	525	G525VBB
516	G516VBB	519	G531VBB						

L526-L556

Leyland Olympian ON2R50C13Z4* Northern Counties   B47/27D   1990 Kentish Bus, 1996
*541/3/4/6-8/50-4 are type ONCL10/1RZA

526	G526VBB	533	G533VBB	539	G539VBB	545	G545VBB	551	G551VBB
527	G527VBB	534	G534VBB	540	G540VBB	546	G546VBB	552	G552VBB
528	G528VBB	535	G535VBB	541	G541VBB	547	G547VBB	553	G553VBB
529	G529VBB	536	G536VBB	542	G542VBB	548	G548VBB	554	G554VBB
530	G530VBB	537	G537VBB	543	G543VBB	549	G549VBB	555	G555VBB
531	G531VBB	538	G538VBB	544	G544VBB	550	G550VBB	556	G556VBB
532	G532VBB								

Arriva London's livery is illustrated here on two generations of the Olympian. Pictured at East Croydon is Leyland-built L225, D225FYM, with Eastern Coachworks body while the lower picture shows Northern Counties-bodied L555, G555VBB working route 176 and passing Elephant & Castle underground station en route for Penge. *Laurie Rufus/Richard Godrey*

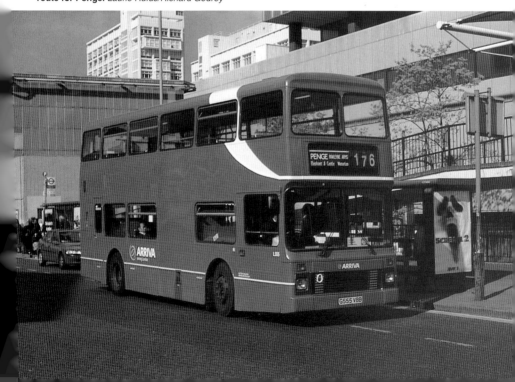

LDR1-21
Dennis Dart 9.8SDL3054 Plaxton Pointer B40F 1995

1	N671GUM	6	N676GUM	10	N680GUM	14	N684GUM	18	N688GUM
2	N672GUM	7	N677GUM	11	N681GUM	15	N685GUM	19	N689GUM
3	N673GUM	8	N678GUM	12	N682GUM	16	N686GUM	20	N680GUM
4	N674GUM	9	N679GUM	13	N683GUM	17	N687GUM	21	N691GUM
5	N675GUM								

LDR22-39
Dennis Dart Plaxton Pointer B40F 1996

22	P822RWU	26	P826RWU	30	P830RWU	34	P834RWU	37	P837RWU
23	P823RWU	27	P827RWU	31	P831RWU	35	P835RWU	38	P838RWU
24	P824RWU	28	P828RWU	32	P832RWU	36	P836RWU	39	P839RWU
25	P825RWU	29	P829RWU	33	P833RWU				

LDR40-55
Dennis Dart Plaxton Pointer B40F 1996

40	P840PWW	44	P844PWW	47	P847PWW	50	P850PWW	53	P853PWW
41	P841PWW	45	P845PWW	48	P848PWW	51	P851PWW	54	P854PWW
42	P842PWW	46	P846PWW	49	P849PWW	52	P852PWW	55	P855PWW
43	P843PWW								

M6-69
MCW Metrobus DR101/8* MCW H43/28D 1978-79 London Buses, 1994
*66/9 are DR101/1

6	WYW 6T	14	WYW14T	49	WYW49T	63	WYW63T	66	WYW66T
7	WYW 7T	38	WYW38T	51w	WYW51T	65	WYW65T	69	WYW69T
10w	WYW10T	40	WYW40T	60	WYW60T				

M132-317
MCW Metrobus DR101/9* MCW H43/28D 1979-80 London Buses, 1994
*208-298 are DR101/12, M170/5, 266 East Herts & Essex, 1998

132	BYX132V	175	BYX175V	232w	BYX232V	280w	BYX280V	290	BYX290V
149	BYX149V	200	BYX200V	263w	BYX263V	282	BYX282V	298	BYX298V
170	BYX170V	205	BYX205V	266	BYX266V	283w	BYX283V	317	BYX317V
173	BYX173V	230	BYX230V						

M346-508
MCW Metrobus DR101/12 MCW H43/28D 1980 London Buses, 1994
M491 East Herts & Essex, 1998

346w	GYE346W	396	GYE396W	441	GYE441W	469	GYE469W	496	GYE496W
365	GYE365W	397	GYE397W	445	GYE445W	474	GYE474W	500	GYE500W
372	GYE372W	398	398CLT	450	GYE450W	478	GYE478W	503	GYE503W
378	GYE378W	419	GYE419W	454	GYE454W	485	GYE485W	507	GYE507W
382	GYE382W	422	GYE422W	456	GYE456W	491	GYE491W	508	GYE508W
384	GYE384W	426	GYE426W	458	GYE458W				

M510-605
MCW Metrobus DR101/14 MCW H43/28D 1981 London Buses, 1994
M537/44/73 East Herts & Essex, 1998

510	GYE510W	529	GYE529W	544	GYE544W	575	GYE575W	590	GYE590W
511	GYE511W	530	GYE530W	547	GYE547W	577	GYE577W	591	GYE591W
515	GYE515W	531	GYE531W	549	GYE549W	580	GYE580W	593	GYE593W
517	GYE517W	534	GYE534W	555	GYE555W	581	GYE581W	596w	GYE596W
518	GYE518W	535	GYE535W	557	GYE557W	582	GYE582W	600	GYE600W
519	GYE519W	536	GYE536W	562	GYE562W	584	GYE584W	601	GYE601W
520	GYE520W	537	GYE537W	567	GYE567W	585	GYE585W	602	GYE602W
521	GYE521W	538	GYE538W	568	GYE568W	586	GYE586W	603	GYE603W
522	GYE522W	540	GYE540W	569	GYE569W	587	GYE587W	605	GYE605W
528	GYE528W	541	GYE541W	573	GYE573W				

M609-631
MCW Metrobus DR101/14 MCW H43/28D 1981 London Buses, 1994
M625 East Herts & Essex, 1998

609	KYO609X	612	KYO612X	619	KYO619X	626	KYO626X	629	KYO629X
610	KYO610X	613	KYO613X	622	KYO622X	627	KYO627X	630	KYO630X
611	KYO611X	617	KYO617X	625	KYO625X	628	KYO628X	631	KYO631X

The displacement of Metrobuses in London commenced during 1998 following the arrival of low-floor double-deck DAF buses. The Metrobuses are being refurbished before joining the provincial fleets. One of the main recipients will be Southern Counties. Pictured in the Capital is M865, OJD865Y, seen operating London Buses route 197 to Croydon. *Gerry Mead*

M632-798		MCW Metrobus DR101/14		MCW		H43/28D		1981-82 London Buses, 1994 649 East Herts & Essex, 1998			
632	KYV632X	669	KYV669X	712	KYV712X	741	KYV741X	774	KYV774X
633	KYV633X	671	KYV671X	713	KYV713X	742	KYV742X	775	KYV775X
634	KYV634X	673	KYV671X	714	KYV714X	743	KYV743X	776	KYV776X
635	KYV635X	675	KYV675X	715	KYV715X	744	KYV744X	777	KYV777X
636	KYV636X	676	KYV676X	716	KYV716X	745	KYV745X	778	KYV778X
637	KYV637X	679	KYV679X	718	KYV718X	746w	KYV746X	780	KYV780X
638	KYV638X	680	KYV680X	719	KYV719X	747	KYV747X	781	KYV781X
641	KYV641X	681	KYV681X	720	KYV720X	749	KYV749X	782	KYV782X
642	KYV642X	682	KYV682X	721	KYV721X	750	KYV750X	783	KYV783X
644	KYV644X	684	KYV684X	722	KYV722X	751	KYV751X	784	KYV784X
645	KYV645X	686	KYV686X	723	KYV723X	752	KYV752X	785	KYV785X
647	KYV647X	688	KYV688X	724	KYV724X	753	KYV753X	786	KYV786X
649	KYV649X	691	KYV691X	726	KYV726X	756	KYV756X	787	KYV787X
650	KYV650X	692	KYV692X	727	KYV727X	757	KYV757X	788	KYV788X
651	KYV651X	694	KYV694X	728	KYV728X	758	KYV758X	789	KYV789X
652	KYV652X	699	KYV699X	729	KYV729X	761	KYV761X	790w	KYV790X
653	KYV653X	700	KYV700X	731	KYV731X	762	KYV762X	791	KYV791X
654	KYV654X	701	KYV701X	732	KYV732X	765	KYV765X	792	KYV792X
657	KYV657X	702	KYV702X	733	KYV733X	766	KYV766X	793	KYV793X
659w	KYV659X	703	KYV703X	734	KYV734X	767	KYV767X	795	KYV795X
661	KYV661X	704	KYV704X	735w	KYV735X	768	KYV768X	796	KYV796X
663	KYV663X	705	KYV705X	736	KYV736X	770	KYV770X	798	KYV798X
664	KYV664X	708	KYV708X	737	KYV737X	771	KYV771X	799	KYV799X
665	KYV665X	710	KYV710X	738	KYV738X	772	KYV772X	803	KYV803X
666	KYV666X	711	KYV711X	740	KYV740X	773	KYV773X	805	KYV805X

M809-954

MCW Metrobus DR101/16 — MCW — B43/28D — 1983 — London Buses, 1994

809	OJD809Y	858	OJD858Y	891	A891SUL	919	A919SUL	936	A936SUL
825	OJD825Y	863	OJD863Y	894	A894SUL	927w	A927SUL	939	A939SUL
827	OJD827Y	865	OJD865Y	895	A895SUL	929	A929SUL	948	A948SUL
850w	OJD850Y	869	OJD869Y	903	A903SUL	930	A930SUL	954	WLT954

M959-1000

MCW Metrobus DR101/17 — MCW — B43/28D — 1983-84 London Buses, 1994

959	A959SYF	984	A984SYF	988w	A988SYF	998	A998SYF	1000	A700THV
973	A973SYF								

M1036	A736THV	MCW Metrobus DR101/17	MCW	BC43/24F	1984	London Buses, 1994
M1044	A744THV	MCW Metrobus DR101/19	MCW	B43/28D	1984	London Buses, 1994
M1062	B62WUL	MCW Metrobus DR101/17	MCW	B43/28D	1984	London Buses, 1994

M1070-1303

MCW Metrobus DR101/17 — MCW — B43/28D — 1984-85 London Buses, 1994
1248 East Herts & Essex, 1998

1070	B70WUL	1102	B102WUL	1136	B136WUL	1214	B214WUL	1278	B278WUL
1074	B74WUL	1103	B103WUL	1137	B137WUL	1216	B216WUL	1279	B279WUL
1075	B75WUL	1104	B104WUL	1138	B138WUL	1217	B217WUL	1280	B280WUL
1084	B84WUL	1105	B105WUL	1139	B139WUL	1219	B219WUL	1281	B281WUL
1085	B85WUL	1109	B109WUL	1140	B140WUL	1221	B221WUL	1282	B282WUL
1086	B86WUL	1112	B112WUL	1152	B152WUL	1227	B227WUL	1283	B283WUL
1087	B87WUL	1116	B116WUL	1154	B154WUL	1228	B228WUL	1285	B285WUL
1088	B88WUL	1121	B121WUL	1155	B155WUL	1229	B229WUL	1286	B286WUL
1089	B89WUL	1122w	B122WUL	1162	B162WUL	1231	B231WUL	1288	B288WUL
1090	B90WUL	1123	B123WUL	1164	B164WUL	1233	B233WUL	1289	B289WUL
1091	B91WUL	1124	B124WUL	1165	B165WUL	1239	B239WUL	1290	B290WUL
1092	B92WUL	1126	B126WUL	1169	B169WUL	1248	B248WUL	1291	B291WUL
1093	B93WUL	1127	B127WUL	1170	B170WUL	1249	B249WUL	1293	B293WUL
1094	B94WUL	1128	B128WUL	1173	B173WUL	1252	B252WUL	1294	B294WUL
1095	B95WUL	1129	B129WUL	1175	B175WUL	1253	B253WUL	1295	B295WUL
1096	B96WUL	1130	B130WUL	1176	B176WUL	1254	B254WUL	1296	B296WUL
1097	B97WUL	1131	B131WUL	1179	B179WUL	1255	B255WUL	1297	B297WUL
1098	B98WUL	1132	B132WUL	1182	B182WUL	1263	B263WUL	1298	B298WUL
1099	B99WUL	1133	B133WUL	1209	B209WUL	1265	B265WUL	1299	B299WUL
1100	B100WUL	1134	B134WUL	1210	B210WUL	1275	B275WUL	1300	B300WUL
1101	B101WUL	1135	B135WUL	1213	B213WUL	1276	B276WUL	1303	B303WUL

A nearside view of M865, OJD865Y this time operating route 466. The Metrobus was sourced for London Buses concurrently with the Leyland Titan though it was very rare for both types to be operated at the same depot. Arriva acquired companies where the Metrobus was based, and only nine of the Titan model are operated by the group: three in London and six with Scotland West.
Gerry Mead

M1307-1424

MCW Metrobus DR101/17 MCW B43/28D* 1985 London Buses, 1994
*1359/67/98 are BC43/28D; 1367/79/98 East Herts & Essex, 1998

1307	C307BUV	1316	C316BUV	1323	C323BUV	1362	C362BUV	1404	C404BUV
1308	C308BUV	1317	C317BUV	1324	C324BUV	1367	C367BUV	1405	C405BUV
1309	C309BUV	1318	C318BUV	1326	C326BUV	1379	VLT88	1406	C406BUV
1310	C310BUV	1319	C319BUV	1327	C327BUV	1398	C398BUV	1407	C407BUV
1312	C312BUV	1320	C320BUV	1332	C332BUV	1399	C399BUV	1413	C413BUV
1313	C313BUV	1321	C321BUV	1354	C354BUV	1401	C401BUV	1417	C417BUV
1314	C314BUV	1322	C322BUV	1359	C359BUV	1402	C402BUV	1424	C424BUV

M1437	VLT12	MCW Metrobus DR102/17	MCW	BC43/24F	1985	East Herts & Essex, 1998
M1441	A441UUV	MCW Metrobus DR102/45	MCW	B43/24F	1984	London Buses, 1994
M1442	A442UUV	MCW Metrobus DR132/5	MCW	B43/24F	1984	London Buses, 1994

MBT713	L713OVX	Iveco TurboDaily 59.12	Marshall C31	B18FL	1994	East Herts & Essex, 1998
MBT714	L714OVX	Iveco TurboDaily 59.12	Marshall C31	B18FL	1994	East Herts & Essex, 1998
MBT715	L715OVX	Iveco TurboDaily 59.12	Marshall C31	B18FL	1994	East Herts & Essex, 1998
MBT716	L716OVX	Iveco TurboDaily 59.12	Marshall C31	B18FL	1994	East Herts & Essex, 1998
MBV951	R951VPU	Mercedes-Benz O814 Vario	Plaxton Beaver 2	B27F	1997	East Herts & Essex, 1998

MD601-612

Mercedes-Benz 811D Reeve Burgess Beaver B28F 1991 East Herts & Essex, 1998

601	J601WHJ	605	J605WHJ	607	J607WHJ	609	J609WHJ	611	J611WHJ
603	J603WHJ	606	J606WHJ	608	J608WHJ	610	J610WHJ	612	J612WHJ
604	J604WHJ						

MR102	F102YVP	MCW MetroRider MF150/115	MCW	B23F	1988	London Buses, 1994
MR104	F104YVP	MCW MetroRider MF150/116	MCW	DP23F	1988	London Buses, 1994
MR105	F105YVP	MCW MetroRider MF150/116	MCW	DP23F	1988	London Buses, 1994
MRL129	F129YVP	MCW MetroRider MF158/16	MCW	B28F	1988	London Buses, 1995
RM5	VLT5	AEC Routemaster R2RH	Park Royal	H36/28R	1959	London Buses, 1994
RM295	VLT295	AEC Routemaster R2RH	Park Royal	H36/28R	1960	London Buses, 1997
RM736	XYJ418	AEC Routemaster R2RH	Park Royal	H36/28R	1961	London Buses, 1997

RM6-719

AEC Routemaster R2RH(Iveco) Park Royal H36/28R 1959-61 London Buses, 1995/97

6	VLT6	311	KGJ142A	432	SVS617	531	WLT531	676	WLT676
25	VLT25	348	WLT348	467	XVS851	664	WLT664	719	WLT719
275	VLT275	385	WLT385						

RML882-901

AEC Routemaster R2RH/1(Cummins) Park Royal H40/32R 1961 London Buses, 1994

882	WLT882	888	WLT888	895	WLT895	897	WLT897	901	WLT901
884	WLT884	892	WLT892	896	WLT896				

RM970-2217

AEC Routemaster R2RH(Iveco) Park Royal H36/28R 1961-65 London Buses, 1995

970	WLT970	1125	KGH858A	1593	593CLT	1811	EGF220B	2179	CUL179C
997	WLT997	1324	324CLT	1725	725DYE	1822	822DYE	2185	CUL185C
1003	3CLT	1361	VYJ808	1734	734DYE	1872	ALD872B	2217	CUL217C
1124	VYJ806	1398	KGJ118A	1801	801DYE	1978	ALD978B		

RM1330	KGH975A	AEC Routemaster R2RH	Park Royal	H36/28R	1962	London Buses, 1997
RMC1453	453CLT	AEC Routemaster R2RH	Park Royal	H36/28R	1962	East Herts & Essex, 1998
RMC1464	464CLT	AEC Routemaster R2RH	Park Royal	H36/28R	1962	East Herts & Essex, 1998

RML2264-2759

AEC Routemaster R2RH/1(Iveco)Park Royal H40/32R 1965-68

2264	CUV264C	2366	JJD366D	2521	JJD521D	2608	NML608E	2726	SMK726F
2307	CUV307C	2375	JJD375D	2545	JJD545D	2636	NML636E	2730	SMK730F
2324	CUV324C	2407	JJD407D	2549	JJD549D	2653	NML653E	2741	SMK741F
2333	CUV333C	2477	JJD477D	2572	JJD572D	2692	SMK692F	2753	SMK753F
2351	CUV351C	2491	JJD491D	2573	JJD573D	2718	SMK718F	2759	SMK759F

RML2261-2359

AEC Routemaster R2RH/1(Cummins) Park Royal   H40/32R   1965   London Buses, 1994

2261	CUV261C	2292	CUV292C	2325	CUV325C	2334	CUV334C	2354	CUV354C
2267	CUV267C	2294	CUV294C	2326	CUV326C	2340	CUV340C	2355	CUV355C
2277	CUV277C	2304	CUV304C	2328	CUV328C	2344	CUV344C	2356	CUV356C
2280	CUV280C	2315	CUV315C	2329	CUV329C	2346	CUV346C	2359	CUV359C
2287	CUV287C	2323	CUV323C	2330	CUV330C	2350	CUV350C		

RML2370-2597

AEC Routemaster R2RH/1   Park Royal   H40/32R   1966   London Buses, 1994

2370	JJD370D	2406	JJD406D	2468	JJD468D	2525	JJD525D	2562	JJD562D
2372	JJD372D	2408	JJD408D	2483	JJD483D	2526	JJD526D	2567	JJD567D
2373	JJD373D	2409	JJD409D	2492	JJD492D	2528	JJD528D	2571	JJD571D
2380	JJD380D	2416	JJD416D	2494	JJD494D	2534	JJD534D	2588	JJD588D
2386	JJD386D	2418	JJD418D	2503	JJD503D	2544	JJD544D	2589	JJD589D
2391	JJD391D	2434	JJD434D	2504	JJD504D	2546	JJD546D	2595	JJD595D
2394	JJD394D	2457	JJD457D	2510	JJD510D	2552	JJD552D	2597	JJD597D
2401	JJD401D	2460	JJD460D	2518	JJD518D				

RML2611-2655

AEC Routemaster R2RH/1   Park Royal   H40/32R   1967   London Buses, 1994

2611	NML611E	2625	NML625E	2632	NML632E	2638	NML638E	2655	NML655E
2617	NML617E	2628	NML628E	2635	NML635E	2643	NML643E		

RML2266-2619

AEC Routemaster R2RH/1(Iveco) Park Royal   H42/30R   1965-67 On extended loan from London Buses

2266	CUV266C	2383	JJD383D	2512	JJD512D	2533	JJD533D	2577	JJD577D
2301	CUV301C	2387	JJD387D	2514	JJD514D	2536	JJD536D	2586	JJD586D
2343	CUV343C	2410	JJD410D	2523	JJD523D	2548	JJD548D	2591	JJD591D
2347	CUV347C	2452	JJD452D	2524	JJD524D	2574	JJD574D	2619	NML619E
2382	JJD382D	2505	JJD505D	2531	JJD531D				

RML2658-2758

AEC Routemaster R2RH/1   Park Royal   H40/32R   1968   London Buses, 1994
2715 has an Iveco engine and is on extended loan from London Buses

2658	SMK658F	2678	SMK678F	2688	SMK688F	2742	SMK742F	2750	SMK750F
2660	SMK660F	2682	SMK682F	2708	SMK708F	2746	SMK746F	2754	SMK754F
2666	SMK666F	2684	SMK684F	2715	SMK715F	2747	SMK747F	2758	SMK758F
2675	SMK675F	2685	SMK685F	2716	SMK716F				

RV1	GJG750D	AEC Regent V 2D3RA	Park Royal	H40/32F	1966	East Herts & Essex, 1998

SLW1-14

Scania N113CRL   Wright Pathfinder   B37D   1994   London Buses, 1994

1	RDZ1701	4	RDZ1704	7	RDZ1707	10	RDZ1710	13	RDZ1713
2	RDZ1702	5	RDZ1705	8	RDZ1708	11	RDZ1711	14	RDZ1714
3	RDZ1703	6	RDZ1706	9	RDZ1709	12	RDZ1712		

T69	UJN335V	Leyland Titan TNLXB2RRSp	Park Royal		O44/26D	1979	East Herts & Essex, 1998
T83	CUL83V	Leyland Titan TNLXB2RRSp	Park Royal		O44/26D	1979	East Herts & Essex, 1998
T100	CUL100V	Leyland Titan TNLXB2RRSp	Park Royal		O44/26D	1979	East Herts & Essex, 1998
TDL54	C254SPC	Leyland Tiger TRCTL11/3RH	Duple 320		C53F	1986	East Herts & Essex, 1998
TPL1	124CLT	Leyland Tiger TRCTL11/3ARZM	Plaxton Paramount 3200 III	C53F	1989	East Herts & Essex, 1998
TPL2	361CLT	Leyland Tiger TRCTL11/3ARZM	Plaxton Paramount 3200 III	C53F	1989	East Herts & Essex, 1998
TPL8	70CLT	Leyland Tiger TRCT10/3ARZA	Plaxton Paramount 3200 III	C53F	1991	East Herts & Essex, 1998
TPL518	530MUY	Leyland Tiger TRCTL11/3ARZ(Vo)	Plaxton Paramount 3500 III	C51FT	1988	East Herts & Essex, 1998
VPL3	185CLT	Volvo B10M-61	Plaxton Paramount 3200 II	C53F	1986	East Herts & Essex, 1998
VPL4	205CLT	Volvo B10M-61	Plaxton Paramount 3200 II	C53F	1986	East Herts & Essex, 1998
VPL503	H903AHS	Volvo B10M-60	Plaxton Paramount 3500 III	C53F	1991	East Herts & Essex, 1998

VA115-158

Volvo Citybus B10M-55   Alexander RV   H46/29D   1988   Grey Green, 1998

116	F116PHM	117	F117PHM	118	F118PHM	123	F123PHM	124	F124PHM

Opposite, top:- **Arriva has applied a traditional paint scheme to the London Routemaster, as illustrated by RML2635, NML635E. The introduction of low-floor buses to central London is likely to see the demise of the Routemaster in coming years.** *Laurie Rufus*

Opposite, bottom:- **An early delivery of low floor buses for London duties saw thirty Wright Pathfinder-bodied Scania N113s delivered in 1994. Scania is one of the leaders in low-floor design, a format that, some five years later, is the standard for buses in Europe.** *Laurie Rufus*

Previous Registrations:

7CLT	D170FYM	815DYE	D215FYM	VLT173	D173FYM
70CLT	H643GRO	EGF220B	811DYE	VLT244	D244FYM
124CLT	G661WMD	JIW3696	E908UOH	VYJ806	124CLT
185CLT	C874CYX	KGH858A	125CLT	VYJ808	361CLT
205CLT	C876CYX	KGH975A	330CLT	WLT372	D172FYM
217CLT	D217FYM	KGJ118A	398CLT	WLT554	D154FYM
319CLT	D190FYM	KGJ142A	WLT311	WLT751	D151FYM
324CLT	324CLT, VYJ807	SVS617	WLT432	WLT807	C808BYY
330CLT	C33CHM	UJN335V	CUL69V, 70CLT	WLT916	C816BYY
361CLT	G662WMD	VLT12	C437BUV	WLT954	A954SUL
398CLT	GYE398W	VLT13	C813BYY	XVS851	WLT467
480CLT	D180FYM	VLT27	C27CHM	XVS997	WLT461
519CLT	D219FYM	VLT32	J354BSH	XYJ418	WLT736
530MUY	E118KFV	VLT47	C47CHM		
656DYE	D156FYM	VLT88	C379BUV		

Allocations and depots:

Barking (Ripple Road) - London North East

Dart	934	935	936	937	938	939	940	941
	950	952	953	954	955	956	957	958
	959	960	961	962	963	964	965	966
	967	968						
Volvo Citybus	104	149	150	151	152	153	154	
Olympian	401	402	403	404	405	406	407	408
	409	410	412	413	414	415		
Scania DD	107	109	110	111	112	113	114	

Battersea (Hester Road) - London South (Sub depot of Brixton)

Routemaster	RML2266	RML2301	RML2343	RML2347	RML2382	RML2383	RML2387	RML2410
	RML2452	RML2505	RML2512	RML2523	RML2524	RML2531	RML2533	RML2536
	RML2548	RML2574	RML2577	RML2586	RML2591	RML2619	RML2715	

Brixton (Streatham Hill) - London South

Dart	DDL1	DDL2	DDL3	DDL4	DDL5	DDL6	DDL7	DDL8
	DDL9	DDL10	DDL11	DDL12	DDL13	DDL14	DDL15	DDL16
	DDL17	DDL18						
Metrobus	M7t	M10t	M38t	M40t	M49t	M60t	M65t	M66
	M132	M149t	M173	M200	M230	M298	M365	M372
	M396	M398	M399	M400	M458	M492	M511	M517
	M562	M580	M584	M753	M634	M724	M741	M803
	M805	M825	M827	M850	M1062	M1075		
Routemaster	RM6	RM25	RM275	RM348	RM385	RM432	RM467	RM531
	RM664	RM676	RM719	RM970	RM997	RM1003	RM1124	RM1324
	RM1361	RM1398	RM1593	RM1734	RM1801	RM1811	RM1822	RM1872
	RM1978	RM2179	RM2217					
	RML892	RML895	RML2264	RML2307	RML2324	RML2333	RML2351	RML2366
	RML2375	RML2407	RML2477	RML2491	RML2514	RML2521	RML2545	RML2549
	RML2572	RML2573	RML2608	RML2636	RML2653	RML2692	RML2718	RML2726
	RML2730	RML2741	RML2753	RML2759				

Clapton (Bohemia Place, Hackney) - London North

Olympian	L315	L316	L317	L318	L319	L320	L321	L322
	L323	L324	L325	L326	L327	L328	L329	L330
	L331	L332	L333	L334	L335	L336	L337	L338
	L339	L340	L341	L342	L343	L344	L345	L346
	L347	L348	L349	L350	L351	L352	L353	L354
	L514	L515	L516	L517	L518	L519	L520	L521
	L522	L523	L524	L525				
Metrobus	M632	M996	M1112	M1121	M1132	M1134	M1138	
MetroRider	MR102	MR104	MR105					
Routemaster	RM5	RM311	RML882	RML884	RML888	RML896	RML897	RML901
	RM1125	RM1725	RM2185	RML2280	RML2287	RML2304	RML2325	RML2326
	RML2328	RML2329	RML2334	RML2344	RML2354	RML2355	RML2356	RML2359

DAF/ALX400	RML2370	RML2386	RML2401	RML2406	RML2409	RML2416	RML2457	RML2483
	RML2492	RML2494	RML2526	RML2534	RML2552	RML2567	RML2597	RML2675
	RML2682	RML2685	RML2688	RML2716	RML2750	RML2754	RML2758	
	DLA2	DLA3	DLA4	DLA5	DLA6	DLA7	DLA8	DLA9
	DLA10	DLA11	DLA12	DLA13	DLA14	DLA15	DLA16	DLA17
	DLA18	DLA19	DLA20	DLA21				

Croydon (Brighton Road, South Croydon) - London South

DAF	DIB1	DIB2	DIB3	DIB4	DIB5			
Dart	LDR26	LDR27	LDR28	LDR29	LDR30	LDR31	LDR32	LDR33
	LDR34	LDR35	LDR36	LDR37	LDR38	LDR39		
Olympian	L1	L2	L3	L4	L8	L14	L17	L27
	L35	L46	L52	L79	L99	L139	L140	L148
	L154	L163	L175	L182	L183	L197	L199	L210
	L213	L218	L228	L232	L235	L246	L248	L249
	L250	L252	L253	L255	L256			
Metrobus	M290	M378	M384	M454	M456	M474	M496	M500
	M503	M507	M508	M515	M518	M519	M520	M521
	M522	M528	M534	M541	M555	M568	M577	M601
	M629	M633	M654	M671	M680	M682	M691	M722
	M729	M731	M799	M809	M858	M863	M865	M869
	M894	M895	M930	M948	M959	M959	M973	M984
	M998	M1036	M1084	M1085	M1086	M1087	M1088	M1089
	M1090	M1091	M1092	M1093	M1094	M1095	M1096	M1097
	M1098	M1099	M1100	M1101	M1102	M1103	M1104	M1105
	M1116	M1354	M1359	M1407	M1441	M1442		

Edmonton (Edmonton Wharf, Lea Valley Trading Estate) - London North

Iveco	MBT713	MBT714	MBT715	MBT716				
Mercedes-Benz	MD601	MD603	MD604	MD605	MD606	MD607	MD608	MD609
	MD610	MD611	MD612	MBV951				
Dart	DP301	DP302	DP303	DP304	DP305	DP306	DP307	DP308
	DP309	DP310	DP311	DP312	DP313	DPP416	DDP417	DPP418
	DDP419	DPP420	DDP421	DPP422	DDP423	DPP424	DDP425	DPP426
	DDP427	DPP428	DDP429	DPP430	DDP431	DW314	DW315	

Edmonton (Edmonton Wharf) - Leaside Travel

Volvo B10M	VPL3	VPL4	VPL503					
Tiger	TPL1	TPL2	TPL8	TDL54	TPL518			
DAF	DPL1	DPL2	DPL3	DIL4	DVH5	DVH6	DVH7	DVH8
Bova	BOV595	BOV596						
AEC RegentV	RV1							
Routemaster	RMC1453	RMC1464						
Metrobus	M170	M175	M266	M441	M491	M537	M544	M573
	M625	M649	M796	M1248	M1367	M1379	M1398	M1437
Titan	T69	T83	T100					

Enfield (Southbury Road, Ponders End) - London North

Dart	DRN115	DRN116	DRN117	DRN118	DRN119	DT59	DT64	LDR1
	LDR3	LDR4	LDR6	LDR8	LDR9	LDR10	LDR11	LDR12
	LDR14	LDR22	LDR23	LDR24	LDR25	LDR40	LDR41	LDR42
	LDR43	LDR44	LDR45					
Metrobus	M6t	M14t	M205t	M282t	M382t	M422t	M426t	M445t
	M450t	M469t	M478t	M485t	M569	M590	M593	M619
	M622	M630	M644	M652	M657	M661	M666	M694
	M700	M701	M702	M703	M704	M712	M713	M715
	M718	M720	M721	M723	M726	M728	M733	M734
	M736	M737	M738	M740	M742	M743	M744	M747
	M749	M751	M752	M761	M762	M765	M770	M774
	M778	M780	M781	M783	M785	M787	M791	M798
	M903	M1000	M1140	M1170	M1179	M1231	M1249	M1253
	M1279	M1320						
Olympian	L700	L701	L702	L703	L704	L744		

Norwood (Knights Hill, West Norwood) - London South

Dart							
DRL38	DRL42	DRL43	DRL44	DRL47	DRL48	DRL147	DRL148
DRL149	DRL150	DRL151	DRL152	DRL153	DRL154	DRL155	DRL156
DRL157	DRL158	DRL210	DRL211	DRL212	DRL213	DRL214	DRL215

Olympian							
L6	L13	L16	L25	L31	L32	L33	L36
L37	L38	L45	L50	L59	L65	L102	L113
L146	L155	L156	L157	L160	L162	L165	L166
L167	L168	L169	L170	L171	L172	L174	L176
L177	L178	L180	L181	L185	L187	L189	L190
L191	L192	L196	L198	L203	L207	L208	L211
L214	L215	L216	L217	L223	L224	L231	L234
L237	L240	L242	L251	L257	L258	L522	L526
L527	L528	L529	L530	L531	L532	L533	L534
L535	L536	L537	L538	L539	L540	L541	L542
L543	L544	L545	L546	L547	L548	L549	L550
L551	L552	L553	L554	L555	L556		

Palmers Green (Regents Avenue) - London North (sub-depot of Wood Green)

Metrobus							
M510	M529	M530	M531	M535	M536	M538	M540
M547	M549	M557	M567	M581	M582	M585	M587
M591	M600	M602	M603	M605	M609	M610	M611
M612	M613	M617	M626	M627	M628	M631	M635
M636	M637	M638	M641	M642	M645	M647	M651
M653	M664	M669					

Citybus							
VA116	VA117	VA118	VA123	VA124			

Stamford Hill (Egerton Road) - London North East

Dart							
969	970	971	972	973	974	975	976
977	978	979	980	981	982	983	

Volvo Citybus							
105	115	119	120	121	122	125	126
127	128	129	130	131	132	133	134
135	136	137	138	139	140	141	142
143	144	145	146	147	148	155	156
157	158	163	164	165	166	167	168
170	171	172	721	723	724	725	726
727	728	729	730	732	733		

Scania DD							
159	160	161	178	179	180	181	182
183							

DAF/ALX400		
DLA38t	DLA39t	

L354, VLT32 is an Alexander-bodied Leyland Olympian seen operating route 253 to Euston Station carrying Leaside livery with the Arriva 'wheels within wheels' motif applied in an early style between decks. This bus is operated by London North.
Richard Godfrey

Thornton Heath (London Road) - London South

MetroRider	MRL129							
Dart	DR20	DR21	DR22	DR23	DR24	DR25	DR26	DR27
	DR28	DR29	DR30	DR31	DRL39	DRL40	DRL41	DRL45
	DRL46	DRL49	DRL50	DRL51	DRL52	DRL216	DRL217	DRL218
	DT58	DT60	DT61	DT62	DT63	DT65	DT66	DT67
	DT68	DT69	DT70	DT132	DT143			
Olympian	L5	L20	L21	L22	L24	L26	L41	L47
	L49	L56	L58	L63	L66	L78	L135	L143
	L147	L149	L150	L151	L152	L153	L158	L159
	L161	L164	L173	L179	L184	L186	L188	L193
	L194	L195	L200	L201	L202	L204	L205	L206
	L209	L212	L219	L220	L221	L222	L225	L226
	L227	L229	L230	L233	L236	L238	L239	L241
	L243	L244	L245	L247	L254	L259		
DAF/ALX400	DLA41t	DLA43t						

Tottenham (Philip Lane) - London North

Metrobus	M317	M727	M782	M1129	M1131	M1133	M1135	M1137
	M1139	M1152	M1154	M1155	M1162	M1164	M1165	M1175
	M1176	M1182	M1210	M1213	M1227	M1228	M1229	M1233
	M1263	M1275	M1280	M1281	M1283	M1285	M1286	M1288
	M1289	M1290	M1291	M1293	M1294	M1295	M1296	M1297
	M1298	M1299	M1307	M1308	M1309	M1399	M1401	M1402
	M1404	M1405	M1406	M1413	M1417	M1424		
Routemaster	RML2261	RML2267	RML2277	RML2292	RML2294	RML2315	RML2323	RML2330
	RML2340	RML2346	RML2350	RML2372	RML2373	RML2380	RML2391	RML2394
	RML2408	RML2418	RML2434	RML2460	RML2468	RML2503	RML2504	RML2510
	RML2518	RML2525	RML2528	RML2544	RML2546	RML2562	RML2571	RML2588
	RML2589	RML2595	RML2611	RML2617	RML2625	RML2628	RML2632	RML2635
	RML2638	RML2643	RML2655	RML2658	RML2660	RML2666	RML2678	RML2684
	RML2708	RML2742	RML2746	RML2747				

Wood Green (High Road) - London North

DAF/Palatine	DBS1	DBS2	DBS3	DBS4	DBS5	DBS6	DBS7	DBS8
	DBS9	DBS10	DBS11	DBS12	DBS13			
DAF/Prestige	DLP1	DLP2	DLP3					
Dart	LDR2	LDR5	LDR7	LDR13	LDR15	LDR16	LDR17	LDR18
	LDR19	LDR20	LDR21	LDR46	LDR47	LDR48	LDR49	LDR50
	LDR51	LDR52	LDR53	LDR54	LDR55			
Metrobus	M575	M586	M650	M663	M665	M673	M675	M676
	M679	M681	M684	M686	M688	M692	M699	M705
	M708	M710	M711	M714	M716	M719	M732	M745
	M750	M756	M757	M758	M766	M767	M768	M771
	M772	M773	M775	M776	M784	M789	M792	M793
	M795	M891	M919	M929	M936	M939	M1044	M1070
	M1074	M1109	M1123	M1124	M1126	M1127	M1128	M1130
	M1136	M1169	M1173	M1209	M1214	M1216	M1217	M1219
	M1221	M1239	M1252	M1254	M1255	M1265	M1276	M1278
	M1282	M1300	M1303	M1310	M1312	M1313	M1314	M1316
	M1317	M1318	M1319	M1321	M1322	M1323	M1324	M1326
	M1327	M1332	M1362					
Scania	SLW1	SLW2	SLW3	SLW4	SLW5	SLW6	SLW7	SLW8
	SLW9	SLW10	SLW11	SLW12	SLW13	SLW14		
DAF/ALX400	DLA1	DLA22	DLA23	DLA24	DLA25	DAL26	DLA27	DLA28
	DLA29	DLA30	DLA31	DLA32	DLA33	DLA34	DLA35	DLA36
	DLA37							

Unallocated

Metrobus	Many Metrobuses are currently in store being prepared for service elsewhere.							
Dart	932	933	942	943	948	949		
Routemaster	RM245	RM736	RM1330					
Citybus	912	913	914	915	916	917	918	919
	920	921	922	923	925			

The Original London Sightseeing Tour

BE112	VDV112S	Bristol VRT/SL3/6LXB	Eastern Coach Works	PO43/31F	1978	Northern Bus, Anston, 1996
BE168	VTV168S	Bristol VRT/SL3/6LXB	Eastern Coach Works	PO43/31F	1978	Northern Bus, Anston, 1996
BE184	AET184T	Bristol VRT/SL3/6LXB	Eastern Coach Works	PO43/31F	1979	Northern Bus, Anston, 1996
BE284	MDM284P	Bristol VRT/SL3/6LXB	Eastern Coach Works	PO43/31F	1975	Northern Bus, Anston, 1996
BW21	PJJ21S	Bristol VRT/SL3/6LXB	Willowbrook	O43/31F	1978	Stagecoach South (EK), 1996
BW75	RVB975S	Bristol VRT/SL3/6LXB	Willowbrook	O43/31F	1978	Stagecoach South (EK), 1994
BW76	RVB976S	Bristol VRT/SL3/6LXB	Willowbrook	O43/31F	1978	Stagecoach South (EK), 1994
BW79	TFN979T	Bristol VRT/SL3/6LXB	Willowbrook	O43/31F	1978	Stagecoach South (SCB), 1996
BW82	TFN982T	Bristol VRT/SL3/6LXB	Willowbrook	O43/31F	1978	Stagecoach South (EK), 1994
BW85	TFN985T	Bristol VRT/SL3/6LXB	Willowbrook	B43/31F	1978	Stagecoach South (SCB), 1996
BW86	TFN986T	Bristol VRT/SL3/6LXB	Willowbrook	O43/31F	1978	Stagecoach South (EK), 1993
BW87	TFN987T	Bristol VRT/SL3/6LXB	Willowbrook	B43/31F	1978	Stagecoach South (SCB), 1994
BW88	TFN988T	Bristol VRT/SL3/6LXB	Willowbrook	O43/31F	1978	Stagecoach South (EK), 1996
BW89	TFN989T	Bristol VRT/SL3/6LXB	Willowbrook	B43/31F	1978	Stagecoach South (EK), 1993
BW91	TFN991T	Bristol VRT/SL3/6LXB	Willowbrook	B43/31F	1978	Stagecoach South (EK), 1993
ERM80	JSJ748	AEC Routemaster R2RH/1	Park Royal	O40/32R	1959	London Buses, 1989
ERM84	JSJ747	AEC Routemaster R2RH/1	Park Royal	O40/32R	1959	London Buses, 1989
ERM90	JSJ746	AEC Routemaster R2RH/1	Park Royal	O40/32R	1959	London Buses, 1989
ERM94	JSJ749	AEC Routemaster R2RH/1	Park Royal	O40/32R	1959	London Buses, 1989
ERM143	VLT143	AEC Routemaster R2RH/1	Park Royal	O40/32R	1959	London Buses, 1989
ERM163	VLT163	AEC Routemaster R2RH/1	Park Royal	O40/32R	1959	London Buses, 1989
ERM235	VLT235	AEC Routemaster R2RH/1	Park Royal	O40/32R	1959	London Buses, 1989
ERM237	VLT237	AEC Routemaster R2RH/1	Park Royal	O40/32R	1959	London Buses, 1989
ERM242	VLT242	AEC Routemaster R2RH/1	Park Royal	O40/32R	1959	London Buses, 1989
ERM281	VLT281	AEC Routemaster R2RH/1	Park Royal	O40/32R	1959	London Buses, 1989
MB20	UKA20V	MCW Metrobus DR101/1	MCW	B43/30F	1980	Meresybus, 1997
MB21	UKA21V	MCW Metrobus DR103/2	MCW	B43/30F	1980	Meresybus, 1997
MB22	UKA22V	MCW Metrobus DR103/2	MCW	B43/30F	1980	Meresybus, 1997
MB23	UKA23V	MCW Metrobus DR103/2	MCW	B43/30F	1980	Meresybus, 1997
MB24	WYW24T	MCW Metrobus DR101/8	MCW	PO43/28D	1979	Cowie Leaside, 1995
MB121	BYX121V	MCW Metrobus DR101/9	MCW	PO43/28D	1979	Cowie South London, 1996
MB123	BYX123V	MCW Metrobus DR101/9	MCW	PO43/28D	1979	Cowie Leaside, 1995
MB143	BYX143V	MCW Metrobus DR101/9	MCW	CPO43/28D	1979	Cowie Leaside, 1996
MB185	BYX185V	MCW Metrobus DR101/9	MCW	PO43/28D	1979	Cowie South London, 1996
MB245	BYX245V	MCW Metrobus DR101/12	MCW	PO43/28D	1980	Cowie Leaside, 1996
MB296	BYX296V	MCW Metrobus DR101/12	MCW	O43/28D	1980	London South, 1998
MB304	BYX304V	MCW Metrobus DR101/12	MCW	CPO43/28D	1980	Cowie South London, 1996
MB310	BYX310V	MCW Metrobus DR101/12	MCW	O43/28D	1979	London North, 1998
MB314	BYX314V	MCW Metrobus DR101/12	MCW	O43/28D	1979	London South, 1998
MB351	GYE351W	MCW Metrobus DR101/12	MCW	O43/28D	1980	London General, 1997
MB353	GYE353W	MCW Metrobus DR101/12	MCW	O43/28D	1980	London South, 1998
MB389	GYE389W	MCW Metrobus DR101/12	MCW	PO43/28D	1980	London South, 1998
MB494	MNC494W	MCW Metrobus DR102/10	MCW	B43/30F	1980	Stagecoach Manchester, 1997
MB495	GYE495W	MCW Metrobus DR101/14	MCW	PO43/28D	1980	Cowie South London, 1996
MB497	MNC497W	MCW Metrobus DR102/10	MCW	B43/30F	1980	Stagecoach Manchester, 1997
MB509	GYE509W	MCW Metrobus DR101/14	MCW	O43/28D	1981	London North, 1998
MB525	GYE525W	MCW Metrobus DR101/14	MCW	O43/28D	1981	London North, 1998
MB533	GYE533W	MCW Metrobus DR101/14	MCW	O43/28D	1981	London South, 1998
MB539	GYE539W	MCW Metrobus DR101/14	MCW	PO43/28D	1981	Cowie South London, 1996
MB553	GYE553W	MCW Metrobus DR101/14	MCW	PO43/28D	1981	Cowie South London, 1996
MB558	GYE558W	MCW Metrobus DR101/14	MCW	PO43/28D	1981	Cowie South London, 1996
MB672	KYV672X	MCW Metrobus DR101/14	MCW	O43/28D	1982	London North, 1998
MB689	KYV689X	MCW Metrobus DR101/14	MCW	O43/28D	1981	London North, 1998
MB707	KYV707X	MCW Metrobus DR101/14	MCW	PO43/28D	1981	London North, 1998
MB744	KYV744X	MCW Metrobus DR101/14	MCW	PO43/28D	1982	London North, 1998
MB748	KYV748X	MCW Metrobus DR101/14	MCW	O43/28D	1982	London North, 1998
MB754	KYV754X	MCW Metrobus DR101/14	MCW	O43/28D	1982	London South, 1998
MB840	OJD840Y	MCW Metrobus DR101/16	MCW	PO43/28D	1983	Cowie South London, 1996
MB927	A927SUL	MCW Metrobus DR101/16	MCW	O43/28D	1983	London South, 1998

Opposite, top:- **The Original London Sightseeing Tour operation was acquired by Arriva during 1998 and brought many interesting vehicle conversions into the group. The principal activity as the name suggests the continuation of London transport's long-established tour that now attracts much competition. Commentary is supplied in many languages. The upper picture shows part-open-top MB389, GYE389W in corporate scheme applied to the type.** *Malcolm King*

Opposite, bottom:- **A colour scheme now disappearing from the London scene is that used by Grey Green, here shown with the Arriva motif on Olympian 156, H156XYU as is passes Euston rail station.** *R Godfrey*

ML5	C915BPW	MCW Metroliner DR130/16	MCW	O63/16F	1986	Ambassador, Great Yarmouth, 1994
ML6	C916BPW	MCW Metroliner DR130/16	MCW	O63/16F	1986	Ambassador, Great Yarmouth, 1994
ML7	C917BPW	MCW Metroliner DR130/16	MCW	O63/16F	1986	Ambassador, Great Yarmouth, 1994
ML8	C918BPW	MCW Metroliner DR130/16	MCW	O63/16F	1986	Ambassador, Great Yarmouth, 1994
ML9	B238LRA	MCW Metroliner DR130/7	MCW	O63/32F	1986	Dunn Line, Nottingham, 1994
ML10	B240LRA	MCW Metroliner DR130/7	MCW	O63/32F	1986	Dunn Line, Nottingham, 1994
ML11	B241LRA	MCW Metroliner DR130/7	MCW	O63/32F	1986	Dunn Line, Nottingham, 1994
RCL2220	CUV220C	AEC Routemaster R2RH/3	Park Royal	CO40/27R	1965	London Buses, 1989
RCL2240	CUV240C	AEC Routemaster R2RH/3	Park Royal	CO36/27R	1965	London Buses, 1989
RCL2241	CUV241C	AEC Routemaster R2RH/3	Park Royal	CO36/27R	1965	London Buses, 1989
RCL2243	CUV243C	AEC Routemaster R2RH/3	Park Royal	CO36/27R	1965	London Buses, 1989
RCL2248	CUV248C	AEC Routemaster R2RH/3	Park Royal	CO36/29R	1965	London Buses, 1989
RCL2259	CUV259C	AEC Routemaster R2RH/3	Park Royal	CO36/27R	1965	London Buses, 1989
RM370	WLT370	AEC Routemaster R2RH/1	Park Royal	CO22/10RL	1960	London Buses, 1989
RM438w	WLT438	AEC Routemaster R2RH/1	Park Royal	O36/28R	1960	London Buses, 1989
RM479w	WLT479	AEC Routemaster R2RH/1	Park Royal	CO36/28R	1960	London Buses, 1989
RM545	WLT545	AEC Routemaster R2RH/1	Park Royal	H36/28R	1960	London Buses, 1989
RM710w	WLT710	AEC Routemaster R2RH/1	Park Royal	CO36/26R	1961	London Buses, 1989
RM752	WLT752	AEC Routemaster R2RH/1	Park Royal	O36/28R	1961	London Buses, 1989
RM753w	WLT753	AEC Routemaster R2RH/1	Park Royal	O36/28R	1960	London Buses, 1989
RM1864	864DYE	AEC Routemaster R2RH/1	Park Royal	O36/28R	1964	London Buses, 1989
RM1919	ALD919B	AEC Routemaster R2RH/1	Park Royal	O36/28R	1964	London Buses, 1989

Ancilliary vehicles:-

VDL891	E891KYW	Volvo B10M-61	Duple 340	C53F	1988	Ex County, 1998

Previous Registrations:-

B238LRA	B903XJO, A3BOB	JSJ746	VLT90	JSJ748	VLT80
B240LRA	B901XJO, A5BOB	JSJ747	VLT84	JSJ749	VLT94
B241LRA	B904XJO, A4BOB				

Liveries:-

Arriva red livery with lettering for the Original London Sightseing Tour. Several of the buses are in overall advertisment liveries with contravision.

London South's DRL157, L157WAG, is pictured at Wallington in September 1998 while working route 410. For London work an orange motif is placed on the red principal colour while a red name and motif are used on the white front panel.
Gerry Mead

ARRIVA SOUTHERN COUNTIES Ltd

Arriva Southern Counties Ltd, Invicta House, Armstrong Road, Maidstone, Kent, ME15 6TY

Arriva Kent Thameside Ltd, Invicta House, Armstrong Road, Maidstone, Kent, ME15 6TY

Arriva Kent & Sussex Ltd, Invicta House, Armstrong Road, Maidstone, Kent, ME15 6TY

New Enterprise Ltd, Invicta House, Armstrong Road, Maidstone, Kent, ME15 6TY

Arriva Croydon & North Surrey Ltd, Linden Court, Lesbourne Road, Reigate, RH2 7LEP

Arriva Guildford & West Surrey Ltd, Linden Court, Lesbourne Road, Reigate, RH2 7LEP

Arriva West Sussex Ltd, Linden Court, Lesbourne Road, Reigate, RH2 7LEP

| 1041w | E41UKL | Mercedes-Benz 609D | Reeve Burgess | B20F | 1987 | | | |
| 1046w | E46UKL | Mercedes-Benz 609D | Reeve Burgess | B20F | 1987 | | | |

1071-1086

		Mercedes-Benz 609D		Reeve Burgess	B20F	1987-90 *1077/8 are B19F			
1071	G71PKR	1074w	G74PKR	1078	G78PKR	1080	G80SKR	1085	G85SKR
1073	G73PKR	1075	G75PKR	1079	G79SKR	1082	G82SKR	1086	G86SKR

1101-1124

		Mercedes-Benz O810 Vario		Plaxton Beaver 2	B27F	1998			
1101	R101TKO	1107	R107TKO	1113	R113TKO	1117	R117TKO	1121	R121TKO
1102	R102TKO	1108	R108TKO	1114	R114TKO	1118	R118TKO	1122	R122TKO
1103	R103TKO	1109	R109TKO	1115	R115TKO	1119	R119TKO	1123	R123TKO
1104	R104TKO	1110	R110TKO	1116	R116TKO	1120	R120TKO	1124	R124TKO
1105	R105TKO	1112	R112TKO						

1201	G201RKK	Mercedes-Benz 709D	Reeve Burgess Beaver	B25F	1989
1202	G202RKK	Mercedes-Benz 709D	Reeve Burgess Beaver	B25F	1989
1203	G203RKK	Mercedes-Benz 709D	Reeve Burgess Beaver	B25F	1989
1204	H204EKO	Mercedes-Benz 709D	Carlyle	B25F	1991
1205	M205SKE	Mercedes-Benz 709D	Plaxton Beaver	B23F	1995
1206	M206SKE	Mercedes-Benz 709D	Plaxton Beaver	B23F	1995

1207-1217

		Mercedes-Benz 709D		Plaxton Beaver	B27F	1996			
1207	N207CKP	1210	P210JKK	1212	P212JKL	1214	P214JKL	1216	P216JKL
1208	N208CKP	1211	P211JKL	1213	P213JKL	1215	P215JKL	1217	P217JKL
1209	N209CKP								

1218-1230

		Mercedes-Benz 711D		Plaxton Beaver	B27F	1997			
1218	P218LKK	1221	P221LKK	1225	P225LKK	1227	P227LKK	1229	P229LKK
1219	P219LKK	1223	P223LKK	1226	P226LKK	1228	P228LKK	1230	P230LKK
1220	P220LKK	1224	P224LKK						

1301	H301FKL	Mercedes-Benz 709D	Reeve Burgess Beaver	BC25F	1991	New Enterprise, 1996
1351	N351YKE	Mercedes-Benz 709D	Plaxton Beaver	BC16FL	1995	
1352	N352BKK	Mercedes-Benz 709D	Plaxton Beaver	BC16FL	1995	
1360	J60MPS	Mercedes-Benz 811D	PMT Ami	BC33F	1992	Mercury, Hoo, 1996

The MetroRider underwent many changes after the model had moved from the Laird group's MCW factory to the Optare group. Pictured with Medway Towns lettering is 1961, J961JNL, from the 1991 delivery of 25 seaters. Southern Counties fleet provides vehicles for several operations that were previously supplied from the London & Country and Maidstone & District fleets. Currently, former fleet numbers are in use, though there are plans to re-number those buses not in a four-digit scheme. *Phillip Stephenson*

1444-1453		Optare MetroRider MR17	Optare		B29F	1994	1444/7-53 ex Londonlinks, 1997		
1444	M444HPF	**1446**	M446HPF	**1448**	M448HPF	**1450**	M450HPF	**1452**	M452HPG
1445	M445HPF	**1447**	M447HPF	**1449**	M449HPF	**1451**	M451HPF	**1453**	M453HPG

1636w	F393DOA	Peugeot-Talbot Pullman	Talbot	B17FL	1989	Kentish Bus, 1997
1680w	L80MPS	Peugeot-Talbot Pullman	TBP	B22F	1994	Mercury, Hoo, 1996
1713w	L287EKK	Iveco TurboDaily 59-12	Dormobile Routemaker	B25F	1994	Kentish Bus, 1996
1714w	L714EKO	Iveco TurboDaily 59-12	Dormobile Routemaker	B25F	1994	Kentish Bus, 1996
1740w	M40MPS	Iveco TurboDaily 59-12	Marshall C31	B26FL	1995	Mercury, Hoo, 1996

1801-1808		Optare MetroRider MR15	Optare		B29F	1996			
1801	N801BKN	**1803**	N803BKN	**1805**	N805BKN	**1807**	N807BKN	**1808**	N808BKN
1802	N802BKN	**1804**	N804BKN	**1806**	N806BKN				

1809-1814		Optare MetroRider MR	Optare		B29F	1998			
1809	R809TKO	**1811**	R811TKO	**1812**	R812TKO	**1813**	R813TKO	**1814**	R814TKO
1810	R810TKO								

1852	N852YKE	Optare MetroRider MR13	Optare	B25F	1995	Londonlinks, 1995
1886w	H886CCU	Optare MetroRider MR03	Optare	B25F	1991	
1887	H887CCU	Optare MetroRider MR03	Optare	B25F	1991	
1889w	H889CCU	Optare MetroRider MR03	Optare	B25F	1991	
1890w	H890CCU	Optare MetroRider MR03	Optare	B25F	1991	

1961-1975		Optare MetroRider	Optare		B25F	1991			
1961	J961JNL	**1970**	J970JNL	**1973**	J973JNL	**1974**	J974JNL	**1975**	J975JNL
1962	J962JNL								

Surrey & West Sussex names have been applied to Mercedes-Benz 132, K132XRE which moved south in 1995, having previously operated with the Stevensons fleet. The picture was taken at North Holmwood and the vehicle is one of eleven allocated to Warnham Station near Horsham. *Richard Godfrey*

1977	L837MWT	Optare MetroRider MR01	Optare	B31F	1993	Darlington, 1995	
1978	L838MWT	Optare MetroRider MR01	Optare	B31F	1993	Londonlinks, 1995	

Western area:

113w	G113TND	Mercedes-Benz 811D	Carlyle	B20FL	1990	Bee Line Buzz, 1992	
132	K132XRE	Mercedes-Benz 709D	Dormobile	B29F	1992	Stevensons, 1995	
154	K154BRF	Mercedes-Benz 709D	Dormobile Routemaker	B29F	1993	Stevensons, 1995	
189	G689OHE	Mercedes-Benz 811D	Reeve Burgess Beaver	B20FL	1990	Metrowest, Coseley, 1992	
190	G690OHE	Mercedes-Benz 811D	Reeve Burgess Beaver	B20FL	1990	Metrowest, Coseley, 1992	
201w	G101TND	Mercedes-Benz 811D	Carlyle	B33F	1990	C-Line, 1991	
402	K402VPK	Mercedes-Benz 709D	Dormobile Routemaker	B25FL	1992		
405	K405VPK	Mercedes-Benz 709D	Dormobile Routemaker	B25FL	1992		
422	L422CPB	Mercedes-Benz 709D	Dormobile Routemaker	B25F	1993		
423	L423CPB	Mercedes-Benz 709D	Dormobile Routemaker	B25F	1993		
427	L427CPB	Mercedes-Benz 709D	Dormobile Routemaker	B27F	1994		
428	L428CPC	Mercedes-Benz 709D	Danescroft	B27F	1994		

430-437

		Mercedes-Benz 811D	Plaxton Beaver	B31F	1994	Londonlinks, 1997	

430	L430CPJ	**433**	L433CPJ	**435**	L435CPJ	**436**	L436CPJ	**437**	L437CPJ
431	L431CPJ	**434**	L434CPJ				

MM438	P438HKN	Mercedes-Benz 811D	Plaxton Beaver	B31F	1996	Londonlinks, 1997	
440	M440HPF	Optare MetroRider MR17	Optare	B29F	1994	Londonlinks, 1997	
441	M441HPF	Optare MetroRider MR17	Optare	B29F	1994	Londonlinks, 1997	
442	M442HPF	Optare MetroRider MR17	Optare	B29F	1994	Londonlinks, 1997	
443	M443HPF	Optare MetroRider MR17	Optare	B29F	1994	Londonlinks, 1997	
461	M461JPA	Mercedes-Benz 811D	Plaxton Beaver	B31F	1995		
462	M462JPA	Mercedes-Benz 811D	Plaxton Beaver	B31F	1995		
463	M463JPA	Mercedes-Benz 709D	Plaxton Beaver	B23F	1995		
464	M464JPA	Mercedes-Benz 709D	Plaxton Beaver	B23F	1995		
466	M466MPM	Mercedes-Benz 709D	Plaxton Beaver	B21F	1995		
467	M467MPM	Mercedes-Benz 709D	Plaxton Beaver	B21F	1995		

469	N469SPA	Mercedes-Benz 709D	Alexander Sprint	B27FL	1995
MR472	P472APJ	Optare MetroRider MR17	Optare	B29F	1996
MM473	P473APJ	Mercedes-Benz 711D	Plaxton Beaver	B23F	1996
MM474	P474APJ	Mercedes-Benz 811D	Plaxton Beaver	B18FL	1996

MM475-480

| | | Mercedes-Benz 711D | Plaxton Beaver | B27F | 1997 |

| 475 | P475DPE | 476 | P476DPE | 477 | P477DPE | 479 | P479DPE | 480 | P480DPE |

| 969 | J969JNL | Optare MetroRider MR03 | Optare | B25F | 1991 | Londonlinks, 1997 |

Coaches

TP91	AEF990Y	Leyland Tiger TRCTL11/2R	Plaxton Paramount 3200	C53F	1983	Shamrock & Rambler, 1988
2031	UJI2338	Scania K113CRB	Plaxton Paramount 3500 III	C49FT	1990	Happy Days, Woodseaves, 1994
2172	YSU895	Leyland Tiger TRCTL11/2R	Plaxton Paramount 3200E	C53F	1983	Kentish Bus, 1997
2174	YSU897	Leyland Tiger TRCTL11/2R	Plaxton Paramount 3200E	C53F	1984	Kentish Bus, 1990
2184w	544XVW	Leyland Tiger TRCTL11/3R	Duple Laser	C53F	1983	
2192	YSU872	Leyland Tiger TRCL10/3RZ	Duple 320	C53F	1989	Park's, Hamilton, 1993
2193	YSU873	Leyland Tiger TRCL10/3RZ	Duple 320	C53F	1989	Park's, Hamilton, 1993
2194	J25UNY	Leyland Tiger TRCL10/3ARZM	Plaxton 321	C53F	1992	Bebb, Llantwit Fardre, 1993
2195	J26UNY	Leyland Tiger TRCL10/3ARZM	Plaxton 321	C53F	1992	Bebb, Llantwit Fardre, 1993
2196	J27UNY	Leyland Tiger TRCL10/3ARZM	Plaxton 321	C53F	1992	Bebb, Llantwit Fardre, 1993
2200w	TSU644	Leyland Tiger TRCTL11/3R	Plaxton Paramount 3200E	C53F	1983	
2210	TSU645	Leyland Tiger TRCTL11/3R	Plaxton Paramount 3200 E	C53F	1983	
2211	494WYA	Leyland Tiger TRCTL11/3R	Plaxton Paramount 3500	C57F	1984	PMT, 1990
2213w	UJI2337	Leyland Tiger TRCTL11/3RH	Plaxton Paramount 3500 II	C49FT	1985	Kentish Bus, 1995
2214	UJI2339	Leyland Tiger TRCTL11/3RH	Plaxton Paramount 3500 II	C49FT	1985	Kentish Bus, 1995
2830	TIB5903	Volvo B10M-61	Van Hool Alizée H	C53F	1988	Jason, St Mary Cray, 1996
2831	TIB5904	Volvo B10M-61	Van Hool Alizée H	C53F	1988	Jason, St Mary Cray, 1996
2835	A11GTA	Volvo B10M-60	Plaxton Paramount 3500 III	C53F	1991	Kentish Bus, 1997
2842	G546NKJ	Volvo B10M-60	Caetano Algarve	C53F	1989	
2843	G998RKN	Volvo B10M-60	Caetano Algarve	C53F	1990	
2844	TIB5901	Volvo B10M-61	Plaxton Paramount 3500 III	C50F	1988	Kentish Bus, 1996
2845	A14GTA	Volvo B10M-60	Plaxton Paramount 3500 III	C50F	1990	Kentish Bus, 1996
2846	H846AHS	Volvo B10M-60	Plaxton Paramount 3500 III	C49FT	1991	Express Travel, Liverpool, 1995
2847	H847AHS	Volvo B10M-60	Plaxton Paramount 3500 III	C51F	1991	Express Travel, Liverpool, 1995
2848	H616UWR	Volvo B10M-60	Plaxton Paramount 3500 III	C53F	1991	Wallace Arnold, 1996
2851	G801BPG	Volvo B10M-60	Plaxton Paramount 3500 III	C37FT	1989	Speedlink, 1997
2852w	G802BPG	Volvo B10M-60	Plaxton Paramount 3500 III	C37FT	1989	Speedlink, 1997
2899	F899GUM	DAF MB230LB615	Plaxton Paramount 3500 III	C53F	1989	O'Sullivan, Killarney, 1997
2900	F621HGO	DAF MB230LT615	Van Hool Alizée H	C53FT	1989	London Coaches (Kent), 1997
2901	F901GUM	DAF MB230LB615	Plaxton Paramount 3500 III	C53F	1989	O'Sullivan, Killarney, 1996
2902	J36GCX	DAF SB2305DHS585	Duple 320	C57F	1992	Eagle, Bristol, 1997

2903-2910

| | | DAF DE33WSSB3000 | Plaxton Prima | C53F | 1998 |

| 2903 | R903BKO | 2905 | R905BKO | 2907 | R907BKO | 2909 | R909BKO | 2910 | R910BKO |
| 2904 | R904BKO | 2906 | R906BKO | 2908 | R908BKO | | | | |

Opposite: - **Pictured in welcome summer sun are two liveries now being displaced by the Arriva corporate scheme. Pictured in Maidstone is low-floor Dennis Dart 3204, P204LKJ, one of the large delivery of the type placed in service in 1997 while the former London & Country livery is carried on East Lancashire-bodied DSL52, P252APM, which was seen passing along Cranford High Street heading for London Heathrow.** *M E Lyons*

The 1999 Arriva Bus Handbook

Highly respected for its coaching operations, Shearings commenced commercial bus services shortly after de-regulation and purchased a fleet of modern Lynx and Volvo buses. Many of these were sold even before the formation and sale of Timeline, part of which Arriva eventually acquired during 1998. One of the early sales comprised four Leyland Lynx that Maidstone added to its fleet in 1991. Pictured in the new colours is 3047, F47ENF. *Gerry Mead*

3040	D108NDW	Leyland Lynx LX112TL11ZR1R	Leyland Lynx	B49F	1987	London Coaches (Kent), 1996	
3041	E885KYW	Leyland Lynx LX112TL11ZR1S	Leyland Lynx	B49F	1987	London Coaches (Kent), 1996	
3042	E886KYW	Leyland Lynx LX112TL11ZR1S	Leyland Lynx	B47F	1987	London Coaches (Kent), 1996	
3043	E887KYW	Leyland Lynx LX112TL11ZR1S	Leyland Lynx	B47F	1987	London Coaches (Kent), 1996	
3044	E890KYW	Leyland Lynx LX1126LXCTZR1S	Leyland Lynx	B47F	1987	London Coaches (Kent), 1996	
3045	F45ENF	Leyland Lynx LX112L10ZR1R	Leyland Lynx	B49F	1988	Shearings, 1991	
3046	F46ENF	Leyland Lynx LX112L10ZR1R	Leyland Lynx	B49F	1988	Shearings, 1991	
3047	F47ENF	Leyland Lynx LX112L10ZR1R	Leyland Lynx	B49F	1988	Shearings, 1991	
3048	F48ENF	Leyland Lynx LX112L10ZR1R	Leyland Lynx	B49F	1988	Shearings, 1991	
3049	H256YLG	Leyland Lynx LX2R11V18Z4R	Leyland Lynx 2	B49F	1990	Aintree Coachline, 1995	
3051	H814EKJ	Leyland Lynx LX2R11C15Z4S	Leyland Lynx 2	B49F	1991	Kentish Bus, 1997	
3052	H816EKJ	Leyland Lynx LX2R11C15Z4S	Leyland Lynx 2	B49F	1991	Kentish Bus, 1997	

3053-3065

Leyland Lynx LX2R11C15Z4S   Leyland Lynx   B49F   1989/91 Ex Boro'line, Maidstone, 1992

3053	H813EKJ	3056w	G36VME	3059	G39VME	3062	G42VME	3064	G44VME
3054	H814EKJ	3057	G37VME	3060	G40VME	3063	G43VME	3065	G45VME
3055	H815EKJ	3058	G38VME	3061	G41VME				

3066	D155HML	Leyland Lynx LX112TL11ZR1S	Leyland Lynx	B49F	1987	Kentish Bus, 1997	
3067	D157HML	Leyland Lynx LX112TL11ZR1S	Leyland Lynx	B49F	1987	Kentish Bus, 1997	
3068	D101NDW	Leyland Lynx LX112TL11ZR1R	Leyland Lynx	B49F	1987	Londonlinks, 1997	
(400)w	D102NDW	Leyland Lynx LX112TL11ZR1R	Leyland Lynx	B49F	1987	Londonlinks, 1997	
LL418w	D156HML	Leyland Lynx LX112TL11ZR1S	Leyland Lynx	B49F	1987	Londonlinks, 1997	
3099	M20MPS	Dennis Dart 9.8SDL3054	Marshall C37	B40F	1994	Mercury, Hoo, 1996	
3100	M30MPS	Dennis Dart 9.8SDL3054	Marshall C37	BC40F	1995	Mercury, Hoo, 1996	
3101	J220HGY	Dennis Dart 9SDL3011	Plaxton Pointer	B35F	1992	Londonlinks, 1997	
3102	J221HGY	Dennis Dart 9SDL3011	Plaxton Pointer	B35F	1992	Londonlinks, 1997	
3103	L500DKT	Dennis Dart 9SDL3032	WSC Portsdown	B43F	1994	Wealden Beeline, 1997	
3104	M501PKJ	Dennis Dart 9SDL3032	WSC Portsdown	B43F	1994	Wealden Beeline, 1997	
3105	M502RKO	Dennis Dart 9SDL3032	WSC Portsdown	B43F	1995	Wealden Beeline, 1997	
3106	L503HKM	Dennis Dart 9SDL3032	WSC Portsdown	B43F	1994	Wealden Beeline, 1997	
3107	L766DPE	Dennis Dart 9.8SDL3034	Wadham Stringer Winchester	C39F	1993	Wealden Beeline, 1997	

The Dennis Dart has become the most popular choice of new vehicle in recent years, with a variety of bodybuilders now building on the type. However, it started life as a Hestair-Duple product with the Blackpool bodybuilder designing the *Dartline* body in a venture with Dennis. On the closure of the Duple business, Carlyle took over the design and tooling. Pictured at Pebblecombe is one of the first Darts to be built after the transfer, DS177, G125RGT. *Richard Godfrey*

3112-3159

		Dennis Dart 9SDL3034		Northern Counties Paladin	B35F	1994				

3112	L112YVK	3131	L131YVK	3138	L138YVK	3145	L145YVK	3154	L154YVK
3113	L113YVK	3132	L132YVK	3139	L139YVK	3146	L146YVK	3155	L155YVK
DS181	L114YVK	3133	L133YVK	3140	L140YVK	3148	L148YVK	3156	L156YVK
DS182	L127YVK	3134	L134YVK	3141	L141YVK	3149	L149YVK	3157	L157YVK
3128	L128YVK	3135	L135YVK	3142	L142YVK	3150	L150YVK	3158	L158BFT
3129	L129YVK	3136	L136YVK	3143	L143YVK	3152	L152YVK	3159	L159BFT
3130	L130YVK	3137	L137YVK	3144	L144YVK	3153	L153YVK		

3163	J463MKL	Dennis Dart 9.8SDL3012	Plaxton Pointer	B40F	1991	
3164	J464MKL	Dennis Dart 9.8SDL3012	Plaxton Pointer	B40F	1991	
3165	J465MKL	Dennis Dart 9.8SDL3012	Plaxton Pointer	B40F	1991	

3166-3171

		Dennis Dart 9.8SDL3017		Plaxton Pointer	B40F	1992	3170 was rebodied in 1995		
3166	J466OKP	3168	J468OKP	3169	K469SKO	3170	K470SKO	3171	K471SKO
3167	J467OKP								

3174	M100CBB	Dennis Dart 9.8SDL3040	Plaxton Pointer	B40F	1995	Cardiff Bluebird, 1996
3175	M200CBB	Dennis Dart 9.8SDL3040	Plaxton Pointer	B40F	1995	Cardiff Bluebird, 1996

3176-3183

		Dennis Dart SLF		Plaxton Pointer	N40F	1996			
3176	P176LKL	3178	P178LKL	3180	P180LKL	3182	P182LKL	3183	P183LKL
3177	P177LKL	3179	P179LKL	3181	P181LKL				

3184	P184LKL	Dennis Dart SLF	Plaxton Pointer 2	N37F	1997
3185	P185LKL	Dennis Dart SLF	Plaxton Pointer 2	N37F	1997

3186-3191

		Dennis Dart SLF		Plaxton Pointer 2	N40F	1997			
3186	P186LKJ	3188	P188LKJ	3189	P189LKJ	3190	P190LKJ	3191	P191LKJ
3187	P187LKJ								

The colour selection illustrated Maidstone & District's Darts in their original colours while 3234, P234MKN, is seen at Mereworth displaying the new corporate scheme. As they have been repainted 'Medways Towns' lettering has been applied to much of the former Maidstone & District fleet. *Richard Godfrey*

3192-3247

Dennis Dart SLF — Plaxton Pointer 2 — N40F — 1997

3192	P192LKJ	3204	P204LKJ	3215	P215LKJ	3227	P227MKL	3238	P238MKN
3193	P193LKJ	3205	P205LKJ	3216	P216LKJ	3228	P228MKL	3239	P239MKN
3194	P194LKJ	3206	P206LKJ	3217	P217MKL	3229	P229MKL	3240	P240MKN
3195	P195LKJ	3207	P207LKJ	3218	P218MKL	3230	P230MKL	3241	P241MKN
3196	P196LKJ	3208	P208LKJ	3219	P219MKL	3231	P231MKL	3242	P242MKN
3197	P197LKJ	3209	P209LKJ	3220	P220MKL	3232	P232MKL	3243	P243MKN
3198	P198LKJ	3210	P210LKJ	3221	P221MKL	3233	P233MKN	3244	P244MKN
3199	P199LKJ	3211	P211LKJ	3223	P223MKL	3234	P234MKN	3245	P245MKN
3201	P201LKJ	3212	P212LKJ	3224	P224MKL	3235	P235MKN	3246	P246MKN
3202	P202LKJ	3213	P213LKJ	3225	P225MKL	3236	P236MKN	3247	P247MKN
3203	P203LKJ	3214	P214LKJ	3226	P226MKL	3237	P237MKN		

3250-3259

Scania L113CRL — Wright Axcess-ultralow — N43F — 1995

3250	N250BKK	3252	N252BKK	3254	N254BKK	3256	N256BKK	3258	N258BKK
3251	N251BKK	3253	N253BKK	3255	N255BKK	3257	N257BKK	3259	N259BKK

3261-3272

Dennis Dart SLF — Plaxton Pointer 2 — N39F — 1998

3261	R261EKO	3264	R264EKO	3267	R267EKO	3269	R269EKO	3271	R271EKO
3262	R262EKO	3265	R265EKO	3268	R268EKO	3270	R270EKO	3272	R272EKO
3263	R263EKO	3266	R266EKO						

3492	RUF42R	Leyland National 11351/2R	B25DL	1977	London Buses, 1993
3493	THX202S	Leyland National 10351A/2R	B21DL	1978	London Buses, 1993
3494	YYE290T	Leyland National 10351A/2R	B21DL	1979	London Buses, 1994

London & Country were enthusiastic about the National Greenway programme and were involved in preparing vehicles before they were shipped to East Lancashire for body re-build. Consequently their own fleet contained many examples. While most have now been dispersed to other fleets over a dozen remain, including 374, PDZ6274 which is fitted with high-back seating. *Richard Godfrey*

3601-3619   Volvo B6-9.9M   Plaxton Pointer   B40F   1994-95

3601	L601EKM	3605	L605EKM	3609	L609EKM	3613	M613PKP	3617	M617PKP
3602	L602EKM	3606	L606EKM	3610	L610EKM	3614	M614PKP	3618	M618PKP
3603	L603EKM	3607	L607EKM	3611	M611PKP	3615	M615PKP	3619	M619PKP
3604	L604EKM	3608	L608EKM	3612	M612PKP	3616	M616PKP		

3701-3706   Dennis Dart SLF (11m)   Plaxton Pointer 2 SPD   N44F   1998

3701	S701VKM	3703	S703VKM	3704	S704VKM	3705	S705VKM	3706	S706VKM
3702	S702VKM								

DS1-24   Dennis Dart 9.8SDL3035*   East Lancashire EL2000   B40F*   1993-96   *10-3/6-18 are B30FL
   *14/15 are 9.8SDL3054; *10-3/6-8 are 9.8SDL3053

1	L503CPB	6	L508CPJ	11	M522MPF	16	N528SPA	21	N541TPK
2	L504CPB	7	L509CPJ	12	M523MPF	17	N529SPA	22	N542TPK
3	L505CPJ	8	L510CPJ	13	M524MPF	18	N530SPA	23	N543TPK
4	L506CPJ	9	L511CPJ	14	M525MPM	19	N539TPF	24	N544TPK
5	L507CPJ	10	M521MPF	15	M526MPM	20	N540TPF		

DSL25-36   Dennis Dart SLF   Plaxton Pointer 2   N35F   1996   North Western (Beeline), 1998

25	N225TPK	28	N228TPK	31	N231TPK	33	N233TPK	35	N235TPK
26	N226TPK	29	N229TPK	32	N232TPK	34	N234TPK	36	N236TPK
27	N227TPK	30	N230TPK						

DSL37-55   Dennis Dart SLF   East Lancashire Spryte   N31F   1996-97

37	N237VPH	41	N241VPH	45	N245VPH	49	N249VPH	53	P253APM
38	N238VPH	42	N242VPH	46	N246VPH	50	P250APM	54	P254APM
39	N239VPH	43	N243VPH	47	N247VPH	51	P251APM	55	P255APM
40	N240VPH	44	N244VPH	48	N248VPH	52	P252APM		

Currently numbered DS4, and carrying DS004 on the front, is East Lancashire bodied Dennis Dart L506CPJ. The vehicle was pictured at Longhead Estate. The vehicle is presently based at Crawley. *Gerry Mead*

DSL68-96

Dennis Dart SLF — Plaxton Pointer 2 — N39F — 1997

68	P268FPK	74	P274FPK	80	P380FPK	86	P286FPK	92	P292FPK
69	P269FPK	75	P275FPK	81	P281FPK	87	P287FPK	93	P293FPK
70	P270FPK	76	P276FPK	82	P282FPK	88	P288FPK	94	P294FPK
71	P271FPK	77	P277FPK	83	P283FPK	89	P289FPK	95	P295FPK
72	P272FPK	78	P278FPK	84	P284FPK	90	P290FPK	96	P296FPK
73	P273FPK	79	P279FPK	85	P285FPK	91	P291FPK		

DSL97-108

Dennis Dart SLF — Plaxton Pointer 2 — B39F — 1997

97	R297CMV	100	R310CMV	103	R303CMV	105	R305CMV	107	R307CMV
98	R298CMV	101	R301CMV	104	R304CMV	106	R296CMV	108	R308CMV
99	R299CMV	102	R302CMV						

DS120-126

Dennis Dart 9SDL3034 — Northern Counties Paladin — B35F — 1994 — Londonlinks, 1997

120	L120YVK	122	L122YVK	124	L124YVK	125	L125YVK	126	L126YVK
121	L121YVK	123	L123YVK						

DS151	L151YVK	Dennis Dart 9SDL3034	Northern Counties Paladin	B35F	1994	Londonlinks, 1997
DP160	M160SKR	Dennis Dart 9SDL3053	Plaxton Pointer	B35F	1995	Londonlinks, 1997
DP161	M161SKR	Dennis Dart 9SDL3053	Plaxton Pointer	B35F	1995	Londonlinks, 1997
DP162	M162SKR	Dennis Dart 9SDL3053	Plaxton Pointer	B35F	1995	Londonlinks, 1997
DP163	M163SKR	Dennis Dart 9SDL3053	Plaxton Pointer	B35F	1995	Londonlinks, 1997

DS164-172

Dennis Dart 9SDL3053 — Plaxton Pointer — B34F — 1995 — Londonlinks, 1997

164	N701GUM	166	N703GUM	168	N705GUM	170	N707GUM	172	N709GUM
165	N702GUM	167	N704GUM	169	N706GUM	171	N708GUM		

DS173	G217LGK	Dennis Dart 9SDL3002	Duple Dartline	B36F	1990	Kent & Sussex, 1998
DS174	G218LGK	Dennis Dart 9SDL3002	Duple Dartline	B36F	1990	Kent & Sussex, 1998
DS175	G122RGT	Dennis Dart 9SDL3002	Carlyle Dartline	B36F	1990	Kent & Sussex, 1998

The 1999 Arriva Bus Handbook

DS176	G123PGT	Dennis Dart 9SDL3002	Carlyle Dartline	B36F	1990	Kent Thameside, 1998
DS178	G126PGT	Dennis Dart 9SDL3002	Carlyle Dartline	B36F	1990	Kent Thameside, 1998
DS179	G127PGT	Dennis Dart 9SDL3002	Carlyle Dartline	B36F	1990	Kent Thameside, 1998

V201-212

Volvo B6-9.9M — Northern Counties Paladin — B39F — 1994 — Londonlinks, 1997

201	L201YCU	204	L204YCU	207	L207YCU	209	L209YCU	211	L211YCU
202	L202YCU	205	L205YCU	208	L208YCU	210	L210YCU	212	L212YCU
203	L203YCU	206	L206YCU						

512-516

Volvo B6-9.9M — Plaxton Pointer — B41F — 1994

512	L512CPJ	513	L513CPJ	514	L514CPJ	515	L515CPJ	516	L516CPJ

LSL5-9

Dennis Lance SLF — Wright Pathfinder — N40F* — 1994-95 *9 is N39F

5	M517KPA	6	M518KPA	7	M519KPA	8	M520KPA	9	N527SPA

LS10-24

Dennis Lance SLF — East Lancashire — N49F — 1996

10	N210TPK	13	N213TPK	16	N216TPK	19	N219TPK	22	N322TPK
11	N211TPK	14	N214TPK	17	N217TPK	20	N220TPK	23	N223TPK
12	N212TPK	15	N215TPK	18	N218TPK	21	N221TPK	24	N224TPK

202	HPK504N	Leyland National 11351/1R	Urban Bus	B49F	1975	Alder Valley, 1990
265	PPM892R	Leyland 11351A/1R(Cummins)	Urban Bus	B49F	1976	Alder Valley, 1990
363	PDZ6263	Leyland 11351A/1R	East Lancs Greenway(1994)	B49F	1977	Tellings Golden-Miller, 1992
364	PDZ6264	Leyland 11351A/1R	East Lancs Greenway(1994)	B49F	1979	Tellings Golden-Miller, 1994
365	PDZ6265	Leyland 11351A/1R	East Lancs Greenway(1994)	B49F	1975	Alder Valley, 1990
366	SJI5066	Leyland 11351A/1R	East Lancs Greenway(1994)	B49F	1977	Tellings Golden-Miller, 1994
368w	LIL2168	Leyland 11351A/1R	East Lancs Greenway(1994)	B49F	1977	Tellings Golden-Miller, 1994
371	SJI5571	Leyland 11351/1R	East Lancs Greenway(1994)	B49F	1976	Midland Fox, 1994
372	SJI5572	Leyland 11351/1R	East Lancs Greenway(1994)	B49F	1976	The Bee Line, 1994
373	PDZ6273	Leyland 11351/1R	East Lancs Greenway(1994)	DP49F	1976	Midland Fox, 1994
374	PDZ6274	Leyland 11351A/1R	East Lancs Greenway(1994)	DP49F	1976	Midland Fox, 1994
375	PDZ6275	Leyland 11351A/2R	East Lancs Greenway(1994)	DP49F	1977	Panther, Crawley, 1991
376	PDZ6276	Leyland 11351A/1R	East Lancs Greenway(1994)	DP49F	1975	Northumbria, 1994
377	PDZ6277	Leyland 11351A/1R	East Lancs Greenway(1994)	DP49F	1978	Alder Valley, 1990
378	RDZ4278	Leyland 11351/1R	East Lancs Greenway(1995)	B49F	1975	Shamrock & Rambler, 1988
379	RDZ4279	Leyland 11351/1R	East Lancs Greenway(1995)	B49F	1975	Alder Valley, 1990
380	LIL2180	Leyland 11351/1R	East Lancs Greenway(1995)	B49F	1975	Alder Valley, 1990
LNB28	JOX528P	Leyland National 11351A/1R		B25F	1976	Shamrock & Rambler, 1988
SNB331	UPB331S	Leyland National 10351A/1R(Volvo)		B41F	1977	Londonlinks, 1997
SNB420	YPL420T	Leyland National 10351A/1R (Cummins) Urban Bus		B41F	1977	
LNB600	NOE600R	Leyland 11351A/1R(Cummins) Urban Bus		B49F	1977	Midland, 1994

Double-deck buses

610-622

Volvo Citybus B10M-50 — East Lancashire — B49/39F — 1989

610	G610BPH	613	G613BPH	616	G616BPH	619	G619BPH	621	G621BPH
611	G611BPH	614	G614BPH	617	G617BPH	620	G620BPH	622	G622BPH
612	G612BPH	615	G615BPH	618	G618BPH				

623-630

Volvo Citybus B10M-50 — Northern Counties — B45/31F — 1989 — Londonlinks, 1997

623	G623BPH	625	G625BPH	627	G627BPH	629	G629BPH	630	G630BPH
624	G624BPH	626	G626BPH	628	G628BPH				

640	G640CHF	Volvo Citybus B10M-50	East Lancashire	B49/39F	1989	Londonlinks, 1997
643	G643CHF	Volvo Citybus B10M-50	East Lancashire	B49/39F	1989	Londonlinks, 1997

694-704

Volvo Olympian YN2RV16Z4 — East Lancashire — B44/30F — 1994 — 694-700 Ex Londonlinks, 1997

694	M694HPF	697	M697HPF	699	M699HPF	701	M701HPF	703	M703HPF
695	M695HPF	698	M698HPF	700	M700HPF	702	M702HPF	704	M704HPF
696	M696HPF								

901	F571SMG	Leyland Olympian ONLXB/1RZ	Alexander RL	B47/32F	1988	Alder Valley, 1990
907	F577SMG	Leyland Olympian ONLXB/1RZ	Alexander RL	B47/32F	1988	Alder Valley, 1990
908	F578SMG	Leyland Olympian ONLXB/1RZ	Alexander RL	B47/32F	1988	Alder Valley, 1990
910	F580SMG	Leyland Olympian ONLXB/1RZ	Alexander RL	B47/32F	1988	Alder Valley, 1990

5111w	PKM111R	Bristol VRT/SL3/6LXB	Eastern Coach Works	B43/31F	1976		
5112w	PKM112R	Bristol VRT/SL3/6LXB	Eastern Coach Works	B43/31F	1976		
5125	WKO125S	Bristol VRT/SL3/6LXB	Eastern Coach Works	B43/31F	1978		
5133	WKO133S	Bristol VRT/SL3/6LXB	Eastern Coach Works	B43/31F	1978		
5137w	WKO137S	Bristol VRT/SL3/6LXB	Eastern Coach Works	B43/31F	1978		
5138w	WKO138S	Bristol VRT/SL3/6LXB	Eastern Coach Works	B43/31F	1978		
5139w	WKO139S	Bristol VRT/SL3/6LXB	Eastern Coach Works	B43/31F	1978		

5201-5210

MCW Metrobus DR102/42 MCW B45/31F 1984

5201	A201OKJ	5203	A203OKJ	5205	A205OKJ	5208	A208OKJ	5210	A210OKJ
5202	A202OKJ	5204	A204OKJ	5207	A207OKJ	5209	A209OKJ		

5557-5565

Volvo Olympian YN2RC16Z4 Northern Counties Palatine II B47/30F 1994

5557	L557YCU	5559	L559YCU	5562	L562YCU	5564	L564YCU	5565	L565YCU
5558	L558YCU	5561	L561YCU	5563	L563YCU				

5601w	WDC219Y	Leyland Olympian ONLXB/1R	Eastern Coach Works	B44/32F	1983	Londonlinks, 1997
5608w	CEF231Y	Leyland Olympian ONLXB/1R	Eastern Coach Works	B45/32F	1983	Londonlinks, 1997
5620w	C257UAJ	Leyland Olympian ONLXB/1R	Eastern Coach Works	B45/32F	1985	Londonlinks, 1997

5751-5761

Leyland Olympian ONLXB/1RH Optare B47/29F 1888/89 Boro'line, Maidstone, 1992

5751	E151OMD	5754	E154OMD	5756	E156OMD	5758	E158OMD	5760	E160OMD
5752	E152OMD	5755	E155OMD	5757	E157OMD	5759	E159OMD	5761	E161OMD
5753	E153OMD								

5765-5770

Leyland Olympian ON2R50C13Z4 Northern Counties B47/30F 1991 Boro'line, Maidstone, 1992

5765	H765EKJ	5767	H767EKJ	5768	H768EKJ	5769	H769EKJ	5770	H770EKJ
5766	H766EKJ								

5824w	VCA461W	Bristol VRT/SL3/6LXB	Eastern Coach Works	B43/31F	1980	Crosville Cymru, 1996
5826	YUM515S	Bristol VRT/SL3/6LXB	Eastern Coach Works	B43/31F	1978	Southend, 1996
5827w	WRC833S	Bristol VRT/SL3/501(6LXB)	Eastern Coach Works	B43/31F	1978	Trent, 1993
5828w	BRC834T	Bristol VRT/SL3/6LXB	Eastern Coach Works	B43/31F	1979	Trent, 1993
5830	BRC837T	Bristol VRT/SL3/6LXB	Eastern Coach Works	B43/31F	1979	Trent, 1993

5831-5853

Bristol VRT/SL3/6LXB Eastern Coach Works B43/31F 1978-79

5831	BKE831T	5846	BKE846T	5848w	BKE848T	5852w	BKE852T	5853	BKE853T
5832w	BKE832T								

5863-5869

Bristol VRT/SL3/6LXB Eastern Coach Works B43/31F 1979

5863	FKM863V	5864	FKM864V	5867w	FKM867V	5868	FKM868V	5869	FKM869V

5870w	ODC470W	Bristol VRT/SL3/6LXB	Eastern Coach Works	B43/31F	1981	West Riding, 1995

5875-5886

Bristol VRT/SL3/6LXB Eastern Coach Works B43/31F 1979-80

5875w	FKM875V	5878w	FKM878V	5883w	HKM883V	5885w	HKM885V	5886w	HKM886V
5877	FKM877V	5882w	FKM882V						

5888	A888PKR	Leyland Olympian ONLXB/1R	Eastern Coach Works	BC42/27F	1984
5889	A889PKR	Leyland Olympian ONLXB/1R	Eastern Coach Works	BC42/27F	1984
5890	A890PKR	Leyland Olympian ONLXB/1R	Eastern Coach Works	BC42/27F	1984

5891-5900

Leyland Olympian ONLXB/1RH Northern Counties B45/30F 1988

5891	E891AKN	5893	F893BKK	5895	F895BKK	5897	F897DKK	5899	F899DKK
5892	F892BKK	5894	F894BKK	5896	F896DKK	5898	F898DKK	5900	F900DKK

Opposite:- **The Southern Counties double-deck fleet comprises a variety of models from Bristol VRs to the latest DAF double-deck buses as the two former groups pursued different purchasing policies. The upper picture shows one of the latest arrivals, DFD3, R203CKO which is pictured in Putney Vale. The type are used from Leatherhead on London Bus route 85 to Kingston. The lower picture shows DD19, F631BKD. Though part of a batch transferred from North Western in 1997, DD19 has a different model chassis from the others and, until recently, had high-back seating fitted. The vehicle is seen on West Sussex service C8, at Crawley.**
Gerry Mead

5901-5905
Leyland Olympian ON2R50G13Z4 Northern Counties Palatine B45/30F   1990

| 5901 | G901SKP | 5902 | G902SKP | 5903 | G903SKP | 5904 | G904SKP | 5905 | G905SKP |

5906-5910
Leyland Olympian ON2R50G13Z4 Northern Counties Palatine B45/30F   1993

| 5906 | K906SKR | 5907 | K907SKR | 5908 | K908SKR | 5909 | K909SKR | 5910 | K910SKR |

5911-5925
Volvo Olympian YN2R50C16Z4   Northern Counties Palatine   B47/30F   1994-95 5913 rebodied 1995

5911	M911MKM	5914	M914MKM	5917	M917MKM	5920	M920MKM	5923	M923PKN
5912	M912MKM	5915	M915MKM	5918	M918MKM	5921	M921PKN	5924	M924PKN
5913	M913MKM	5916	M916MKM	5919	M919MKM	5922	M922PKN	5925	M925PKN

5926-5943
Volvo Olympian   Northern Counties Palatine B47/30F*   1997   *5938-43 are H45/30F

5926	P926MKL	5930	P930MKL	5934	P934MKL	5938	P938MKL	5941	P941MKL
5927	P927MKL	5931	P931MKL	5935	P935MKL	5939	P939MKL	5942	P942MKL
5928	P928MKL	5932	P932MKL	5936	P936MKL	5940	P940MKL	5943	P943MKL
5929	P929MKL	5933	P933MKL	5937	P937MKL				

6172w	XPG172T	Leyland Atlantean AN68A/1R	Park Royal	B43/30F	1978	Londonlinks, 1997
6220w	EPH220V	Leyland Atlantean AN68A/1R	Roe	B43/30F	1980	Londonlinks, 1997
6232w	EPH232V	Leyland Atlantean AN68A/1R	Roe	B43/30F	1980	Londonlinks, 1997
6270	KPJ270W	Leyland Atlantean AN68B/1R	Roe	B43/30F	1981	
6274w	KPJ274W	Leyland Atlantean AN68B/1R	Roe	B43/30F	1981	
6277	KPJ277W	Leyland Atlantean AN68B/1R	Roe	B43/30F	1981	
6283w	KPJ283W	Leyland Atlantean AN68B/1R	Roe	B43/30F	1981	
6666w	THX291S	Leyland Fleetline FE30ALR	MCW	O44/24F	1977	Cowie Leaside, 1997

7631-7643
Volvo Citybus B10M-50   Northern Counties   B45/31F   1989   639-43 ex Londonlinks, 1997

7631w	G631BPH	7634w	G634BPH	7637	G637BPH	7640	G640BPH	7642	G642BPH
7632	G632BPH	7635	G635BPH	7638	G638BPH	7641	G641BPH	7643	G643BPH
7633	G633BPH	7636	G636BPH	7639	G639BPH				

7702-7709
Volvo Citybus B10M-50   East Lancashire   B49/39F   1989-90 North Western, 1996

| 7702 | G641CHF | 7706 | G648EKA | 7707 | G649EKA | 7708 | G659DTJ | 7709 | G660DTJ |
| 7703 | G642CHF | | | | | | | | |

7722	F102TML	Volvo Citybus B10M-50	Alexander RV	B47/29D	1989	Londonlinks, 1997
7731	F111TML	Volvo Citybus B10M-50	Alexander RV	B47/29D	1989	Londonlinks, 1997
7734	F114TML	Volvo Citybus B10M-50	Alexander RV	B47/29D	1989	Londonlinks, 1997
7764w	E164OMD	Volvo Citybus B10M-50	Alexander RV	B47/37F	1988	Boro'line, Maidstone, 1992

AD1-8
Dennis Arrow   East Lancashire Pyoneer B45/35F   1996

| 1 | N801TPK | 3 | N803TPK | 5 | N805TPK | 7 | N807TPK | 8 | N808TPK |
| 2 | N802TPK | 4 | N804TPK | 6 | N806TPK | | | | |

| AD10 | N810TPK | Dennis Arrow | East Lancashire Pyoneer | BC45/31F | 1996 | |
| AN262 | KPJ262W | Leyland Atlantean AN68B/1R | Roe | B43/30F | 1981 | Londonlinks, 1997 |

| DD5w | F605RPG | Dennis Dominator DDA1026 | East Lancashire | B45/31F | 1989 | |
| DD8w | F608RPG | Dennis Dominator DDA1026 | East Lancashire | B45/31F | 1989 | |

DD10-16
Dennis Dominator DDA2005*   East Lancashire   B45/31F   1993-96 *13-16 are DDA2004; 10-12 Mayne, 1996

| 10 | K36XNE | 12 | K38YVM | 14 | N714TPK | 15 | N715TPK | 16 | N716TPK |
| 11 | K37XNE | 13 | N713TPK | | | | | | |

DD17-22
Dennis Dominator DDA1031*   East Lanacshire   B43/25F   1989-90 North Western, 1997
                                                             *19 is type DDA1026

| 17 | G626EKA | 19 | F631BKD | 20 | G663FKA | 21 | G664FKA | 22 | G665FKA |
| 18 | G628EKA | | | | | | | | |

DFD1-13
DAF DE23RSDB250   Northern Counties Palatine 2 B43/24D   1998

1	R201CKO	4	R204CKO	7	R207CKO	10	R210CKO	12	R212CKO
2	R201CKO	5	R205CKO	8	R208CKO	11	R211CKO	13	R213CKO
3	R201CKO	6	R206CKO	9	R209CKO				

LR14	TPD114X	Leyland Olympian ONLXB/1R	Roe		B43/29F	1982	
LR28	TPD128X	Leyland Olympian ONLXB/1R	Roe		B43/29F	1982	
LR501	G501SFT	Leyland Olympian ONCL10/1R	Northern Counties		B47/30F	1989	Kentish Bus, 1992
LR502	G502SFT	Leyland Olympian ONCL10/1R	Northern Counties		B43/29F	1989	Kentish Bus, 1992
LR503	G503SFT	Leyland Olympian ONCL10/1R	Northern Counties		B43/29F	1989	Kentish Bus, 1992
LR504	G504SFT	Leyland Olympian ONCL10/1R	Northern Counties		B43/29F	1989	Kentish Bus, 1992

| M168 | BYX168V | MCW Metrobus DR101/9 | MCW | B43/28D | 1979 | London South, 1999 |

M388-717

| | | MCW Metrobus DR101/14* | MCW | B43/28D | 1981-82 London South, 1999 |

388	GYE388W	548	GYE548W	614	KYO614X	658	KYO658X	709	KYV709X
395	GYE395W	551	GYE551W	615	KYO615X	660	KYO660X	717	KYV717X
417	GYE417W	559	GYE559W	648	KYO648X				

| M996 | A996SYF | MCW Metrobus DR101/17 | MCW | B43/28D | 1984 | London South, 1999 |

Heritage Vehicle:-

| RT3775 | NLE882 | AEC Regent III O961 | Park Royal | H30/26R | 1953 | preservation, 1994 |

Ancilliary vehicles:

A22	OLS540P	Leyland Leopard PSU3C/4R	Alexander AYS	BC53F	1975	Londonlinks, 1997
VCB89	C89NNV	Volvo B10M-61	Caetano Stagecoach	B57F	1986	Tellings-Golden Miller, 1995
BS407	YPH407T	Bedford YMT	Plaxton Supreme III	C53F	1978	Blue Saloon, Guildford, 1996
BS820	YPB820T	Bedford YMT	Plaxton Supreme III	C53F	1978	Blue Saloon, Guildford, 1996
	HNB27N	Leyland Atlantean AN68A/1R	Northern Counties	B43/27F	1974	
AN135	UPK135S	Leyland Atlantean AN68A/1R	Park Royal	B43/30F	1978	
ZFD257	NPJ478R	Leyland National 11351A/1R		B49F	1976	Alder Valley, 1990
SNB511	EPD511V	Leyland National 10351B/1R		B41F	1979	
P5	CVA110V	Bedford YMT	Plaxton Supreme IV	C53F	1980	New Enterprise, Tonbridge, 1995
P9	AKP430T	Bedford YMT	Plaxton Supreme IV	C53F	1978	New Enterprise, Tonbridge, 1995
P10	FKM713L	Leyland Atlantean PDR1/1	MCW	O45/33F	1972	
ZDT40	A829JLT	Mercedes-Benz L609D	Mercedes-Benz	M10	1984	private owner, 1987
P43	D387VKJ	Renault-Dodge S56	?	B/F	1986	
P44	E836BKL	Renault-Dodge S56	?	B/F	1987	
ZFB136	E136KYW	MCW MetroRider MF150/38	MCW	B25F	1987	Londonlinks, 1997
P49	E141KYW	MCW MetroRider MF150/38	MCW	B25F	1987	Londonlinks, 1997
P50	E145KYW	MCW MetroRider MF150/38	MCW	B25F	1987	Londonlinks, 1997
ZDT954	D954VCN	Freight Rover Sherpa	Dormobile	B16F	1986	Londonlinks, 1997
YFB42	E42UKL	Mercedes-Benz 609D	Reeve Burgess	B20F	1987	
YFB58	E58UKL	Mercedes-Benz L608D	Reeve Burgess	B20F	1989	
YFB69	G69PKR	Mercedes-Benz L608D	Reeve Burgess	B20F	1989	
YFB70	G70PKR	Mercedes-Benz L608D	Reeve Burgess	B20F	1989	
YFB72	G72PKR	Mercedes-Benz L608D	Reeve Burgess	B20F	1989	
ZDT252	JCK852W	Leyland 2 NL106AL11/1R	East Lancs Greenway (1991)	B44F	1981	North Western, 1991
ZDT339	SIB6709	Leyland NL106AL11/1R	East Lancs Greenway(1992)	B41F	1981	Londonlinks, 1997
ZDT341	SIB6711	Leyland 10351/1R/SC	East Lancs Greenway(1992)	B41F	1975	Londonlinks, 1997
ZDT343	SIB6713	Leyland 1051/1R/0402	East Lancs Greenway(1992)	B41F	1974	Londonlinks, 1997
ZDT344	SIB6714	Leyland 10351/R/SC	East Lancs Greenway(1992)	B41F	1974	Londonlinks, 1997

Named vehicles: 2830 *Silver Fox*; 2831 *Silver Link*

Previous Registrations:

494WYA	A420HND, 507EXA, A268MEH	PDZ6265	GPJ891N	TSU644	FKL174Y
544XVW	A184MKE	RDZ4278	JOX481P	TSU645	FLK173Y
J60MPS	J457JFS, J10FTG	SJI5066	NEN961R	UJI2337	C205PPE, XSV691, C895YKJ
L80MPS	L140FOJ	SJI5571	SCK709P	UJI2338	G897EDH
L503HKM	L10FUG	SJI5572	LPF601P	UJI2339	C202PPE, XSV689,C894YKJ
LIL2168	SGR134R	TIB5901	E301UUB, HIL2280,E848WWU	YSU872	G795RNC
LIL2180	KPA375P	TIB5903	E316OPR	YSU873	G796RNC
PDZ6263	NOE562R	TIB5904	E319OPR	YSU895	A114EPA
PDZ6264	ERP551T	TIB5905	C261SPC	YSU897	A140EPA

Allocations and liveries

Cranleigh (Mansfield Park) - West Sussex

Lance	LS20	LS21	LS22	LS23	LS24
Dominator	DD19	DD20	DD21	DD22	

Crawley (Wheatstone Close) - West Sussex

Mercedes-Benz	422	466	467					
Dart	DS1	DS2	DS8	DSL68	DSL69	DSL70	DSL71	DSL72
	DSL73	DSL74	DSL75	DSL76	DSL77	DSL86	DSL87	DSL88
	DSL89	DSL101	DSL102	DSL103	DSL104			
Volvo B6	V205	V209	V210	V211	V212			
National	202	265	SNB420					
Greenway	373	374	375	376	377	379		
Olympian	LR14	LR28	LR502	LR503	LR504			
Volvo Citybus	617	622						
Arrow	AD1	AD2	AD3	AD4	AD5	AD6	AD7	AD8
	AD10							

Croydon (Beddington Farm Road) - Croydon & North Surrey

Mercedes-Benz	430	431	433	434	435	436	437	
MetroRider	440	441	442	443				
Dart	DS22	DS23	DS24	DS120	DS121	DS122	DS123	DS124
	DS125	DS126	DS151	DP160	DP161	DP162	DP163	DS164
	DS165	DS166	DS167	DS168	DS169	DS170	DS171	DS172
National	366	372						
Lance	LS10	LS11	LS12	LS13	LS14	LS15	LS16	LS17
	LS18	LS19						
Atlantean	AN262							
Olympian	694	695	696	697	698	699	700	701
	702	703	704					
Volvo Citybus	618	619	620	629	640	643		

Dartford (Central Road) - Kent Thameside

MetroRider	1448	1449	1450	1801	1802	1803	1804	1805
	1806	1807	1808	1974	1975	1978		
Mercedes	1154							
Dart	3112	3128	3139	3140	3141	3146	3148	3149
	3150	3152	3159	3179	3217	3261	3262	3263
	3264	3265	3266	3267	3268	3269	3270	3271
	3272							
Lynx	3059	3061	3062	3063	3064	3065		
Citybus	7702	7703	7706	7707	7708	7709	7722	

Gillingham (Nelson Road) - Kent & Sussex

Mercedes-Benz	1073	1075	1078	1079	1080	1082	1085	1086
	1101	1102	1103	1104	1105	1107	1108	1109
	1110	1112	1113	1114	1115	1116	1117	1118
	1119	1120	1121	1122	1123	1124	1204	1205
	1217							
MetroRider	1961	1962	1970	1973				
Dart	3099	3100	3174	3175	3178	3180	3182	3183
	3213	3214	3216	3219	3220	3221	3223	3224
	3225	3226	3227	3228	3229	3230	3231	3232
	3233	3234	3235	3236	3237	3238	3239	3240
	3241	3242	3243	3244	3245			
Lynx	3052	3057	3058					
Olympian	5765	5766	5767	5768	5769	5770	5911	5912
	5913	5914	5915	5916	5917	5919	5920	5921
	5938	5939	5940	5941	5942	5943		
Citybus	7631	7632	7633	7634	7635	7636	7637	7638
	7639	7640	7641	7642	7643			

Guildford (Leas Road) - Guildford & West Surrey

Mercedes-Benz	423	427	469	MM480				
Dart	DS14	DS15	DSL25	DSL26	DSL32	DSL33	DSL34	DSL35
	DSL36	DSL78	DSL79	DSL80	DSL81	DSL82	DSL85	DSL97
	DSL98	DSL99	DSL100	DSL105	DSL107	DSL108	DS173	DS174
	DS175	DS176	DS178	DS179	DS181	DS182		
National	LNB28							
Dominator	DD10	DD11	DD12	DD13	DD14	DD15	DD16	DD17
	DD18							

Hawkhurst (Sandhurst Road) - Kent & Sussex

Outstation at Tenterden

Mercedes-Benz	1351	1352						
Dart	3107	3167	3168	3169				
Volvo B6	3614	3615						
Tiger	2174							
Lynx	3047							
Bristol VR	5846							
Olympian	5888	5889	5890	5898	5899	5900	5922	5923
	5924	5925						

Hounslow (Albion Road) - Croydon & North Surrey

Mercedes-Benz	189	190	402	405	MM473	MM474	
MetroRider	MR472	969					
Dart	DS10	DS11	DS12	DS13	DS16	DS17	DS18

Leatherhead (Guildford Road) - Croydon & North Surrey

Dart	DSL90	DSL91	DSL92	DSL93	DSL94	DSL95	DSL96	
Lance	LSL5	LSL6	LSL7	LSL8	LSL9			
National	378	380						
Volvo Citybus	610	611	612	613	614	615	616	
DAF/Palatine	DFD1	DFD2	DFD3	DFD4	DFD5	DFD6	DFD7	DFD8
	DFD9	DFD10	DFD11	DFD12	DFD13			

Gillingham's allocation contains 5941, P941MLK which was photographed at Maidstone while carrying lettering for service 101. The vehicle is a Northern Counties-bodied Volvo Olympian from a batch of eighteen delivered in 1997. *Gerry Mead*

Maidstone (Armstrong Road) - Kent & Sussex

Mercedes-Benz	1201	1202	1203	1210				
Volvo	2844	2845	2846	2847	2848			
DAF	2903	2904	2905	2906	2907	2908	2909	2910
Dart	3101	3102	3163	3164	3166	3170	3171	3176
	3177	3181	3192	3193	3194	3195	3196	3201
	3202	3203	3204	3205	3206	3207	3208	3209
	3210	3211	3212	3215	3246	3247	3701	3702
	3703	3704	3705	3706				
Lynx	3045	3046	3048	3049				
Bristol VR	5125	5877						
Metrobus	5201	5202	5203	5204	5205	5207	5208	5209
	5210							
Olympian	5891	5909	5910	5926	5927	5928	5929	5930
	5931	5932	5933	5934	5935	5936	5937	

Merstham (Station Road) - Croydon & North Surrey

Mercedes-Benz	428	MM475	MM476	MM477	MM479			
Volvo B6	V201	V202	V203	V204	V206	V207	V208	512
	513	514	515	516				
Tiger	TP91							
National	SNB331							
Greenway	363	364	365	371				
Volvo Citybus	623	624	625	626	627	628	630	

The 1999 Arriva Bus Handbook

Pictured at Woolwich while operating Kent Thameside's service 272 is Volvo Citybus 7702, G641CHF. The vehicle is one of several transferred to London & Country from North Western. Interestingly, more than half of this batch, comprising those vehicles that latterly operated with Londonlinks, has been renumbered into the main numbering scheme. *Richard Godfrey*

Northfleet (London Road) - Kent Thameside

MetroRider	1444	1445	1446	1447	1452	1453	1809	1810
	1811	1812	1813	1814	1852	1887		
Dart	3113	3129	3130	3131	3132	3133	3134	3135
	3136	3137	3138	3142	3143	3144	3145	3153
	3154	3155	3156	3157	3158	3186	3187	3188
	3189	3190	3191	3218				
Lynx	3053	3054						
Scania	3250	3251	3252	3253	3254	3255	3256	3257
	3258	3259						
National	3492	3493	3494					
Coach	2830							
Atlantean	6270	6277						
Olympian	5557	5558	5559	5561	5562	5754	5755	5756

Sheerness (Bridge Road) - Kent & Sussex

Tiger	2172							
Bristol VR	5863	5864						
Olympian	5751	5752	5753	5757	5758	5759	5760	5761
	5918							

Sittingbourne (Crown Quay Lane) - Kent & Sussex

Mercedes-Benz	1207	1208	1209	1211	1212	1213	1214	1215
	1216							
Dart	3165	3197	3198	3199				

Tonbridge (Cannon Bridge Works, Cannon Lane) - New Enterprise

Mercedes-Benz	1301	1360						
Volvo B6	3619							
Coach	2031	2192	2193	2194	2195	2196	2210	2211
	2214	2831	2835	2842	2843	2851	2899	2900
	2901	2902						
Bristol VR	5133	5826	5830	5868				

Tunbridge Wells (St John's Road) - Kent & Sussex; Kent Thameside

Mercedes-Benz	1071	1206	1218	1219	1220	1221	1223	1224
	1225	1226	1227	1228	1229	1230		
MetroRider	1451	1977						
Volvo B6	3601	3602	3603	3604	3605	3606	3607	3608
	3609	3610	3611	3612	3613	3616	3617	3618
Dart	3103	3104	3105	3106	3184	3185		
Lynx	3040	3041	3042	3043	3044	3051	3060	3066
	3067	3068						
Bristol VR	5831	5853	5869					
Olympian	5892	5893	5894	5895	5896	5897	5901	5902
	5903	5904	5905	5906	5907	5908		

Horsham (Warnham Station) - West Sussex

Mercedes-Benz	132	154			
Dart	DSL37				
National	LNB600				
Volvo B6	DS4	DS7			
Olympian	LR501	901	907	908	910

Woking (Goldsworth Park Industrial Estate) - Guildford & West Surrey

Mercedes-Benz	461	462	463	464					
Volvo B6	DS3	DS5	DS6	DS9	DS19	DS20	DS21		
Dart	DSL27	DSL28	DSL29	DSL30	DSL31	DSL38	DSL39	DSL40	
	DSL41	DSL42	DSL43	DSL45	DSL46	DSL47	DSL48	DSL49	
	DSL50	DSL51	DSL52	DSL53	DSL54	DSL55	DSL84		

Withdrawn and unallocated

Mercedes-Benz	113	201	MM438	1041	1046	1074	1636	1680
MetroRider	1886	1889	1890					
Iveco	1713	1714	1740					
Coach	2184	2213	2852					
Dart	DSL44	DSL106						
National	368							
Lynx	400	LL418	3056					
Bristol VR	5111	5112	5137	5138	5139	5824	5827	5828
	5832	5848	5852	5867	5870	5878	5882	5883
	5885	5886						
Atlantean	6172	6220	6232	6274	6283			
Fleetline	6666		Heritage		RT3775			
Olympian	5563	5564	5565	5601	5608	5620		
Volvo Citybus	621	7764		Dominator		DD5	DD8	
Metrobus	M168	M388	M395	M417	M548	M551	M559	M614
	M615	M648	M658	M660	M709	M717	M996	

UNIBUS

Unibus, København, Denmark.

10B	NU 97 824	Volvo B10M		C49F	1985	Acquired 1998
15B	LC 92 311	Volvo B10M		C47F	1983	Acquired 1998
17B	MY 90 746	Mercedes-Benz 608D	Mercedes-Benz	M16	19	Acquired 1998
22B	JH 90 189	Volvo B10M		C47F	1982	Acquired 1998
23B	MZ 90 944	Volvo B10M		C57F	1981	Acquired 1998
24B	MY 90 923	Mercedes-Benz 307	Mercedes-Benz	C14FL	1984	Acquired 1998
26B	NN 91 567	Volvo B10M		C49F	1984	Acquired 1998
32B	NM 94 111	DAB-	DAB	C51F	1981	Acquired 1998
12	KR 89 881	Volvo B10M		C42D	1986	SAS Livery
14	KR 89 880	Volvo B10M		C42D	1986	SAS Livery
16	LJ 96 639	Volvo B10M		C42D	1986	SAS Livery
17	LP 94 320	Volvo B10M		C42D	1986	SAS Livery
18	LM 90 737	Volvo B10M		C42D	1986	SAS Livery
19	LP 94 306	Volvo B10M		C42D	1986	SAS Livery
20	LJ 96 640	Volvo B10M		C42D	1986	SAS Livery
21	MC 94 113	Volvo B10M		C42D	1986	SAS Livery
22	MC 94 114	Volvo B10M		C42D	1986	SAS Livery
23	MC 94 115	Volvo B10M		C42D	1986	SAS Livery
24	MC 94 116	Volvo B10M		C42D	1986	SAS Livery
25	MC 94 117	Volvo B10M		C42D	1986	SAS Livery
63	KU 91 015	Leyland-DAB 7-1200L	DAB	B37D	1986	
66	LT 91 504	DAF-DAB 7-1200L	DAB	B37D	1989	
67	LT 91 505	DAF-DAB 7-1200L	DAB	B37D	1989	
68	NY 93 040	Leyland-DAB 7-1200L	DAB	B37D	1984	
70	LY 91 088	DAF-DAB 7-1200L	DAB	B37D	1989	
74	ML 93 782	Leyland-DAB 7-1200L	DAB	B37D	1984	
75	NY 93 318	Leyland-DAB 7-1200L	DAB	B37D	1984	
79	NJ 97 904	DAF-DAB 7-1200L	DAB	B37D	1990	
80	NJ 97 905	DAF-DAB 7-1200L	DAB	B37D	1990	
81	NY 93 044	MAN	MRK 2	B37D	1994	
82	NY 93 045	MAN	MRK 2	B37D	1994	
83	NX 92 949	MAN	MRK 2	B37D	1994	
84	NX 92 950	MAN	MRK 2	B37D	1994	
85	NX 92 951	MAN	MRK 2	B37D	1994	
86	NX 92 952	MAN	MRK 2	B37D	1994	
87	NZ 93 971	MAN	MRK 2	B37D	1995	
88	NZ 93 972	MAN	MRK 2	B37D	1995	
89	OM 90 436	MAN	MRK 2	B35D	1994	
90	OS 89 278	MAN	MRK 2	B37D	1996	
151	ME 94 576	DAB-Silkeborg 11-0860S	DAB	B37D	1990	Hovedstadsområdets Trafikselskab,
155	MY 91 485	DAB-Silkeborg 11-0860S	DAB	B37D	1992	Hovedstadsområdets Trafikselskab,
156	MY 91 486	DAB-Silkeborg 11-0860S	DAB	B37D	1992	Hovedstadsområdets Trafikselskab,
165	MN 92 651	DAB-Silkeborg 11-0860S	DAB	B37D	1991	Hovedstadsområdets Trafikselskab,
166	NJ 89 343	DAB-Silkeborg 11-0860S	DAB	B37D	1993	Linjebuss
170	MY 91 536	DAB-Silkeborg 11-0860S	DAB	B37D	1992	Linjebuss
171	MY 91 537	DAB-Silkeborg 11-0860S	DAB	B37D	1992	Linjebuss
175	NJ 97 918	DAB-Silkeborg 11-0860S	DAB	B37D	1993	Hovedstadsområdets Trafikselskab,
7016	MB 92 556	Leyland-DAB 7-2	DAB	B..D	1983	Søndergaard, Fjerritslev, 1993
7018	MB 92 555	Leyland-DAB 7-1200L	DAB	B..D	1985	Kirsten Jensen, Hallund, 1998
7019	MB 92 527	Leyland-DAB 7-1200L	DAB	B..D	1984	
7026	MV 95 774	Scania N113CLB	WIIMA K202L	B35D	1992	
7027	MV 95 777	Scania N113CLB	WIIMA K202L	B35D	1992	
7028	MV 95 782	Scania N113CLB	WIIMA K202L	B35D	1992	
7029	MV 95 794	Scania N113CLB	WIIMA K202L	B35D	1992	
7030	MV 95 793	Scania N113CLB	WIIMA K202L	B35D	1992	
7036	MV 91 360	DAB-Silkeborg 7-1200B	DAB RS2001	B34D	1992	
7037	MV 91 402	DAB-Silkeborg 7-1200B	DAB RS2001	B34D	1992	
7038	MV 91 401	DAB-Silkeborg 7-1200B	DAB RS2001	B34D	1992	
7039	MS 91 259	Leyland-DAB 7-1200B	DAB	B33D	1986	
7040	MY 91 327	Leyland-DAB 7-1200B	DAB	B35D	1986	

7045	NC 97 438	DAB-Silkeborg 7-1200B	DAB RS2001	B26T	1993
7046	NC 97 439	DAB-Silkeborg 7-1200B	DAB RS2001	B26T	1993
7047	NC 97 440	DAB-Silkeborg 7-1200B	DAB RS2001	B26T	1993
7048	NC 97 441	DAB-Silkeborg 7-1200B	DAB RS2001	B26T	1993
7049	NR 96 580	DAB-Silkeborg 7-1200B	DAB RS2001	B35T	1986
7051	NJ 89 354	DAB-Silkeborg 7-1200B	DAB RS2001	B26T	1993
7052	NJ 89 355	DAB-Silkeborg 7-1200B	DAB RS2001	B26T	1993
7053	NJ 89 356	DAB-Silkeborg 7-1200B	DAB RS2001	B26T	1993
7054	NJ 97 966	DAB-Silkeborg 7-1200B	DAB RS2001	B26T	1993
7055	NJ 97 967	DAB-Silkeborg 7-1200B	DAB RS2001	B26T	1993
7056	NJ 97 968	DAB-Silkeborg 7-1200B	DAB RS2001	B26T	1993
7057	NN 96 579	Leyland-DAB 7-1200B	DAB 1200L	B35T	1989
7058	NN 96 576	Leyland-DAB 7-1200B	DAB 1200L	B35T	1988
7059	NR 96 580	Leyland-DAB 7-1200L	DAB	B35T	1986
7060	NR 96 578	Leyland-DAB 7-1200L	DAB	B35T	1986 .. 1994
7061	NN 97 769	Leyland-DAB 7-1200B	DAB 1200L	B35T	1986
7062	NR 96 577	Leyland-DAB 7-1200B	DAB 1200L	B35T	1987
7063	NR 96 575	Leyland-DAB 7-1200B	DAB 1200L	B35T	1987
7064	NR 96 581	DAB-Silkeborg 7-1200B	DAB	B41T	1989
7070	NR 96 626	DAB 7-1200B	DAB 1200L	B35T	1985
7071	NR 96 600	DAB 7-1200B	DAB 1200L	B35T	1989
7072	NR 96 555	DAB-Silkeborg 12-1200B	DAB	B30T	1994
7073	NR 96 556	DAB-Silkeborg 12-1200B	DAB	B30T	1994
7074	NR 96 557	DAB-Silkeborg 12-1200B	DAB	B30T	1994
7075	NR 96 558	DAB-Silkeborg 12-1200B	DAB	B30T	1994
7076	NR 96 559	DAB-Silkeborg 12-1200B	DAB	B30T	1994
7077	NR 96 601	Leyland-DAB 7-1200B	DAB 1200L	B35T	1985
7078	NR 96 602	Leyland-DAB 7-1200B	DAB 1200L	B35T	1985
7079	NR 96 603	Leyland-DAB 7-1200B	DAB 1200L	B35T	1986
7080	NR 96 622	Leyland-DAB 7-1200B	DAB 1200L	B35T	1986
7081	NR 96 641	Leyland-DAB 7-1200B	DAB 1200L	B35T	1986
7082	NR 96 642	Leyland-DAB 7-1200B	DAB 1200L	B35T	1986
7083	NN 96 604	Leyland-DAB 7-1200B	DAB 1200L	B35T	1987
7084	NR 96 627	Leyland-DAB 7-1200B	DAB 1200L	B35T	1988
7085	NS 91 555	Leyland-DAB 7-1200B	DAB 1200L	B41T	1988
7086	NR 96 624	Leyland-DAB 7-1200B	DAB 1200L	B41T	1988
7087	NR 96 625	Scania N112CL	Aabenraa	B38T	1987
7088	NR 96 589	DAB-Silkeborg 15-1200C	DAB Citybus 2	B35T	1994
7089	NR 96 590	DAB-Silkeborg 15-1200C	DAB Citybus 2	B35T	1994
7090	NR 96 591	DAB-Silkeborg 15-1200C	DAB Citybus 2	B35T	1994
7091	NR 96 592	DAB-Silkeborg 15-1200C	DAB Citybus 2	B35T	1994
7092	NR 96 593	DAB-Silkeborg 15-1200C	DAB Citybus 2	B35T	1994
7093	NR 96 594	DAB-Silkeborg 15-1200C	DAB Citybus 2	B35T	1994
7094	NR 96 595	DAB-Silkeborg 15-1200C	DAB Citybus 2	B35T	1994
7095	NR 96 618	DAB-Silkeborg 15-1200C	DAB Citybus 2	B35T	1994
7096	NR 96 619	DAB-Silkeborg 15-1200C	DAB Citybus 2	B35T	1994
7097	NR 96 620	DAB-Silkeborg 15-1200C	DAB Citybus 2	B35T	1994
7098	NR 96 643	DAB-Silkeborg 15-1200C	DAB Citybus 2	B35T	1994
7099	NR 96 621	DAB-Silkeborg 15-1200C	DAB Citybus 2	B35T	1994
7100	NR 96 674	DAB-Silkeborg 15-1200C	DAB Citybus 2	B35T	1994
7101	NS 95 940	DAB-Silkeborg 15-1200C	DAB Citybus 2	B35T	1994
7102	NS 95 941	DAB-Silkeborg 15-1200C	DAB Citybus 2	B35T	1994
7103	NS 95 942	DAB-Silkeborg 15-1200C	DAB Citybus 2	B35T	1994
7104	NS 95 943	DAB-Silkeborg 15-1200C	DAB Citybus 2	B35T	1994
7105	NS 95 944	DAB-Silkeborg 15-1200C	DAB Citybus 2	B35T	1994
7106	NS 95 973	DAB-Silkeborg 15-1200C	DAB Citybus 2	B35T	1994
7107	NS 95 974	DAB-Silkeborg 15-1200C	DAB Citybus 2	B35T	1994
7108	NS 96 987	DAB-Silkeborg 15-1200C	DAB Citybus 2	B35T	1994
7109	NS 95 988	DAB-Silkeborg 15-1200C	DAB Citybus 2	B35T	1994
7110	NS 95 989	DAB-Silkeborg 15-1200C	DAB Citybus 2	B35T	1994
7111	NS 95 990	DAB-Silkeborg 15-1200C	DAB Citybus 2	B35T	1994
7112	NS 96 012	DAB-Silkeborg 15-1200C	DAB Citybus 2	B35T	1994
7113	NS 96 013	DAB-Silkeborg 15-1200C	DAB Citybus 2	B35T	1994
7114	NS 96 034	DAB-Silkeborg 15-1200C	DAB Citybus 2	B35T	1994
7115	NS 96 035	DAB-Silkeborg 15-1200C	DAB Citybus 2	B35T	1994
7116	NS 96 052	DAB-Silkeborg 15-1200C	DAB Citybus 2	B35T	1994
7117	NS 96 053	DAB-Silkeborg 15-1200C	DAB Citybus 2	B35T	1994
7118	NS 96 073	DAB-Silkeborg 15-1200C	DAB Citybus 2	B35T	1994
7119	NS 96 074	DAB-Silkeborg 15-1200C	DAB Citybus 2	B35T	1994
7122	NV 93 256	DAB-Silkeborg 15-1200C	DAB Citybus 2	B28T	1994

Unibus operate a proportion of the city services in Copenhagen, which are operated on a tendering scheme. Vehicle are painted in the required yellow scheme. Pictured in the Danish capital some time ago, and not one of the present Arriva vehicles is a standard DAB emblazoned with a British Airways overall advertisement.
Bill Potter

7127	NY 90 312	Mercedes-Benz 602	Mercedes-Benz	B9C	1995	
7128	NY 90 313	Mercedes-Benz 602	Mercedes-Benz	B9C	1995	
7129	NY 90 314	Mercedes-Benz 602	Mercedes-Benz	B9C	1995	
7130	NY 90 315	Mercedes-Benz 602	Mercedes-Benz	B9C	1995	
7131	NY 90 316	Mercedes-Benz 602	Mercedes-Benz	B9C	1995	
7132	NY 90 317	Mercedes-Benz 602	Mercedes-Benz	B9C	1995	
7133	NY 90 318	Mercedes-Benz 602	Mercedes-Benz	B9C	1995	
7136	NZ 95 428	Mercedes-Benz 602	Mercedes-Benz	B9C	1995	
7137	NZ 95 429	Mercedes-Benz 602	Mercedes-Benz	B9C	1995	
7138	NU 91 449	Mercedes-Benz 602	Mercedes-Benz	B9C	1995	
7143	OL 88 190	Volvo B10L-60	Säffle-Aabenraa	B29T	1996	
7144	OL 88 191	Volvo B10L-60	Säffle-Aabenraa	B29T	1996	
7145	OL 88 192	Volvo B10L-60	Säffle-Aabenraa	B29T	1996	
7146	PC 95 824	Volvo B10L-60	Säffle-Aabenraa	B30T	1996	
7147	OL 88 194	Volvo B10L-60	Säffle-Aabenraa	B29T	1996	
7148	OL 88 238	Volvo B10L-60	Säffle-Aabenraa	B29T	1996	
7149	OL 88 239	Volvo B10L-60	Säffle-Aabenraa	B29T	1996	
7150	OL 88 240	Volvo B10L-60	Säffle-Aabenraa	B29T	1996	
7151	OL 88 241	Volvo B10L-60	Säffle-Aabenraa	B29T	1996	
7152	OL 88 242	Volvo B10L-60	Säffle-Aabenraa	B29T	1996	
7153	OL 88 243	Volvo B10L-60	Säffle-Aabenraa	B29T	1996	
7154	OL 88 250	Volvo B10L-60	Säffle-Aabenraa	B29T	1996	
7155	OL 88 260	Volvo B10L-60	Säffle-Aabenraa	B29T	1996	
7156	OL 88 261	Volvo B10L-60	Säffle-Aabenraa	B29T	1996	
7157	OL 88 262	Volvo B10L-60	Säffle-Aabenraa	B29T	1996	
7158	OL 88 279	Volvo B10L-60	Säffle-Aabenraa	B29T	1996	
7159	OL 88 280	Volvo B10L-60	Säffle-Aabenraa	B29T	1996	
7160	NY 90 163	Mercedes-Benz 309D	Mercedes-Benz	B9CL	1995	
7161	HV 89 713	Volvo B10M-70	Säffle		1982	Vejle, 1996
7162	HV 89 714	Volvo B10M-70	Säffle		1982	Vejle, 1996
7163	JC 94 330	Leyland-DAB 7-2	DAB		1983	Vejle, 1996
7165	JK 93 651	Leyland-DAB 7-1200B	DAB		1984	Vejle, 1996
7166	OM 94 884	Mercedes-Benz 309D	Mercedes-Benz	M..	1982	
7167	JR 89 516	Volvo B10M-70	Säffle		1996	Vejle, 1996

7168	HP 91 335	Leyland-DAB LS575-690	DAB		1981	Vejle, 1996
7169	OU 96 504	Mercedes-Benz Sprinter 312TD	Mercedes-Benz	B9CL	1997	
7170	OU 96 508	Mercedes-Benz Sprinter 312TD	Mercedes-Benz	B9CL	1997	
7171	OU 96 503	Mercedes-Benz Sprinter 312TD	Mercedes-Benz	B9CL	1997	
7172	OU 96 506	Mercedes-Benz Sprinter 312TD	Mercedes-Benz	B9CL	1997	
7173	OU 96 490	Mercedes-Benz Sprinter 312TD	Mercedes-Benz	B9CL	1997	
7174	OU 96 501	Mercedes-Benz Sprinter 312TD	Mercedes-Benz	B9CL	1997	
7175	OU 96 489	Mercedes-Benz Sprinter 312TD	Mercedes-Benz	B9CL	1997	
7176	OU 96 509	Mercedes-Benz Sprinter 312TD	Mercedes-Benz	B9CL	1997	
7177	OU 96 505	Mercedes-Benz Sprinter 312TD	Mercedes-Benz	B9CL	1997	
7178	OU 96 502	Mercedes-Benz Sprinter 312TD	Mercedes-Benz	B9CL	1997	
7179	OU 96 510	Mercedes-Benz Sprinter 312TD	Mercedes-Benz	B9CL	1997	
7180	OU 96 512	Mercedes-Benz Sprinter 312TD	Mercedes-Benz	B9CL	1997	
7181	OU 96 511	Mercedes-Benz Sprinter 312TD	Mercedes-Benz	B9CL	1997	
7182	OU 96 507	Mercedes-Benz Sprinter 312TD	Mercedes-Benz	B9CL	1997	
7183	OU 96 578	Mercedes-Benz Sprinter 312TD	Mercedes-Benz	B9CL	1997	
7184	OU 96 571	Mercedes-Benz Sprinter 312TD	Mercedes-Benz	B9CL	1997	
7185	OX 90 560	Mercedes-Benz Sprinter 312TD	Mercedes-Benz	B9CL	1997	
7186	OU 96 647	Mercedes-Benz Sprinter 312TD	Mercedes-Benz	B9CL	1997	
7187	OX 90 566	Mercedes-Benz Sprinter 312TD	Mercedes-Benz	B9CL	1997	
7188	OX 90 518	Mercedes-Benz Sprinter 312TD	Mercedes-Benz	B9CL	1997	
7189	OU 96 661	Mercedes-Benz Sprinter 312TD	Mercedes-Benz	B9CL	1997	
7190	OX 90 486	Mercedes-Benz Sprinter 312TD	Mercedes-Benz	B9CL	1997	
7191	OU 96 660	Mercedes-Benz Sprinter 312TD	Mercedes-Benz	B9CL	1997	
7192	OU 96 662	Mercedes-Benz Sprinter 312TD	Mercedes-Benz	B9CL	1997	
7193	OU 96 648	Mercedes-Benz Sprinter 312TD	Mercedes-Benz	B9CL	1997	
7194	OX 90 567	Mercedes-Benz Sprinter 312TD	Mercedes-Benz	B9CL	1997	
7195	OX 90 510	Mercedes-Benz Sprinter 312TD	Mercedes-Benz	B9CL	1997	
7196	OX 90 636	Mercedes-Benz Sprinter 312TD	Mercedes-Benz	B9CL	1997	
7197	OX 90 635	Mercedes-Benz Sprinter 312TD	Mercedes-Benz	B9CL	1997	
7198	OX 90 633	Mercedes-Benz Sprinter 312TD	Mercedes-Benz	B9CL	1997	
7199	OX 90 632	Mercedes-Benz Sprinter 312TD	Mercedes-Benz	B9CL	1997	
7200	OX 90 698	Mercedes-Benz Sprinter 312TD	Mercedes-Benz	B9CL	1997	
7201	KU 90 832	DAB-Silkeborg 15-1200C	DAB Citybus	B38D	1994	
7202	KU 90 813	DAB-Silkeborg 15-1200C	DAB Citybus	B38D	1994	
7203	KU 90 811	DAB-Silkeborg 15-1200C	DAB Citybus	B38D	1994	
7204	KU 90 814	DAB-Silkeborg 15-1200C	DAB Citybus	B38D	1994	
7205	OZ 90 990	DAB-Silkeborg 15-1200C	DAB Citybus	B38D	1994	
7206	NB 97 584	DAB-Silkeborg 15-1200C	DAB Citybus	B37T	1992	
7207	NB 97 585	DAB-Silkeborg 15-1200C	DAB Citybus	B37T	1992	
7208	NR 96 200	Volvo B10L-60		B39T	1994	
7209	NN 91 908	Volvo B10L-60		B39T	1994	
7210	NX 90 841	Volvo B10L-60		B39T	1994	
7211	OB 94 391	Volvo B10L-60	Säffle-Aabenraa	B34T	1995	
7212	OL 88 346	Volvo B10L-60	Säffle-Aabenraa	B34T	1996	
7213	OV 92 039	Volvo B10L-60	Säffle-Aabenraa	B34T	1997	

Livery: Operations within Københaven carry Hovedstadsområdets Trafikselskab's yellow livery onto which Unibus have applied a blue and white striped banner to the roof-line. The open-top double-decks operate as 'Copenhagen Pride' in a red and grey livery.

Operations:

Gilleleje Turistart AF 1994:-

7165	7167	7168

Unibus Handicapbefordring A/s

7127	7128	7129	7130	7131	7132	7133	7136	7137	7138
7139	7140	7160	7166	7169	7170	7171	7172	7173	7174
7175	7176	7177	7178	7179	7180	7181	7182	7183	7184
7186	7189	7191	7192	7193	+ 5 un-numbered and 2 undelivered				

Unibus Rutetrafik:- remainder

ARRIVA Groningen

Arriva Groningen, Sonweg 13, NL-9723 AT, Groningen, Nederlands

1	BN-56-XV	DAF SB201DKDL554	Hainje CSA-II	B32D	1985
2	BN-98-ZR	DAF SB201DKDL554	Hainje CSA-II	B32D	1985
3	BP-10-DV	DAF SB201DKDL554	Hainje CSA-II	B32D	1985
4	BP-44-FZ	DAF SB201DKDL554	Hainje CSA-II	B32D	1985
5	BP-08-GP	DAF SB201DKDL554	Hainje CSA-II	B32D	1985
6	BP-36-HP	DAF SB201DKDL554	Hainje CSA-II	B32D	1985
7	BP-38-HP	DAF SB201DKDL554	Hainje CSA-II	B32D	1985
8	BP-07-GP	DAF SB201DKDL554	Hainje CSA-II	B32D	1985
9	BS-94-ZG	DAF SB201DKDL554	Hainje CSA-II	B32D	1986
10	BS-95-ZG	DAF SB201DKDL554	Hainje CSA-II	B32D	1986
11	BS-96-ZG	DAF SB201DKDL554	Hainje CSA-II	B32D	1986
12	BT-86-BS	DAF SB201DKDL554	Hainje CSA-II	B32D	1986
13	BT-85-BS	DAF SB201DKDL554	Hainje CSA-II	B32D	1986
14	BT-84-BS	DAF SB201DKDL554	Hainje CSA-II	B32D	1986
15	BV-67-HF	DAF SB201DKDL554	Hainje CSA-II	B32D	1987
17	BV-16-JL	DAF SB201DKDL554	Hainje CSA-II	B32D	1987
18	BV-18-JL	DAF SB201DKDL554	Hainje CSA-II	B32D	1987
19	BV-68-HF	DAF SB201DKDL554	Hainje CSA-II	B32D	1987
20	BY-64-FJ	DAF SB220LD550	Hainje CAOV	B32D	1987
90	BJ-93-LS	DAF SB201DKDL554	Hainje CSA-II	B32D	1984
91	BJ-88-NJ	DAF SB201DKDL554	Hainje CSA-II	B32D	1984
92	BJ-85-NJ	DAF SB201DKDL554	Hainje CSA-II	B32D	1984
93	BJ-64-PF	DAF SB201DKDL554	Hainje CSA-II	B32D	1984
94	BJ-67-PF	DAF SB201DKDL554	Hainje CSA-II	B32D	1984
95	BJ-75-PZ	DAF SB201DKDL554	Hainje CSA-II	B32D	1984
96	BJ-85-PZ	DAF SB201DKDL554	Hainje CSA-II	B32D	1984
97	BJ-41-RT	DAF SB201DKDL554	Hainje CSA-II	B32D	1984
120	BY-85-FY	Mercedes-Benz O405	Mercedes-Benz	B30F	1987
123	VF-11-VX	Mercedes-Benz O405	Berkhof	B38F	1989
124	VF-52-XJ	Mercedes-Benz O405	Berkhof	B38F	1989
125	VG-24-BH	Mercedes-Benz O405	Berkhof	B38F	1989
126	VF-37-ZX	Mercedes-Benz O405	Berkhof	B38F	1989
127	VF-26-YS	Mercedes-Benz O405	Berkhof	B38F	1989
128	VF-25-YS	Mercedes-Benz O405	Berkhof	B38F	1989
129	VF-39-ZX	Mercedes-Benz O405	Berkhof	B38F	1989
130	VF-37-ZX	Mercedes-Benz O405	Berkhof	B38F	1989
131	VF-27-YS	Mercedes-Benz O405	Berkhof	B38F	1989
132	VG-19-BH	Mercedes-Benz O405	Berkhof	B38F	1989
133	VJ-58-LT	Mercedes-Benz O405G	Mercedes-Benz	AB49F	1990
134	VJ-77-TK	Mercedes-Benz O405G	Mercedes-Benz	AB49F	1990
135	VJ-71-ZV	Mercedes-Benz O405G	Mercedes-Benz	AB49F	1990
136	VJ-75-TK	Mercedes-Benz O405G	Mercedes-Benz	AB49F	1990
137	VN-59-GX	Mercedes-Benz O405G	Mercedes-Benz	AB49F	1991
138	VN-19-HG	Mercedes-Benz O405G	Mercedes-Benz	AB49F	1991
139	VN-72-JX	Mercedes-Benz O405	Mercedes-Benz	B38F	1991
140	VN-63-GX	Mercedes-Benz O405	Mercedes-Benz	B37F	1991
141	VN-15-HG	Mercedes-Benz O405	Mercedes-Benz	B37F	1991
142	VR-27-LR	Mercedes-Benz O405G	Mercedes-Benz	AB49F	1992
143	VR-12-JT	Mercedes-Benz O405G	Mercedes-Benz	AB49F	1992
144	VR-09-XS	Mercedes-Benz O405G	Mercedes-Benz	AB49F	1992
145	VR-13-XS	Mercedes-Benz O405G	Mercedes-Benz	AB49F	1992
146	VR-85-JS	Mercedes-Benz O405G	Mercedes-Benz	AB49F	1992
147	VR-98-JS	Mercedes-Benz O405G	Mercedes-Benz	AB49F	1992
148	VR-06-XS	Mercedes-Benz O405G	Mercedes-Benz	AB49F	1992
149	VR-09-LR	Mercedes-Benz O405G	Mercedes-Benz	AB49F	1992
150	VR-39-DF	Mercedes-Benz O405G	Mercedes-Benz	AB49F	1992
151	VR-58-FJ	Mercedes-Benz O405G	Mercedes-Benz	AB49F	1992
152	VR-10-LR	Mercedes-Benz O405G	Mercedes-Benz	AB49F	1992
153	VV-69-XH	Mercedes-Benz O405G	Mercedes-Benz	AB49F	1993
154	VV-72-XH	Mercedes-Benz O405G	Mercedes-Benz	AB49F	1993
155	VV-64-XH	Mercedes-Benz O405G	Mercedes-Benz	AB49F	1993
156	VV-99-XB	Mercedes-Benz O405G	Mercedes-Benz	AB49F	1993

157	VV-65-XH	Mercedes-Benz O405G	Mercedes-Benz	AB49F	1993	
200	BV-66-HF	DAF SB220DKDL554	Hainje CSA-II	B29D	1987	LPG bus
201	BD-FZ-03	DAF DE02LB SB220	Berkhof 2000NL	N36D	1995	LPG bus
202	BD-FZ-10	DAF DE02LB SB220	Berkhof 2000NL	N36D	1995	LPG bus
203	BD-FZ-01	DAF DE02LB SB220	Berkhof 2000NL	N36D	1995	LPG bus
204	BD-FZ-05	DAF DE02LB SB220	Berkhof 2000NL	N36D	1995	LPG bus
205	BD-FZ-08	DAF DE02LB SB220	Berkhof 2000NL	N36D	1995	LPG bus
206	BD-FZ-09	DAF DE02LB SB220	Berkhof 2000NL	N36D	1995	LPG bus

ARRIVA ZUID-LIMBURG

Arriva Zuid-Limburg, Mastrict.

900	RS-BG-36	Mercedes-Benz 212D-KA	Mercedes Sprinter/Kusters	M8	1997	Vancom, 1998
901	BB-ZN-39	DAF SB220LT575	Berkhof ST2000NL	B43D	1995	Vancom, 1998
902	BB-ZR-05	DAF SB220LT575	Berkhof ST2000NL	B43D	1995	Vancom, 1998
903	BB-ZL-95	DAF SB220LT575	Berkhof ST2000NL	B43D	1995	Vancam, 1998
904	BB-ZL-98	DAF SB220LT575	Berkhof ST2000NL	B43D	1995	Vancom, 1998
905	BB-ZN-37	DAF SB220LT575	Berkhof ST2000NL	B43D	1995	Vancom, 1998
906	BB-ZL-97	DAF SB220LT575	Berkhof ST2000NL	B43D	1995	Vancom, 1998
907	BB-ZL-96	DAF SB220LT575	Berkhof ST2000NL	B43D	1995	Vancom, 1998
908	BB-ZN-41	DAF SB220LT575	Berkhof ST2000NL	B43D	1995	Vancom, 1998
909	BB-ZL-93	DAF SB220LT575	Berkhof ST2000NL	B43D	1995	Vancom, 1998
910	BB-ZL-92	DAF SB220LT575	Berkhof ST2000NL	B43D	1995	Vancom, 1998
911	VF-14-VX	Mercedes-Benz O405	Mercedes-Benz	B38D	1989	Vancom, 1998
912	VF-51-XJ	Mercedes-Benz O405	Mercedes-Benz	B38D	1989	Vancom, 1998
913	VN-01-BS	Mercedes-Benz O408	Mercedes-Benz	B38D	1991	Veonn, 1999
914	BF-GJ-34	Iveco EuroRider 391.12.29A	Berkhof 2000NL	B44D+34	1997	Vancom, 1999
915	JG-RR-88	Mercedes-Benz 208D	Mercedes aanpassing Q-Bus	M8	1994	Vancom, 1998
949	BK-30-TT	Volvo B10R-55	Hainje CSA-II	B32D	1984	Vancom, 1997

Opposite:- **Limberg is the province in the south-west corner of Der Nederland, that forms a divide between Belgium and Germany. One of the main towns in the area is Maastricht, escallated to fame following the latest EU treaty. The upper picture shows Zuid Limberg's 912, VF-51-XJ, an integral Mercedes-Benz O405 complete with the current Arriva names. The principal model for the Zuid-Limberg duties are locally-produced Berkhof-bodied DAF SB220s.** *Arriva Nederland*

The first site of Arriva corporate colours appeared on Mercedes-Benz 139, VN-72-JX, when, by cleverly using a zip feature shows the new style being revealed under the former red colours. Repainting the fleet commenced as the this edition was going to press.
Fred Huppertz

ARRIVA NEDERLAND BV

This operation, Groninger Autobusdienst Onderneming (GAOD), has recently been acquired by Arriva and provides services in the provinces of Friesland, Groningen and Drenthe, through rural bus services and demand-response taxi. We appreciate the efforts of Arriva Nederlands and the Dutch enthusiast groups in the preparation of this listing.

VEONN

14	BB-TD-03	Iveco EuroRider 391.12.29A	Berkhof 3000NL	C49FT	1994
15	BB-GF-85	Bova FHD12.340	Bova Futura	C51FT	1994
16	VR-71-GZ	Bova FHD12.290	Bova Futura	C47FT	1992
19	VD-17-BH	Bova FHD12.290	Bova Futura	C49FT	1996
58	BB-HB-77	Mercedes-Benz O404/15RHD	Mercedes-Benz	C29T	1994
61	VT-95-VP	DAF SB3000	Berkhof Excellence 1000LD	C50FT	1993
62	VT-86-VP	DAF SB3000	Berkhof Excellence 1000LD	C50FT	1993
63	VT-82-VP	DAF SB3000	Berkhof Excellence 1000LD	C50FT	1993
64	BB-LV-58	Iveco 380.12.	Berkhof 3000NL	C49FT	1995
65	BD-BZ-68	DAF SBR3015	Berkhof Excellence 3000-15	C66FT	1995
66	BD-FV-42	Iveco 380	Iveco Orlandi	C49F	1995
67	BF-DH-41	Iveco 380	Iveco Orlandi	C45F	1995
68	BX-97-JS	DAF MB230DKVL615	Smit Joure	C52D+27	1987
450	VV-82-GZ	Bova FHD12.290	Bova Futura	C47FT	1993
451	VV-78-GZ	Bova FHD12.290	Bova Futura	C47FT	1993
452	VV-69-GZ	Bova FHD12.290	Bova Futura	C47FT	1993
453	BB-LT-71	Iveco 380.12.35 Euroclass	Berkhof Excellence 3000HD	C48FT	1994
454	BB-LT-69	Iveco 380.12.35 Euroclass	Berkhof Excellence 3000HD	C48FT	1994
455	BB-VN-42	Iveco 380.12.35 Euroclass	Berkhof Excellence 3000HD	C48FT	1995
456	BD-BZ-70	Iveco 380.12.35 Euroclass	Berkhof Excellence 3000HD	C40FT	1995
513	BB-85-DK	DAF MB220 DKDL564	Den Oudsten	B43D+36	1981
515	BB-97-DS	DAF MB220 DKDL564	Den Oudsten	B43D+36	1981
516	BD-42-PG	DAF MB220 DKDL564	Den Oudsten	B40D+41	1981
524	BD-02-NX	DAF MB220 DKDL564	Den Oudsten	B40D+41	1981
525	BD-93-NV	DAF MB220 DKDL564	Den Oudsten	B40D+41	1981
526	BD-08-NX	DAF MB220 DKDL564	Den Oudsten	B40D+41	1981
528	BD-48-PG	DAF MB220 DKDL564	Den Oudsten	B40D+41	1981
534	BG-76-JY	DAF MB220 DKDL564	Den Oudsten	B40D+42	1981
535	BG-73-KN	DAF MB220 DKDL564	Den Oudsten	B40D+42	1981
536	BJ-54-NZ	DAF MB220 DKDL564	Den Oudsten	B40D+42	1981
537	BJ-90-PV	DAF MB220 DKDL564	Den Oudsten	B40D+42	1981
878	BY-96-JV	Bova FHD12.290	Bova Futura	C58F	1987
1078	BD-BF-74	Volvo B10M-55	Den Oudsten Interliner	B35D+33	1995
1079	BD-BF-70	Volvo B10M-55	Den Oudsten Interliner	B35D+33	1995
1080	BD-BG-94	Volvo B10M-55	Berkhof 2000NL	B45D+34	1995
1081	BD-BG-33	Volvo B10M-55	Berkhof 2000NL	B45D+34	1995
1082	BD-BG-92	Volvo B10M-55	Berkhof 2000NL	B45D+34	1995
1083	BD-BG-26	Volvo B10M-55	Berkhof 2000NL	B45D+34	1995
1084	BD-BG-29	Volvo B10M-55	Berkhof 2000NL	B45D+34	1995
1085	BD-BG-98	Volvo B10M-55	Berkhof 2000NL	B45D+34	1995
1086	BD-BG-96	Volvo B10M-55	Berkhof 2000NL	B45D+34	1995
1087	BD-NN-44	Iveco EuroRider 391.12.29A	Berkhof 2000NL	B45D+34	1995
1088	BD-NN-21	Iveco EuroRider 391.12.29A	Berkhof 2000NL	B44D+34	1996
1089	BD-NN-51	Iveco EuroRider 391.12.29A	Berkhof 2000NL	B44D+34	1996
1090	BD-NN-46	Iveco EuroRider 391.12.29A	Berkhof 2000NL	B44D+34	1996
1091	BD-NN-47	Iveco EuroRider 391.12.29A	Berkhof 2000NL	B44D+34	1996
1092	BD-NN-48	Iveco EuroRider 391.12.29A	Berkhof 2000NL	B44D+34	1996
1093	BD-NN-49	Iveco EuroRider 391.12.29A	Berkhof 2000NL	B44D+34	1996
1094	BD-NN-50	Iveco EuroRider 391.12.29A	Berkhof 2000NL	B44D+34	1996
1095	BD-NN-52	Iveco EuroRider 391.12.29A	Berkhof 2000NL	B44D+34	1996
1096	BD-NN-42	Iveco EuroRider 391.12.29A	Berkhof 2000NL	B44D+34	1996
1138	BD-JB-29	Iveco EuroRider	Den Oudsten B89	B45D+31	1995
1139	BD-HV-12	Iveco EuroRider	Den Oudsten B89	B45D+31	1995
1140	BD-HV-13	Iveco EuroRider	Den Oudsten B89	B45D+31	1995
1141	BD-HV-14	Iveco EuroRider	Den Oudsten B89	B45D+31	1995
1142	BD-JB-28	Iveco EuroRider	Den Oudsten B89	B45D+31	1995
1143	BD-NV-24	Iveco EuroRider	Den Oudsten B89	B45D+31	1995
1144	BD-JP-95	Iveco EuroRider	Den Oudsten B89	B45D+31	1995

1145	BD-JP-96	Iveco EuroRider	Den Oudsten B89	B45D+31	1995
1146	BD-JP-94	Iveco EuroRider	Den Oudsten B89	B45D+31	1995
1147	BD-NV-26	Iveco EuroRider	Den Oudsten B89	B45D+31	1995
1254	BD-ZJ-61	Den Oudsten	Den Oudsten B96	AB32D+62	1996
1255	BD-ZJ-52	Den Oudsten	Den Oudsten B96	AB32D+62	1996
1256	BD-ZJ-51	Den Oudsten	Den Oudsten B96	AB32D+62	1996
1257	BD-ZJ-66	Den Oudsten	Den Oudsten B96	AB32D+62	1996
1279	BF-GJ-28	Iveco EuroRider 391.12.29A	Berkhof 2000NL	B44D+34	1997
1280	BF-GJ-38	Iveco EuroRider 391.12.29A	Berkhof 2000NL	B44D+34	1997
1281	BF-GJ-36	Iveco EuroRider 391.12.29A	Berkhof 2000NL	B44D+34	1997
1282	BF-GJ-34	Iveco EuroRider 391.12.29A	Berkhof 2000NL	B44D+34	1997
1283	BF-GJ-31	Iveco EuroRider 391.12.29A	Berkhof 2000NL	B44D+34	1997
1284	BF-GJ-30	Iveco EuroRider 391.12.29A	Berkhof 2000NL	B44D+34	1997
1285	BF-GJ-29	Iveco EuroRider 391.12.29A	Berkhof 2000NL	B44D+34	1997
1286	BF-GJ-26	Iveco EuroRider 391.12.29A	Berkhof 2000NL	B44D+34	1997
1287	BF-GJ-86	Iveco EuroRider 391.12.29A	Berkhof 2000NL	B44D+34	1997
1288	BF-GJ-13	Iveco EuroRider 391.12.29A	Berkhof 2000NL	B44D+34	1997
1989	BN-69-JN	DAF Midi	?		1985
1994	BP-32-VY	DAF Midi	?		1986
2217	BF-XV-78	Den Oudsten OM580	Den Oudsten B95	B45D+32	1997
2218	BF-XV-24	Den Oudsten OM580	Den Oudsten B95	B45D+32	1997
2219	BF-XV-23	Den Oudsten OM580	Den Oudsten B95	B45D+32	1997
2220	BF-XV-22	Den Oudsten OM580	Den Oudsten B95	B45D+32	1997
2221	BF-XV-21	Den Oudsten OM580	Den Oudsten B95	B45D+32	1997
3500	BN-18-PT	DAF MB200 DKDL600	Den Oudsten	B45D/33	1985
3501	BN-16-PT	DAF MB200 DKDL600	Den Oudsten	B45D/33	1985
3502	BN-13-PT	DAF MB200 DKDL600	Den Oudsten	B45D/33	1985
3503	BN-14-PT	DAF MB200 DKDL600	Den Oudsten	B45D/33	1985
3504	BN-55-RG	DAF MB200 DKDL600	Den Oudsten	B45D/33	1985
3505	BN-51-RG	DAF MB200 DKDL600	Den Oudsten	B45D/33	1985
3506	BN-48-RG	DAF MB200 DKDL600	Den Oudsten	B45D/33	1985
3507	BN-45-RG	DAF MB200 DKDL600	Den Oudsten	B45D/33	1985
3508	BN-96-RN	DAF MB200 DKDL600	Den Oudsten	B45D/33	1985
3509	BN-33-SK	DAF MB200 DKDL600	Den Oudsten	B45D/33	1985
3510	BN-34-SK	DAF MB200 DKDL600	Den Oudsten	B45D/33	1985
3511	BN-35-SK	DAF MB200 DKDL600	Den Oudsten	B45D/33	1985
3512	BN-32-SK	DAF MB200 DKDL600	Den Oudsten	B45D/33	1985
3513	BN-03-SZ	DAF MB200 DKDL600	Den Oudsten	B45D/33	1985
3514	BN-76-SY	DAF MB200 DKDL600	Den Oudsten	B45D/33	1985
3515	BN-73-SY	DAF MB200 DKDL600	Den Oudsten	B45D/33	1985
3516	BN-65-SY	DAF MB200 DKDL600	Den Oudsten	B45D/33	1985
3517	BN-59-SY	DAF MB200 DKDL600	Den Oudsten	B45D/33	1985
3518	BN-30-TJ	DAF MB200 DKDL600	Den Oudsten	B45D/33	1985
3581	BP-76-NJ	DAF MB200 DKDL600	Den Oudsten	B47D/28	1986
3582	BR-22-PN	DAF MB200 DKDL600	Den Oudsten	B47D/28	1986
3583	BR-19-PN	DAF MB200 DKDL600	Den Oudsten	B47D/28	1986
3584	BR-41-SK	DAF MB200 DKDL600	Den Oudsten	B47D/28	1986
3585	BR-59-TD	DAF MB200 DKDL600	Den Oudsten	B47D/28	1986
3596	BP-20-TR	DAF MB200 DKDL600	Den Oudsten	B44D/34	1986
3597	BP-56-SV	DAF MB200 DKDL600	Den Oudsten	B44D/34	1986
3598	BP-53-SV	DAF MB200 DKDL600	Den Oudsten	B44D/34	1986
3599	BP-44-SV	DAF MB200 DKDL600	Den Oudsten	B44D/34	1986
3600	BP-94-TT	DAF MB200 DKDL600	Den Oudsten	B44D/34	1986
3601	BP-96-TT	DAF MB200 DKDL600	Den Oudsten	B44D/34	1986
3602	BP-89-TT	DAF MB200 DKDL600	Den Oudsten	B44D/34	1986
3603	BP-86-VS	DAF MB200 DKDL600	Den Oudsten	B44D/34	1986
3604	BP-94-VS	DAF MB200 DKDL600	Den Oudsten	B44D/34	1986
3605	BP-96-VS	DAF MB200 DKDL600	Den Oudsten	B44D/34	1986
3606	BP-01-VT	DAF MB200 DKDL600	Den Oudsten	B44D/34	1986
3607	BP-45-VY	DAF MB200 DKDL600	Den Oudsten	B44D/34	1986
3608	BP-50-VY	DAF MB200 DKDL600	Den Oudsten	B44D/34	1986
3609	BP-43-VY	DAF MB200 DKDL600	Den Oudsten	B44D/34	1986
3610	BP-02-XN	DAF MB200 DKDL600	Den Oudsten	B44D/34	1986
3654	BS-51-GD	DAF MB200 DKDL600	Den Oudsten	B44D/34	1986
3655	BS-02-FP	DAF MB200 DKDL600	Den Oudsten	B44D/34	1986
3656	BS-01-FP	DAF MB200 DKDL600	Den Oudsten	B44D/34	1986
3657	BS-52-GD	DAF MB200 DKDL600	Den Oudsten	B44D/34	1986
3658	BS-37-GT	DAF MB200 DKDL600	Den Oudsten	B44D/34	1986
3659	BS-38-GT	DAF MB200 DKDL600	Den Oudsten	B44D/34	1986
3660	BS-71-HL	DAF MB200 DKDL600	Den Oudsten	B44D/34	1986
3661	BS-74-HL	DAF MB200 DKDL600	Den Oudsten	B44D/34	1986
3662	BS-60-HT	DAF MB200 DKDL600	Den Oudsten	B44D/34	1986
3663	BS-52-JN	DAF MB200 DKDL600	Den Oudsten	B44D/34	1986

Pictured in Veonn livery is 1143, BD-HV-24, one of the Den Oudsten B89-bodied Iveco EuroRider models that joined the fleet in 1995. The body style retaines features that Den Oudsten have used in their integral design.
Fred Huppertz

3665	BS-49-JN	DAF MB200 DKDL600	Den Oudsten	B44D/34	1986
3666	BS-50-JN	DAF MB200 DKDL600	Den Oudsten	B44D/34	1986
3667	BS-19-RB	DAF MB200 DKDL600	Den Oudsten	B44D/34	1986
3754	BV-48-KJ	DAF MB200 DKDL600	Den Oudsten	B47D/28	1987
3755	BV-49-KJ	DAF MB200 DKDL600	Den Oudsten	B47D/28	1987
3756	BV-47-KJ	DAF MB200 DKDL600	Den Oudsten	B47D/28	1987
3757	BV-65-KT	DAF MB200 DKDL600	Den Oudsten	B47D/28	1987
3815	BV-78-VD	DAF MB200 DKDL600	Den Oudsten	B44D/36	1987
3816	BV-85-VR	DAF MB200 DKDL600	Den Oudsten	B44D/36	1987
3817	BV-86-VR	DAF MB200 DKDL600	Den Oudsten	B44D/36	1987
3818	BV-22-XP	DAF MB200 DKDL600	Den Oudsten	B44D/36	1987
3819	BV-23-XP	DAF MB200 DKDL600	Den Oudsten	B44D/36	1987
3820	BV-24-XP	DAF MB200 DKDL600	Den Oudsten	B44D/36	1987
3821	BV-25-XP	DAF MB200 DKDL600	Den Oudsten	B44D/36	1987
3822	BV-21-XP	DAF MB200 DKDL600	Den Oudsten	B44D/36	1987
3823	BV-73-XX	DAF MB200 DKDL600	Den Oudsten	B44D/36	1987
3824	BV-25-YS	DAF MB200 DKDL600	Den Oudsten	B44D/36	1987
3825	BV-72-XX	DAF MB200 DKDL600	Den Oudsten	B44D/36	1987
3826	BV-71-XX	DAF MB200 DKDL600	Den Oudsten	B44D/36	1987
3827	BV-26-YS	DAF MB200 DKDL600	Den Oudsten	B44D/36	1987
3828	BV-27-YS	DAF MB200 DKDL600	Den Oudsten	B44D/36	1987
3829	BV-28-YS	DAF MB200 DKDL600	Den Oudsten	B44D/36	1987
3884	BY-83-LJ	DAF MB200 DKDL600	Den Oudsten	B44D/36	1987
3885	BY-81-LJ	DAF MB200 DKDL600	Den Oudsten	B44D/36	1987
3886	BY-82-LJ	DAF MB200 DKDL600	Den Oudsten	B44D/36	1987
3887	BY-85-LJ	DAF MB200 DKDL600	Den Oudsten	B44D/36	1987
3888	BY-84-LJ	DAF MB200 DKDL600	Den Oudsten	B44D/36	1987
3889	BY-45-ND	DAF MB200 DKDL600	Den Oudsten	B44D/36	1987
3890	BY-75-TK	DAF MB200 DKDL600	Den Oudsten	B44D/36	1988
3891	BY-97-TK	DAF MB200 DKDL600	Den Oudsten	B44D/36	1988
3892	BY-96-TK	DAF MB200 DKDL600	Den Oudsten	B44D/36	1988
3893	BY-68-VV	DAF MB200 DKDL600	Den Oudsten	B44D/36	1988

3893	BY-68-VV	DAF MB200 DKDL600	Den Oudsten		B44D/36	1988
3894	BY-53-XB	DAF MB200 DKDL600	Den Oudsten		B44D/36	1988
3935	BY-51-XB	DAF MB200 DKDL584	Zabo		B44D/36	1984
3936	BY-52-XB	DAF MB200 DKDL584	Zabo		B44D/36	1984
3943	BH-68-LG	DAF MB200 DKDL584	Zabo		B44D/36	1984
3944	BJ-58-KF	DAF MB200 DKDL584	Zabo		B44D/36	1984
3945	BJ-77-HY	DAF MB200 DKDL584	Zabo		B44D/36	1984
3946	BJ-96-TT	DAF MB200 DKDL584	Zabo		B49D/33	1984
3947	BJ-16-SP	DAF MB200 DKDL600	Zabo		B49D/33	1984
3948	BN-95-SY	DAF MB200 DKDL600	Zabo		B49D/33	1985
3949	BN-75-XR	DAF MB200 DKDL600	Zabo		B49D/33	1985
3998	BP-91-BL	DAF MB200 DKDL600	Zabo		B49D/33	1985
3999	BP-22-GJ	DAF MB200 DKDL600	Zabo		B49D/33	1985
4014	BZ-71-SV	DAF MB230 LC615	Den Oudsten B88		B45D+31	1988
4015	BZ-74-SV	DAF MB230 LC615	Den Oudsten B88		B45D+31	1988
4016	BZ-73-SV	DAF MB230 LC615	Den Oudsten B88		B45D+31	1988
4017	BZ-72-SV	DAF MB230 LC615	Den Oudsten B88		B45D+31	1988
4018	BZ-46-SP	DAF MB230 LC615	Den Oudsten B88		B45D+31	1988
4019	BZ-45-SP	DAF MB230 LC615	Den Oudsten B88		B45D+31	1988
4020	BZ-47-SP	DAF MB230 LC615	Den Oudsten B88		B45D+31	1988
4021	BZ-48-SP	DAF MB230 LC615	Den Oudsten B88		B45D+31	1988
4022	BZ-49-SP	DAF MB230 LC615	Den Oudsten B88		B45D+31	1988
4023	BZ-50-SP	DAF MB230 LC615	Den Oudsten B88		B45D+31	1988
4024	BZ-44-SP	DAF MB230 LC615	Den Oudsten B88		B45D+31	1988
4025	BZ-94-VJ	DAF MB230 LC615	Den Oudsten B88		B45D+31	1988
4039	BZ-03-ZV	DAF MB230 LC615	Den Oudsten B88		B45D+31	1988
4040	BZ-04-ZV	DAF MB230 LC615	Den Oudsten B88		B45D+31	1988
4041	BZ-05-ZV	DAF MB230 LC615	Den Oudsten B88		B45D+31	1988
4042	BZ-06-ZV	DAF MB230 LC615	Den Oudsten B88		B45D+31	1988
4043	BZ-07-ZV	DAF MB230 LC615	Den Oudsten B88		B45D+31	1988
4044	BZ-98-ZT	DAF MB230 LC615	Den Oudsten B88		B45D+31	1988
4045	VB-71-BN	DAF MB230 LC615	Den Oudsten B88		B45D+31	1988
4046	VB-35-BY	DAF MB230 LC615	Den Oudsten B88		B45D+31	1988
4047	VB-73-BN	DAF MB230 LC615	Den Oudsten B88		B45D+31	1988
4048	VB-26-DY	DAF MB230 LC615	Den Oudsten B88		B47D+29	1988
4049	VB-25-DY	DAF MB230 LC615	Den Oudsten B88		B47D+29	1988
4065	VB-98-KJ	DAF MB230 LC615	Den Oudsten B88		B45D+31	1988
4066	VB-97-KJ	DAF MB230 LC615	Den Oudsten B88		B45D+31	1988
4067	VB-96-KJ	DAF MB230 LC615	Den Oudsten B88		B45D+31	1988
4068	VB-95-KJ	DAF MB230 LC615	Den Oudsten B88		B45D+31	1988
4069	VB-94-KJ	DAF MB230 LC615	Den Oudsten B88		B45D+31	1988
4070	VB-92-KJ	DAF MB230 LC615	Den Oudsten B88		B45D+31	1988
4071	VB-93-KJ	DAF MB230 LC615	Den Oudsten B88		B45D+31	1988
4072	VB-91-KJ	DAF MB230 LC615	Den Oudsten B88		B45D+31	1988
4073	VB-66-KJ	DAF MB230 LC615	Den Oudsten B88		B45D+31	1988
4074	VB-34-KS	DAF MB230 LC615	Den Oudsten B88		B45D+31	1988
4075	VB-65-KJ	DAF MB230 LC615	Den Oudsten B88		B45D+31	1988
4076	VB-64-KJ	DAF MB230 LC615	Den Oudsten B88		B45D+31	1988
4116	VF-37-JG	DAF MB230 LC615	Den Oudsten B88		B45D+32	1989
4117	VF-11-HY	DAF MB230 LC615	Den Oudsten B88		B45D+32	1989
4118	VF-06-HY	DAF MB230 LC615	Den Oudsten B88		B45D+32	1989
4119	VF-71-HX	DAF MB230 LC615	Den Oudsten B88		B45D+32	1989
4120	VF-14-HY	DAF MB230 LC615	Den Oudsten B88		B45D+32	1989
4121	VF-21-HY	DAF MB230 LC615	Den Oudsten B88		B45D+32	1989
4122	VF-20-HY	DAF MB230 LC615	Den Oudsten B88		B45D+32	1989
4123	VF-18-HY	DAF MB230 LC615	Den Oudsten B88		B45D+32	1989
4142	VF-16-GH	DAF MB230 LC615	Den Oudsten B88		B47D+31	1989
4143	VF-08-GH	DAF MB230 LC615	Den Oudsten B88		B47D+31	1989
4144	VF-12-GH	DAF MB230 LC615	Den Oudsten B88		B47D+31	1989
4145	VF-74-GG	DAF MB230 LC615	Den Oudsten B88		B45D+32	1989
4146	VF-99-GG	DAF MB230 LC615	Den Oudsten B88		B45D+32	1989
4147	VF-95-GG	DAF MB230 LC615	Den Oudsten B88		B45D+32	1989
4148	VF-92-GG	DAF MB230 LC615	Den Oudsten B88		B45D+32	1989
4149	VF-86-GG	DAF MB230 LC615	Den Oudsten B88		B45D+32	1989
4150	VF-02-GH	DAF MB230 LC615	Den Oudsten B88		B45D+32	1989
4151	VF-27-GK	DAF MB230 LC615	Den Oudsten B88		B45D+32	1989
4152	VF-94-GG	DAF MB230 LC615	Den Oudsten B88		B45D+32	1989
4153	VF-87-GG	DAF MB230 LC615	Den Oudsten B88		B45D+32	1989
4154	VF-32-PP	DAF MB230 LC615	Den Oudsten B88		B45D+32	1989
4155	VF-91-NP	DAF MB230 LC615	Den Oudsten B88		B45D+32	1989
4233	VH-91-JX	DAF MB230 LC615	Den Oudsten B88		B41D+31	1990
4234	VH-01-JY	DAF MB230 LC615	Den Oudsten B88		B41D+31	1990
4239	VH-69-HF	DAF MB230 LC615	Den Oudsten B88		B45D+32	1990

4240	VH-72-HF	DAF MB230 LC615	Den Oudsten B88	B45D+32	1990
4241	VH-31-HG	DAF MB230 LC615	Den Oudsten B88	B45D+32	1990
4242	VH-35-HG	DAF MB230 LC615	Den Oudsten B88	B45D+32	1990
4243	VH-42-HG	DAF MB230 LC615	Den Oudsten B88	B45D+32	1990
4244	VH-44-HG	DAF MB230 LC615	Den Oudsten B88	B45D+32	1990
4245	VH-88-HF	DAF MB230 LC615	Den Oudsten B88	B45D+32	1990
4246	VH-92-HF	DAF MB230 LC615	Den Oudsten B88	B45D+32	1990
4247	VH-93-HF	DAF MB230 LC615	Den Oudsten B88	B45D+32	1990
4248	VH-94-HF	DAF MB230 LC615	Den Oudsten B88	B45D+32	1990
4249	VH-92-KD	DAF MB230 LC615	Den Oudsten B88	B45D+32	1990
4250	VH-89-KB	DAF MB230 LC615	Den Oudsten B88	B45D+32	1990
4251	VH-94-KD	DAF MB230 LC615	Den Oudsten B88	B45D+32	1990
4299	VS-31-RB	Mercedes-Benz O408	Mercedes-Benz/Zabo	B49D+31	1992
4300	VH-29-NK	DAF MB230 LC615	Den Oudsten B88	B45D+32	1990
4301	VH-32-NK	DAF MB230 LC615	Den Oudsten B88	B45D+32	1990
4302	VH-33-NK	DAF MB230 LC615	Den Oudsten B88	B45D+32	1990
4303	VH-04-NX	DAF MB230 LC615	Den Oudsten B88	B45D+32	1990
4304	VH-35-NK	DAF MB230 LC615	Den Oudsten B88	B45D+32	1990
4305	VH-37-SV	DAF MB230 LC615	Den Oudsten B88	B45D+32	1990
4306	VH-27-TF	DAF MB230 LC615	Den Oudsten B88	B45D+32	1990
4307	VH-26-SV	DAF MB230 LC615	Den Oudsten B88	B45D+32	1990
4308	VH-25-SV	DAF MB230 LC615	Den Oudsten B88	B45D+32	1990
4309	VH-23-SV	DAF MB230 LC615	Den Oudsten B88	B45D+32	1990
4310	VH-35-SV	DAF MB230 LC615	Den Oudsten B88	B45D+32	1990
4311	VH-18-SV	DAF MB230 LC615	Den Oudsten B88	B45D+32	1990
4327	VH-93-VX	DAF MB230 LC615	Den Oudsten B88	B45D+32	1990
4328	VH-82-XG	DAF MB230 LC615	Den Oudsten B88	B45D+32	1990
4437	VK-65-TS	Mercedes-Benz O408	Mercedes-Benz/Zabo	B49D+31	1991
4438	VK-05-VN	Mercedes-Benz O408	Mercedes-Benz/Zabo	B49D+31	1991
4439	VK-01-VN	Mercedes-Benz O408	Mercedes-Benz/Zabo	B49D+31	1991
4440	VK-12-YN	Mercedes-Benz O408	Mercedes-Benz/Zabo	B49D+31	1991
4441	VK-19-ZZ	Mercedes-Benz O408	Mercedes-Benz/Zabo	B49D+31	1991
4442	VK-21-ZZ	Mercedes-Benz O408	Mercedes-Benz/Zabo	B49D+31	1991
4443	VL-60-PB	Mercedes-Benz O408	Mercedes-Benz/Zabo	B49D+31	1991
4444	VL-62-LD	Mercedes-Benz O408	Mercedes-Benz/Zabo	B49D+31	1991
4445	VL-13-SB	Mercedes-Benz O408	Mercedes-Benz/Zabo	B49D+31	1991
4446	VL-11-SB	Mercedes-Benz O408	Mercedes-Benz/Zabo	B49D+31	1991
4447	VL-57-PG	Mercedes-Benz O408	Mercedes-Benz/Zabo	B49D+31	1991
4448	VL-97-GG	Mercedes-Benz O408	Mercedes-Benz/Zabo	B49D+31	1991
4449	VL-99-GG	Mercedes-Benz O408	Mercedes-Benz/Zabo	B49D+31	1991
4450	VL-35-JB	Mercedes-Benz O408	Mercedes-Benz/Zabo	B49D+31	1991
4451	VL-40-LN	Mercedes-Benz O408	Mercedes-Benz/Zabo	B49D+31	1991
4452	VL-49-LS	Mercedes-Benz O408	Mercedes-Benz/Zabo	B49D+31	1991
4453	VL-30-TV	Mercedes-Benz O408	Mercedes-Benz/Zabo	B49D+31	1991
4454	VN-85-NN	Mercedes-Benz O408	Mercedes-Benz/Zabo	B49D+31	1991
4455	VL-29-SY	Mercedes-Benz O408	Mercedes-Benz/Zabo	B49D+31	1991
4456	VN-71-BB	Mercedes-Benz O408	Mercedes-Benz/Zabo	B49D+31	1991
4457	VN-01-BS	Mercedes-Benz O408	Mercedes-Benz/Zabo	B49D+31	1991
4458	VN-09-DF	Mercedes-Benz O408	Mercedes-Benz/Zabo	B49D+31	1991
4459	VN-77-DL	Mercedes-Benz O408	Mercedes-Benz/Zabo	B49D+31	1991
4460	VN-75-DL	Mercedes-Benz O408	Mercedes-Benz/Zabo	B49D+31	1991
4461	VN-61-DL	Mercedes-Benz O408	Mercedes-Benz/Zabo	B49D+31	1991
4462	VL-01-GH	Mercedes-Benz O408	Mercedes-Benz/Zabo	B49D+31	1991
4463	VL-98-GG	Mercedes-Benz O408	Mercedes-Benz/Zabo	B49D+31	1991
4464	VL-45-GG	Mercedes-Benz O408	Mercedes-Benz/Zabo	B49D+31	1991
4465	VL-62-PB	Mercedes-Benz O408	Mercedes-Benz/Zabo	B49D+31	1991
4466	VL-03-SZ	Mercedes-Benz O408	Mercedes-Benz/Zabo	B49D+31	1991
4467	VN-68-BB	Mercedes-Benz O408	Mercedes-Benz/Zabo	B49D+31	1991
4468	VL-31-TV	Mercedes-Benz O408	Mercedes-Benz/Zabo	B49D+31	1991
4469	VL-25-SY	Mercedes-Benz O408	Mercedes-Benz/Zabo	B49D+31	1991
4470	VL-19-VH	Mercedes-Benz O408	Mercedes-Benz/Zabo	B49D+31	1991
4471	VN-69-GF	Mercedes-Benz O408	Mercedes-Benz/Zabo	B49D+31	1991
4472	VN-63-GF	Mercedes-Benz O408	Mercedes-Benz/Zabo	B49D+31	1991
4473	VL-81-NZ	Mercedes-Benz O408	Mercedes-Benz/Zabo	B49D+31	1991
4474	VL-36-JB	Mercedes-Benz O408	Mercedes-Benz/Zabo	B49D+31	1991
4475	VL-14-SB	Mercedes-Benz O408	Mercedes-Benz/Zabo	B49D+31	1991
4476	VL-37-LN	Mercedes-Benz O408	Mercedes-Benz/Zabo	B49D+31	1991
4477	VL-33-VV	Mercedes-Benz O408	Mercedes-Benz/Zabo	B49D+31	1991
4478	VN-03-BS	Mercedes-Benz O408	Mercedes-Benz/Zabo	B49D+31	1991
4479	VN-61-DF	Mercedes-Benz O408	Mercedes-Benz/Zabo	B49D+31	1991
4480	VN-07-DF	Mercedes-Benz O408	Mercedes-Benz/Zabo	B49D+31	1991
4481	VN-80-FF	Mercedes-Benz O408	Mercedes-Benz/Zabo	B49D+31	1991
4482	VN-62-DL	Mercedes-Benz O408	Mercedes-Benz/Zabo	B49D+31	1991

Den Oudsten introduced the Alliance single-deck bus around the time Optare launched the Delta, both using the DAF SB220 chassis. The Alliance is also available on the articulated version and has been successful in exporting the type to tendered operations, notable at Wansee between Berlin and Potsdam where they carry Berlin livery. Shown here in Veonn's white livery is 4840, BB-NL-23. *Fred Huppertz*

4484	VL-87-PG	Mercedes-Benz O408	Mercedes-Benz/Zabo	B49D+31	1991
4485	VL-86-PG	Mercedes-Benz O408	Mercedes-Benz/Zabo	B49D+31	1991
4486	VL-02-SZ	Mercedes-Benz O408	Mercedes-Benz/Zabo	B49D+31	1991
4487	VL-21-VH	Mercedes-Benz O408	Mercedes-Benz/Zabo	B49D+31	1991
4488	VN-74-BB	Mercedes-Benz O408	Mercedes-Benz/Zabo	B49D+31	1991
4489	VN-64-DL	Mercedes-Benz O408	Mercedes-Benz/Zabo	B49D+31	1991
4577	VL-49-SY	DAF MB230 LC615	Den Oudsten B88	B47D+31	1991
4578	VL-52-SY	DAF MB230 LC615	Den Oudsten B88	B47D+31	1991
4579	VL-47-SY	DAF MB230 LC615	Den Oudsten B88	B45D+34	1991
4596	VL-05-SB	DAF MB230 LC615	Den Oudsten B88	B45D+34	1991
4597	VL-04-SB	DAF MB230 LC615	Den Oudsten B88	B45D+34	1991
4598	VL-01-SB	DAF MB230 LC615	Den Oudsten B88	B45D+34	1991
4599	VL-98-RZ	DAF MB230 LC615	Den Oudsten B88	B45D+34	1991
4600	VL-96-RZ	DAF MB230 LC615	Den Oudsten B88	B45D+34	1991
4601	VL-38-TL	DAF MB230 LC615	Den Oudsten B88	B45D+34	1991
4602	VL-20-SB	DAF MB230 LC615	Den Oudsten B88	B45D+34	1991
4603	VR-03-GJ	DAF MB230 LO615	Den Oudsten Alliance	B45D+34	1992
4604	VR-58-HH	DAF MB230 LO615	Den Oudsten Alliance	B45D+34	1992
4605	VR-11-GJ	DAF MB230 LO615	Den Oudsten Alliance	B45D+34	1992
4606	VR-09-GJ	DAF MB230 LO615	Den Oudsten Alliance	B45D+34	1992
4607	VR-06-GJ	DAF MB230 LO615	Den Oudsten Alliance	B45D+34	1992
4608	VR-18-GN	DAF MB230 LO615	Den Oudsten Alliance	B45D+34	1992
4609	VR-24-GN	DAF MB230 LO615	Den Oudsten Alliance	B45D+34	1992
4610	VR-21-GN	DAF MB230 LO615	Den Oudsten Alliance	B45D+34	1992
4611	VR-22-GN	DAF MB230 LO615	Den Oudsten Alliance	B45D+34	1992
4612	VR-27-GN	DAF MB230 LO615	Den Oudsten Alliance	B45D+34	1992
4613	VR-30-GN	DAF MB230 LO615	Den Oudsten Alliance	B45D+34	1992
4614	VR-28-GN	DAF MB230 LO615	Den Oudsten Alliance	B45D+34	1992
4615	VP-80-XJ	DAF MB230 LO615	Den Oudsten Alliance	B45D+34	1992
4616	VP-44-XJ	DAF MB230 LO615	Den Oudsten Alliance	B45D+34	1992
4617	VP-77-XJ	DAF MB230 LO615	Den Oudsten Alliance	B45D+34	1992
4618	VP-72-XJ	DAF MB230 LO615	Den Oudsten Alliance	B45D+34	1992

4618	VP-72-XJ	DAF MB230 LO615	Den Oudsten Alliance	B45D+34	1992
4619	VP-48-XJ	DAF MB230 LO615	Den Oudsten Alliance	B45D+34	1992
4620	VP-53-XJ	DAF MB230 LO615	Den Oudsten Alliance	B45D+34	1992
4621	VP-12-XN	DAF MB230 LO615	Den Oudsten Alliance	B45D+34	1992
4622	VP-56-XJ	DAF MB230 LO615	Den Oudsten Alliance	B45D+34	1992
4623	VP-59-XK	DAF MB230 LO615	Den Oudsten Alliance	B45D+34	1992
4624	VP-43-XK	DAF MB230 LO615	Den Oudsten Alliance	B45D+34	1992
4625	VP-78-XX	DAF MB230 LO615	Den Oudsten Alliance	B45D+34	1992
4626	VP-60-XJ	DAF MB230 LO615	Den Oudsten Alliance	B45D+34	1992
4627	VP-64-XJ	DAF MB230 LO615	Den Oudsten Alliance	B45D+34	1992
4628	VP-41-XJ	DAF MB230 LO615	Den Oudsten Alliance	B45D+34	1992
4629	VP-14-YP	DAF MB230 LO615	Den Oudsten Alliance	B45D+34	1992
4630	VP-05-YP	DAF MB230 LO615	Den Oudsten Alliance	B45D+34	1992
4631	VP-78-YN	DAF MB230 LO615	Den Oudsten Alliance	B45D+34	1992
4632	VP-61-YN	DAF MB230 LO615	Den Oudsten Alliance	B45D+34	1992
4700	VR-23-GJ	DAF MB230 LO615	Den Oudsten Alliance	B45D+34	1992
4701	VR-25-GJ	DAF MB230 LO615	Den Oudsten Alliance	B45D+34	1992
4735	VS-75-LN	Mercedes-Benz O408	Mercedes-Benz/Zabo	B49D+31	1992
4736	VS-84-LN	Mercedes-Benz O408	Mercedes-Benz/Zabo	B49D+31	1992
4738	VV-14-XD	Volvo B10M-61	Berkhof 2000NL	B45D+35	1993
4739	VV-17-XD	Volvo B10M-61	Berkhof 2000NL	B45D+35	1993
4740	VV-20-XD	Volvo B10M-61	Berkhof 2000NL	B45D+35	1993
4741	VV-22-XD	Volvo B10M-61	Berkhof 2000NL	B45D+35	1993
4742	VV-23-XD	Volvo B10M-61	Berkhof 2000NL	B45D+35	1993
4743	VV-24-XD	Volvo B10M-61	Berkhof 2000NL	B45D+35	1993
4744	VV-25-XD	Volvo B10M-61	Berkhof 2000NL	B45D+35	1993
4745	VV-26-XD	Volvo B10M-61	Berkhof 2000NL	B45D+35	1993
4746	VV-27-XD	Volvo B10M-61	Berkhof 2000NL	B45D+35	1993
4747	VV-29-XD	Volvo B10M-61	Berkhof 2000NL	B45D+35	1993
4748	VX-66-DY	Volvo B10M-61	Berkhof 2000NL	B45D+35	1993
4749	VX-36-DL	Volvo B10M-61	Berkhof 2000NL	B45D+35	1993
4750	VX-09-DL	Volvo B10M-61	Berkhof 2000NL	B45D+35	1993
4751	VX-18-DL	Volvo B10M-61	Berkhof 2000NL	B45D+35	1993
4752	VX-58-DK	Volvo B10M-61	Berkhof 2000NL	B45D+35	1993
4753	VX-27-GJ	Mercedes-Benz O408	Mercedes-Benz/Zabo	B49D+31	1993
4754	VX-35-GJ	Mercedes-Benz O408	Mercedes-Benz/Zabo	B49D+31	1993
4755	VX-17-GJ	Mercedes-Benz O408	Mercedes-Benz/Zabo	B49D+31	1993
4756	VX-15-GJ	Mercedes-Benz O408	Mercedes-Benz/Zabo	B49D+31	1993
4757	VX-23-GJ	Mercedes-Benz O408	Mercedes-Benz/Zabo	B49D+31	1993
4833	BB-LB-10	DAF SB220 LC575	Den Ousten B89 Alliance	B43D+40	1992
4834	BB-LB-11	DAF SB220 LC575	Den Ousten B89 Alliance	B43D+40	1992
4835	BB-JX-59	DAF SB220 LC575	Den Ousten B89 Alliance	B47D+36	1992
4836	BB-JZ-94	DAF SB220 LC575	Den Ousten B89 Alliance	B43D+40	1992
4837	BB-LB-60	DAF SB220 LC575	Den Ousten B89 Alliance	B43D+40	1992
4838	BB-JV-77	DAF SB220 LC575	Den Ousten B89 Alliance	B43D+40	1992
4839	BB-NL-24	DAF SB220 LC575	Den Ousten B89 Alliance	B47D+36	1992
4840	BB-NL-23	DAF SB220 LC575	Den Ousten B89 Alliance	B43D+40	1992
4841	BB-JZ-95	DAF SB220 LC575	Den Ousten B89 Alliance	B43D+40	1992
4842	BB-JV-80	DAF SB220 LC575	Den Ousten B89 Alliance	B47D+36	1992
4843	BB-JV-89	DAF SB220 LC575	Den Ousten B89 Alliance	B47D+36	1992
4845	BB-LB-13	DAF SB220 LC575	Den Ousten B89 Alliance	B47D+36	1992
4846	VX-07-LK	DAF SB220 LC575	Den Ousten B89 Alliance	B47D+36	1992
4847	BB-LB-14	DAF SB220 LC575	Den Ousten B89 Alliance	B47D+36	1992
4848	BB-LB-61	DAF SB220 LC575	Den Ousten B89 Alliance	B47D+36	1992
5531	VV-23-JP	DAF SB MF580	Den Oudsten Alliance Intercity	B45D+32	1993
5532	VV-14-JP	DAF SB MF580	Den Oudsten Alliance Intercity	B45D+32	1993
5533	VV-16-JP	DAF SB MF580	Den Oudsten Alliance Intercity	B45D+32	1993
5534	VV-07-JV	DAF SB MF580	Den Oudsten Alliance Intercity	B45D+32	1993
5535	VV-35-JV	DAF SB MF580	Den Oudsten Alliance Intercity	B45D+32	1993
5536	VV-25-JP	DAF SB MF580	Den Oudsten Alliance Intercity	B45D+32	1993
5537	VV-19-JP	DAF SB MF580	Den Oudsten Alliance Intercity	B45D+32	1993
5538	VV-11-JP	DAF SB MF580	Den Oudsten Alliance Intercity	B45D+32	1993
5567	BB-HJ-86	DAF SB DM580	Den Oudsten Alliance Intercity	B45D+32	1994
5568	BB-HJ-78	DAF SB DM580	Den Oudsten Alliance Intercity	B45D+32	1994
5569	BB-HJ-76	DAF SB DM580	Den Oudsten Alliance Intercity	B45D+32	1994
5570	BB-HJ-73	DAF SB DM580	Den Oudsten Alliance Intercity	B45D+32	1994
5571	BB-HJ-90	DAF SB DM580	Den Oudsten Alliance Intercity	B45D+32	1994
5572	BB-HJ-88	DAF SB DM580	Den Oudsten Alliance Intercity	B45D+32	1994
5573	BB-HJ-87	DAF SB DM580	Den Oudsten Alliance Intercity	B45D+32	1994
5574	BB-HJ-82	DAF SB DM580	Den Oudsten Alliance Intercity	B45D+32	1994
5575	BB-HJ-80	DAF SB DM580	Den Oudsten Alliance Intercity	B45D+32	1994
5576	BB-HJ-69	DAF SB DM580	Den Oudsten Alliance Intercity	B45D+32	1994
5702	BB-PD-64	DAF SBR3000	Den Oudsten Interliner 500NL	BC44D+35	1995

5703	BB-PD-63	DAF SBR3000	Den Oudsten Interliner 500NL BC44D+35		1995
5704	BB-PD-62	DAF SBR3000	Den Oudsten Interliner 500NL BC44D+35		1995
5747	BB-HH-19	DAF SBR3000	Den Oudsten Interliner 500NL BC44D+35		1995
5748	BB-HG-38	DAF SBR3000	Den Oudsten Interliner 500NL BC44D+35		1995
5783	BF-XR-66	DAF DR33WS15	Den Oudsten Interliner 500NL BC56D		1997
5784	BF-XR-65	DAF DR33WS15	Den Oudsten Interliner 500NL BC56D		1997
5785	BF-XR-63	DAF DR33WS15	Den Oudsten Interliner 500NL BC56D		1997
6009	VL-29-XS	Van Hool A508	Van Hool	B24D+32	1991
6010	VL-26-XS	Van Hool A508	Van Hool	B24D+32	1991
6012	VL-59-LF	Van Hool A508	Van Hool	B24D+32	1992
6013	VL-17-KX	Van Hool A508	Van Hool	B24D+32	1992
6014	VL-81-KX	Van Hool A508	Van Hool	B24D+32	1992
6015	VP-79-KX	Van Hool A508	Van Hool	B24D+32	1992
6313	VF-68-RL	Volvo B10M-G8 5000	Hainje	AB29D+42	1989
6314	VF-85-RK	Volvo B10M-G8 5000	Hainje	AB29D+42	1989
6315	VF-43-PP	Volvo B10M-G8 5000	Hainje	AB29D+42	1989
6316	VF-51-PR	Volvo B10M-G8 5000	Hainje	AB29D+42	1989
6317	VF-70-PP	Volvo B10M-G8 5000	Hainje	AB29D+42	1989
6318	VF-84-RL	Volvo B10M-G8 5000	Hainje	AB29D+42	1989
6319	VF-63-PP	Volvo B10M-G8 5000	Hainje	AB29D+42	1989
6320	VF-50-PY	Volvo B10M-G8 5000	Hainje	AB29D+42	1989
6321	VF-43-PY	Volvo B10M-G8 5000	Hainje	AB29D+42	1989
6322	VF-82-RV	Volvo B10M-G8 5000	Hainje	AB29D+42	1989
6323	VF-91-RK	Volvo B10M-G8 5000	Hainje	AB29D+42	1989
6324	VF-25-RL	Volvo B10M-G8 5000	Hainje	AB29D+42	1989
6325	VG-26-DJ	Hainje10-metre	Hainje	B27D+32	1989
6326	VG-31-DJ	Hainje10-metre	Hainje	B27D+32	1989
6327	VG-76-HR	Hainje10-metre	Hainje	B27D+32	1989
6340	VJ-58-TD	Volvo B10M-50	Berkhof	B29D+43	1990
6341	VJ-32-TB	Volvo B10M-50	Berkhof	B29D+43	1990
6342	VJ-05-TD	Volvo B10M-50	Berkhof	B29D+43	1990
6343	VJ-47-XR	Volvo B10M-50	Berkhof	B29D+43	1990
6344	VJ-48-XR	Volvo B10M-50	Berkhof	B29D+43	1990
6345	VJ-76-YZ	Volvo B10M-50	Berkhof	B29D+43	1990
6381	BD-VV-35	Iveco Daily A45.10	Iveco	B17D+3	1996
6382	BD-VV-36	Iveco Daily A45.10	Iveco	B17D+3	1996
6387	BF-XL-12	MAN 11.220	Berkhof 2000NLE	B25D+24	1997
6388	BF-XL-09	MAN 11.220	Berkhof 2000NLE	B25D+24	1997
6490	BH-38-PN	DAF MB220 DKDL500	Den Ousten	B28D+44	1983
6519	BP-46-DT	DAF MB220 DKDL536	Den Ousten	B34D+42	1985
6520	BP-11-DY	DAF MB220 DKDL536	Den Ousten	B34D+42	1985
6525	BV-11-PK	Hainje10-metre	Hainje	B27D+32	1987
6526	BV-98-SY	Hainje10-metre	Hainje	B27D+32	1987
6721	BT-92-NP	Hainje10-metre	Hainje	B27D+32	1987
6722	BT-99-NP	Hainje10-metre	Hainje	B27D+32	1987
6723	BT-01-PD	Hainje10-metre	Hainje	B27D+32	1987
6724	BT-64-PZ	Hainje10-metre	Hainje	B27D+32	1987
6725	BT-36-PP	Hainje10-metre	Hainje	B27D+32	1987
7624	BX-35-SL	DAF MBG205 DKFL530	Den Ousten	AB58D+55	1987
7625	BX-36-SL	DAF MBG205 DKFL530	Den Ousten	AB58D+55	1987
7626	BX-26-SG	DAF MBG205 DKFL530	Den Ousten	AB58D+55	1987
7627	BX-33-YS	DAF MBG205 DKFL530	Den Ousten	AB58D+55	1987
7628	BX-72-YZ	DAF MBG205 DKFL530	Den Ousten	AB58D+55	1987
7629	BX-73-YZ	DAF MBG205 DKFL530	Den Ousten	AB58D+55	1987
7657	VF-41-DL	Volvo B10MG-60	Hainje-Ouvedec	AB65D+54	1989
7658	VF-76-HB	Volvo B10MG-60	Hainje-Ouvedec	AB65D+54	1989
7659	VF-36-HG	Volvo B10MG-60	Hainje-Ouvedec	AB65D+54	1989
7660	VF-39-HG	Volvo B10MG-60	Hainje-Ouvedec	AB65D+54	1989
7661	VF-81-HB	Volvo B10MG-60	Hainje-Ouvedec	AB65D+54	1989
7668	VJ-36-KH	Volvo B10MG-55	Berkhof	AB65D+59	1990
7669	VJ-18-LD	Volvo B10MG-55	Berkhof	AB65D+59	1990
7670	VJ-98-KV	Volvo B10MG-55	Berkhof	AB65D+59	1990
7671	VJ-16-PJ	Volvo B10MG-55	Berkhof	AB65D+59	1990
7672	VJ-13-PJ	Volvo B10MG-55	Berkhof	AB65D+59	1990
7752	VL-88-PB	Volvo B10MG-55 III	Berkhof	AB65D+59	1991
7753	VL-21-SB	Volvo B10MG-55 III	Berkhof	AB65D+59	1991
7754	VL-33-SB	Volvo B10MG-55 III	Berkhof	AB65D+59	1991
7755	VL-97-SY	Volvo B10MG-55 III	Berkhof	AB65D+59	1991
7756	VL-48-TH	Volvo B10MG-55 III	Berkhof	AB65D+59	1991
7757	VL-98-SY	Volvo B10MG-55 III	Berkhof	AB65D+59	1991
7758	VL-31-LN	Volvo B10MG-55 III	Berkhof	AB65D+59	1991
7759	VL-17-LN	Volvo B10MG-55 III	Berkhof	AB65D+59	1991

8726	BB-84-DF	DAF MB200 DKDL564	Den Ousten	B43D+36	1981
9310	BF-72-DX	DAF MB200 DKDL564	Den Ousten	B40D+41	1982
9311	BF-70-DX	DAF MB200 DKDL564	Den Ousten	B40D+41	1982
9383	BG-19-HV	DAF MB200 DKDL564	Den Ousten	B40D+42	1983
9384	BG-17-HV	DAF MB200 DKDL564	Den Ousten	B40D+42	1983
9388	BG-36-JF	DAF MB200 DKDL564	Den Ousten	B40D+42	1983
9390	BG-52-JH	DAF MB200 DKDL564	Den Ousten	B40D+42	1983
9393	BG-08-JS	DAF MB200 DKDL564	Den Ousten	B40D+42	1983
9394	BG-09-JS	DAF MB200 DKDL564	Den Ousten	B40D+42	1983
9396	BG-11-JS	DAF MB200 DKDL564	Den Ousten	B40D+42	1983
9398	BG-78-JY	DAF MB200 DKDL564	Den Ousten	B40D+42	1983
9425	BF-72-ZZ	DAF MB200 DKDL564	Den Ousten	B40D+42	1983
9426	BF-73-ZZ	DAF MB200 DKDL564	Den Ousten	B40D+42	1983
9427	BG-14-BJ	DAF MB200 DKDL564	Den Ousten	B40D+42	1983
9428	BG-16-BJ	DAF MB200 DKDL564	Den Ousten	B40D+42	1983
9429	BG-76-BN	DAF MB200 DKDL564	Den Ousten	B40D+42	1983
9430	BG-82-BN	DAF MB200 DKDL564	Den Ousten	B40D+42	1983
9431	BG-79-BN	DAF MB200 DKDL564	Den Ousten	B40D+42	1983
9432	BG-81-BN	DAF MB200 DKDL564	Den Ousten	B40D+42	1983
9653	BJ-47-NZ	DAF MB200 DKDL564	Den Ousten	B40D+42	1984
9655	BJ-56-NZ	DAF MB200 DKDL564	Den Ousten	B40D+42	1984
9656	BJ-50-PJ	DAF MB200 DKDL564	Den Ousten	B40D+42	1984
9657	BJ-51-PJ	DAF MB200 DKDL564	Den Ousten	B40D+42	1984
9658	BJ-92-PV	DAF MB200 DKDL564	Den Ousten	B40D+42	1984
9661	BJ-86-PV	DAF MB200 DKDL564	Den Ousten	B40D+42	1984
9662	BJ-66-TR	DAF MB200 DKDL564	Den Ousten	B40D+42	1984
9663	BJ-57-TR	DAF MB200 DKDL564	Den Ousten	B40D+42	1984
9664	BJ-83-TT	DAF MB200 DKDL564	Den Ousten	B40D+42	1984
9680	BJ-91-LS	DAF MB200 DKDL564	Den Ousten	B40D+42	1984
9681	BJ-85-NF	DAF MB200 DKDL564	Den Ousten	B40D+42	1984
9682	BJ-84-NF	DAF MB200 DKDL564	Den Ousten	B40D+42	1984
9683	BJ-86-NF	DAF MB200 DKDL564	Den Ousten	B40D+42	1984
9684	BJ-92-RN	DAF MB200 DKDL564	Den Ousten	B40D+42	1984
9685	BJ-99-RN	DAF MB200 DKDL564	Den Ousten	B40D+42	1984
9702	BK-79-BF	DAF MB200 DKDL564	Den Ousten	B40D+42	1984
9703	BK-85-BL	DAF MB200 DKDL564	Den Ousten	B40D+42	1984
9705	BK-55-BN	DAF MB200 DKDL564	Den Ousten	B40D+42	1984
9742	BK-93-HL	DAF MB200 DKDL564	Den Ousten	B40D+42	1984
9743	BK-88-JB	DAF MB200 DKDL564	Den Ousten	B40D+42	1984
9744	BK-74-JB	DAF MB200 DKDL564	Den Ousten	B40D+42	1984
9745	BK-92-JB	DAF MB200 DKDL564	Den Ousten	B40D+42	1984
9746	BK-90-JB	DAF MB200 DKDL564	Den Ousten	B40D+42	1984
9747	BK-53-JJ	DAF MB200 DKDL564	Den Ousten	B40D+42	1984
9748	BK-55-JJ	DAF MB200 DKDL564	Den Ousten	B40D+42	1984
9749	BK-16-JV	DAF MB200 DKDL564	Den Ousten	B40D+42	1984
9751	BK-26-JV	DAF MB200 DKDL564	Den Ousten	B40D+42	1984
9752	BK-21-JV	DAF MB200 DKDL564	Den Ousten	B40D+42	1984
9847	BL-50-DH	DAF MB200 DKDL564	Den Ousten	B40D+42	1985
9848	BL-20-DV	DAF MB200 DKDL564	Den Ousten	B40D+42	1985
9849	BL-19-DV	DAF MB200 DKDL564	Den Ousten	B40D+42	1985
9850	BL-72-FF	DAF MB200 DKDL564	Den Ousten	B40D+42	1985
9851	BL-73-FF	DAF MB200 DKDL564	Den Ousten	B40D+42	1985
9852	BL-40-FT	DAF MB200 DKDL564	Den Ousten	B40D+42	1985
9854	BL-80-FP	DAF MB200 DKDL564	Den Ousten	B40D+42	1985
9855	BL-78-FP	DAF MB200 DKDL564	Den Ousten	B40D+42	1985
9856	BL-44-GD	DAF MB200 DKDL564	Den Ousten	B40D+42	1985
9857	BL-38-GD	DAF MB200 DKDL564	Den Ousten	B40D+42	1985
9858	BL-40-GD	DAF MB200 DKDL564	Den Ousten	B40D+42	1985
9859	BL-47-GD	DAF MB200 DKDL564	Den Ousten	B40D+42	1985
9860	BL-89-GT	DAF MB200 DKDL564	Den Ousten	B40D+42	1985
9861	BL-92-GT	DAF MB200 DKDL564	Den Ousten	B40D+42	1985

Late in 1998 the acquisition of Veonn and Hanze, two subsidiaries of the state owned VSN group, increased the activity in northern Netherlands. A policy in the Dutch transportation market of moving to competitive tender for transport operations saw the need to reduce the market share of VSN companies to encourage competition for tenders in the future. GADO is one of the two operator names used, seen here on Den Oudsten B88-bodied DAF MB230, number 4582, V-85-PB, parked at Groningen. *Fred Huppertz*

GADO Winschoten

1123	BD-FT-09	Mercedes-Benz O405	Mercedes-Benz	B49D+31	1996
1124	BD-FT-06	Mercedes-Benz O405	Mercedes-Benz	B49D+31	1996
1154	BD-BS-15	Den Oudsten	Den Oudsten B91	B47D+30	1996
1266	BD-ZF-16	Mercedes-Benz O408	Mercedes-Benz	B49D+30	1996
1267	BD-ZB-15	Mercedes-Benz O408	Mercedes-Benz	B49D+30	1996
1275	BD-TS-72	Den Oudsten B95	Den Oudsten Alliance	B45D+33	1997
1276	BD-TS-67	Den Oudsten B95	Den Oudsten Alliance	B45D+33	1997
2201	BF-LG-41	Den Oudsten B95	Den Oudsten Alliance	B45D+33	1997
3540	BP-52-BZ	DAF MB200 DKDL584	Den Oudsten	B45D+33	1985
3541	BP-36-BZ	DAF MB200 DKDL584	Den Oudsten	B45D+33	1985
3544	BP-82-BY	DAF MB200 DKDL584	Den Oudsten	B45D+33	1985
3621	BR-51-HP	DAF MB200 DKDL584	Den Oudsten	B44D+34	1986
3626	BR-15-JN	DAF MB200 DKDL584	Den Oudsten	B44D+34	1986
3627	BR-16-KP	DAF MB200 DKDL584	Den Oudsten	B44D+34	1986
3630	BR-15-KP	DAF MB200 DKDL584	Den Oudsten	B44D+34	1986
3632	BR-11-KP	DAF MB200 DKDL584	Den Oudsten	B44D+34	1986
4126	VF-19-GN	DAF MB230 LC615	Den Oudsten B88	B45D+32	1989
4129	VF-28-HG	DAF MB230 LC615	Den Oudsten B88	B45D+32	1989
4131	VF-26-HG	DAF MB230 LC615	Den Oudsten B88	B45D+32	1989
4257	VH-95-KB	DAF MB230 LC615	Den Oudsten B88	B45D+32	1990
4266	VH-41-NR	DAF MB230 LC615	Den Oudsten B88	B45D+32	1990
4267	VH-42-NR	DAF MB230 LC615	Den Oudsten B88	B45D+32	1990
4586	VL-93-PK	DAF MB230 LC615	Den Oudsten B88	B45D+32	1991
4587	VL-66-PB	DAF MB230 LC615	Den Oudsten B88	B45D+32	1991
4589	VL-75-PB	DAF MB230 LC615	Den Oudsten B88	B45D+32	1991
5584	BB-GR-97	Den Oudsten B91 DM580	Den Oudsten Alliance	B47D+32	1993
9169	BD-34-LG	DAF MB200 DKDL584	Den Oudsten	B44D+34	1982
9173	BD-83-LX	DAF MB200 DKDL584	Den Oudsten	B44D+34	1982
9176	BD-87-LX	DAF MB200 DKDL584	Den Oudsten	B44D+34	1982
9181	BD-98-NH	DAF MB200 DKDL584	Den Oudsten	B44D+34	1982
9182	BD-04-NZ	DAF MB200 DKDL584	Den Oudsten	B44D+34	1982
9987	BN-81-PN	DAF MB200 DKDL584	Den Oudsten	B45D+33	1985

GADO Appingedam en Uithuizen

1125	BD-FT-05	Mercedes-Benz O405	Mercedes-Benz	B49D+31	1996
1126	BD-FT-03	Mercedes-Benz O405	Mercedes-Benz	B49D+31	1996
1156	BD-BS-11	Den Oudsten	Den Oudsten B91	B47D+30	1996
1160	BD-BS-20	Den Oudsten	Den Oudsten B91	B47D+30	1996
1161	BD-BS-09	Den Oudsten	Den Oudsten B91	B47D+30	1996
1261	BD-ZF-13	Mercedes-Benz O408	Mercedes-Benz	B49D+30	1996
1262	BD-ZF-05	Mercedes-Benz O408	Mercedes-Benz	B49D+30	1996
1263	BD-ZF-08	Mercedes-Benz O408	Mercedes-Benz	B49D+30	1996
1268	BD-TS-78	Den Oudsten B95	Den Oudsten Alliance	B45D+33	1997
1269	BD-TS-63	Den Oudsten B95	Den Oudsten Alliance	B45D+33	1997
1557	BH-06-NH	DAF MB200 DKDL564	Hainje	B42D+40	1983
2197	BF-LG-87	Den Oudsten B95	Den Oudsten Alliance	B45D+33	1997
2198	BF-LG-83	Den Oudsten B95	Den Oudsten Alliance	B45D+33	1997
2199	X-20-09	Den Oudsten B95	Den Oudsten Alliance	B45D+33	1997
3538	BP-51-BZ	DAF MB200 DKDL584	Den Oudsten	B44D+34	1985
3629	BR-13-KP	DAF MB200 DKDL584	Den Oudsten	B44D+34	1986
3631	BV-46-VK	DAF MB200 DKDL584	Den Oudsten	B44D+34	1986
3830	BY-42-NO	DAF MB200 DKDL584	Den Oudsten	B44D+34	1987
3831	BY-43-NO	DAF MB200 DKDL584	Den Oudsten	B44D+34	1987
3832	BY-44-NO	DAF MB200 DKDL584	Den Oudsten	B44D+34	1987
3833	BY-44-NJ	DAF MB200 DKDL584	Den Oudsten	B44D+34	1987
4125	VF-23-GN	DAF MB230 LC615	Den Oudsten B88	B45D+32	1989
4130	VF-25-HG	DAF MB230 LC615	Den Oudsten B88	B45D+32	1989
4253	VH-79-KB	DAF MB230 LC615	Den Oudsten B88	B45D+32	1990
4254	VH-65-KO	DAF MB230 LC615	Den Oudsten B88	B45D+32	1990
4582	VL-54-PG	DAF MB230 LC615	Den Oudsten B88	B45D+32	1991
4583	VL-52-PG	DAF MB230 LC615	Den Oudsten B88	B45D+32	1991
4584	VL-51-PG	DAF MB230 LC615	Den Oudsten B88	B45D+32	1991
4585	VL-07-PB	DAF MB230 LC615	Den Oudsten B88	B45D+32	1991
4592	VL-85-PB	DAF MB230 LC615	Den Oudsten B88	B45D+32	1991
4593	VL-79-PB	DAF MB230 LC615	Den Oudsten B88	B45D+32	1991
4594	VL-83-PB	DAF MB230 LC615	Den Oudsten B88	B45D+32	1991
4772	BB-DL-31	Mercedes-Benz O408	Mercedes-Benz	B49D+31	1993
5585	BB-GT-03	Den Oudsten B91 DM580	Den Oudsten Alliance	B47D+32	1993
5586	BB-GS-23	Den Oudsten B91 DM580	Den Oudsten Alliance	B47D+32	1993
7291	RZ-XG-70	Mercedes-Benz 208D	Mercedes-Benz	M8	1997
7301	SN-FZ-80	Mercedes-Benz 208D	Mercedes-Benz	M8	1997
7566	NT-64-BP	Mercedes-Benz 208D	Mercedes-Benz	M8	1985
7620	BX-78-PT	DAF MBG200DKFL530	Den Oudsten	AB68D+55	1987
7642	BZ-36-KT	DAF MBG200 DKFL530	Den Oudsten	AB68D+56	1988
7643	BZ-37-KT	DAF MBG200 DKFL530	Den Oudsten	AB68D+56	1988
7649	BZ-79-LJ	DAF MBG200 DKFL530	Den Oudsten	AB68D+56	1988
7650	BZ-75-LJ	DAF MBG200 DKFL530	Den Oudsten	AB68D+56	1988
9500	BG-11-KP	DAF MB200 DKDL584	Den Oudsten	B44D+34	1983
9501	BG-60-KY	DAF MB200 DKDL584	Den Oudsten	B44D+34	1983
9502	BG-63-KY	DAF MB200 DKDL584	Den Oudsten	B44D+34	1983
9982	BN-45-NY	DAF MB200 DKDL584	Den Oudsten	B44D+34	1985

GADO Zoutkamp

1157	BD-BS-13	Den Oudsten	Den Oudsten B91	B47D+30	1996
1158	BD-BS-12	Den Oudsten	Den Oudsten B91	B47D+30	1996
1260	BD-ZF-03	Mercedes-Benz O408	Mercedes-Benz	B49D+30	1996
1272	BD-TS-69	Den Oudsten B95	Den Oudsten Alliance	B45D+33	1997
3619	BD-85-HB	DAF MB200 DKDL584	Den Oudsten	B44D+34	1986
3620	BD-55-HP	DAF MB200 DKDL584	Den Oudsten	B44D+34	1986
4680	VS-96-BZ	Mercedes-Benz O408	Mercedes-Benz/Zabo	B49D+31	1992
4683	VS-87-BZ	Mercedes-Benz O408	Mercedes-Benz/Zabo	B49D+31	1992
4771	BB-DL-39	Mercedes-Benz O408	Mercedes-Benz/Zabo	B49D+31	1992
5578	BB-GS-54	Den Oudsten B91 DM580	Den Oudsten Alliance	B47D+32	1993
5579	BB-GS-02	Den Oudsten B91 DM580	Den Oudsten Alliance	B47D+32	1993
5582	BB-BR-99	Den Oudsten B91 DM580	Den Oudsten Alliance	B47D+32	1993
7622	BX-80-PT	DAF MBG200 DKFL530	Den Oudsten	AB68D+56	1987
7623	BX-03-RG	DAF MBG200 DKFL530	Den Oudsten	AB68D+56	1987
8889	BB-50-TF	DAF MB200 DKDL584	Den Oudsten	B44D+34	1981
9506	BG-55-LG	DAF MB200 DKDL584	Den Oudsten	B44D+34	1983
9986	BN-84-PN	DAF MB200 DKDL584	Den Oudsten	B44D+34	1985

GADO Groningen

1117	BD-FS-86	Mercedes-Benz O405	Mercedes-Benz	B49D+31	1996
1119	BD-FS-88	Mercedes-Benz O405	Mercedes-Benz	B49D+31	1996
1155	BD-BS-18	Den Oudsten	Den Oudsten B91	B47D+30	1996
1159	BD-BS-21	Den Oudsten	Den Oudsten B91	B47D+30	1996
1162	BD-RX-20	Den Oudsten	Den Oudsten B91	B47D+30	1996
1258	BD-ZB-16	Mercedes-Benz O408	Mercedes-Benz	B49D+30	1996
1259	BD-ZF-18	Mercedes-Benz O408	Mercedes-Benz	B49D+30	1996
1270	BD-TS-64	Den Oudsten B95	Den Oudsten Alliance	B45D+33	1997
1271	BD-TS-66	Den Oudsten B95	Den Oudsten Alliance	B45D+33	1997
2194	BF-LG-44	Den Oudsten B95	Den Oudsten Alliance	B45D+33	1997
2195	BF-LG-43	Den Oudsten B95	Den Oudsten Alliance	B45D+33	1997
2196	BF-LG-89	Den Oudsten B95	Den Oudsten Alliance	B45D+33	1997
3625	BR-36-JN	DAF MB200 DKDL600	Den Oudsten	B44D+34	1986
3628	BR-14-KP	DAF MB200 DKDL600	Den Oudsten	B44D+34	1986
4252	VH-66-KD	DAF MB230 LC615	Den Oudsten B88	B45D+32	1990
4256	VH-81-KB	DAF MB230 LC615	Den Oudsten B88	B45D+32	1990
4258	VH-04-KD	DAF MB230 LC615	Den Oudsten B88	B45D+32	1990
4259	VH-43-KD	DAF MB230 LC615	Den Oudsten B88	B45D+32	1990
4262	VH-26-KD	DAF MB230 LC615	Den Oudsten B88	B45D+32	1990
4591	VL-90-PB	DAF MB230 LC615	Den Oudsten B88	B45D+32	1990
4595	VL-92-PB	DAF MB230 LC615	Den Oudsten B88	B45D+32	1990
4677	VR-60-VG	Mercedes-Benz O408	Mercedes-Benz/Zabo	B49D+31	1992
4678	VR-61-VG	Mercedes-Benz O408	Mercedes-Benz/Zabo	B49D+31	1992
4679	VS-01-DB	Mercedes-Benz O408	Mercedes-Benz/Zabo	B49D+31	1992
5580	BB-GS-03	Den Oudsten B91 DM580	Den Oudsten Alliance	B47D+32	1993
5700	BB-PP-08	DAF SBR3000 WS680	Berkhof Excellence 500NL	B48D+31	1994
5701	BF-PP-11	DAF SBR3000 WS680	Berkhof Excellence 500NL	B48D+31	1994
5742	BD-HG-61	DAF SBR3015 WS580	Berkhof Excellence 500NL	B44D+35	1995
7119	VT-55-FG	DAF SBG200 LB506	Den Oudsten Alliance	AB61D+63	1992
7644	BZ-24-KF	DAF MBG200 DKFL530	Den Oudsten	AB68D+56	1988
7645	BZ-40-KT	DAF MBG200 DKFL530	Den Oudsten	AB68D+56	1988
7647	BZ-32-KT	DAF MBG200 DKFL530	Den Oudsten	AB68D+56	1988
7651	BZ-76-LJ	DAF MBG200 DKFL530	Den Oudsten	AB68D+56	1988
9171	BD-60-LN	DAF MB200 DKDL584	Den Oudsten	B44D+34	1982
9777	BK-19-LY	DAF MB200 DKDL584	Den Oudsten	B44D+34	1984
9778	BK-63-NH	DAF MB200 DKDL584	Den Oudsten	B44D+34	1984
9779	BK-64-NH	DAF MB200 DKDL584	Den Oudsten	B44D+34	1984
9979	BN-21-NR	DAF MB200 DKDL584	Den Oudsten	B44D+34	1985
9980	BN-13-NR	DAF MB200 DKDL584	Den Oudsten	B44D+34	1985
9981	BN-46-NY	DAF MB200 DKDL584	Den Oudsten	B44D+34	1985

GADO Veendam

1122	BD-TV-38	Mercedes-Benz O408	Mercedes-Benz	B49D+30	1995
1152	BD-BS-19	Den Oudsten	Den Oudsten B91	B47D+30	1996
1265	BD-ZF-14	Mercedes-Benz O408	Mercedes-Benz	B49D+30	1996
1274	BD-TS-71	Den Oudsten B95	Den Oudsten Alliance	B45D+33	1997
2203	BF-LH-20	Den Oudsten B95	Den Oudsten Alliance	B45D+33	1997
3618	BR-84-HB	DAF MB200 DKDL584	Den Oudsten	B44D+34	1986
3622	BR-45-HP	DAF MB200 DKDL584	Den Oudsten	B44D+34	1986
3623	BR-39-JN	DAF MB200 DKDL584	Den Oudsten	B44D+34	1986
4127	VF-79-GN	DAF MB230 LC615	Den Oudsten B88	B45D+32	1989
4128	VF-30-HG	DAF MB230 LC615	Den Oudsten B88	B45D+32	1989
4581	VL-62-PG	DAF MB230 LC615	Den Oudsten B88	B45D+32	1989
4588	VL-74-PB	DAF MB230 LC615	Den Oudsten B88	B45D+32	1989
4681	VS-94-BZ	Mercedes-Benz O408	Mercedes-Benz/Zabo	B49D+31	1992
4682	VS-90-BZ	Mercedes-Benz O408	Mercedes-Benz/Zabo	B49D+31	1992
4684	VS-85-BZ	Mercedes-Benz O408	Mercedes-Benz/Zabo	B49D+31	1992
4774	BB-DL-33	Mercedes-Benz O408	Mercedes-Benz	B49D+31	1993
4775	BB-DL-35	Mercedes-Benz O408	Mercedes-Benz	B49D+31	1993
5743	BD-HG-59	DAF SBR3015 WS580	Berkhof Excellence 500NL	B44D+33	1995
5744	BD-HG-64	DAF SBR3015 WS580	Berkhof Excellence 500NL	B44D+33	1995
5745	BD-HG-69	DAF SBR3015 WS580	Berkhof Excellence 500NL	B44D+33	1995
5746	BD-HH-22	DAF SBR3015 WS580	Berkhof Excellence 500NL	B44D+33	1992
7120	VT-54-LD	DAF SBG200 LB506	Den Oudsten Alliance	AB61D+63	1992
7646	BZ-39-KT	DAF MBG200 DKFL530	Den Oudsten	AB68D+56	1988
7648	BZ-48-LD	DAF MBG200 DKFL530	Den Oudsten	AB68D+56	1988
9570	BJ-65-SF	DAF DAF MB200 DKDL584	Den Oudsten	B44D+34	1984

GADO Openbaar Vervoer

9167	BD-38-LG	DAF MB200 DKDL584	Den Oudsten	B40D+41	1982

GADO Stadskanaal

101	VH-65-KO	Mercedes-Benz 609D	Mercedes-Benz	M16	1988
1118	BD-FS-87	Mercedes-Benz O405	Mercedes-Benz	B49D+31	1996
1120	BD-FX-84	Mercedes-Benz O405	Mercedes-Benz	B49D+31	1996
1121	BD-FV-88	Mercedes-Benz O405	Mercedes-Benz	B49D+31	1996
1153	BD-BS-16	Den Oudsten	Den Oudsten B91	B47D+30	1996
1264	BD-ZF-10	Mercedes-Benz O408	Mercedes-Benz	B49D+30	1996
1273	BD-TS-70	Den Oudsten B95	Den Oudsten Alliance	B45D+33	1997
2200	BF-LG-40	Den Oudsten B95	Den Oudsten Alliance	B45D+33	1997
2202	BF-LG-42	Den Oudsten B95	Den Oudsten Alliance	B45D+33	1997
3539	BP-81-BL	DAF MB200 DKDL584	Den Oudsten	B44D+34	1985
3542	BP-83-BY	DAF MB200 DKDL584	Den Oudsten	B44D+34	1985
3624	BD-FS-87	DAF MB200 DKDL584	Den Oudsten	B44D+34	1986
4255	VH-14-KP	DAF MB230 LC615	Den Oudsten B88	B45D+32	1990
4260	VH-47-KD	DAF MB230 LC615	Den Oudsten B88	B45D+32	1990
4261	VH-91-KB	DAF MB230 LC615	Den Oudsten B88	B45D+32	1990
4263	VH-34-KD	DAF MB230 LC615	Den Oudsten B88	B45D+32	1990
4564	VH-37-KD	DAF MB230 LC615	Den Oudsten B88	B45D+32	1990
4565	VH-44-NR	DAF MB230 LC615	Den Oudsten B88	B45D+32	1990
4580	VH-59-PG	DAF MB230 LC615	Den Oudsten B88	B45D+32	1991
4590	VH-98-PK	DAF MB230 LC615	Den Oudsten B88	B45D+32	1991
4773	BB-DL-76	Mercedes-Benz O408	Mercedes-Benz	B49D+31	1993
4776	BB-DL-86	Mercedes-Benz O408	Mercedes-Benz	B49D+31	1993
4777	BB-DL-37	Mercedes-Benz O408	Mercedes-Benz	B49D+31	1993
5569		Den Oudsten B91 DM580	Den Oudsten Alliance	B47D+32	1994
5577	BB-GS-55	Den Oudsten B91 DM580	Den Oudsten Alliance	B47D+32	1993
5581	BB-GS-01	Den Oudsten B91 DM580	Den Oudsten Alliance	B47D+32	1993
5583	BB-GR-98	Den Oudsten B91 DM580	Den Oudsten Alliance	B47D+32	1993
7262	NG-JR-51	Mercedes-Benz 208D	Mercedes-Benz	M8	1996
7290	RG-NL-80	Mercedes-Benz 208D	Mercedes-Benz	M8	1997
7316	TS-VV-22	Mercedes-Benz 208D	Mercedes-Benz	M8	1998
7621	BX-77-PT	DAF MBG200 DKFL530	Den Oudsten	AB68D+56	1987
9498	BG-15-KP	DAF MB200 DKDL584	Den Oudsten	B44D+34	1983
9499	BG-42-KP	DAF MB200 DKDL584	Den Oudsten	B44D+34	1983
9503	BG-57-KY	DAF MB200 DKDL584	Den Oudsten	B44D+34	1983
9571	BJ-63-SF	DAF MB200 DKDL584	Den Oudsten	B44D+34	1984
9983	BN-47-NY	DAF MB200 DKDL584	Den Oudsten	B44D+34	1985
9984	BN-03-PN	DAF MB200 DKDL584	Den Oudsten	B44D+34	1985
9985	BN-02-PN	DAF MB200 DKDL584	Den Oudsten	B44D+34	1985

GADO Touring BV

178	VB-72-KP	DAF SB3000 DKV585	Smit Joure	C50FT	1993
181	VH-83-NK	DAF SB3000 DKV585	Smit Joure	C50FT	1993
182	VJ-58-ZB	DAF SB3000 DKV585	Smit Joure	C50FT	1993
183	VL-63-GS	DAF SB3000 DKV585	Smit Joure	C50FT	1993
184	VL-91-GG	DAF SB3000 DKV585	Smit Joure	C50FT	1993
185	VR-77-LK	Bova FHD12.290	Bova Futura	C47FT	1992
186	VV-85-KK	DAF SB3000 DKV585	Smit Joure Orion GL	C50FT	1993
187	VV-80-PL	Mercedes-Benz OH1834L	Smit Joure	C50FT	1993
188	BB-ZP-53	Mercedes-Benz O350	Mercedes-Benz (Turkey)	C50FT	1995
189	BB-ZP-54	Mercedes-Benz O350	Mercedes-Benz (Turkey)	C50FT	1995
190	BD-RX-88	Mercedes-Benz O350	Mercedes-Benz (Turkey)	C50FT	1996
191	BF-LH-16	Mercedes-Benz O350	Mercedes-Benz (Turkey)	C50FT	1997
192	BG-NP-90	Mercedes-Benz O350	Mercedes-Benz (Turkey)	C50FT	1997
339	VJ-47-ZB	Volvo B10M-60	Berkhof Excellence 1000LD	C48F	1993
342	VJ-31-TB	DAF SB3000 DKV585	Smit Joure	C46F	1990
345	VJ-33-ZB	DAF SB3000 DKV585	Smit Joure	C46F	1990
346	VJ-26-ZB	DAF SB3000 DKV585	Smit Joure	C46F	1990
349	VK-10-BB	DAF SB3000 DKV585	Smit Joure	C46F	1991
2783	VK-10-BB	Leyland Leopard	Den Ousten	C48F	1975
6650	BV-63-ND	DAF MB200 DKDL584	Den Oudsten	B44D+34	1987
6651	BV-62-ND	DAF MB200 DKDL584	Den Oudsten	B44D+34	1987

The 1999 Arriva Bus Handbook

Reg	Region	Reg	Region	Reg	Region	Reg	Region
3CLT	London	A139SMA	North West	A518EVN	North Midlands	ADZ4731	Fox County
7CLT	London	A140FDC	North East	A542PCW	North East	ADZ4731	The Shires
49XBF	North West	A140MRN	North West	A543PCW	North East	AEF221Y	Cymru
70CLT	London	A140SMA	North West	A562KWY	Yorkshire	AEF222Y	Cymru
109CRC	Fox County	A141DPE	The Shires	A563KWY	North East	AEF223Y	North East
111XKT	Fox County	A141EPA	The Shires	A564KWY	Yorkshire	AEF224Y	Cymru
123TKM	North Midlands	A141MRN	North West	A565NWX	Yorkshire	AEF225Y	North East
124CLT	London	A141SMA	North West	A566NWX	Yorkshire	AEF226Y	North East
124YTW	North Midlands	A142FDC	North East	A567NWX	Scotland West	AEF227Y	North East
185CLT	London	A142SMA	North West	A568NWX	Yorkshire	AEF228Y	North East
205CLT	London	A143DPE	The Shires	A569NWX	Yorkshire	AEF229Y	Cymru
217CLT	London	A143EPA	The Shires	A570NWX	Yorkshire	AEF990Y	Southern Counties
319CLT	London	A144OFR	North West	A571NWX	Yorkshire	AET184T	OLST
324CLT	London	A146EPA	North East	A572NWX	Yorkshire	AFB593V	Northumbria
361CLT	London	A146FPG	North Midlands	A573NWX	Yorkshire	AHW206V	North Midlands
398CLT	London	A146OFR	North West	A574NWX	Yorkshire	AJA118	North West
422AKN	North Midlands	A147FPG	Scotland West	A575NWX	Yorkshire	AJA142B	North West
445YMU	North East	A147OFR	North West	A576NWX	Cymru	AJA144B	Cymru
453CLT	London	A148FPG	North Midlands	A577NWX	Yorkshire	AKP430T	Southern Counties
464CLT	London	A148UDM	North West	A578NWX	Yorkshire	ALD872B	London
479BOC	North Midlands	A149FPG	The Shires	A579NWX	Yorkshire	ALD919B	OLST
480CLT	London	A149UDM	North West	A580NWX	Yorkshire	ALD978B	London
488BDN	North Midlands	A14GTA	Southern Counties	A581NWX	Yorkshire	AOL11T	North West
494WYA	Southern Counties	A150FPG	North Midlands	A583NWX	Yorkshire	APT810W	Northumbria
519CLT	London	A150UDM	North Midlands	A584NWX	Yorkshire	APT811W	Northumbria
530MUY	London	A151FPG	The Shires	A584NWX	Yorkshire	APT816W	Northumbria
544WRA	The Shires	A151UDM	North West	A584NWX	The Shires	APT817W	Northumbria
544XVW	Southern Counties	A152EPA	North Midlands	A585NWX	Yorkshire	ARN895Y	North East
565LON	North Midlands	A152EPA	The Shires	A586NWX	Yorkshire	ARN896Y	North East
593CLT	London	A152FPG	The Shires	A587NWX	Yorkshire	ARN897Y	North East
614WEH	North Midlands	A152UDM	North Midlands	A588NWX	Yorkshire	ARN898Y	North East
648WHK	North East	A153EPA	North Midlands	A589NWX	Yorkshire	ARP612X	The Shires
656DYE	London	A153FPG	The Shires	A590NWX	Yorkshire	ARP613X	The Shires
662NKR	Fox County	A153UDM	North West	A698EAU	The Shires	ARP614X	The Shires
681CXM	North East	A154FPG	The Shires	A699EAU	The Shires	ARP615X	The Shires
725DYE	London	A154UDM	North Midlands	A700THV	London	ARP616X	The Shires
734DYE	London	A155FPG	The Shires	A701HVT	North Midlands	ARP617X	The Shires
796UHT	Fox County	A155UDM	North Midlands	A702HVT	North Midlands	ARP618X	The Shires
801DYE	London	A157EPA	The Shires	A703HVT	North Midlands	ARP619X	The Shires
803HOM	North Midlands	A160EPA	North Midlands	A704HVT	North Midlands	ARP620X	The Shires
815DYE	London	A172VFM	North Midlands	A705HVT	North Midlands	B45NDX	North East
822DYE	London	A195KKF	North Midlands	A706HVT	North Midlands	B62WUL	London
864DYE	OLST	A201OKJ	Southern Counties	A707HVT	North Midlands	B70WUL	London
869SVX	Northumbria	A202OKJ	Southern Counties	A708HVT	North Midlands	B74WUL	London
904AXY	North Midlands	A203OKJ	Southern Counties	A709HVT	North Midlands	B75WUL	London
A39SMA	North Midlands	A204OKJ	Southern Counties	A736THV	London	B83SWX	The Shires
A42SMA	North Midlands	A205OKJ	Southern Counties	A744THV	London	B84SWX	The Shires
A101EPA	North Midlands	A207OKJ	Southern Counties	A829JLT	Southern Counties	B84WUL	London
A101SYE	London	A208OKJ	Southern Counties	A855UYM	The Shires	B85WUL	London
A102SYE	London	A209OKJ	Southern Counties	A856UYM	The Shires	B86WUL	London
A103OUG	Cymru	A210OKJ	Southern Counties	A858YOX	North Midlands	B87WUL	London
A103SYE	London	A215PEV	North Midlands	A859YOX	North Midlands	B88WUL	London
A104OUG	Cymru	A233GHN	North East	A888PKR	Southern Counties	B89WUL	London
A110FDL	The Shires	A234GHN	North East	A889PKR	Southern Counties	B90WUL	London
A113EPA	North Midlands	A235GHN	North East	A890PKR	Southern Counties	B91WUL	London
A115EPA	North Midlands	A236GHN	North East	A891SUL	London	B92WUL	London
A117EPA	North East	A237GHN	North East	A894SUL	London	B93WUL	London
A118EPA	North Midlands	A238GHN	North East	A895SUL	London	B94WUL	London
A119EPA	North East	A240GHN	North East	A898KAH	North Midlands	B95WUL	London
A11GTA	Southern Counties	A241GHN	North East	A903SUL	London	B96WUL	London
A121EPA	North Midlands	A242GHN	North East	A909LWU	North East	B97WUL	London
A122EPA	North East	A243GHN	North East	A919SUL	London	B98WUL	London
A124EPA	The Shires	A244GHN	North East	A927SUL	London	B99WUL	London
A125EPA	Fox County	A246SVW	The Shires	A929SUL	London	B100WUL	London
A129DTO	Fox County	A247SVW	The Shires	A930SUL	London	B100XTW	The Shires
A130DTO	Fox County	A248SVW	The Shires	A936SUL	London	B101WUL	London
A130FDC	North East	A249SVW	The Shires	A939SUL	London	B102KPF	North Midlands
A131DTO	Fox County	A250SVW	The Shires	A948SUL	London	B102WUL	London
A131FDC	North East	A441UUV	London	A949KAJ	North East	B103KPF	North Midlands
A132DTO	Fox County	A442UUV	London	A959SYF	London	B103WUL	London
A132SMA	Fox County	A501EJF	Fox County	A973SYF	London	B104KPF	North Midlands
A133DTO	Fox County	A502EJF	Fox County	A984SYF	London	B104WUL	London
A133SMA	Fox County	A503EJF	Fox County	A988SYF	London	B105KPF	North Midlands
A134FDC	North East	A504EJF	Fox County	A996SYF	Southern Counties	B105WUL	London
A134SMA	Fox County	A505EJF	Fox County	A998SYF	London	B108KPF	North Midlands
A135FDC	North East	A507EJF	Fox County	AAL303A	North Midlands	B109KPF	North Midlands
A135SMA	North East	A508EJF	Fox County	AAL404A	North Midlands	B109WUL	London
A136EPA	North Midlands	A509EJF	Fox County	AAX590A	North Midlands	B110GRR	North East
A136FDC	North East	A50LHG	North West	ACM706X	Fox County	B111GRR	North East
A137FDC	North East	A510EJF	Fox County	ACM707X	Fox County	B112GRR	North East
A138FDC	North East	A511EJF	Fox County	ACM710X	Fox County	B112WUL	London
A139EPA	North Midlands	A516EVN	North East	ACM711X	Fox County	B113GRR	North East
A139MRN	North West	A517EVN	North East	ACW764R	North West	B114GRR	North East

Reg	Operator	Reg	Operator	Reg	Operator	Reg	Operator
B115GRR	North East	B245NVN	North East	B860XYR	The Shires	BYX280V	London
B116WUL	London	B246NVN	North East	B861XYR	The Shires	BYX282V	London
B121WUL	London	B247NVN	North East	B863XYR	London	BYX283V	London
B122WUL	London	B248WUL	London	B864XYR	London	BYX290V	London
B123WUL	London	B249WUL	London	B865XYR	London	BYX296V	OLST
B124WUL	London	B251NVN	North East	B866XYR	London	BYX298V	London
B126WUL	London	B252PHN	North East	B867XYR	London	BYX299V	The Shires
B127WUL	London	B252WUL	London	B868XYR	London	BYX301V	The Shires
B128WUL	London	B253PHN	North East	B870XYR	London	BYX304V	OLST
B129WUL	London	B253WUL	London	B871XYR	London	BYX310V	OLST
B130WUL	London	B254WUL	London	B872XYR	London	BYX314V	OLST
B131SED	Cymru	B255RAJ	North East	B907RVF	North East	BYX317V	London
B131WUL	London	B255WUL	London	B908RVF	North East	C21CHM	London
B132SED	Cymru	B262KPF	Northumbria	B911NBF	North Midlands	C22CHM	London
B132WUL	London	B262LPH	The Shires	B912NBF	North Midlands	C24CHM	London
B133WUL	London	B263WUL	London	B913NBF	North Midlands	C26CHM	London
B134GAU	Fox County	B265KPF	Northumbria	B962WRN	North West	C31CHM	London
B134WUL	London	B265WUL	London	B963WRN	North West	C32CHM	London
B135GAU	Fox County	B266KPF	North East	B964WRN	North West	C34CWT	North East
B135WUL	London	B270LPH	The Shires	B965WRN	North West	C35CHM	London
B136GAU	Fox County	B271LPH	The Shires	B966WRN	North West	C35CWT	North East
B136WUL	London	B272LPH	The Shires	B967WRN	North West	C36CHM	London
B137GAU	Fox County	B273KPF	Northumbria	B968WRN	North West	C36CWT	North Midlands
B137WUL	London	B273LPH	The Shires	B969WRN	North West	C37CHM	London
B138GAU	Fox County	B274LPH	North Midlands	BAZ6869	The Shires	C37CWT	North Midlands
B138WUL	London	B275LPH	North Midlands	BAZ7384	The Shires	C37WBF	North Midlands
B139GAU	Fox County	B275WUL	London	BHS206X	Scotland West	C38CHM	London
B139WUL	London	B276KPF	Northumbria	BHS207X	Scotland West	C38CWT	North East
B140GAU	Fox County	B276WUL	London	BKE831T	Southern Counties	C39CWT	North East
B140WUL	London	B277KPF	Northumbria	BKE832T	Southern Counties	C40CWT	North Midlands
B141GAU	Fox County	B278WUL	London	BKE840T	Southern Counties	C41CHM	London
B142GAU	Fox County	B279KPF	Northumbria	BKE846T	Southern Counties	C41CWT	North East
B143GAU	Fox County	B279WUL	London	BKE847T	The Shires	C41HHJ	The Shires
B145ALG	North Midlands	B280WUL	London	BKE848T	Southern Counties	C42CWT	North East
B147ALG	North Midlands	B281KPF	North East	BKE852T	Southern Counties	C42HHJ	Fox County
B148TRN	North West	B281WUL	London	BKE853T	Southern Counties	C43CWT	North East
B149TRN	North West	B282WUL	London	BMA522W	Cymru	C45CHM	London
B150ALG	North Midlands	B283KPF	North East	BMA523W	North Midlands	C46CHM	London
B150TRN	North West	B283WUL	London	BMA524W	Cymru	C49CHM	London
B151TRN	North West	B284KPF	Northumbria	BMA527W	Cymru	C49OCM	Cymru
B152WUL	London	B285WUL	London	BPF135Y	The Shires	C50CHM	London
B153TRN	North West	B286WUL	London	BPF136Y	The Shires	C52CHM	London
B154TRN	North West	B288WUL	London	BPR48Y	North East	C56CHM	London
B154WUL	London	B289WUL	London	BPR49Y	North East	C58CHM	London
B155TRN	North West	B290WUL	London	BPR102Y	North Midlands	C59CHM	London
B155WUL	London	B291WUL	London	BPR108Y	Fox County	C63CHM	London
B162WUL	London	B293WUL	London	BPT919S	Northumbria	C63JTU	Cymru
B164WUL	London	B294WUL	London	BPT923S	Northumbria	C65CHM	London
B165WUL	London	B295WUL	London	BRC834T	Southern Counties	C66CHM	London
B169WUL	London	B296WUL	London	BRC837T	Southern Counties	C75UHN	North East
B170WUL	London	B297WUL	London	BSJ899T	Scotland West	C78CHM	London
B173WUL	London	B298WUL	London	BSJ916T	Scotland West	C78WRE	North Midlands
B175WUL	London	B299WUL	London	BSJ925T	Scotland West	C79CHM	London
B176WUL	London	B300WUL	London	BTX152T	The Shires	C89NNV	Southern Counties
B179WUL	London	B303WUL	London	BVP763V	North Midlands	C99CHM	London
B182WUL	London	B504PRF	North Midlands	BVP765V	North Midlands	C102CHM	London
B183BLG	The Shires	B512LFP	Fox County	BVP767V	North Midlands	C103UHO	Yorkshire
B184BLG	The Shires	B513LFP	Cymru	BVP785V	Fox County	C104UHO	Yorkshire
B185BLG	The Shires	B514LFP	Fox County	BVP813V	Fox County	C113CHM	London
B186BLG	Cymru	B516OEH	North Midlands	BVV545T	The Shires	C131HJN	North East
B187BLG	Fox County	B51XFV	North West	BYW359V	North West	C132HJN	North East
B189BLG	The Shires	B593SWX	Yorkshire	BYW367V	North West	C133HJN	North East
B190BLG	Fox County	B593SWX	Yorkshire	BYW379V	North West	C141SPB	North Midlands
B191BLG	Cymru	B593SWX	Yorkshire	BYW402V	North West	C144NRR	Fox County
B192BLG	Cymru	B594SWX	Yorkshire	BYW406V	North West	C145NRR	Fox County
B193BLG	Cymru	B595SWX	Yorkshire	BYW412V	North West	C146NRR	Fox County
B194BLG	Cymru	B596SWX	Yorkshire	BYW413V	North West	C147NRR	Fox County
B196BLG	Cymru	B597SWX	Yorkshire	BYW430V	North West	C148NRR	Fox County
B197DTU	North Midlands	B598SWX	North East	BYW432V	North West	C206EKJ	Scotland West
B198DTU	North Midlands	B599SWX	Yorkshire	BYW437V	North West	C208GTU	Cymru
B203DTU	North Midlands	B600UUM	Yorkshire	BYX121V	OLST	C209GTU	Cymru
B204DTU	North Midlands	B601UUM	Yorkshire	BYX123V	OLST	C210GTU	Cymru
B209WUL	London	B602UUM	Yorkshire	BYX132V	London	C211GTU	Cymru
B210WUL	London	B603UUM	Yorkshire	BYX143V	OLST	C212GTU	Cymru
B213WUL	London	B604OEH	North Midlands	BYX168V	Southern Counties	C214UPD	Scotland West
B214WUL	London	B604UUM	Yorkshire	BYX170V	London	C218EKJ	North Midlands
B216WUL	London	B605UUM	The Shires	BYX173V	London	C220EKJ	Cymru
B217WUL	London	B606OEH	North Midlands	BYX175V	London	C221EKJ	Cymru
B219WUL	London	B606UUM	Yorkshire	BYX185V	OLST	C255SPC	The Shires
B221WUL	London	B607OEH	North Midlands	BYX200V	London	C257UAJ	Southern Counties
B227WUL	London	B607UUM	Yorkshire	BYX205V	London	C258UAJ	Cymru
B228WUL	London	B608UUM	Yorkshire	BYX208V	The Shires	C259UAJ	Northumbria
B229WUL	London	B609UUM	Yorkshire	BYX222V	The Shires	C25CHM	London
B231WUL	London	B724AGD	Scotland West	BYX230V	London	C260UAJ	Northumbria
B233WUL	London	B725AGD	Scotland West	BYX232V	The Shires	C261UAJ	Northumbria
B238LRA	OLST	B85SWX	The Shires	BYX232V	London	C262SPC	North Midlands
B239WUL	London	B857XYR	The Shires	BYX245V	OLST	C262UAJ	Northumbria
B240LRA	OLST	B858XYR	The Shires	BYX263V	London	C263FGG	Scotland West
B241LRA	OLST	B859XYR	The Shires	BYX266V	London	C263XEF	Northumbria

Reg	Location	Reg	Location	Reg	Location	Reg	Location
C264FGG	Scotland West	CUB60Y	North East	D45OKH	The Shires	D211FYM	London
C264XEF	Northumbria	CUB61Y	North East	D59TLV	Fox County	D212FYM	London
C265SPC	The Shires	CUB63Y	North East	D80UTF	Fox County	D213FYM	London
C265XEF	North East	CUB64Y	North East	D82VCC	Cymru	D214FYM	London
C266XEF	North East	CUB66Y	North East	D85VCC	Scotland West	D216FYM	London
C267XEF	North East	CUB68Y	North East	D89VCC	Cymru	D218FYM	London
C268XEF	North East	CUB69Y	North East	D98VCC	Scotland West	D220FYM	London
C307BUV	London	CUB71Y	North East	D101NDW	Southern Counties	D221FYM	London
C308BUV	London	CUL83V	London	D102NDW	Southern Counties	D222FYM	London
C309BUV	London	CUL88V	Scotland West	D108NDW	Southern Counties	D223FYM	London
C310BUV	London	CUL94V	Scotland West	D135FYM	London	D223SKD	Fox County
C312BUV	London	CUL95V	Scotland West	D135NUS	North Midlands	D224FYM	London
C313BUV	London	CUL100V	London	D139FYM	London	D224SKD	Fox County
C314BUV	London	CUL143V	Scotland West	D140FYM	London	D225FYM	London
C316BUV	London	CUL152V	Scotland West	D143FYM	London	D226FYM	London
C317BUV	London	CUL179C	London	D146FYM	London	D226SKD	Fox County
C318BUV	London	CUL185C	London	D147FYM	London	D227FYM	London
C319BUV	London	CUL217C	London	D148FYM	London	D228FYM	London
C320BUV	London	CUV220C	OLST	D149FYM	London	D229FYM	London
C321BUV	London	CUV240C	OLST	D150FYM	London	D230FYM	London
C322BUV	London	CUV241C	OLST	D152FYM	London	D231FYM	London
C323BUV	London	CUV243C	OLST	D153FYM	London	D232FYM	London
C324BUV	London	CUV248C	OLST	D154THG	North West	D233FYM	London
C326BUV	London	CUV259C	OLST	D155FYM	London	D234FYM	London
C327BUV	London	CUV261C	London	D155HML	Southern Counties	D235FYM	London
C332BUV	London	CUV264C	London	D156HML	Southern Counties	D236FYM	London
C354BUV	London	CUV266C	London	D157FYM	London	D237FYM	London
C359BUV	London	CUV267C	London	D157HML	Southern Counties	D238FYM	London
C362BUV	London	CUV277C	London	D158FYM	London	D239FYM	London
C367BUV	London	CUV280C	London	D159FYM	London	D240FYM	London
C379BUV	London	CUV287C	London	D160FYM	London	D241FYM	London
C398BUV	London	CUV292C	London	D161FYM	London	D242FYM	London
C399BUV	London	CUV294C	London	D162FYM	London	D243FYM	London
C401BUV	London	CUV301C	London	D163FYM	London	D245FYM	London
C402BUV	London	CUV304C	London	D164FYM	London	D246FYM	London
C404BUV	London	CUV307C	London	D165FYM	London	D247FYM	London
C405BUV	London	CUV315C	London	D166FYM	London	D248FYM	London
C406BUV	London	CUV323C	London	D167FYM	London	D249FYM	London
C407BUV	London	CUV324C	London	D168FYM	London	D250FYM	London
C413BUV	London	CUV325C	London	D168VRP	Scotland West	D251FYM	London
C417BUV	London	CUV326C	London	D169FYM	London	D252FYM	London
C424BUV	London	CUV328C	London	D170VRP	Scotland West	D253FYM	London
C449BKM	Scotland West	CUV329C	London	D171FYM	London	D254FYM	London
C450BKM	Scotland West	CUV330C	London	D171VRP	Scotland West	D255FYM	London
C451BKM	Scotland West	CUV333C	London	D174FYM	London	D256FYM	London
C452GKE	Scotland West	CUV334C	London	D174VRP	Scotland West	D257FYM	London
C453GKE	Scotland West	CUV340C	London	D175FYM	London	D258FYM	London
C454GKE	Scotland West	CUV343C	London	D176FYM	London	D259FYM	London
C475TAY	Fox County	CUV344C	London	D176LNA	North Midlands	D387VKJ	Southern Counties
C514MDS	Scotland West	CUV346C	London	D177FYM	London	D401MHS	North Midlands
C610ANW	Yorkshire	CUV347C	London	D178FYM	London	D409NNA	North West
C611ANW	Yorkshire	CUV350C	London	D179FYM	London	D431NNA	North West
C612ANW	Yorkshire	CUV351C	London	D181FYM	London	D433UHC	Scotland West
C613ANW	Northumbria	CUV354C	London	D182FYM	London	D438UHC	Scotland West
C614ANW	Northumbria	CUV355C	London	D183FYM	London	D441RKE	Cymru
C616ANW	Northumbria	CUV356C	London	D184FYM	London	D442UHC	Scotland West
C617ANW	Northumbria	CUV359C	London	D185FYM	London	D443UHC	Cymru
C632PAU	Fox County	CVA110V	Southern Counties	D186FYM	London	D445NNA	North West
C707JMB	Scotland West	CWR505Y	North East	D187FYM	London	D466EAJ	North East
C802SDY	North Midlands	CWR506Y	Cymru	D188FYM	London	D479EAJ	North East
C804BYY	London	CWR507Y	Cymru	D188VRP	Scotland West	D534FAE	North Midlands
C805BYY	London	CWR508Y	Cymru	D189FYM	London	D538FAE	North Midlands
C806BYY	London	CWR509Y	Cymru	D191FYM	London	D603ACW	The Shires
C814BYY	London	CWR510Y	Cymru	D192FYM	London	D648CVN	North East
C817BYY	London	CWR511Y	Scotland West	D193FYM	London	D711SKB	Cymru
C820BYY	London	CWR512Y	Cymru	D194FYM	London	D906MVU	Fox County
C823SDY	North Midlands	CWR513Y	Cymru	D195FYM	London	D954VCN	Southern Counties
C915BPW	OLST	CWR514Y	Scotland West	D196FYM	London	D959UDY	Scotland West
C916BPW	OLST	CWR515Y	Scotland West	D197FYM	London	DBV133Y	North West
C917BPW	OLST	CWR516Y	The Shires	D198FYM	London	DBV135Y	North West
C918BPW	OLST	CWR517Y	Yorkshire	D199FYM	London	DBV136Y	North West
C920FMP	Yorkshire	CWR518Y	Scotland West	D200FYM	London	DCA528X	Cymru
CAZ6852	The Shires	CWR519Y	Scotland West	D201FYM	London	DCA530X	Cymru
CBD897T	The Shires	CWR520Y	Yorkshire	D202FYM	London	DCA532X	Cymru
CBD899T	The Shires	CWR521Y	Yorkshire	D202SKD	Scotland West	DCA533X	The Shires
CBD904T	The Shires	CWR522Y	Cymru	D203FYM	London	DDX741T	The Shires
CBV792S	North West	CWR523Y	Cymru	D204FBK	Yorkshire	DJN25X	North Midlands
CCY819V	North East	CWR524Y	Yorkshire	D204FYM	London	DOC20V	North West
CCY820V	Cymru	CWR527Y	Cymru	D204SKD	Scotland West	DOC21V	North West
CEF230Y	Cymru	CWR528Y	Yorkshire	D205FYM	London	DOC22V	North West
CEF231Y	Southern Counties	CWR529Y	Yorkshire	D205SKD	Scotland West	DOC26V	North Midlands
CEF232Y	Cymru	CWU326T	North East	D206FYM	London	DOC29V	North Midlands
CFM350S	North West	D25KKP	Scotland West	D206SKD	Scotland West	DOC30V	North West
CKS386X	Fox County	D28KKP	Cymru	D207FYM	London	DOC31V	North East
CPT734S	Northumbria	D31RWC	Cymru	D208FYM	London	DOC32V	North West
CPT736S	Northumbria	D32RWC	Cymru	D208SKD	The Shires	DOC33V	North West
CPT738S	Northumbria	D36KKP	Scotland West	D209FYM	London	DOC36V	North West
CPT739S	Northumbria	D43RWC	The Shires	D210FYM	London	DOC37V	North Midlands
CTN637V	Southern Counties	D44RWC	Fox County	D210SKD	The Shires	DOC38V	North West

DOC43V	North West	E254TUB	Cymru	E885KYW	Southern Counties	F51ENF	North Midlands
DOC45V	North West	E255TUB	Yorkshire	E886KYW	Southern Counties	F52ENF	North Midlands
DOC47V	North West	E255TUB	Yorkshire	E887KYW	Southern Counties	F61SMC	The Shires
DTG366V	The Shires	E256TUB	Cymru	E888KYW	The Shires	F62SMC	The Shires
DTG367V	The Shires	E257TUB	Yorkshire	E889KYW	The Shires	F63SMC	The Shires
DUP745S	Northumbria	E258TUB	Cymru	E890KYW	Southern Counties	F66BKK	Cymru
DUP747S	Northumbria	E259TUB	Yorkshire	E891AKN	Southern Counties	F66FKW	Cymru
DUP753S	Northumbria	E260TUB	Yorkshire	E963PME	North East	F67FKW	Cymru
E21ECH	Fox County	E261TUB	Yorkshire	E965PME	The Shires	F68BKK	North Midlands
E23ECH	Fox County	E262TUB	Cymru	E966PME	The Shires	F68BKK	Southern Counties
E24ECH	Fox County	E263TUB	Yorkshire	E967PME	Cymru	F68FKW	Cymru
E25ECH	Fox County	E264TUB	Yorkshire	E968PME	Cymru	F69FKW	Cymru
E25UNE	North Midlands	E265WUB	Yorkshire	E969PME	The Shires	F70FKW	Cymru
E26ECH	Fox County	E266KEF	North East	E970NMK	The Shires	F77ERJ	North Midlands
E26UNE	North Midlands	E266WUB	Yorkshire	E970PME	The Shires	F96PRE	North Midlands
E27UNE	North Midlands	E267KEF	North East	E980NMK	Cymru	F97PRE	North Midlands
E28UNE	North Midlands	E267WUB	Yorkshire	E990DNK	The Shires	F101TML	London
E29UNE	North Midlands	E268KEF	North East	E990NMK	North Midlands	F102TML	Southern Counties
E30UNE	North Midlands	E268WUB	Yorkshire	E992NMK	North Midlands	F102YVP	London
E31UNE	North Midlands	E269KEF	North East	E993NMK	North Midlands	F103TML	London
E32UNE	North Midlands	E269WUB	Yorkshire	EDZ215	Northumbria	F104TML	London
E33EVW	Cymru	E270KEF	North East	EEH901Y	Northumbria	F104YVP	London
E34EVW	Cymru	E270WUB	Yorkshire	EEH902Y	North Midlands	F105TML	London
E34NEF	Southern Counties	E271KEF	North East	EEH903Y	North Midlands	F105YVP	London
E35EVW	Cymru	E271WUB	Yorkshire	EEH904Y	North Midlands	F106TML	London
E36EVW	Cymru	E272KEF	North East	EEH905Y	North Midlands	F107TML	London
E37EVW	Cymru	E273KEF	North East	EEH906Y	North Midlands	F108TML	London
E41UKL	Southern Counties	E274KEF	North East	EEH907Y	North Midlands	F109TML	London
E42UKL	Southern Counties	E275KEF	North East	EEH908Y	Northumbria	F110SRF	North Midlands
E43UKL	Cymru	E290OMG	Cymru	EEH909Y	North Midlands	F110TML	London
E44UKL	North West	E323OMG	The Shires	EEH910Y	North Midlands	F111TML	Southern Counties
E45UKL	Cymru	E324WYS	Scotland West	EGF220B	London	F112TML	London
E46UKL	Southern Counties	E328OMG	Cymru	EJC447X	Cymru	F113TML	London
E47UKL	North West	E332WYS	Scotland West	EMB366S	North West	F114TML	Southern Counties
E48UKL	Cymru	E335DRO	The Shires	EMB367S	North West	F115PHM	London
E49UKL	Cymru	E339WYS	Scotland West	EON831V	Fox County	F116PHM	London
E49WEM	Cymru	E341DRO	The Shires	EPD511V	Southern Counties	F117PHM	London
E50UKL	Cymru	E353WYS	Scotland West	EPH210V	Fox County	F117XTX	Yorkshire
E51UKL	Cymru	E355WYS	Scotland West	EPH212V	Fox County	F118PHM	London
E52UKL	North West	E420EBH	The Shires	EPH220V	Southern Counties	F118XTX	Yorkshire
E53UKL	North West	E478NSC	North Midlands	EPH232V	Southern Counties	F119PHM	London
E54UKL	North West	E564BNK	The Shires	EWF474V	Fox County	F120PHM	London
E55UKL	North West	E564YBU	North Midlands	EWF484V	Fox County	F121PHM	London
E56UKL	North West	E565BNK	The Shires	EWT206Y	North East	F121TRU	The Shires
E57UKL	North West	E641VFY	Cymru	EWT207Y	Cymru	F122PHM	London
E58UKL	Southern Counties	E642VFY	Cymru	EWT208Y	North East	F122TRU	The Shires
E59UKL	Cymru	E667YDT	The Shires	EWT209Y	Cymru	F122TRU	The Shires
E60UKL	Cymru	E676DCU	Northumbria	EWT210Y	North East	F123PHM	London
E62UKL	Fox County	E677DCU	Cymru	EWW539Y	Yorkshire	F123TRU	The Shires
E63UKL	North West	E678DCU	Cymru	EWW541Y	Yorkshire	F124PHM	London
E64UKL	North West	E701XKR	Fox County	EWW542Y	Yorkshire	F124TRU	The Shires
E65XKE	North West	E702XKR	Fox County	EWW545Y	Yorkshire	F125PHM	London
E69UKL	Southern Counties	E801BTN	Northumbria	EWW546Y	The Shires	F125TRU	The Shires
E70UKL	Southern Counties	E803BTN	Northumbria	EWW546Y	The Shires	F126PHM	London
E72KBF	North Midlands	E804BTN	Northumbria	EWW547Y	Yorkshire	F127PHM	London
E72UKL	Southern Counties	E805BTN	Northumbria	EWW548Y	Yorkshire	F128PHM	London
E96WCM	North Midlands	E806BTN	Northumbria	EWW551Y	The Shires	F128TRU	The Shires
E99WCM	North Midlands	E810BTN	Northumbria	EWW552Y	Yorkshire	F129PHM	London
E104JYV	London	E812BTN	Northumbria	EWX211Y	Cymru	F129YVP	London
E105JYV	London	E813BTN	Northumbria	EWX212Y	Cymru	F130PHM	London
E107JYV	London	E814BTN	Northumbria	EWX213Y	Cymru	F131PHM	London
E109JYV	London	E815BTN	Northumbria	EWX214Y	Cymru	F132PHM	London
E110JYV	London	E816BTN	Northumbria	EWX215Y	Cymru	F133PHM	London
E111KYN	London	E817BTN	Northumbria	EWX530Y	Yorkshire	F134PHM	London
E112KYN	London	E818BTN	Northumbria	EWX531Y	Cymru	F135PHM	London
E113KYN	London	E819BTN	Northumbria	EWX532Y	Yorkshire	F136PHM	London
E114KYN	London	E820BTN	Northumbria	EWX534Y	Yorkshire	F137PHM	London
E116UTX	Yorkshire	E821BTN	Northumbria	EWX535Y	Yorkshire	F138PHM	London
E136KYW	Southern Counties	E822BTN	Northumbria	EWX536Y	Yorkshire	F139PHM	London
E141KYW	Southern Counties	E823BTN	Northumbria	EWX536Y	The Shires	F140PHM	London
E145KYW	Southern Counties	E824BTN	Northumbria	EWX537Y	Yorkshire	F141PHM	London
E149BTO	Fox County	E825BTN	Northumbria	EWX543Y	The Shires	F142PHM	London
E150BTO	Fox County	E826BTN	Northumbria	EYE336V	The Shires	F143PHM	London
E151BTO	Fox County	E827BTN	Northumbria	F27JRC	Fox County	F144PHM	London
E151OMD	Southern Counties	E829AWA	North Midlands	F26XVP	Fox County	F151KGS	The Shires
E152BTO	Fox County	E829BTN	Northumbria	F27XVP	Fox County	F152KGS	The Shires
E152OMD	Southern Counties	E830BTN	Northumbria	F28JRC	Fox County	F153DET	Fox County
E153BTO	Fox County	E831BTN	Northumbria	F29XVP	Fox County	F153KGS	The Shires
E153OMD	Southern Counties	E832BTN	Northumbria	F33ENF	North Midlands	F154DET	Fox County
E154OMD	Southern Counties	E833BTN	Northumbria	F34ENF	North Midlands	F154DKU	The Shires
E155OMD	Southern Counties	E834BTN	Northumbria	F35ENF	North Midlands	F155DET	Fox County
E156OMD	Southern Counties	E836BKL	Southern Counties	F36ENF	North Midlands	F155DKU	North Midlands
E157OMD	Southern Counties	E836BTN	Northumbria	F39ENF	North Midlands	F156DET	Fox County
E158OMD	Southern Counties	E840BTN	Northumbria	F40ENF	North Midlands	F157DET	Fox County
E159OMD	Southern Counties	E841BTN	Northumbria	F44XVP	Fox County	F158DET	Fox County
E160OMD	Southern Counties	E844BTN	Northumbria	F45ENF	Southern Counties	F170DET	North Midlands
E161OMD	Southern Counties	E845BTN	Northumbria	F46ENF	Southern Counties	F181YDA	North Midlands
E164OMD	Southern Counties	E881YKY	The Shires	F47ENF	Southern Counties	F185PRE	North Midlands
E205TUB	Yorkshire	E882YKY	The Shires	F48ENF	Southern Counties	F186PRE	North Midlands

Reg	Operator	Reg	Operator	Reg	Operator	Reg	Operator
F187REH	North Midlands	F379UCP	Fox County	F836BCW	North Midlands	G97VMM	The Shires
F188HKK	Northumbria	F393DOA	Southern Counties	F892BKK	Southern Counties	G98VMM	North Midlands
F188REH	North Midlands	F400PUR	The Shires	F893BKK	Southern Counties	G100TND	North West
F189HKK	Northumbria	F401PUR	The Shires	F894BKK	Southern Counties	G101TND	Southern Counties
F189RRF	North Midlands	F402PUR	The Shires	F895BKK	Southern Counties	G102TND	North West
F190RRF	North Midlands	F403PUR	The Shires	F896DKK	Southern Counties	G104TND	North West
F191SRF	North Midlands	F404PUR	The Shires	F897DKK	Southern Counties	G106TND	North West
F192VFA	North Midlands	F406DUG	Fox County	F898DKK	Southern Counties	G107TND	North West
F210DCC	Cymru	F407DUG	Fox County	F899DKK	Southern Counties	G108OUG	Yorkshire
F211DCC	Cymru	F424EJC	Cymru	F899GUM	Southern Counties	G108TND	North West
F212DCC	Cymru	F425EJC	Cymru	F900DKK	Southern Counties	G109OUG	Yorkshire
F213DCC	Cymru	F425UVW	The Shires	F901GUM	Southern Counties	G109TND	North West
F214DCC	Cymru	F426EJC	Cymru	F905RPG	Southern Counties	G109YRE	North Midlands
F215DCC	Cymru	F427EJC	Cymru	F907PFH	North Midlands	G110OUG	Yorkshire
F216DCC	Cymru	F428EJC	Cymru	F908RPG	Southern Counties	G110TND	North West
F217DCC	Cymru	F467UVW	The Shires	F956XCK	North Midlands	G111TND	North Midlands
F218DCC	Cymru	F484EJC	North Midlands	F969GKJ	The Shires	G113PGT	North West
F219DCC	Cymru	F485EJC	North Midlands	F985EDS	North Midlands	G113TND	Southern Counties
F220DCC	Cymru	F486EJC	North Midlands	F985GKJ	The Shires	G114TND	North Midlands
F221DCC	Cymru	F506OYW	The Shires	F991UME	Southern Counties	G115TND	North Midlands
F222DCC	Cymru	F523UVW	The Shires	FAZ2784	Fox County	G116TND	North West
F223DCC	Cymru	F571SMG	Southern Counties	FAZ3194	North Midlands	G117TND	North Midlands
F245MTW	The Shires	F572SMG	The Shires	FAZ3195	North Midlands	G118TND	North West
F246MTW	The Shires	F572UPB	The Shires	FAZ5181	North Midlands	G119TND	North West
F258GWJ	North Midlands	F573SMG	The Shires	FAZ5279	North Midlands	G120TJA	Cymru
F266CEY	The Shires	F574SMG	The Shires	FCA10X	North West	G121TJA	North Midlands
F272AWW	Yorkshire	F575SMG	The Shires	FEV178	The Shires	G122RGT	Southern Counties
F272OPX	Fox County	F576SMG	The Shires	FIL3451	Fox County	G122TJA	North Midlands
F273AWW	Yorkshire	F577SMG	Southern Counties	FIL3452	Fox County	G123PGT	Southern Counties
F273CEY	The Shires	F578SMG	Southern Counties	FIL4919	The Shires	G123TND	North West
F274AWW	Yorkshire	F579SMG	The Shires	FKM713L	Southern Counties	G124TJA	North West
F275AWW	Yorkshire	F580SMG	Southern Counties	FKM863V	Southern Counties	G125PGT	Southern Counties
F276AWW	Yorkshire	F598CET	The Shires	FKM864V	Southern Counties	G125TJA	North West
F277AWW	Yorkshire	F601EHA	North Midlands	FKM866V	The Shires	G126PGT	Southern Counties
F278AWW	Yorkshire	F602EHA	North Midlands	FKM867V	Southern Counties	G126TJA	North Midlands
F278HOD	North Midlands	F603EHA	North Midlands	FKM868V	Southern Counties	G127PGT	Southern Counties
F279AWW	Yorkshire	F604EHA	North Midlands	FKM869V	Southern Counties	G127TJA	North Midlands
F280AWW	Yorkshire	F605EHA	North Midlands	FKM874V	The Shires	G128PGT	Southern Counties
F281AWW	Yorkshire	F606EHA	North Midlands	FKM875V	Southern Counties	G128TJA	North Midlands
F282AWW	Yorkshire	F607EHA	North Midlands	FKM877V	Southern Counties	G129YEV	The Shires
F283AWW	Yorkshire	F608EHA	North Midlands	FKM878V	Southern Counties	G130YEV	The Shires
F284AWW	Yorkshire	F609EHA	North Midlands	FKM882V	Southern Counties	G131YWC	The Shires
F285AWW	Yorkshire	F610EHA	North Midlands	G21HHG	North East	G132YWC	The Shires
F286AWW	Yorkshire	F611EHA	North Midlands	G32OHS	Scotland West	G141GOL	North Midlands
F287AWW	Yorkshire	F612EHA	North Midlands	G34HKY	North West	G142GOL	Fox County
F288AWW	Yorkshire	F613EHA	North Midlands	G34VME	Cymru	G143GOL	Fox County
F289AWW	Yorkshire	F615EHA	North Midlands	G34VME	Southern Counties	G145GOL	The Shires
F290AWW	Yorkshire	F616EHA	North Midlands	G35HKY	North West	G145TYT	London
F291AWW	Yorkshire	F619EHA	North Midlands	G35VME	Cymru	G146GOL	The Shires
F292AWW	Yorkshire	F61PRE	North Midlands	G36HKY	North West	G146TYT	London
F293AWW	Yorkshire	F620EHA	North Midlands	G36VME	Southern Counties	G147TYT	London
F294AWW	Yorkshire	F621HGO	Southern Counties	G37HKY	North West	G148CHP	Yorkshire
F295AWW	Yorkshire	F622EHA	North Midlands	G37VME	Southern Counties	G148GOL	The Shires
F296AWW	Yorkshire	F625EHA	North Midlands	G38HKY	North West	G148TYT	London
F297AWW	Yorkshire	F626EHA	North Midlands	G38VME	Southern Counties	G149CHP	Yorkshire
F298AWW	Yorkshire	F630BKD	North West	G38YHJ	Cymru	G149TYT	London
F299AWW	Yorkshire	F632BKD	North West	G39VME	Southern Counties	G150TYT	London
F300AWW	Yorkshire	F633BKD	North West	G39YHJ	Cymru	G151FJC	Cymru
F301AWW	Yorkshire	F633LMJ	The Shires	G40OHS	The Shires	G151TYT	London
F301RUT	Fox County	F634BKD	North West	G40VME	Southern Counties	G152FJC	Cymru
F302AWW	Yorkshire	F634LMJ	The Shires	G40YHJ	Cymru	G152TYT	London
F302MNK	Cymru	F635BKD	North West	G41HKY	North Midlands	G153TYT	London
F302RUT	Fox County	F635LMJ	The Shires	G41VME	Southern Counties	G154TYT	London
F303AWW	Yorkshire	F636LMJ	The Shires	G42VME	Southern Counties	G160YRE	Cymru
F303JTY	Northumbria	F637LMJ	The Shires	G43VME	Southern Counties	G161YRE	Cymru
F303MNK	Cymru	F638LMJ	The Shires	G44VME	Southern Counties	G162YRE	Cymru
F304AWW	Yorkshire	F639LMJ	The Shires	G45VME	Southern Counties	G163YRE	Cymru
F304JTY	Northumbria	F640LMJ	The Shires	G49CVC	Yorkshire	G164YRE	North Midlands
F305AWW	Yorkshire	F641LMJ	The Shires	G58BEL	The Shires	G165YRE	North Midlands
F305JTY	Northumbria	F642LMJ	The Shires	G69PKR	Southern Counties	G166YRE	North Midlands
F306AWW	Yorkshire	F643LMJ	The Shires	G70PKR	Southern Counties	G167YRE	North Midlands
F306JTY	Northumbria	F644LMJ	The Shires	G71PKR	Southern Counties	G168YRE	North Midlands
F307AWW	Yorkshire	F700LCA	North Midlands	G73PKR	Southern Counties	G169FJC	Cymru
F307JTY	Northumbria	F701ECC	Northumbria	G74PKR	Southern Counties	G169YRE	North Midlands
F308AWW	Yorkshire	F701KMA	Cymru	G75PKR	Southern Counties	G170FJC	Cymru
F308JTY	Northumbria	F702ECC	Northumbria	G76PKR	Cymru	G170YRE	North Midlands
F309AWW	Yorkshire	F702KMA	Cymru	G77PKR	Southern Counties	G171FJC	Cymru
F309JTY	Northumbria	F703KFM	North Midlands	G78SKR	Southern Counties	G171YRE	Cymru
F310AWW	Yorkshire	F704KMA	Cymru	G79SKR	Southern Counties	G172FJC	Cymru
F310JTY	Northumbria	F705KFM	North Midlands	G80SKR	Southern Counties	G172YRE	North Midlands
F311AWW	Yorkshire	F713CWJ	The Shires	G82SKR	Southern Counties	G173FJC	Cymru
F311JTY	Northumbria	F714CWJ	The Shires	G83OTU	Fox County	G173YRE	North Midlands
F312AWW	Yorkshire	F715CWJ	The Shires	G84OTU	Fox County	G174FJC	Cymru
F312JTY	Northumbria	F718CWJ	The Shires	G84SKR	Southern Counties	G174YRE	Northumbria
F313AWW	Yorkshire	F719CWJ	The Shires	G85SKR	Southern Counties	G175DRF	Northumbria
F314AWW	Yorkshire	F747XCS	The Shires	G86OTU	Fox County	G175FJC	Cymru
F314RMH	The Shires	F760VNH	Scotland West	G86SKR	Southern Counties	G176FJC	Cymru
F326PPO	North Midlands	F792DWT	North Midlands	G87OTU	Fox County	G177FJC	Cymru
F367CHE	The Shires	F822GDT	North Midlands	G87SKR	Cymru	G183DRF	North Midlands

G184DRF	North Midlands	G386EKA	North West	G621YMG	The Shires	G905SKP	Southern Counties
G193NWY	Scotland West	G387EKA	North West	G622BPH	Southern Counties	G905TYR	London
G196NWY	Scotland West	G388EKA	North West	G623BPH	Southern Counties	G906TYR	London
G201RKK	Southern Counties	G399FSF	North Midlands	G624BPH	Southern Counties	G907TYR	London
G202RKK	Southern Counties	G501SFT	Southern Counties	G625BPH	Southern Counties	G908TYR	London
G203RKK	Southern Counties	G502SFT	Southern Counties	G626BPH	Southern Counties	G916LHA	North Midlands
G209HCP	North East	G503SFT	Southern Counties	G626EKA	Southern Counties	G917LHA	North Midlands
G210HCP	North East	G504SFT	Southern Counties	G627BPH	Southern Counties	G918LHA	North Midlands
G211HCP	North East	G505SFT	North Midlands	G628BPH	Southern Counties	G919LHA	North Midlands
G212HCP	North East	G506SFT	Fox County	G628EKA	Southern Counties	G924WGS	The Shires
G214HCP	North East	G507SFT	North Midlands	G629BPH	Southern Counties	G925WGS	The Shires
G218LGK	Southern Counties	G508EAJ	North East	G630BPH	Southern Counties	G926WGS	The Shires
G229FJC	Cymru	G508SFT	Fox County	G631BPH	Southern Counties	G932WGS	The Shires
G230FJC	Cymru	G509EAJ	North East	G632BPH	Southern Counties	G998RKN	Southern Counties
G232EOA	Fox County	G509SFT	Fox County	G633BPH	Southern Counties	GBU1V	The Shires
G232FJC	Cymru	G510EAJ	North East	G634BPH	Southern Counties	GBU4V	The Shires
G233FJC	Cymru	G510SFT	North Midlands	G635BPH	Southern Counties	GBU5V	The Shires
G234FJC	Cymru	G511EAJ	North East	G636BPH	Southern Counties	GBU8V	The Shires
G235FJC	Cymru	G511SFT	North Midlands	G637BPH	Southern Counties	GBU9V	The Shires
G236EOA	Fox County	G512EAJ	North East	G638BPH	Southern Counties	GCS56V	Scotland West
G236FJC	Cymru	G512SFT	Fox County	G639BPH	Southern Counties	GDZ795	North Midlands
G237FJC	Cymru	G513SFT	Fox County	G640BPH	Southern Counties	GEY389Y	Cymru
G238FJC	Cymru	G514VBB	London	G640CHF	Southern Counties	GFM107X	North Midlands
G239FJC	Cymru	G515VBB	London	G641BPH	Southern Counties	GFM110X	North West
G240FJC	Cymru	G516VBB	London	G641CHF	Southern Counties	GFR799W	The Shires
G241GCC	Cymru	G520VBB	London	G642BPH	Southern Counties	GGE156T	Southern Counties
G242GCC	Cymru	G521VBB	London	G642CHF	Southern Counties	GGR406N	North West
G243GCC	Cymru	G521WJF	Fox County	G643BPH	Southern Counties	GHB574V	The Shires
G251SRG	Northumbria	G522VBB	London	G643CHF	Southern Counties	GIL6253	Fox County
G252SRG	Northumbria	G522WJF	Fox County	G644BPH	North Midlands	GIL6949	Fox County
G253SRG	Northumbria	G523VBB	London	G644EVN	North West	GJG750D	London
G254SRG	Northumbria	G523VBB	London	G645BPH	North Midlands	GKE442Y	Scotland West
G255UVK	Northumbria	G523WJF	Fox County	G645UPP	The Shires	GMB372T	North Midlands
G256UVK	Northumbria	G524VBB	London	G646BPH	North Midlands	GMB373T	North Midlands
G257UVK	Northumbria	G524VBB	London	G646UPP	The Shires	GMB376T	North Midlands
G258UVK	Northumbria	G524WJF	Fox County	G647BPH	North Midlands	GMB378T	North Midlands
G277HDW	The Shires	G525VBB	London	G647EKA	North West	GMB380T	North West
G281UMJ	The Shires	G525WJF	Fox County	G647UPP	The Shires	GMB383T	North Midlands
G282UMJ	The Shires	G526VBB	London	G648EKA	Southern Counties	GMB390T	North Midlands
G283UMJ	The Shires	G527VBB	London	G648UPP	The Shires	GMB392T	North West
G284UMJ	The Shires	G528VBB	London	G649EKA	Southern Counties	GSU347	Northumbria
G285UMJ	The Shires	G529VBB	London	G649UPP	The Shires	GSU854T	North Midlands
G286UMJ	The Shires	G530VBB	London	G64SNN	Fox County	GTO48V	Fox County
G287UMJ	The Shires	G531VBB	London	G650EKA	North West	GTO49V	Fox County
G288UMJ	The Shires	G531VBB	London	G650UPP	The Shires	GTO301V	Fox County
G289UMJ	The Shires	G532VBB	London	G651EKA	North West	GTO302V	Fox County
G290UMJ	The Shires	G533VBB	London	G651UPP	The Shires	GTO304V	Fox County
G291UMJ	The Shires	G534VBB	London	G652EKA	North West	GTO305V	Fox County
G292UMJ	The Shires	G535VBB	London	G652UPP	The Shires	GTO306V	Fox County
G293UMJ	The Shires	G536VBB	London	G653EKA	North West	GTO307V	Fox County
G294UMJ	The Shires	G537VBB	London	G653UPP	The Shires	GUW441W	The Shires
G295UMJ	The Shires	G538VBB	London	G654UPP	The Shires	GUW447W	The Shires
G301DPA	North Midlands	G539VBB	London	G655UPP	The Shires	GUW456W	The Shires
G301RJA	Fox County	G540VBB	London	G656UPP	The Shires	GUW457W	The Shires
G302DPA	North West	G541VBB	London	G657UPP	The Shires	GUW461W	The Shires
G303DPA	North West	G542GAC	Yorkshire	G659DTJ	Southern Counties	GUW462W	The Shires
G304DPA	North West	G542VBB	London	G65SNN	Fox County	GUW465W	The Shires
G305DPA	North West	G543VBB	London	G660DTJ	Southern Counties	GUW475W	The Shires
G306DPA	North Midlands	G544VBB	London	G661DTJ	North West	GUW494W	The Shires
G307DPA	North Midlands	G545JOG	London	G689OHE	Southern Counties	GYE346W	London
G308DPA	North Midlands	G545VBB	London	G690OHE	Southern Counties	GYE351W	OLST
G309DPA	North Midlands	G546NKJ	Southern Counties	G711LKW	North West	GYE353W	OLST
G310DPA	North Midlands	G546VBB	London	G714LKW	North West	GYE365W	London
G311DPA	Cymru	G547VBB	London	G727RGA	North Midlands	GYE372W	London
G312DPA	Cymru	G548VBB	London	G735PGA	The Shires	GYE378W	London
G313DPA	Cymru	G549VBB	London	G754UYT	North East	GYE382W	London
G314DPA	Cymru	G550VBB	London	G755UYT	North East	GYE384W	London
G315DPA	Cymru	G551VBB	London	G756UYT	North East	GYE388W	Southern Counties
G316DPA	Cymru	G552VBB	London	G757UYT	North East	GYE389W	OLST
G317NNW	Yorkshire	G553VBB	London	G758UYT	North East	GYE395W	Southern Counties
G319NNW	Yorkshire	G554VBB	London	G759UYT	North East	GYE396W	London
G321NNW	Yorkshire	G555VBB	London	G760UYT	North East	GYE399W	London
G322NNW	Yorkshire	G556VBB	London	G761UYT	North East	GYE417W	Southern Counties
G324NNW	Yorkshire	G610BPH	Southern Counties	G762UYT	North East	GYE419W	The Shires
G324NUM	Yorkshire	G610CFA	North Midlands	G785PWL	North Midlands	GYE422W	London
G326NUM	Yorkshire	G611BPH	Southern Counties	G801BPG	Southern Counties	GYE426W	London
G327NUM	Yorkshire	G611CFA	North Midlands	G801THA	North Midlands	GYE441W	London
G327PHA	North Midlands	G612BPH	Southern Counties	G802BPG	Southern Counties	GYE445W	London
G328PHA	North Midlands	G612CFA	North Midlands	G802THA	North Midlands	GYE454W	London
G329NUM	Yorkshire	G613BPH	Southern Counties	G807FJX	North Midlands	GYE458W	London
G330NUM	Yorkshire	G614BPH	Southern Counties	G896TGG	The Shires	GYE459W	London
G331NUM	Yorkshire	G615BPH	Southern Counties	G897TGG	North Midlands	GYE474W	London
G332NUM	Yorkshire	G616BPH	Southern Counties	G900TJA	North Midlands	GYE478W	London
G360FOP	The Shires	G616WGS	North Midlands	G901MNS	North Midlands	GYE485W	London
G381EKA	North West	G617BPH	Southern Counties	G901SKP	Southern Counties	GYE492W	London
G382EKA	North West	G618BPH	Southern Counties	G902MNS	Scotland West	GYE493W	The Shires
G383EKA	North West	G619BPH	Southern Counties	G902SKP	Southern Counties	GYE495W	OLST
G384EKA	North West	G620BPH	Southern Counties	G903SKP	Southern Counties	GYE496W	London
G385EKA	North West	G621BPH	Southern Counties	G904SKP	Southern Counties	GYE500W	London

Reg	Operator	Reg	Operator	Reg	Operator	Reg	Operator
GYE503W	London	H108GEV	London	H266CFT	Northumbria	H658GPF	North Midlands
GYE507W	London	H108RWT	Yorkshire	H267CFT	Northumbria	H659GPF	Fox County
GYE508W	London	H109GEV	London	H278LEF	North East	H660GPF	North West
GYE509W	OLST	H110GEV	London	H279LEF	North East	H661GPF	North West
GYE510W	London	H112DDS	North Midlands	H301FKL	Southern Counties	H662GPF	North West
GYE511W	London	H112GEV	London	H313WUA	North Midlands	H663GPF	Fox County
GYE515W	London	H113GEV	London	H314WUA	North Midlands	H664GPF	Fox County
GYE517W	London	H114GEV	London	H330DHA	North Midlands	H665GPF	North West
GYE518W	London	H115GEV	London	H331DHA	North Midlands	H667GPF	North West
GYE519W	London	H120THE	London	H332DHA	North Midlands	H668GPF	Scotland West
GYE520W	London	H122THE	London	H334DHA	North Midlands	H671GPF	Fox County
GYE521W	London	H123THE	London	H334TYG	Yorkshire	H672GPF	Fox County
GYE522W	London	H123WFM	The Shires	H335DHA	North Midlands	H674GPF	Fox County
GYE525W	OLST	H124THE	London	H335TYG	Yorkshire	H675AGD	Scotland West
GYE528W	London	H125THE	London	H336DHA	North Midlands	H675GPF	Scotland West
GYE529W	London	H126THE	London	H336TYG	Yorkshire	H676GPF	Scotland West
GYE530W	London	H127THE	London	H337DHA	North Midlands	H677GPF	Fox County
GYE531W	London	H128THE	London	H337TYG	Yorkshire	H679GPF	North West
GYE533W	OLST	H129CDB	North West	H338DHA	North Midlands	H680GPF	Fox County
GYE534W	London	H129THE	London	H338TYG	Yorkshire	H681GPF	Scotland West
GYE535W	London	H130CDB	North West	H338UWT	Yorkshire	H682GPF	Fox County
GYE536W	London	H130LPU	Cymru	H339UWT	Yorkshire	H684GPF	Fox County
GYE537W	London	H130THE	London	H341UWT	Yorkshire	H695KKV	Fox County
GYE538W	London	H131CDB	North Midlands	H342UWT	Yorkshire	H697KKV	Fox County
GYE539W	OLST	H131THE	London	H343UWT	Yorkshire	H701UNW	Scotland West
GYE540W	London	H132CDB	North Midlands	H343UWX	Yorkshire	H702UNW	Scotland West
GYE541W	London	H132MOB	London	H344UWX	Yorkshire	H703UNW	Scotland West
GYE544W	London	H133CDB	North Midlands	H345UWX	Yorkshire	H704UNW	Scotland West
GYE547W	London	H134CDB	North Midlands	H346UWX	Yorkshire	H705UNW	Scotland West
GYE548W	Southern Counties	H135CDB	North Midlands	H347UWX	Yorkshire	H706UNW	Scotland West
GYE549W	London	H136CDB	North Midlands	H350PNO	The Shires	H707UNW	Yorkshire
GYE551W	Southern Counties	H143MOB	London	H355WWX	Yorkshire	H708LOL	North Midlands
GYE553W	OLST	H149NOJ	Cymru	H356WWX	Yorkshire	H708UNW	Scotland West
GYE555W	London	H155XYU	London	H357WWX	Yorkshire	H709LOL	North Midlands
GYE558W	OLST	H156XYU	London	H358WWY	Yorkshire	H709UNW	Scotland West
GYE559W	Southern Counties	H157XYU	London	H359WWY	Yorkshire	H710UNW	Scotland West
GYE562W	London	H158XYU	London	H372PHK	The Shires	H711UNW	Scotland West
GYE567W	London	H166MFA	North Midlands	H393WWY	Yorkshire	H712UNW	Scotland West
GYE568W	London	H176JVT	North Midlands	H406FGS	The Shires	H713UNW	Scotland West
GYE569W	London	H177JVT	North Midlands	H407BVR	Cymru	H729LOL	North Midlands
GYE573W	London	H183CNS	Scotland West	H407ERO	The Shires	H731LOL	North Midlands
GYE575W	London	H185CNS	Scotland West	H407FGS	The Shires	H733HWK	Cymru
GYE577W	London	H185DHA	North Midlands	H408BVR	The Shires	H755WWW	Yorkshire
GYE580W	London	H186EHA	North Midlands	H408ERO	The Shires	H756WWW	Yorkshire
GYE581W	London	H187EHA	North Midlands	H408FGS	The Shires	H757WWW	Yorkshire
GYE582W	London	H188EHA	North Midlands	H408YMA	North Midlands	H765EKJ	Southern Counties
GYE584W	London	H189EHA	North Midlands	H409BVR	The Shires	H766EKJ	Southern Counties
GYE585W	London	H191EHA	North Midlands	H409ERO	The Shires	H767EKJ	Southern Counties
GYE586W	London	H192JNF	North Midlands	H410ERO	The Shires	H768EKJ	Southern Counties
GYE587W	London	H196GRO	The Shires	H433DHA	North Midlands	H769EKJ	Southern Counties
GYE590W	London	H196JVT	North Midlands	H458UGO	London	H770EKJ	Southern Counties
GYE591W	London	H197GRO	The Shires	H459UGO	London	H801SKY	North Midlands
GYE593W	London	H197JVT	North Midlands	H460UGO	London	H802SKY	North Midlands
GYE596W	London	H198AOD	The Shires	H460WWY	Yorkshire	H803AHA	North Midlands
GYE600W	London	H198GRO	The Shires	H461UGO	London	H803RWJ	North West
GYE601W	London	H198JVT	North Midlands	H462UGO	London	H804AHA	North Midlands
GYE602W	London	H199AOD	The Shires	H463UGO	London	H804RWJ	North West
GYE603W	London	H199GRO	The Shires	H464UGO	London	H805AHA	North Midlands
GYE604W	London	H199KEH	North Midlands	H465UGO	London	H805RWJ	North West
GYE605W	London	H201LRF	North Midlands	H466UGO	London	H806AHA	North Midlands
H28MJN	Cymru	H202GRO	The Shires	H467UGO	London	H813EKJ	Southern Counties
H29MJN	Cymru	H202LRF	North Midlands	H468UGO	London	H814EKJ	Southern Counties
H31PAJ	North East	H203GRO	The Shires	H469UGO	London	H815EKJ	Southern Counties
H32PAJ	North East	H204EKO	Southern Counties	H470UGO	London	H816EKJ	Southern Counties
H34PAJ	North East	H231KBH	North West	H475KSG	The Shires	H840UUA	Northumbria
H35DGD	The Shires	H242MUK	Scotland West	H501GHA	North Midlands	H845AHS	The Shires
H47MJN	The Shires	H243MUK	The Shires	H523SWE	The Shires	H846AHS	Southern Counties
H48MJN	The Shires	H244MUK	The Shires	H566MPD	The Shires	H847AHS	Southern Counties
H49MJN	The Shires	H245MUK	The Shires	H567MPD	The Shires	H848AUS	The Shires
H73DVM	North Midlands	H251GEV	The Shires	H575DVM	North Midlands	H851NOC	North Midlands
H74DVM	North Midlands	H252GEV	The Shires	H577DVM	North Midlands	H880NFS	North Midlands
H76DVM	North Midlands	H253GEV	The Shires	H580DVM	North Midlands	H886CCU	Southern Counties
H78DVM	North West	H253PAJ	North East	H588DVM	North West	H887CCU	Southern Counties
H79DVM	North West	H254GEV	The Shires	H598CNL	Northumbria	H889CCU	Southern Counties
H81DVM	North Midlands	H254PAJ	North East	H614CGG	The Shires	H890CCU	Southern Counties
H82DVM	North Midlands	H255GEV	The Shires	H616UWR	Southern Counties	H901GNC	Scotland West
H83DVM	North Midlands	H256GEV	The Shires	H621TKU	London	H903AHS	London
H84DVM	North Midlands	H256YLG	Southern Counties	H641UWE	The Shires	H912KUD	Fox County
H85DVM	North West	H257GEV	The Shires	H642UWE	The Shires	H912XYT	London
H86DVM	North West	H258GEV	The Shires	H648GPF	North Midlands	H913XYT	London
H87DVM	North West	H259CFT	Northumbria	H649GPF	North Midlands	H914XYT	London
H101GEV	London	H261CFT	Northumbria	H650GPF	Fox County	H915XYT	London
H102GEV	London	H262CFT	Northumbria	H651GPF	North Midlands	H916XYT	London
H103GEV	London	H262GEV	The Shires	H652GPF	Fox County	H917XYT	London
H104GEV	London	H263CFT	Northumbria	H653GPF	Fox County	H918XYT	London
H105GEV	London	H263GEV	The Shires	H654GPF	Fox County	H919XYT	London
H106RWT	Yorkshire	H264CFT	Northumbria	H655GPF	Fox County	H920XYT	London
H107GEV	London	H264GEV	The Shires	H656GPF	North Midlands	H921XYT	London
		H265GEV	The Shires	H657GPF	North Midlands	H922LOX	The Shires

Reg	Location	Reg	Location	Reg	Location	Reg	Location
H922XYT	London	J247MFP	Fox County	J382BWU	Yorkshire	JDE972X	Fox County
H923LOX	The Shires	J248SHP	Fox County	J401FNS	Fox County	JDJ350N	Fox County
H923XYT	London	J249SHP	Fox County	J401XVX	The Shires	JEY554Y	Cymru
H925LOX	The Shires	J255TJW	Fox County	J402XVX	The Shires	JHE153W	Fox County
H925XYT	London	J292NNB	North West	J403XVX	The Shires	JHE167W	Fox County
H926LOX	The Shires	J293NNB	North West	J404XVX	The Shires	JHE177W	Fox County
HDZ8354	The Shires	J296NNB	North West	J413NCP	London	JHE179W	Fox County
HED204V	North East	J297NNB	North West	J414NCP	London	JHE189W	Fox County
HED205V	North East	J298NNB	North West	J433BSH	London	JHE192W	Fox County
HFM186N	North West	J299NNB	North West	J463MKL	Southern Counties	JHK495N	The Shires
HFM581D	Cymru	J301WHJ	London	J464MKL	Southern Counties	JIL2156	Fox County
HIL2148	Cymru	J302WHJ	London	J465MKL	Southern Counties	JIL2157	Fox County
HIL3652	North Midlands	J303WHJ	London	J465UFS	The Shires	JIL2158	Fox County
HIL7592	Cymru	J304WHJ	London	J466OKP	Southern Counties	JIL2159	Fox County
HIL7593	Cymru	J305WHJ	London	J467OKP	Southern Counties	JIL2160	Fox County
HIL7594	Fox County	J306WHJ	London	J468OKP	Southern Counties	JIL2161	Fox County
HIL7595	The Shires	J307WHJ	London	J473RDU	Fox County	JIL2162	Fox County
HIL7597	The Shires	J308WHJ	London	J474RDU	Fox County	JIL2163	Fox County
HIL8438	Scotland West	J309WHJ	London	J480XHL	Southern Counties	JIL2164	Fox County
HIL8439	Scotland West	J310WHJ	London	J556GTP	North Midlands	JIL2165	Fox County
HKM883V	Southern Counties	J311WHJ	London	J601WHJ	London	JIL2190	Fox County
HKM884V	Southern Counties	J312WHJ	London	J603WHJ	London	JIL2193	Fox County
HKM885V	Southern Counties	J313WHJ	London	J604WHJ	London	JIL2194	The Shires
HKM886V	Southern Counties	J314XVX	London	J605WHJ	London	JIL2195	The Shires
HNB27N	Southern Counties	J315BSH	London	J606WHJ	London	JIL2196	Fox County
HPK504N	Southern Counties	J315XVX	London	J607WHJ	London	JIL2197	Fox County
HSB948Y	Scotland West	J316BSH	London	J608WHJ	London	JIL2198	Fox County
HSB949Y	Scotland West	J316XVX	The Shires	J609WHJ	London	JIL2199	Fox County
HUP757T	Northumbria	J317BSH	London	J610WHJ	London	JIL5367	Fox County
HUP758T	Northumbria	J317XVX	The Shires	J611WHJ	London	JIW3696	London
HUP759T	Northumbria	J318BSH	London	J612WHJ	London	JJD366D	London
HXI3006	North Midlands	J319BSH	London	J620UHN	North East	JJD370D	London
HXI3007	North Midlands	J320BSH	London	J649OWK	Fox County	JJD372D	London
HXI3008	North Midlands	J321BSH	London	J650OWK	Fox County	JJD373D	London
HXI3009	North Midlands	J322BSH	London	J651OWK	Fox County	JJD375D	London
HXI3010	North Midlands	J323BSH	London	J651UHN	North East	JJD380D	London
HXI3011	North Midlands	J324BSH	London	J652UHN	North East	JJD382D	London
HXI3012	North Midlands	J325BSH	London	J653UHN	North East	JJD383D	London
IAZ2314	The Shires	J326BSH	London	J654UHN	North East	JJD386D	London
IAZ3977	The Shires	J327BSH	London	J655OWK	Fox County	JJD387D	London
IAZ4037	The Shires	J327VAW	North Midlands	J655UHN	North East	JJD391D	London
IDZ8561	North Midlands	J328BSH	London	J656OWK	Fox County	JJD394D	London
IIL4821	The Shires	J328VAW	North Midlands	J656UHN	North East	JJD401D	London
IIL4822	The Shires	J329BSH	London	J657OWK	Fox County	JJD406D	London
IIL4823	The Shires	J330BSH	London	J657UHN	North East	JJD407D	London
IIL4824	The Shires	J331BSH	London	J658UDU	Fox County	JJD408D	London
IIL9168	Cymru	J332BSH	London	J658UHN	North East	JJD409D	London
IIL9169	Cymru	J334BSH	London	J659UDU	Fox County	JJD410D	London
J3SLT	North West	J335BSH	London	J661UHN	North East	JJD416D	London
J4SLT	North West	J336BSH	London	J701NHA	North Midlands	JJD418D	London
J6SLT	North West	J337BSH	London	J714CUM	Yorkshire	JJD434D	London
J7SLT	North West	J338BSH	London	J715CUM	Cymru	JJD452D	London
J8SLT	North West	J339BSH	London	J716CUM	Yorkshire	JJD457D	London
J9SLT	North West	J340BSH	London	J717CUM	Yorkshire	JJD460D	London
J10SLT	North West	J341BSH	London	J718CUM	Cymru	JJD468D	London
J20NMS	Northumbria	J342BSH	London	J719CUM	Cymru	JJD477D	London
J25UNY	Southern Counties	J343BSH	London	J720CUM	Yorkshire	JJD483D	London
J26UNY	Southern Counties	J344BSH	London	J721CUM	Cymru	JJD491D	London
J27UNY	Southern Counties	J345BSH	London	J722CUM	Cymru	JJD492D	London
J31SFA	North Midlands	J346BSH	London	J734MFY	North West	JJD494D	London
J32SFA	North Midlands	J347BSH	London	J735MFY	North West	JJD503D	London
J32UTG	The Shires	J348BSH	London	J766SOC	Fox County	JJD504D	London
J34SRF	North Midlands	J349BSH	London	J866UPY	North East	JJD505D	London
J36GCX	Southern Counties	J350BSH	London	J867UPY	North East	JJD510D	London
J36SRF	North Midlands	J351BSH	London	J917HGD	The Shires	JJD512D	London
J37VDW	The Shires	J352BSH	London	J917VHP	Fox County	JJD514D	London
J56GCX	The Shires	J353BSH	London	J918VHP	Fox County	JJD518D	London
J60MPS	Southern Counties	J362YWX	Yorkshire	J926CYL	The Shires	JJD521D	London
J64BJN	The Shires	J363BNW	Northumbria	J927CYL	The Shires	JJD523D	London
J65BJN	The Shires	J363YWX	Yorkshire	J929CYL	London	JJD524D	London
J65UNA	The Shires	J364YWX	Yorkshire	J930CYL	London	JJD525D	London
J78MHF	North West	J365YWX	Yorkshire	J931CYL	London	JJD526D	London
J143SRF	North Midlands	J366BNW	Northumbria	J933WHJ	The Shires	JJD528D	London
J151WEH	Fox County	J366YWX	Yorkshire	J934WHJ	The Shires	JJD531D	London
J154NKN	Southern Counties	J367YWX	Yorkshire	J935WHJ	The Shires	JJD533D	London
J162REH	North Midlands	J368YWX	Yorkshire	J936WHJ	The Shires	JJD534D	London
J169REH	North Midlands	J369YWX	Yorkshire	J937WHJ	The Shires	JJD536D	London
J171GGG	The Shires	J370YWX	Yorkshire	J938WHJ	The Shires	JJD544D	London
J203REH	North Midlands	J371AWT	Yorkshire	J961JNL	Southern Counties	JJD545D	London
J204REH	North Midlands	J371YWX	Yorkshire	J961TOF	Fox County	JJD546D	London
J205REH	North Midlands	J372AWT	Yorkshire	J962JNL	Southern Counties	JJD548D	London
J206REH	North Midlands	J373AWT	Yorkshire	J963TOF	Fox County	JJD549D	London
J207REH	North Midlands	J374AWT	Yorkshire	J964NLL	The Shires	JJD552D	London
J208SRF	North Midlands	J375AWT	Yorkshire	J969JNL	Southern Counties	JJD562D	London
J209SRF	North Midlands	J376AWT	Yorkshire	J970JNL	Southern Counties	JJD567D	London
J218HDS	Scotland West	J377AWT	Yorkshire	J973JNL	Southern Counties	JJD571D	London
J220HGY	Southern Counties	J379BWU	Yorkshire	J974JNL	Southern Counties	JJD572D	London
J221HGY	Southern Counties	J380BWU	Yorkshire	J975JNL	Southern Counties	JJD573D	London
J246MFP	Fox County	J381BWU	Yorkshire	JCK852W	Southern Counties	JJD574D	London

Reg	Location	Reg	Location	Reg	Location	Reg	Location
JJD577D	London	K403VPK	North Midlands	K803HWW	Yorkshire	KYV654X	London
JJD586D	London	K404HWW	Yorkshire	K804HWW	Yorkshire	KYV657X	London
JJD588D	London	K404VPK	North Midlands	K805HWX	Yorkshire	KYV658X	Southern Counties
JJD589D	London	K405FHJ	The Shires	K851RBB	Northumbria	KYV659X	London
JJD591D	London	K405HWX	Yorkshire	K852RBB	Northumbria	KYV660X	Southern Counties
JJD595D	London	K405VPK	Southern Counties	K853RBB	Northumbria	KYV661X	London
JJD597D	London	K406FHJ	The Shires	K854RBB	Northumbria	KYV663X	London
JOX480P	North Midlands	K407FHJ	The Shires	K876UDB	North West	KYV664X	London
JOX515P	North West	K408BHN	North East	K877UDB	North West	KYV665X	London
JOX517P	North Midlands	K408FHJ	The Shires	K878UDB	North West	KYV666X	London
JOX528P	Southern Counties	K409BHN	North East	K879UDB	North West	KYV669X	London
JPE233V	The Shires	K409FHJ	The Shires	K882UDB	North West	KYV671X	London
JPE236V	The Shires	K410BHN	North East	K884UDB	North West	KYV672X	OLST
JSJ746	OLST	K410FHJ	The Shires	K887UDB	North West	KYV673X	London
JSJ747	OLST	K411BHN	North East	K906SKR	Southern Counties	KYV675X	London
JSJ748	OLST	K411FHJ	The Shires	K907SKR	Southern Counties	KYV676X	London
JSJ749	OLST	K412BHN	North East	K908SKR	Southern Counties	KYV679X	London
JSK994	North Midlands	K412FHJ	The Shires	K909SKR	Southern Counties	KYV680X	London
JTD390P	Cymru	K413BHN	North East	K910SKR	Southern Counties	KYV681X	London
JTD392P	The Shires	K413FHJ	The Shires	K945SGG	Scotland West	KYV682X	London
JTD395P	Cymru	K414BHN	North East	K946SGG	Scotland West	KYV684X	London
JTL804V	Cymru	K414FHJ	The Shires	K947BRE	North Midlands	KYV686X	London
JUP111T	North East	K415BHN	North East	K947SGG	Scotland West	KYV688X	London
JUR818V	Southern Counties	K416BHN	North East	K981KGY	Cymru	KYV689X	OLST
K1SLT	North West	K417BHN	North East	K982KGY	Cymru	KYV691X	London
K2SLT	North West	K447XPA	The Shires	K983KGY	Cymru	KYV692X	London
K3SLT	North West	K448XPA	The Shires	KGH858A	London	KYV694X	London
K8BUS	The Shires	K457EVC	North West	KGH975A	London	KYV699X	London
K25WND	The Shires	K469SKO	Southern Counties	KGJ118A	London	KYV700X	London
K26WND	The Shires	K470SKO	Southern Counties	KGJ142A	London	KYV701X	London
K27EWC	Cymru	K471SKO	Southern Counties	KJW296W	North Midlands	KYV702X	London
K27WND	The Shires	K503BHN	North East	KJW301W	North Midlands	KYV703X	London
K28WND	The Shires	K504BHN	North East	KJW305W	North Midlands	KYV704X	London
K29WND	The Shires	K505BHN	North East	KJW310W	North Midlands	KYV705X	London
K31WND	The Shires	K506BHN	North East	KJW318W	North Midlands	KYV707X	OLST
K32WND	The Shires	K507BHN	North East	KJW320W	North Midlands	KYV708X	London
K36XNE	Southern Counties	K508BHN	North East	KKG109W	Scotland West	KYV709X	Southern Counties
K37XNE	Southern Counties	K509BHN	North East	KMA395T	North West	KYV710X	London
K38XNE	Southern Counties	K510BHN	North East	KMA396T	North West	KYV711X	London
K73SRG	North West	K511BHN	North East	KMA397T	North West	KYV712X	London
K74SRG	North West	K512BHN	North East	KMA400T	North West	KYV713X	London
K75SRG	North West	K513BHN	North East	KMA401T	North Midlands	KYV714X	London
K91RGA	Scotland West	K514BHN	North East	KMA402T	North Midlands	KYV715X	London
K92RGA	Scotland West	K515BHN	North East	KNV514P	North West	KYV716X	London
K95RGA	Scotland West	K516BHN	North East	KPJ248W	The Shires	KYV717X	Southern Counties
K96RGA	Scotland West	K517BHN	North East	KPJ262W	Southern Counties	KYV718X	London
K124TCP	The Shires	K518BHN	North East	KPJ270W	Southern Counties	KYV719X	London
K131FKW	Northumbria	K538ORH	London	KPJ274W	Southern Counties	KYV720X	London
K131XRE	Fox County	K539ORH	London	KPJ277W	Southern Counties	KYV721X	London
K132FKW	Northumbria	K540ORH	London	KPJ282W	Southern Counties	KYV722X	London
K132XRE	Southern Counties	K541ORH	London	KPJ283W	Southern Counties	KYV723X	London
K136ARE	North Midlands	K542ORH	London	KRS536V	Scotland West	KYV724X	London
K137ARE	North Midlands	K543OGA	The Shires	KUB671V	North Midlands	KYV726X	London
K138BRF	North Midlands	K543ORH	London	KYO609X	London	KYV727X	London
K139BRF	North Midlands	K544ORH	London	KYO610X	London	KYV728X	London
K140BFA	North Midlands	K545ORH	London	KYO611X	London	KYV729X	London
K140RYS	North Midlands	K546ORH	London	KYO612X	London	KYV731X	London
K141BFA	North Midlands	K547ORH	London	KYO613X	London	KYV732X	London
K142BFA	North Midlands	K548ORH	London	KYO614X	Southern Counties	KYV733X	London
K148BRF	Fox County	K549ORH	London	KYO615X	Southern Counties	KYV734X	London
K150BRF	North Midlands	K550ORH	London	KYO617X	London	KYV735X	London
K154BRF	Southern Counties	K551ORH	London	KYO619X	London	KYV737X	London
K155CRE	Cymru	K552ORH	London	KYO622X	London	KYV738X	London
K156BRF	Cymru	K578YOJ	The Shires	KYO625X	London	KYV740X	London
K157BRF	Cymru	K579YOJ	The Shires	KYO626X	London	KYV741X	London
K158HRF	Fox County	K580YOJ	The Shires	KYO627X	London	KYV742X	London
K184GDU	The Shires	K707FNO	The Shires	KYO628X	London	KYV743X	London
K202FEH	The Shires	K708FNO	The Shires	KYO629X	London	KYV744X	OLST
K203FEH	The Shires	K709FNO	The Shires	KYO630X	London	KYV745X	London
K211UHA	North Midlands	K710FNO	The Shires	KYO631X	London	KYV746X	London
K212UHA	North Midlands	K711FNO	The Shires	KYV408X	Scotland West	KYV747X	London
K213UHA	North Midlands	K712FNO	The Shires	KYV632X	London	KYV748X	OLST
K214UHA	North Midlands	K723HUG	Cymru	KYV633X	London	KYV749X	London
K215UHA	North Midlands	K724HUG	Cymru	KYV634X	London	KYV750X	London
K216UHA	North Midlands	K725HUG	Yorkshire	KYV635X	London	KYV751X	London
K217UHA	North Midlands	K726HUG	Cymru	KYV636X	London	KYV752X	London
K218UHA	North Midlands	K727HUG	Cymru	KYV637X	London	KYV754X	OLST
K219UHA	North Midlands	K728HUG	Cymru	KYV638X	London	KYV756X	London
K318CVX	The Shires	K729HUG	Cymru	KYV641X	London	KYV757X	London
K319CVX	The Shires	K741CWK	Fox County	KYV642X	London	KYV758X	London
K320CVX	The Shires	K742CWK	Fox County	KYV644X	London	KYV761X	London
K321CVX	The Shires	K745CWK	Fox County	KYV645X	London	KYV762X	London
K322CVX	The Shires	K746CWK	Fox County	KYV647X	London	KYV765X	London
K323CVX	The Shires	K760JVX	The Shires	KYV648X	London	KYV766X	London
K390NGG	Fox County	K761JVX	The Shires	KYV649X	London	KYV767X	London
K401HWW	Yorkshire	K762JVX	The Shires	KYV650X	London	KYV768X	London
K402HWW	Yorkshire	K787VNR	North West	KYV651X	London	KYV770X	London
K402VPK	Southern Counties	K801HWW	Yorkshire	KYV652X	London	KYV771X	London
K403HWW	Yorkshire	K802HWW	Yorkshire	KYV653X	London	KYV772X	London

Reg	Location	Reg	Location	Reg	Location	Reg	Location
KYV773X	London	L146NHP	Fox County	L305NFA	North Midlands	L514BNX	North Midlands
KYV774X	London	L146YVK	Southern Counties	L306AUT	Fox County	L514CPJ	Southern Counties
KYV775X	London	L148NHP	Fox County	L306HPP	The Shires	L515BNX	North Midlands
KYV776X	London	L148WAG	London	L307AUT	Fox County	L515CPJ	Southern Counties
KYV777X	London	L148YVK	Southern Counties	L307HPP	The Shires	L516BNX	North Midlands
KYV778X	London	L149NHP	Fox County	L308AUT	Fox County	L516CPJ	Southern Counties
KYV780X	London	L149WAG	London	L308HPP	The Shires	L517BNX	North Midlands
KYV781X	London	L149YVK	Southern Counties	L309AUT	Fox County	L519BNX	North Midlands
KYV782X	London	L150SBG	North West	L309HPP	The Shires	L519FHN	North East
KYV783X	London	L150WAG	London	L310AUT	Fox County	L520FHN	North East
KYV784X	London	L150YVK	Southern Counties	L310HPP	The Shires	L521BNX	North Midlands
KYV785X	London	L151FRJ	North West	L311AUT	Fox County	L521FHN	North East
KYV786X	London	L151SBG	North West	L311HPP	The Shires	L522BNX	North Midlands
KYV787X	London	L151WAG	London	L312AUT	Fox County	L522FHN	North East
KYV788X	London	L151YVK	Southern Counties	L312HPP	The Shires	L523BNX	North Midlands
KYV789X	London	L152FRJ	North West	L313AUT	Fox County	L523FHN	North East
KYV790X	London	L152SBG	North West	L313HPP	The Shires	L524FHN	North East
KYV791X	London	L152WAG	London	L314AUT	Fox County	L525FHN	North East
KYV792X	London	L152YVK	Southern Counties	L314HPP	The Shires	L526FHN	North East
KYV793X	London	L153FRJ	North West	L315AUT	Fox County	L527FHN	North East
KYV795X	London	L153UEM	North West	L315HPP	The Shires	L528FHN	North East
KYV796X	London	L153UKB	North West	L316AUT	Fox County	L529FHN	North East
KYV798X	London	L153WAG	London	L316HPP	The Shires	L529XNR	North West
KYV799X	London	L153YVK	Southern Counties	L317AUT	Fox County	L530FHN	North East
KYV803X	London	L154FRJ	North West	L318AUT	Fox County	L531FHN	North East
KYV805X	London	L154UEM	North West	L319AUT	Fox County	L532EHD	Northumbria
L1SLT	North West	L154UKB	North West	L320AUT	Fox County	L532FHN	North East
L2SLT	North West	L154WAG	London	L321AUT	Fox County	L533EHD	Northumbria
L11SLT	North West	L154YVK	Southern Counties	L322AUT	Fox County	L533FHN	North East
L33NMS	Northumbria	L155UEM	North West	L323AUT	Fox County	L534FHN	North East
L34PNN	Fox County	L155UKB	North West	L324AUT	Fox County	L535FHN	North East
L35OKV	Cymru	L155WAG	London	L325AUT	Fox County	L536FHN	North East
L35PNN	Fox County	L155YVK	Southern Counties	L326AUT	The Shires	L537FHN	North East
L36OKV	Cymru	L156UEM	North West	L327AUT	The Shires	L538FHN	North East
L36PNN	Fox County	L156UKB	North West	L328AUT	The Shires	L539FHN	North East
L37OKV	Cymru	L156WAG	London	L400BUS	The Shires	L540FHN	North East
L37PNN	Fox County	L156YVK	Southern Counties	L406NUA	Yorkshire	L541FHN	North East
L38OKV	Cymru	L157WAG	London	L407NUA	Yorkshire	L542FHN	North East
L38PNN	Fox County	L157YVK	Southern Counties	L408NUA	Yorkshire	L543FHN	North East
L43MEH	The Shires	L158BFT	Southern Counties	L409NUA	Yorkshire	L544GHN	North East
L51LSG	Scotland West	L158WAG	London	L415NHJ	The Shires	L545GHN	North East
L52LSG	Scotland West	L159BFT	Southern Counties	L418FHN	North East	L546GHN	North East
L53LSG	Scotland West	L159GYL	London	L419FHN	North East	L547GHN	North East
L54LSG	Scotland West	L160GYL	London	L420FHN	North East	L548GHN	North East
L80MPS	Southern Counties	L161GYL	London	L421CPB	Cymru	L549GHN	North East
L94HRF	Fox County	L193DBC	North West	L421FHN	North East	L550GHN	North East
L95HRF	Fox County	L200BUS	The Shires	L422CPB	Southern Counties	L551GHN	North East
L100BUS	The Shires	L201YCU	Southern Counties	L422FHN	North East	L557YCU	Southern Counties
L100SBS	North Midlands	L202YCU	Southern Counties	L423CPB	Southern Counties	L558YCU	Southern Counties
L102MEH	North Midlands	L203YCU	Southern Counties	L424CPB	Southern Counties	L559YCU	Southern Counties
L112YVK	Southern Counties	L204YCU	Southern Counties	L425CPB	Southern Counties	L561YCU	Southern Counties
L113YVK	Southern Counties	L205YCU	Southern Counties	L426CPB	The Shires	L562YCU	Southern Counties
L114YVK	Southern Counties	L206YCU	Southern Counties	L427CPB	Southern Counties	L563YCU	Southern Counties
L115YVK	London	L207YCU	Southern Counties	L428CPC	Southern Counties	L564YCU	Southern Counties
L116YVK	London	L208YCU	Southern Counties	L429CPC	The Shires	L565YCU	Southern Counties
L117YVK	London	L209YCU	Southern Counties	L430CPJ	Southern Counties	L588JSG	Scotland West
L118YVK	London	L210YCU	Southern Counties	L431CPJ	Southern Counties	L600BUS	The Shires
L119YVK	London	L211YCU	Southern Counties	L433CPJ	Southern Counties	L601EKM	Southern Counties
L120YVK	Southern Counties	L212YCU	Southern Counties	L434CPJ	Southern Counties	L601FHN	North East
L121YVK	Southern Counties	L226JFA	North Midlands	L435CPJ	Southern Counties	L602EKM	Southern Counties
L122YVK	Southern Counties	L227HRF	Fox County	L436CPJ	Southern Counties	L602FHN	North East
L123YVK	Southern Counties	L228HRF	Fox County	L437CPJ	Southern Counties	L603EKM	Southern Counties
L124YVK	Southern Counties	L229HRF	North Midlands	L438FPA	Cymru	L603FHN	North East
L125YVK	Southern Counties	L230HRF	North Midlands	L439FPA	Cymru	L604EKM	Southern Counties
L126YVK	Southern Counties	L231HRF	Fox County	L500BUS	The Shires	L604FHN	North East
L127YVK	Southern Counties	L232HRF	North Midlands	L500DKT	Southern Counties	L605BNX	North Midlands
L128YVK	Southern Counties	L233HRF	Fox County	L502BNX	North Midlands	L605EKM	Southern Counties
L129YVK	Southern Counties	L247WAG	London	L503BNX	North Midlands	L605FHN	North East
L130YVK	Southern Counties	L253NFA	North Midlands	L503CPB	Southern Counties	L606EKM	Southern Counties
L131YVK	Southern Counties	L254NFA	North Midlands	L503HKM	Southern Counties	L607EKM	Southern Counties
L132NHP	Fox County	L255NFA	North Midlands	L504BNX	North Midlands	L608EKM	Southern Counties
L132YVK	Southern Counties	L25LSX	Scotland West	L504CPB	Southern Counties	L609EKM	Southern Counties
L133HVS	The Shires	L263VSU	Scotland West	L505CPJ	Southern Counties	L610EKM	Southern Counties
L133NHP	Fox County	L271FVN	North East	L506BNX	North Midlands	L613LVX	The Shires
L133YVK	Southern Counties	L272FVN	North East	L506CPJ	Southern Counties	L614LVX	The Shires
L134YVK	Southern Counties	L273FVN	North East	L507BNX	North Midlands	L618BNX	North Midlands
L135YVK	Southern Counties	L274FVN	North East	L507CPJ	Southern Counties	L620BNX	North Midlands
L136YVK	Southern Counties	L275FVN	North East	L508BNX	North Midlands	L638DNA	Cymru
L137YVK	Southern Counties	L287EKK	Southern Counties	L508CPJ	Southern Counties	L641DNA	North West
L138YVK	Southern Counties	L300BUS	The Shires	L509BNX	North Midlands	L642DNA	North West
L139YVK	Southern Counties	L300SBS	North Midlands	L509CPJ	Southern Counties	L643DNA	North West
L140YVK	Southern Counties	L301NFA	North Midlands	L510BNX	North Midlands	L646DNA	North West
L141YVK	Southern Counties	L302NFA	North Midlands	L510CPJ	Southern Counties	L647DNA	North West
L142YVK	Southern Counties	L303AUT	Fox County	L511BNX	North Midlands	L648DNA	North West
L143NHP	Fox County	L303NFA	North Midlands	L511CPJ	Southern Counties	L649DNA	North West
L143YVK	Southern Counties	L304AUT	Fox County	L512BNX	North Midlands	L700BUS	The Shires
L144YVK	Southern Counties	L304NFA	North Midlands	L512CPJ	Southern Counties	L705AGA	Scotland West
L145NHP	Fox County	L305AUT	Fox County	L513BNX	North Midlands	L713OVX	London
L145YVK	Southern Counties	L305HPP	The Shires	L513CPJ	Southern Counties	L714EKO	Southern Counties

L714OVX	London	L941GYL	London	M157LNC	North West	M205SKE	Southern Counties
L715OVX	London	L970VGE	Scotland West	M157RBH	The Shires	M205YKA	North West
L715WCC	Cymru	LAZ5785	Scotland West	M157WKA	North West	M206SKE	Southern Counties
L716OVX	London	LAZ5929	Scotland West	M157WWM	North West	M206YKA	North West
L716WCC	Cymru	LAZ5962	Scotland West	M158RBH	The Shires	M207YKA	North West
L717OVX	The Shires	LAZ5964	Scotland West	M158WKA	North West	M208YKA	North West
L717WCC	Cymru	LBD837P	The Shires	M158WWM	North West	M209YKA	North West
L718OVX	The Shires	LFR875X	North Midlands	M159GRY	Fox County	M20MPS	Southern Counties
L724PHK	The Shires	LHO992Y	North East	M159RBH	The Shires	M210YKA	North West
L730MWW	Yorkshire	LIL2168	Southern Counties	M159WKA	North West	M211YKD	North West
L731MWW	Yorkshire	LIL2180	Southern Counties	M160GRY	Fox County	M212YKD	North West
L732MWW	Yorkshire	LJI5632	Fox County	M160RBH	The Shires	M213YKD	North West
L733MWW	Yorkshire	LJI8157	Fox County	M160WKA	North West	M214YKD	North West
L734MWW	Yorkshire	LMA412T	North West	M160WTJ	North West	M215YKD	North West
L735PUA	Yorkshire	LPB218P	Southern Counties	M161GRY	Fox County	M216YKD	North West
L736PUA	Yorkshire	LPF600P	Southern Counties	M161SKR	Southern Counties	M217AKB	North West
L737PUA	Yorkshire	LPT701T	Northumbria	M161WKA	North West	M218AKB	North West
L738PUA	Yorkshire	LPT703T	North East	M162GRY	Fox County	M219AKB	North West
L739PUA	Yorkshire	LPT707T	Northumbria	M162LNC	North Midlands	M220AKB	North West
L740PUA	Yorkshire	LRB206W	Cymru	M162SKR	Southern Counties	M221AKB	North West
L741PUA	Yorkshire	M2SLT	North West	M162WKA	North West	M223AKB	North West
L766DPE	Southern Counties	M5SLT	North West	M163GRY	Fox County	M224AKB	North West
L771RWW	Yorkshire	M30MPS	Southern Counties	M163LNC	North Midlands	M225AKB	North West
L772RWW	Yorkshire	M38WUR	The Shires	M163SKR	Southern Counties	M226AKB	North West
L773RWW	Yorkshire	M39WUR	The Shires	M163WKA	North West	M227AKB	North West
L774RWW	Yorkshire	M40MPS	Southern Counties	M164GRY	Fox County	M228AKB	North West
L775RWW	Yorkshire	M41WUR	The Shires	M164LNC	North Midlands	M229AKB	North West
L776RWW	Yorkshire	M42WUR	The Shires	M164WKA	North West	M230AKB	North West
L778RWW	Yorkshire	M43WUR	The Shires	M165GRY	Fox County	M231AKB	North West
L779RWW	Yorkshire	M45WUR	The Shires	M165LNC	North Midlands	M232AKB	North West
L800BUS	The Shires	M46WUR	The Shires	M165WKA	North West	M236KNR	Southern Counties
L801KNO	The Shires	M47WUR	The Shires	M166GRY	Fox County	M239XLV	The Shires
L802KNO	The Shires	M51AWW	Yorkshire	M166LNC	North West	M240XLV	The Shires
L803KNO	The Shires	M52AWW	Yorkshire	M166WKA	North West	M247WWX	Yorkshire
L804KNO	The Shires	M53AWW	Yorkshire	M166WTJ	North West	M248SPP	Scotland West
L805OVX	The Shires	M54AWW	Yorkshire	M167GRY	Fox County	M250SPP	Scotland West
L806NNW	Yorkshire	M583SSX	The Shires	M167LNC	North West	M251SPP	Scotland West
L807NNW	Yorkshire	M59WKA	North West	M167WKA	North West	M255BDM	Yorkshire
L808NNW	Yorkshire	M61WKA	North West	M168GRY	Fox County	M266VPU	The Shires
L809NNW	Yorkshire	M62WKA	North West	M168WKA	North West	M267VPU	The Shires
L810NNW	Yorkshire	M63WKA	North West	M169GRY	Fox County	M268VPU	The Shires
L811NNW	Yorkshire	M64WKA	North West	M169WKA	North West	M269VPU	The Shires
L812NNW	Yorkshire	M65FDS	Scotland West	M170GRY	Fox County	M276FNS	Scotland West
L813NNW	Yorkshire	M65WKA	North West	M170WKA	North West	M277FNS	Scotland West
L814NNW	Yorkshire	M67FDS	Scotland West	M171GRY	Fox County	M278FNS	Scotland West
L815NNW	Yorkshire	M67WKA	North West	M171YKA	North West	M290AJC	The Shires
L816NWY	Yorkshire	M95EGE	Scotland West	M172GRY	Fox County	M291AJC	The Shires
L817NWY	Yorkshire	M100CBB	Southern Counties	M172YKA	North West	M301SAJ	North East
L818NWY	Yorkshire	M101WKA	North West	M173GRY	Fox County	M302SAJ	North East
L819NWY	Yorkshire	M102RMS	Scotland West	M173YKA	North West	M303SAJ	North East
L820NWY	Yorkshire	M102WKA	North West	M174GRY	Fox County	M304SAJ	North East
L821NWY	Yorkshire	M103RMS	Scotland West	M174YKA	North West	M305SAJ	North East
L822NWY	Yorkshire	M103WKA	North West	M175GRY	Fox County	M322AKB	North West
L823NWY	Yorkshire	M104RMS	Scotland West	M175YKA	North West	M331MRW	Fox County
L824NWY	Yorkshire	M104WKA	North West	M176GRY	Fox County	M332MRW	Fox County
L825NWY	Yorkshire	M105RMS	Scotland West	M176YKA	North West	M363KVR	North West
L826NYG	Yorkshire	M105WKA	North West	M177GRY	Fox County	M364KVR	North West
L827NYG	Yorkshire	M106RMS	Scotland West	M177YKA	North West	M365KVR	North West
L828NYG	Yorkshire	M107RMS	Scotland West	M178GRY	Fox County	M366KVR	North West
L829NYG	Yorkshire	M108RMS	Scotland West	M178LYP	London	M367KVR	North West
L830NYG	Yorkshire	M109RMS	Scotland West	M178YKA	North West	M368KVR	North West
L837MWT	Southern Counties	M110RMS	Scotland West	M179LYP	London	M369KVR	North West
L838MWT	Southern Counties	M112RMS	Scotland West	M179YKA	North West	M370FTY	Northumbria
L855WRG	Northumbria	M113RMS	Scotland West	M180LYP	London	M370KVR	North West
L856WRG	Northumbria	M114RMS	Scotland West	M180YKA	North West	M371EFD	North Midlands
L857WRG	Northumbria	M115RMS	Scotland West	M181YKA	North West	M371FTY	Northumbria
L858WRG	Northumbria	M116RMS	Scotland West	M182YKA	North West	M371KVR	North West
L860LFS	Scotland West	M117RMS	Scotland West	M183YKA	North West	M372EFD	North Midlands
L861LFS	Scotland West	M118RMS	Scotland West	M184YKA	North West	M372FTY	Northumbria
L862LFS	Scotland West	M119RMS	Scotland West	M185YKA	North West	M372KVR	North West
L863BEA	The Shires	M120RMS	Scotland West	M186YKA	North West	M373EFD	North Midlands
L863LFS	Scotland West	M120YCM	North West	M187YKA	North West	M373FTY	Northumbria
L864BEA	The Shires	M121RMS	Scotland West	M188YKA	North West	M374EFD	North Midlands
L864LFS	Scotland West	M121YCM	North West	M189YKA	North West	M374FTY	Northumbria
L865LFS	Scotland West	M122UUB	Northumbria	M190YKA	North West	M375EFD	North Midlands
L866LFS	Scotland West	M122YCM	North West	M191YKA	North West	M375FTY	Northumbria
L867LFS	Scotland West	M124YCM	North West	M192YKA	North West	M376EFD	North Midlands
L868LFS	Scotland West	M125YCM	North West	M193YKA	North West	M376FTY	Northumbria
L869LFS	Scotland West	M126YCM	North West	M194YKA	North West	M377EFD	North Midlands
L870LFS	Scotland West	M127YCM	North West	M195YKA	North West	M377FTY	Northumbria
L922LJO	The Shires	M128YCM	North West	M196YKA	North West	M378EFD	North Midlands
L923LJO	The Shires	M129YCM	North West	M197YKA	North West	M379EFD	North Midlands
L934GYL	London	M150RBH	The Shires	M198YKA	North West	M380EFD	North Midlands
L935GYL	London	M151RBH	The Shires	M199YKA	North West	M381EFD	North Midlands
L936GYL	London	M152RBH	The Shires	M200CBB	Southern Counties	M385KVR	Cymru
L937GYL	London	M153RBH	The Shires	M201YKA	North West	M394KVR	Cymru
L938GYL	London	M154RBH	The Shires	M202YKA	North West	M401EFD	North Midlands
L939GYL	London	M156LNC	North West	M203YKA	North West	M402EFD	North Midlands
L940GYL	London	M156RBH	The Shires	M204YKA	North West	M403EFD	North Midlands

Reg	Location	Reg	Location	Reg	Location	Reg	Location
M404EFD	North Midlands	M615PKP	Southern Counties	M799EUS	Scotland West	M943UDT	Cymru
M410UNW	Yorkshire	M615XLG	North West	M802MOJ	North Midlands	M944LYR	Cymru
M411BEY	Cymru	M616PKP	Southern Counties	M803MOJ	North Midlands	M945LYR	Cymru
M411UNW	Yorkshire	M617PKP	Southern Counties	M804MOJ	North Midlands	M946LYR	The Shires
M412BEY	Cymru	M618PKP	Southern Counties	M805MOJ	North Midlands	M947LYR	The Shires
M412UNW	Yorkshire	M619PKP	Southern Counties	M831SDA	North Midlands	M948LYR	The Shires
M413BEY	Cymru	M651ERW	Fox County	M832SDA	North Midlands	M949LYR	The Shires
M413UNW	Yorkshire	M652ERW	Fox County	M833SDA	North Midlands	M950LYR	London
M414UNW	Yorkshire	M685HPF	Northumbria	M834SDA	North Midlands	M951LYR	The Shires
M415UNW	Yorkshire	M686HPF	Northumbria	M835SDA	North Midlands	M998XRF	North West
M416UNW	Yorkshire	M687HPF	Northumbria	M841DDS	The Shires	MBZ6455	The Shires
M417UNW	Yorkshire	M688HPF	Northumbria	M841RCP	North West	MDM284P	OLST
M418UNW	Yorkshire	M689FJF	North West	M842DDS	The Shires	MEF822W	North East
M419UNW	Yorkshire	M689HPF	Northumbria	M842RCP	North West	MEF823W	North East
M420UNW	Yorkshire	M690HPF	Northumbria	M843DDS	The Shires	MEV83V	The Shires
M421UNW	Yorkshire	M691HPF	Northumbria	M843RCP	North West	MEV84V	The Shires
M422GUS	Scotland West	M692HPF	Northumbria	M844DDS	The Shires	MEV85V	The Shires
M422UNW	Yorkshire	M693HPF	Northumbria	M845DDS	The Shires	MEV86V	The Shires
M423GUS	Scotland West	M694HPF	Southern Counties	M846DDS	The Shires	MEV87V	The Shires
M423UNW	Yorkshire	M695HPF	Southern Counties	M847DDS	The Shires	MEY395	Cymru
M424UNW	Yorkshire	M696HPF	Southern Counties	M847RCP	Cymru	MGR659P	Scotland West
M425UNW	Yorkshire	M697HPF	Southern Counties	M849RCP	Cymru	MIL2350	The Shires
M426UNW	Yorkshire	M698HPF	Southern Counties	M859KCU	Northumbria	MIL5573	North West
M427UNW	Yorkshire	M699HPF	Southern Counties	M860KCU	Northumbria	MIL5574	North West
M428UNW	Yorkshire	M700HPF	Southern Counties	M861KCU	Northumbria	MIL5575	North West
M429UNW	Yorkshire	M701HPF	Southern Counties	M862KCU	Northumbria	MIL5580	North West
M430UNW	Yorkshire	M702HPF	Southern Counties	M863KCU	Northumbria	MIL5581	North West
M431UNW	Yorkshire	M703HPF	Southern Counties	M864KCU	Northumbria	MIL5582	North West
M432UNW	Yorkshire	M704HPF	Southern Counties	M865KCU	Northumbria	MIL6676	North West
M433UNW	Yorkshire	M710OMJ	The Shires	M866KCU	Northumbria	MIL6678	North West
M440HPF	Southern Counties	M711OMJ	The Shires	M867KCU	Northumbria	MIL6679	North West
M441HPF	Southern Counties	M711YJC	Cymru	M868KCU	Northumbria	MIL6680	North West
M442HPF	Southern Counties	M712OMJ	The Shires	M869KCU	Northumbria	MIL6681	North West
M443HPF	Southern Counties	M712YJC	Cymru	M870KCU	Northumbria	MIL7612	North West
M444HPF	Southern Counties	M713OMJ	The Shires	M871KCU	Northumbria	MIL7614	North West
M445HPF	Southern Counties	M713YJC	Cymru	M872LBB	Northumbria	MIL7617	North West
M446HPF	Southern Counties	M714OMJ	The Shires	M873LBB	Northumbria	MIL7620	North West
M447HPF	Southern Counties	M714YJC	Cymru	M874LBB	Northumbria	MIL7621	North West
M448HPF	Southern Counties	M715OMJ	The Shires	M875LBB	Northumbria	MIL7622	North West
M449HPF	Southern Counties	M716OMJ	The Shires	M876LBB	Northumbria	MIL7623	North West
M450HPF	Southern Counties	M717OMJ	The Shires	M878DDS	Scotland West	MIL7624	North West
M451EDH	North Midlands	M718OMJ	The Shires	M880DDS	Scotland West	MNC494W	OLST
M451HPF	Southern Counties	M719OMJ	The Shires	M883DDS	Scotland West	MNC497W	OLST
M452EDH	North Midlands	M719UTW	The Shires	M890DHP	Fox County	MRJ231W	The Shires
M452HPG	Southern Counties	M720OMJ	The Shires	M901DHP	Fox County	MRJ232W	The Shires
M453EDH	North Midlands	M720UTW	The Shires	M903DHP	Fox County	MRJ233W	The Shires
M453HPG	Southern Counties	M721OMJ	The Shires	M904DHP	Fox County	MRJ234W	The Shires
M454EDH	North Midlands	M721UTW	The Shires	M905DHP	Fox County	MRJ235W	The Shires
M454HPG	Southern Counties	M722OMJ	The Shires	M906DHP	Fox County	MRJ236W	The Shires
M455EDH	North Midlands	M723OMJ	The Shires	M907DHP	Fox County	MRJ237W	The Shires
M455HPG	Cymru	M724OMJ	The Shires	M908DHP	Fox County	MRJ238W	The Shires
M456EDH	North Midlands	M725OMJ	The Shires	M909DHP	Fox County	MRJ239W	The Shires
M456HPG	Cymru	M725UTW	The Shires	M910DHP	Fox County	MRJ240W	The Shires
M457EDH	North Midlands	M726OMJ	The Shires	M911DHP	Fox County	MRJ241W	The Shires
M457HPG	Cymru	M726UTW	The Shires	M911MKM	Southern Counties	MRJ242W	The Shires
M458EDH	North Midlands	M727OMJ	The Shires	M912DHP	Fox County	MRO993P	North Midlands
M458JPA	Cymru	M727UTW	The Shires	M912MKM	Southern Counties	MSU433	Fox County
M459EDH	North Midlands	M728OMJ	The Shires	M913DHP	Fox County	MTU117Y	Fox County
M459HPG	Southern Counties	M728UTW	The Shires	M913MKM	Southern Counties	MTU118Y	Fox County
M460EDH	North Midlands	M729OMJ	The Shires	M914DHP	Fox County	MTU119Y	Fox County
M460HPG	Southern Counties	M729UTW	The Shires	M914MKM	Southern Counties	MTU121Y	Fox County
M461EDH	North Midlands	M730AOO	The Shires	M915DHP	Fox County	MTV309W	Fox County
M461JPA	Southern Counties	M731AOO	The Shires	M915MKM	Southern Counties	MTV310W	Fox County
M462JPA	Southern Counties	M732AOO	The Shires	M916DHP	Fox County	MTV311W	Fox County
M463JPA	Southern Counties	M733AOO	The Shires	M916MKM	Southern Counties	MTV312W	Fox County
M464JPA	Southern Counties	M734AOO	The Shires	M917DHP	Fox County	MTV313W	Fox County
M465LPG	Southern Counties	M735AOO	The Shires	M917MKM	Southern Counties	MTV314W	Fox County
M466MPM	Southern Counties	M736AOO	The Shires	M918DHP	Fox County	MTV315W	Fox County
M467MPM	Southern Counties	M737AOO	The Shires	M918MKM	Southern Counties	MUH281X	The Shires
M501AJC	North East	M738AOO	The Shires	M919DHP	Fox County	MUH283X	The Shires
M501PKJ	Southern Counties	M742UUA	Yorkshire	M919MKM	Southern Counties	MUH284X	The Shires
M502AJC	North East	M743UUA	Yorkshire	M920DHP	Fox County	MUH285X	The Shires
M502RKO	Southern Counties	M744UUA	Yorkshire	M920MKM	Southern Counties	MUH286X	The Shires
M503AJC	North East	M745UUA	Yorkshire	M921PKN	Southern Counties	MUH287X	The Shires
M504AJC	North East	M746WWX	Yorkshire	M922PKN	Southern Counties	MUH290X	The Shires
M517KPA	Southern Counties	M748WWX	Yorkshire	M923PKN	Southern Counties	MUP712T	Northumbria
M518KPA	Southern Counties	M749WWR	Yorkshire	M924PKN	Southern Counties	MUP713T	Cymru
M519KPA	Southern Counties	M750WWR	Yorkshire	M925PKN	Southern Counties	N24FWU	Cymru
M520KPA	Southern Counties	M751WWR	Yorkshire	M927EYS	North West	N25FWU	Cymru
M521MPF	Southern Counties	M752WWR	Yorkshire	M928EYS	North West	N26KYS	Scotland West
M522MPF	Southern Counties	M753WWR	Yorkshire	M929EYS	North West	N27KYS	Scotland West
M523MPF	Southern Counties	M761JPA	The Shires	M930EYS	North West	N28KGS	The Shires
M524MPF	Southern Counties	M762JPA	The Shires	M931EYS	North West	N29KGS	The Shires
M525MPM	Southern Counties	M763JPA	The Shires	M932EYS	North West	N31KGS	The Shires
M526MPM	Southern Counties	M764JPA	The Shires	M933EYS	North West	N32KGS	The Shires
M611PKP	Southern Counties	M791EUS	Scotland West	M934EYS	North West	N35JPP	The Shires
M612PKP	Southern Counties	M792EUS	Scotland West	M935EYS	North West	N36JPP	The Shires
M613PKP	Southern Counties	M793EUS	Scotland West	M936EYS	North West	N38JPP	The Shires
M614PKP	Southern Counties	M794EUS	Scotland West	M942LYR	The Shires	N37JPP	The Shires

Reg	Operator	Reg	Operator	Reg	Operator	Reg	Operator
N39JPP	The Shires	N203NHS	Scotland West	N258BKK	Southern Counties	N466EHA	North Midlands
N41JPP	The Shires	N204NHS	Scotland West	N258CKA	North West	N467EHA	North Midlands
N42JPP	The Shires	N205NHS	Scotland West	N258PGD	Scotland West	N468EHA	North Midlands
N43JPP	The Shires	N206NHS	Scotland West	N259BKK	Southern Counties	N468SPA	Southern Counties
N45JPP	The Shires	N207CKP	Southern Counties	N259CKA	North West	N469EHA	North Midlands
N46JPP	The Shires	N207NHS	Scotland West	N260CKA	North West	N469SPA	Southern Counties
N81PUS	Scotland West	N208CKP	Southern Counties	N261CKA	North West	N470EHA	North Midlands
N82PUS	Scotland West	N208NHS	Scotland West	N262CKA	North West	N470SPA	Cymru
N101YVU	North West	N209CKP	Southern Counties	N263CKA	North West	N471EHA	North Midlands
N103YVU	North West	N210TPK	Southern Counties	N264CKA	North West	N472EHA	North Midlands
N104YVU	North West	N211DWM	North West	N281NCN	Northumbria	N472XRC	Fox County
N105YVU	North West	N211TBC	Fox County	N282NCN	Northumbria	N473MUS	Scotland West
N106DWM	North West	N211TPK	Southern Counties	N283NCN	Northumbria	N473XRC	Fox County
N107DWM	North West	N212TBC	Fox County	N284NCN	Northumbria	N474MUS	Scotland West
N108DWM	North West	N212TPK	Southern Counties	N285NCN	Northumbria	N474XRC	Fox County
N109DWM	North West	N213TPK	Southern Counties	N286NCN	Northumbria	N475XRC	Fox County
N110DWM	North West	N214TPK	Southern Counties	N287NCN	Northumbria	N476XRC	Fox County
N112DWM	North West	N215TPK	Southern Counties	N288NCN	Northumbria	N477XRC	Fox County
N113DWM	North West	N216TPK	Southern Counties	N289NCN	Northumbria	N478XRC	Fox County
N114DWM	North West	N217TPK	Southern Counties	N290NCN	Northumbria	N479XRC	Fox County
N115DWM	North West	N218TPK	Southern Counties	N301ENX	North Midlands	N480XRC	Fox County
N116DWM	North West	N219TPK	Southern Counties	N302ENX	North Midlands	N481XRC	Fox County
N117DWM	North West	N220TPK	Southern Counties	N303ENX	North Midlands	N511XVN	North East
N118DWM	North West	N221TPK	Southern Counties	N304ENX	North Midlands	N512XVN	North East
N119DWM	North West	N223TPK	Southern Counties	N305ENX	North Midlands	N513XVN	North East
N120DWM	North West	N224TPK	Southern Counties	N322TPK	Southern Counties	N514XVN	North East
N121DWM	North West	N225TPK	Southern Counties	N331OFP	Fox County	N515XVN	North East
N122DWM	North West	N226TPK	Southern Counties	N344OBC	Fox County	N516XVN	North East
N123DWM	North West	N227TPK	Southern Counties	N345OBC	Fox County	N517XVN	North East
N124DWM	North West	N228MUS	Scotland West	N346OBC	Fox County	N518XVN	North East
N124GNM	The Shires	N228TPK	Southern Counties	N347OBC	Fox County	N519XVN	North East
N125DWM	North West	N229TPK	Southern Counties	N348OBC	Fox County	N520XVN	North East
N126DWM	North West	N230TPK	Southern Counties	N349OBC	Fox County	N521XVN	North East
N127DWM	North West	N231TPK	Southern Counties	N350OBC	Fox County	N522XVN	North East
N128DWM	North West	N232TPK	Southern Counties	N351OBC	Fox County	N523XVN	North East
N129DWM	North West	N233CKA	North West	N351YKE	Southern Counties	N524XVN	North East
N130DWM	North West	N233TPK	Southern Counties	N352BKK	Southern Counties	N525XVN	North East
N131DWM	North West	N234CKA	North West	N352OBC	Fox County	N527SPA	Southern Counties
N132DWM	North West	N234TPK	Southern Counties	N353OBC	Fox County	N528SPA	Southern Counties
N133DWM	North West	N235CKA	North West	N354OBC	Fox County	N529SPA	Southern Counties
N134DWM	North West	N235TPK	Southern Counties	N355OBC	Fox County	N530SPA	Southern Counties
N160VVO	Fox County	N236CKA	North West	N356OBC	Fox County	N539TPF	Southern Counties
N161VVO	Fox County	N236TPK	Southern Counties	N357OBC	Fox County	N540TPF	Southern Counties
N162VVO	Fox County	N237CKA	North West	N358OBC	Fox County	N541TPF	Southern Counties
N163VVO	Fox County	N237VPH	Southern Counties	N366JGS	The Shires	N542TPK	Southern Counties
N164VVO	Fox County	N238CKA	North West	N367JGS	The Shires	N543TPK	Southern Counties
N165XVO	Fox County	N238VPH	Southern Counties	N368JGS	The Shires	N544TPK	Southern Counties
N166PUT	Fox County	N239CKA	North West	N369JGS	The Shires	N551LUA	London
N166XVO	Fox County	N239VPH	Southern Counties	N370JGS	The Shires	N552LUA	London
N167PUT	Fox County	N240CKA	North West	N371JGS	The Shires	N601DWY	London
N168LNF	North Midlands	N240VPH	Southern Counties	N372JGS	The Shires	N602DWY	London
N168PUT	Fox County	N241CKA	North West	N373JGS	The Shires	N603DWY	London
N169LNF	North Midlands	N241VPH	Southern Counties	N374JGS	The Shires	N604DWY	London
N169PUT	Fox County	N242CKA	North West	N375JGS	The Shires	N605DWY	London
N170LNF	North Midlands	N242VPH	Southern Counties	N376JGS	The Shires	N606DWY	London
N170PUT	Fox County	N243CKA	North West	N377JGS	The Shires	N607DWY	London
N171PUT	Fox County	N243VPH	Southern Counties	N378JGS	The Shires	N608DWY	London
N171WNF	North Midlands	N244CKA	North West	N379JGS	The Shires	N609DWY	London
N172PUT	Fox County	N244VPH	Southern Counties	N380JGS	The Shires	N610DWY	London
N172WNF	North Midlands	N245CKA	North West	N381JGS	The Shires	N611DWY	London
N173PUT	Fox County	N245VPH	Southern Counties	N381OTY	Northumbria	N612DWY	London
N174PUT	Fox County	N246CKA	North West	N382JGS	The Shires	N613DWY	London
N175DWM	North West	N246VPH	Southern Counties	N382OTY	Northumbria	N621KUA	Yorkshire
N175PUT	Fox County	N247CKA	North West	N383JGS	The Shires	N622KUA	Yorkshire
N176DWM	North West	N247VPH	Southern Counties	N383OTY	Northumbria	N623KUA	Yorkshire
N176PUT	Fox County	N248CKA	North West	N384JGS	The Shires	N671GUM	London
N177DWM	North West	N248VPH	Southern Counties	N384OTY	Northumbria	N671TPF	Cymru
N177PUT	Fox County	N249CKA	North West	N385JGS	The Shires	N672GUM	London
N178DWM	North West	N249VPH	Southern Counties	N385OTY	Northumbria	N673GUM	London
N178PUT	Fox County	N250BKK	Southern Counties	N386JGS	The Shires	N674GUM	London
N179DWM	North West	N250CKA	North West	N386OTY	Northumbria	N675GUM	London
N179PUT	Fox County	N251BKK	Southern Counties	N387JGS	The Shires	N676GUM	London
N181OYH	London	N251CKA	North West	N387OTY	Northumbria	N677GUM	London
N182OYH	London	N252BKK	Southern Counties	N388OTY	Northumbria	N678GUM	London
N183OYH	London	N252CKA	North West	N389OTY	Northumbria	N679GUM	London
N186EMJ	The Shires	N253BKK	Southern Counties	N390OTY	Northumbria	N680GUM	London
N187EMJ	The Shires	N253CKA	North West	N391OTY	Northumbria	N680GUM	London
N188EMJ	The Shires	N253PGD	Scotland West	N392OTY	Northumbria	N681GUM	London
N189EMJ	The Shires	N254BKK	Southern Counties	N393OTY	Northumbria	N682GUM	London
N190EMJ	The Shires	N254CKA	North West	N429XRC	Fox County	N683GUM	London
N191EMJ	The Shires	N254PGD	Scotland West	N430XRC	Fox County	N684GUM	London
N192EMJ	The Shires	N255BKK	Southern Counties	N431XRC	Fox County	N685GUM	London
N192RVK	Northumbria	N255CKA	North West	N432XRC	Fox County	N686GUM	London
N193EMJ	The Shires	N256BKK	Southern Counties	N433XRC	Fox County	N687GUM	London
N194EMJ	The Shires	N256CKA	North West	N439GHG	Scotland West	N688GUM	London
N195EMJ	The Shires	N256PGD	Scotland West	N440GHG	Scotland West	N689GUM	London
N196EMJ	The Shires	N257BKK	Southern Counties	N463EHA	North Midlands	N691GUM	London
N201NHS	Scotland West	N257CKA	North West	N464EHA	North Midlands	N693EUR	The Shires
N202NHS	Scotland West	N257PGD	Scotland West	N465EHA	North Midlands	N694EUR	The Shires

N695EUR	The Shires	N808BKN	Southern Counties	OCU809R	Northumbria	P115HCH	Fox County
N696EUR	The Shires	N808EHA	North Midlands	OCU810R	Northumbria	P116HCH	Fox County
N697EUR	The Shires	N808PDS	Scotland West	OCU812R	Northumbria	P117HCH	Fox County
N698EUR	The Shires	N808TPK	Southern Counties	OCY916R	The Shires	P118HCH	Fox County
N699EUR	The Shires	N808XHN	North East	ODC470W	Southern Counties	P119HCH	Fox County
N701EUR	Southern Counties	N809PDS	Scotland West	OHE274X	The Shires	P120HCH	Fox County
N701GUM	Southern Counties	N809TPK	Southern Counties	OHE280X	The Shires	P121HCH	Fox County
N702EUR	The Shires	N809XHN	North East	OJD809Y	London	P122HCH	Fox County
N702GUM	Southern Counties	N810TPK	Southern Counties	OJD825Y	London	P123HCH	Fox County
N703EUR	The Shires	N810XHN	North East	OJD827Y	London	P124HCH	Fox County
N703GUM	Southern Counties	N852YKE	Southern Counties	OJD840Y	OLST	P125HCH	Fox County
N704EUR	The Shires	N877RTN	Northumbria	OJD850Y	London	P126HCH	Fox County
N704GUM	Southern Counties	N878RTN	Northumbria	OJD858Y	London	P135GND	North West
N705EUR	The Shires	N879RTN	Northumbria	OJD863Y	London	P136GND	North West
N705GUM	Southern Counties	N880RTN	Northumbria	OJD865Y	London	P137GND	North West
N705TPK	The Shires	N881RTN	Northumbria	OJD869Y	London	P138GND	North West
N706EUR	The Shires	N882RTN	Northumbria	OJN357P	The Shires	P139GND	North West
N706GUM	Southern Counties	N883RTN	Northumbria	OKY822X	North Midlands	P140GND	North West
N706TPK	The Shires	N884RTN	Northumbria	OLS540P	Southern Counties	P167BTV	Fox County
N707EUR	The Shires	N885RTN	Northumbria	ONH925V	The Shires	P168BTV	Fox County
N707GUM	Southern Counties	N886RTN	Northumbria	ONH928V	The Shires	P169BTV	Fox County
N707TPK	The Shires	N887RTN	Northumbria	ONH929V	The Shires	P170VUA	Yorkshire
N708EUR	The Shires	N889RTN	Northumbria	OOV761X	North Midlands	P171VUA	Yorkshire
N708GUM	Southern Counties	N890RTN	Northumbria	OOX801R	North West	P172VUA	Yorkshire
N708TPK	The Shires	N891RTN	Northumbria	OOX802R	North West	P173VUA	Yorkshire
N709EUR	The Shires	N906ETM	The Shires	OOX803R	North West	P174VUA	Yorkshire
N709GUM	Southern Counties	N907ETM	The Shires	OOX805R	North West	P175SRO	The Shires
N709TPK	The Shires	N908ETM	The Shires	OOX807R	North West	P175VUA	Yorkshire
N710EUR	The Shires	N909ETM	The Shires	OOX809R	North West	P176LKL	Southern Counties
N710GUM	London	N910ETM	The Shires	OOX810R	North West	P176SRO	The Shires
N711EUR	The Shires	N911ETM	The Shires	OOX811R	North West	P176VUA	Yorkshire
N711GUM	London	N912ETM	The Shires	OOX813R	North West	P177LKL	Southern Counties
N712EUR	The Shires	N913ETM	The Shires	OOX818R	North West	P177SRO	The Shires
N712GUM	London	N914ETM	The Shires	OVV851R	The Shires	P177VUA	Yorkshire
N713EUR	The Shires	N915ETM	The Shires	OVV852R	The Shires	P178FNF	North West
N713TPK	Southern Counties	N916ETM	The Shires	OVV853R	The Shires	P178LKL	Southern Counties
N714EUR	The Shires	N917ETM	The Shires	OVV855R	The Shires	P178SRO	The Shires
N714TPK	Southern Counties	N918ETM	The Shires	P3SLT	North West	P178VUA	Yorkshire
N715EUR	The Shires	N919ETM	The Shires	P26KOP	The Shires	P179FNF	North West
N715TPK	Southern Counties	N935ETU	The Shires	P28LOE	Fox County	P179LKL	Southern Counties
N716EUR	The Shires	N936ETU	The Shires	P29HOF	Fox County	P179SRO	The Shires
N716TPK	Southern Counties	N941MGG	Scotland West	P29LOE	Fox County	P179VUA	Yorkshire
N718DJC	Cymru	N942MGG	Scotland West	P31XUG	Yorkshire	P180FNF	North West
N719DJC	Cymru	N991KUS	Scotland West	P36LOE	Fox County	P180GND	North West
N739AVW	The Shires	N993CCC	Cymru	P37LOE	Fox County	P180LKL	Southern Counties
N740AVW	The Shires	N994CCC	Cymru	P41MVU	North West	P180SRO	The Shires
N741AVW	The Shires	N995CCC	Cymru	P42MVU	North West	P180VUA	Yorkshire
N742AVW	The Shires	N996CCC	Cymru	P43MVU	North West	P181FNF	North West
N743ANW	The Shires	N996KUS	Cymru	P52HOJ	North Midlands	P181GND	North West
N744AVW	The Shires	N997CCC	Cymru	P52MVU	North West	P181LKL	Southern Counties
N750LUS	Scotland West	NEY819	Cymru	P53HOJ	North Midlands	P181SRO	The Shires
N752LUS	Scotland West	NGR681P	North Midlands	P53MVU	North West	P181VUA	Yorkshire
N753LUS	Scotland West	NGR685P	Northumbria	P54HOJ	North Midlands	P182FNF	North West
N754LUS	Scotland West	NIB8459	The Shires	P56HOJ	North Midlands	P182GND	North West
N754LWW	Yorkshire	NIW6507	The Shires	P56MVU	North West	P182LKL	Southern Counties
N755LWW	Yorkshire	NIW6508	The Shires	P56XTN	Northumbria	P182SRO	The Shires
N756LWW	Yorkshire	NIW6509	The Shires	P57HOJ	North Midlands	P182VUA	Yorkshire
N757LWW	Yorkshire	NIW6510	The Shires	P56LOE	Fox County	P183FNF	North West
N779EUA	Yorkshire	NIW6511	The Shires	P57LOE	Fox County	P183GND	North West
N780EUA	Yorkshire	NIW6512	The Shires	P57XTN	Northumbria	P183LKL	Southern Counties
N781EUA	Yorkshire	NJF204W	The Shires	P58HOJ	North Midlands	P183SRO	The Shires
N782EUA	Yorkshire	NLE882	Southern Counties	P58LOE	Fox County	P183VUA	Yorkshire
N783EUA	Yorkshire	NLG35Y	North East	P58MVU	North West	P184GND	North West
N784EUA	Yorkshire	NML608E	London	P58XTN	Northumbria	P184LKL	Southern Counties
N801BKN	Southern Counties	NML611E	London	P59HOJ	North Midlands	P184SRO	The Shires
N801PDS	Scotland West	NML617E	London	P59XTN	Northumbria	P184VUA	Yorkshire
N801TPK	Southern Counties	NML619E	London	P61HOJ	North Midlands	P185LKL	Southern Counties
N802BKN	Southern Counties	NML625E	London	P61MVU	North West	P185SRO	The Shires
N802PDS	Scotland West	NML628E	London	P61XTN	Northumbria	P185VUA	Yorkshire
N802TPK	Southern Counties	NML632E	London	P94MOX	Fox County	P186LKJ	Southern Counties
N803BKN	Southern Counties	NML635E	London	P95HOF	Fox County	P186SRO	The Shires
N803PDS	Scotland West	NML636E	London	P95MOX	Fox County	P186VUA	Yorkshire
N803TPK	Southern Counties	NML638E	London	P96HOF	Fox County	P187LKJ	Southern Counties
N804BKN	Southern Counties	NML643E	London	P96MOX	Fox County	P187SRO	The Shires
N804PDS	Scotland West	NML653E	London	P100LOW	The Shires	P187VUA	Yorkshire
N804TPK	Southern Counties	NML655E	London	P101HCH	Fox County	P188LKJ	Southern Counties
N805BKN	Southern Counties	NMS700	Northumbria	P102HCH	Fox County	P188SRO	The Shires
N805PDS	Scotland West	NOE600R	Southern Counties	P103HCH	Fox County	P188VUA	Yorkshire
N805TPK	Southern Counties	NPJ478R	Southern Counties	P104HCH	Fox County	P189LKJ	Southern Counties
N806BKN	Southern Counties	NPK242P	North West	P105HCH	Fox County	P189SRO	The Shires
N806EHA	North Midlands	NPK245P	North West	P106HCH	Fox County	P189VUA	Yorkshire
N806PDS	Scotland West	NPK250R	North West	P107HCH	Fox County	P190LKJ	Southern Counties
N806TPK	Southern Counties	NRP581V	The Shires	P108HCH	Fox County	P190SRO	The Shires
N806XHN	North East	NTU11Y	North East	P109HCH	Fox County	P190VUA	Yorkshire
N807BKN	Southern Counties	NTU12Y	North East	P110HCH	Fox County	P191LKJ	Southern Counties
N807EHA	North Midlands	NTU13Y	North East	P111MML	Fox County	P191VUA	Yorkshire
N807PDS	Scotland West	NTU15Y	North West	P112HCH	Fox County	P192LKJ	Southern Counties
N807TPK	Southern Counties	OBN505R	Northumbria	P113HCH	Fox County	P192VUA	Yorkshire
N807XHN	North East	OBR769T	Northumbria	P114HCH	Fox County	P193LKJ	Southern Counties

Marshall-bodied Volvo Citybus B135GAU joined Arriva with the Derby City Transport fleet which, in January 1996 was incorporated into the Midland Fox group. The Arriva branding has vehicles carrying the 'Arriva serving the Fox County', or 'Arriva serving Derby' identities as appropriate.

P193VUA	Yorkshire	P216LKJ	Southern Counties	P234MKN	Southern Counties	P271VRG	Northumbria
P194LKJ	Southern Counties	P217JKL	Southern Counties	P235MKN	Southern Counties	P272FPK	Southern Counties
P194VUA	Yorkshire	P217MKL	Southern Counties	P236MKN	Southern Counties	P272VRG	Northumbria
P195LKJ	Southern Counties	P217SGB	Scotland West	P237MKN	Southern Counties	P273FPK	Southern Counties
P195VUA	Yorkshire	P218LKK	Southern Counties	P238MKN	Southern Counties	P273VRG	Northumbria
P196LKJ	Southern Counties	P218MKL	Southern Counties	P239MKN	Southern Counties	P274FPK	Southern Counties
P196VUA	Yorkshire	P218SGB	Scotland West	P240MKN	Southern Counties	P274VRG	Northumbria
P197LKJ	Southern Counties	P219LKK	Southern Counties	P241MKN	Southern Counties	P275FPK	Southern Counties
P197VUA	Yorkshire	P219MKL	Southern Counties	P242MKN	Southern Counties	P275VRG	Northumbria
P198LKJ	Southern Counties	P219SGB	Scotland West	P243MKN	Southern Counties	P276FPK	Southern Counties
P198VUA	Yorkshire	P220LKK	Southern Counties	P244MKN	Southern Counties	P276VRG	Northumbria
P199LKJ	Southern Counties	P220MKL	Southern Counties	P244NBA	North West	P277FPK	Southern Counties
P199VUA	Yorkshire	P220SGB	Scotland West	P245MKN	Southern Counties	P277VRG	Northumbria
P201HRY	Fox County	P221LKK	Southern Counties	P246MKN	Southern Counties	P278FPK	Southern Counties
P201LKJ	Southern Counties	P221MKL	Southern Counties	P247MKN	Southern Counties	P278VRG	Northumbria
P202HRY	Fox County	P221SGB	Scotland West	P250APM	Southern Counties	P279FPK	Southern Counties
P202LKJ	Southern Counties	P222MML	Fox County	P250NBA	North West	P279VRG	Northumbria
P203HRY	Fox County	P223LKK	Southern Counties	P251APM	Southern Counties	P281FPK	Southern Counties
P203LKJ	Southern Counties	P223MKL	Southern Counties	P252APM	Southern Counties	P282FPK	Southern Counties
P204HRY	Fox County	P223SGB	Scotland West	P253APM	Southern Counties	P283FPK	Southern Counties
P204LKJ	Southern Counties	P224LKK	Southern Counties	P254APM	Southern Counties	P284FPK	Southern Counties
P205HRY	Fox County	P224MKL	Southern Counties	P255APM	Southern Counties	P285FPK	Southern Counties
P205LKJ	Southern Counties	P224SGB	Scotland West	P255HOJ	North Midlands	P286FPK	Southern Counties
P206HRY	Fox County	P225LKK	Southern Counties	P256FPK	The Shires	P287FPK	Southern Counties
P206LKJ	Southern Counties	P225MKL	Southern Counties	P257FPK	The Shires	P288FPK	Southern Counties
P207LKJ	Southern Counties	P225SGB	Scotland West	P258FPK	The Shires	P289FPK	Southern Counties
P208LKJ	Southern Counties	P226LKK	Southern Counties	P259FPK	The Shires	P290FPK	Southern Counties
P209LKJ	Southern Counties	P226MKL	Southern Counties	P260FPK	The Shires	P291FPK	Southern Counties
P210JKK	Southern Counties	P226SGB	Scotland West	P260HOJ	North Midlands	P292FPK	Southern Counties
P210LKJ	Southern Counties	P227LKK	Southern Counties	P260NBA	North West	P293FPK	Southern Counties
P211JKL	Southern Counties	P227MKL	Southern Counties	P261FPK	The Shires	P294FPK	Southern Counties
P211LKJ	Southern Counties	P227SGB	Scotland West	P262FPK	The Shires	P295FPK	Southern Counties
P212JKL	Southern Counties	P228LKK	Southern Counties	P263FPK	The Shires	P296FPK	Southern Counties
P212LKJ	Southern Counties	P228MKL	Southern Counties	P264FPK	The Shires	P306FEA	North Midlands
P213JKL	Southern Counties	P229LKK	Southern Counties	P265FPK	The Shires	P307FEA	North Midlands
P213LKJ	Southern Counties	P229MKL	Southern Counties	P266FPK	The Shires	P308FEA	North Midlands
P214JKL	Southern Counties	P230LKK	Southern Counties	P267FPK	The Shires	P309FEA	North Midlands
P214LKJ	Southern Counties	P230MKL	Southern Counties	P268FPK	Southern Counties	P310FEA	North Midlands
P215JKL	Southern Counties	P231MKL	Southern Counties	P269FPK	Southern Counties	P311FEA	North Midlands
P215LKJ	Southern Counties	P232MKL	Southern Counties	P270FPK	Southern Counties	P312FEA	North Midlands
P216JKL	Southern Counties	P233MKN	Southern Counties	P271FPK	Southern Counties	P313FEA	North Midlands

The Arriva branding for the vehicles based at the Leatherhead depot of Southern Counties carry the 'Arriva serving Croydon & North Surrey as shown on DFD003, R203CKD. Pictured at Kingston Hill, the batch are normally found on London Transport service 85. As we go to press the first fifteen Metrobuses have arrived for this fleet and these are expected to displace other double-deck types during 1999. *Gerry Mead*

P314FEA	North Midlands	P401FEA	North Midlands	P487CAL	Fox County	P622FHN	North East
P315FAW	North Midlands	P410CCU	Northumbria	P488CAL	Fox County	P623FHN	North East
P315FEA	North Midlands	P411CCU	Northumbria	P490CAL	Fox County	P624FHN	North East
P316FAW	North Midlands	P412CCU	Northumbria	P490TGA	Scotland West	P625FHN	North East
P316FEA	North Midlands	P413CCU	Northumbria	P491CAL	Fox County	P626FHN	North East
P317FEA	North Midlands	P414CCU	Northumbria	P491TGA	Scotland West	P627FHN	North East
P318FEA	North Midlands	P415CCU	Northumbria	P492CAL	Fox County	P628FHN	North East
P319HOJ	North Midlands	P416CCU	Northumbria	P492TGA	Scotland West	P629FHN	North East
P320HOJ	North Midlands	P417CCU	Northumbria	P49MVU	North West	P630FHN	North East
P321HOJ	North Midlands	P418CCU	Northumbria	P51HOJ	North Midlands	P631FHN	North East
P322HOJ	North Midlands	P419CCU	Northumbria	P526UGA	Scotland West	P632FHN	North East
P323HOJ	North Midlands	P419HVX	The Shires	P527UGA	Scotland West	P633FHN	North East
P324HOJ	North Midlands	P420CCU	Northumbria	P528UGA	Scotland West	P634FHN	North East
P324HVX	The Shires	P420HVX	The Shires	P529UGA	Scotland West	P635FHN	North East
P325HOJ	North Midlands	P421HVX	The Shires	P570TBH	The Shires	P636FHN	North East
P325HVX	The Shires	P422HVX	The Shires	P571TBH	The Shires	P637FHN	North East
P326HOJ	North Midlands	P423HVX	The Shires	P601CAY	Fox County	P638FHN	North East
P326HVX	The Shires	P424HVX	The Shires	P602CAY	Fox County	P639FHN	North East
P327HOJ	North Midlands	P425HVX	The Shires	P603CAY	Fox County	P640FHN	North East
P328HVX	The Shires	P426HVX	The Shires	P604CAY	Fox County	P641FHN	North East
P329HVX	The Shires	P427HVX	The Shires	P605CAY	Fox County	P642FHN	North East
P330HVX	The Shires	P428HVX	The Shires	P606CAY	Fox County	P643FHN	North East
P331HVX	The Shires	P429HVX	The Shires	P606FHN	North East	P644FHN	North East
P332HVX	The Shires	P430HVX	The Shires	P607CAY	Fox County	P645FHN	North East
P334HVX	The Shires	P431HVX	The Shires	P607FHN	North East	P658KEY	Cymru
P380FPK	Southern Counties	P438HKN	Southern Counties	P608CAY	Fox County	P669PNM	The Shires
P382FEA	North Midlands	P452BPH	North West	P608FHN	North East	P670PNM	The Shires
P383FEA	North Midlands	P45MVU	North West	P609CAY	Fox County	P671OPP	The Shires
P384FEA	North Midlands	P46MVU	North West	P609FHN	North East	P671PNM	The Shires
P385FEA	North Midlands	P472APJ	Southern Counties	P610CAY	Fox County	P672OPP	The Shires
P386FEA	North Midlands	P473APJ	Southern Counties	P610FHN	North East	P673OPP	The Shires
P387FEA	North Midlands	P474APJ	Southern Counties	P611CAY	Fox County	P674OPP	The Shires
P388FEA	North Midlands	P475DPE	Southern Counties	P611FHN	North East	P688KCC	Cymru
P389FEA	North Midlands	P476DPE	Southern Counties	P612CAY	Fox County	P753RWU	London
P390FEA	North Midlands	P477DPE	Southern Counties	P612FHN	North East	P754RWU	London
P391FEA	North Midlands	P478DPE	The Shires	P613CAY	Fox County	P801RWU	Scotland West
P392FEA	North Midlands	P479DPE	Southern Counties	P613FHN	North East	P802RWU	Scotland West
P393FEA	North Midlands	P480DPE	Southern Counties	P614FHN	North East	P803RWU	Scotland West
P394FEA	North Midlands	P481DPE	The Shires	P615FHN	North East	P804RWU	Scotland West
P395FEA	North Midlands	P482CAL	Fox County	P616FHN	North East	P805RWU	Scotland West
P396FEA	North Midlands	P482DPE	The Shires	P617FHN	North East	P806DBS	Scotland West
P397FEA	North Midlands	P483CAL	Fox County	P618FHN	North East	P807DBS	Scotland West
P398FEA	North Midlands	P484CAL	Fox County	P619FHN	North East	P808DBS	Scotland West
P399FEA	North Midlands	P485CAL	Fox County	P620FHN	North East	P809DBS	Scotland West
		P486CAL	Fox County	P621FHN	North East	P810DBS	Scotland West

Reg	Operator	Reg	Operator	Reg	Operator	Reg	Operator
P811DBS	Scotland West	P930MKL	Southern Counties	R105TKO	Southern Counties	R187DNM	The Shires
P812DBS	Scotland West	P930YSB	Scotland West	R107TKO	Southern Counties	R188DNM	The Shires
P813DBS	Scotland West	P931MKL	Southern Counties	R108TKO	Southern Counties	R189DNM	The Shires
P814DBS	Scotland West	P931YSB	Scotland West	R109TKO	Southern Counties	R190DNM	The Shires
P814VTY	Northumbria	P932MKL	Southern Counties	R110GNW	Scotland West	R191DNM	The Shires
P815DBS	Scotland West	P932YSB	Scotland West	R110TKO	Southern Counties	R191RBM	The Shires
P816GMS	Scotland West	P933MKL	Southern Counties	R112GNW	Scotland West	R192DNM	The Shires
P817GMS	Scotland West	P934MKL	Southern Counties	R112TKO	Southern Counties	R192RBM	The Shires
P818GMS	Scotland West	P935MKL	Southern Counties	R113GNW	Scotland West	R193DNM	The Shires
P819GMS	Scotland West	P936MKL	Southern Counties	R113TKO	Southern Counties	R193RBM	The Shires
P820GMS	Scotland West	P936YSB	Scotland West	R114TKO	Southern Counties	R194DNM	The Shires
P821GMS	Scotland West	P937MKL	Southern Counties	R115TKO	Southern Counties	R194RBM	The Shires
P822GMS	Scotland West	P937YSB	Scotland West	R116TKO	Southern Counties	R195DNM	The Shires
P822RWU	London	P938MKL	Southern Counties	R117TKO	Southern Counties	R195RBM	The Shires
P823GMS	Scotland West	P939HVX	The Shires	R118TKO	Southern Counties	R196DNM	The Shires
P823RWU	London	P939MKL	Southern Counties	R119TKO	Southern Counties	R196RBM	The Shires
P824GMS	Scotland West	P940MKL	Southern Counties	R120TKO	Southern Counties	R197DNM	The Shires
P824RWU	London	P941MKL	Southern Counties	R121TKO	Southern Counties	R197RBM	The Shires
P825KES	Scotland West	P942MKL	Southern Counties	R122TKO	Southern Counties	R198DNM	The Shires
P825RWU	London	P943MKL	Southern Counties	R123TKO	Southern Counties	R198RBM	The Shires
P826KES	Scotland West	P952RUL	London	R124TKO	Southern Counties	R199RBM	The Shires
P826RWU	London	P953RUL	London	R127LNR	Fox County	R201CKO	Southern Counties
P827KES	Scotland West	P954RUL	London	R128LNR	Fox County	R201CKO	Southern Counties
P827RWU	London	P955RUL	London	R129GNW	Scotland West	R201CKO	Southern Counties
P828KES	Scotland West	P956RUL	London	R129LNR	Fox County	R201RBM	The Shires
P828RWU	London	P957RUL	London	R130GNW	Scotland West	R201VPU	The Shires
P829KES	Scotland West	P958RUL	London	R130LNR	Fox County	R202RBM	The Shires
P829RWU	London	P959RUL	London	R131LNR	Fox County	R202VPU	The Shires
P830KES	Scotland West	P960RUL	London	R132LNR	Fox County	R203RBM	The Shires
P830RWU	London	P961RUL	London	R133LNR	Fox County	R203VPU	The Shires
P831KES	Scotland West	P962RUL	London	R134LNR	Fox County	R204CKO	Southern Counties
P831RWU	London	P963RUL	London	R135LNR	Fox County	R204RBM	The Shires
P832KES	Scotland West	P964RUL	London	R136LNR	Fox County	R204VPU	The Shires
P832RWU	London	P965RUL	London	R137LNR	Fox County	R205CKO	Southern Counties
P833HVX	The Shires	P966RUL	London	R138LNR	Fox County	R205VPU	The Shires
P833KES	Scotland West	P967RUL	London	R139LNR	Fox County	R206CKO	Southern Counties
P833RWU	London	P968RUL	London	R140LNR	Fox County	R206GMJ	The Shires
P834KES	Scotland West	P981PKX	The Shires	R141LNR	Fox County	R206VPU	The Shires
P834RWU	London	PAJ827X	Northumbria	R142LNR	Fox County	R207CKO	Southern Counties
P835KES	Scotland West	PAJ829X	Northumbria	R143LNR	Fox County	R207GMJ	The Shires
P835RWU	London	PDZ6261	North East	R144LNR	Fox County	R207VPU	The Shires
P836KES	Scotland West	PDZ6262	North East	R145LNR	Fox County	R208CKO	Southern Counties
P836RWU	London	PDZ6263	Southern Counties	R146LNR	Fox County	R208GMJ	The Shires
P837KES	Scotland West	PDZ6264	Southern Counties	R147UAL	Fox County	R208VPU	The Shires
P837RWU	London	PDZ6265	Southern Counties	R148UAL	Fox County	R209CKO	Southern Counties
P838KES	Scotland West	PFM126Y	North West	R149UAL	Fox County	R209GMJ	The Shires
P838RWU	London	PFM128Y	North West	R150UAL	Fox County	R209VPU	The Shires
P839KES	Scotland West	PFM129Y	North West	R151GNW	London	R210CKO	Southern Counties
P839RWU	London	PFM130Y	North Midlands	R151UAL	Fox County	R210GMJ	The Shires
P840KES	Scotland West	PJJ21S	OLST	R152GNW	London	R211CKO	Southern Counties
P840PWW	London	PKM111R	Southern Counties	R152UAL	Fox County	R211GMJ	The Shires
P841PWW	London	PKM112R	Southern Counties	R153GNW	London	R212CKO	Southern Counties
P842PWW	London	PKM116R	Southern Counties	R153UAL	Fox County	R212GMJ	The Shires
P843PWW	London	PRJ486R	Northumbria	R154UAL	Fox County	R213CKO	Southern Counties
P844PWW	London	PRJ488R	Northumbria	R155UAL	Fox County	R213GMJ	The Shires
P845PWW	London	PRJ489R	Northumbria	R156UAL	Fox County	R214GMJ	The Shires
P846PWW	London	PRJ490R	Northumbria	R157UAL	Fox County	R215GMJ	The Shires
P847PWW	London	PRJ492R	Northumbria	R158UAL	Fox County	R233AEY	Cymru
P848PWW	London	PRJ494R	Northumbria	R159UAL	Fox County	R234AEY	Cymru
P849PWW	London	PRP802M	The Shires	R160UAL	Fox County	R235AEY	Cymru
P850PWW	London	PTD639S	Northumbria	R161UAL	Fox County	R236AEY	Cymru
P851PWW	London	PUK637R	North Midlands	R162UAL	Fox County	R237AEY	Cymru
P852PWW	London	PUK639R	North Midlands	R163UAL	Fox County	R238AEY	Cymru
P853PWW	London	PUK647R	North Midlands	R164UAL	Fox County	R239AEY	Cymru
P854PWW	London	PUK652R	North Midlands	R165GNW	The Shires	R251JNL	Northumbria
P855PWW	London	PUS226P	Scotland West	R165UAL	Fox County	R255WRJ	North West
P860PBH	The Shires	PWE534R	Fox County	R166UAL	Fox County	R261EKO	Southern Counties
P861PBH	The Shires	Q124VOE	North Midlands	R167UAL	Fox County	R262EKO	Southern Counties
P865VYT	The Shires	Q125VOE	North Midlands	R168UAL	Fox County	R263EKO	Southern Counties
P892XCU	Northumbria	Q126VOE	North Midlands	R169GNW	The Shires	R264EKO	Southern Counties
P893XCU	Northumbria	Q475MEV	The Shires	R169UAL	Fox County	R265EKO	Southern Counties
P894XCU	Northumbria	Q476MEV	The Shires	R170GNW	The Shires	R266EKO	Southern Counties
P895XCU	Northumbria	Q552MEV	The Shires	R170UUT	Fox County	R267EKO	Southern Counties
P896XCU	Northumbria	Q553MEV	The Shires	R171VBM	The Shires	R268EKO	Southern Counties
P902DRG	Northumbria	Q554MEV	The Shires	R172VBM	The Shires	R269EKO	Southern Counties
P903DRG	Northumbria	R32JYG	Yorkshire	R173VBM	The Shires	R270EKO	Southern Counties
P904DRG	Northumbria	R45VJF	Fox County	R174VBM	The Shires	R271EKO	Southern Counties
P905JNL	Northumbria	R46VJF	Fox County	R175VBM	The Shires	R272EKO	Southern Counties
P906JNL	Northumbria	R47XVM	North West	R176VBM	The Shires	R278VOK	Fox County
P913PWW	London	R48XVM	North West	R177VBM	The Shires	R279VOK	Fox County
P914PWW	London	R51XVM	North West	R178VBM	The Shires	R288VOK	Fox County
P915PWW	London	R54XVM	North West	R179VBM	The Shires	R289VOK	Fox County
P916PWW	London	R57XVM	North West	R180VBM	The Shires	R291KRG	Northumbria
P917PWW	London	R59XVM	North West	R181VBM	The Shires	R292KRG	Northumbria
P918PWW	London	R101GNW	London	R182VBM	The Shires	R293KRG	Northumbria
P926MKL	Southern Counties	R101TKO	Southern Counties	R183VBM	The Shires	R294KRG	Northumbria
P927MKL	Southern Counties	R102TKO	Southern Counties	R184VBM	The Shires	R296CMV	Southern Counties
P928MKL	Southern Counties	R103TKO	Southern Counties	R185DNM	The Shires	R297CMV	Southern Counties
P929MKL	Southern Counties	R104TKO	Southern Counties	R186DNM	The Shires		

Reg	Region	Reg	Region	Reg	Region	Reg	Region
R298CMV	Southern Counties	R434RPY	North East	R709MHN	North East	R920JNL	Northumbria
R299CMV	Southern Counties	R435RPY	North East	R710MHN	North East	R921JNL	Northumbria
R301CMV	Southern Counties	R436RPY	North East	R711MHN	North East	R922JNL	Northumbria
R301CVU	North West	R437RPY	North East	R712MHN	North East	R923JNL	Northumbria
R302CMV	Southern Counties	R438RPY	North East	R713MHN	North East	R940VPU	The Shires
R302CVU	North West	R439RPY	North East	R714MHN	North East	R941VPU	The Shires
R303CMV	Southern Counties	R440GWY	Yorkshire	R715MHN	North East	R942VPU	The Shires
R303CVU	North West	R440RPY	North East	R716MHN	North East	R943VPU	The Shires
R304CMV	Southern Counties	R441KWT	Yorkshire	R717MHN	North East	R944VPU	The Shires
R304CVU	North West	R442KWT	Yorkshire	R718MHN	North East	R945VPU	The Shires
R305CMV	Southern Counties	R443KWT	Yorkshire	R719MHN	North East	R946VPU	The Shires
R305CVU	North West	R445KWT	Yorkshire	R720MHN	North East	R947VPU	The Shires
R307CMV	Southern Counties	R446KWT	Yorkshire	R721MHN	North East	R948VPU	The Shires
R307CVU	North West	R447KWT	Yorkshire	R722MHN	North East	R949VPU	The Shires
R308CMV	Southern Counties	R447SKX	The Shires	R723MHN	North East	R950VPU	The Shires
R308CVU	North West	R448KWT	Yorkshire	R724MHN	North East	R951VPU	London
R309CVU	North West	R448SKX	The Shires	R725MHN	North East	R952VPU	The Shires
R310CMV	Southern Counties	R449KWT	Yorkshire	R758DUB	Yorkshire	R953VPU	The Shires
R310CVU	North West	R449SKX	The Shires	R760DUB	Yorkshire	R954VPU	The Shires
R311CVU	North West	R450KWT	Yorkshire	R761DUB	Yorkshire	RBC500W	Fox County
R312CVU	North West	R450SKX	The Shires	R762DUB	Yorkshire	RDS83W	The Shires
R313CVU	North West	R451KWT	Yorkshire	R763DUB	Yorkshire	RDS84W	The Shires
R329TJW	North Midlands	R451SKX	The Shires	R764DUB	Yorkshire	RDZ1701	London
R330TJW	North Midlands	R452KWT	Yorkshire	R765DUB	Yorkshire	RDZ1702	London
R331TJW	North Midlands	R452SKX	The Shires	R766DUB	Yorkshire	RDZ1703	London
R332TJW	North Midlands	R453KWT	Yorkshire	R767DUB	Yorkshire	RDZ1704	London
R334TJW	North Midlands	R453SKX	The Shires	R768DUB	Yorkshire	RDZ1705	London
R335TJW	North Midlands	R454KWT	Yorkshire	R769DUB	Yorkshire	RDZ1706	London
R336TJW	North Midlands	R454SKX	The Shires	R770DUB	Yorkshire	RDZ1707	London
R337TJW	North Midlands	R455KWT	Yorkshire	R785DUB	Yorkshire	RDZ1708	London
R338TJW	North Midlands	R455SKX	The Shires	R787DUB	Yorkshire	RDZ1709	London
R339TJW	North Midlands	R456KWT	Yorkshire	R788DUB	Yorkshire	RDZ1710	London
R340TJW	North Midlands	R456SKX	The Shires	R789DUB	Yorkshire	RDZ1711	London
R341KGG	Scotland West	R457KWT	Yorkshire	R790DUB	Yorkshire	RDZ1712	London
R341TJW	North Midlands	R458KWT	Yorkshire	R791DUB	Yorkshire	RDZ1713	London
R342TJW	North Midlands	R459KWT	Yorkshire	R792DUB	Yorkshire	RDZ1714	London
R343TJW	North Midlands	R460KWT	Yorkshire	R793DUB	Yorkshire	RDZ4278	Southern Counties
R344KGG	Scotland West	R461KWT	Yorkshire	R794DUB	Yorkshire	REU323S	Cymru
R344TJW	North Midlands	R486UCC	Cymru	R795DUB	Yorkshire	RHG882X	North East
R381JYS	Scotland West	R487UCC	Cymru	R796DUB	Yorkshire	RJI6861	The Shires
R382JYS	Scotland West	R521UCC	Cymru	R797DUB	Yorkshire	RJI6862	The Shires
R383JYS	Scotland West	R522UCC	Cymru	R798DUB	Yorkshire	RLG429V	Cymru
R384JYS	Scotland West	R601MHN	North East	R799DUB	Yorkshire	RMO202Y	North East
R385JYS	Scotland West	R602MHN	North East	R801YJC	Cymru	RMO204Y	North East
R415TJW	North Midlands	R603MHN	North East	R802YJC	Cymru	RRA219X	North East
R416COO	London	R603MHN	North East	R803YJC	Cymru	RUF42R	Southern Counties
R416HVX	The Shires	R604MHN	North East	R804YJC	Cymru	RUJ351R	North Midlands
R416TJW	North Midlands	R606FBU	North West	R805YJC	Cymru	RVB975S	OLST
R417COO	London	R606MHN	North East	R807YJC	Cymru	RVB976S	OLST
R417HVX	The Shires	R607MHN	North East	R808YJC	Cymru	RVW88W	The Shires
R417TJW	North Midlands	R614MNU	Fox County	R809TKO	Southern Counties	RVW89W	The Shires
R418COO	London	R615MNU	Fox County	R809YJC	Cymru	RVW90W	The Shires
R418HVX	The Shires	R616MNU	Fox County	R810TKO	Southern Counties	S146KNK	The Shires
R418TJW	North Midlands	R617MNU	Fox County	R810YJC	Cymru	S147KNK	The Shires
R419COO	London	R618MNU	Fox County	R811TKO	Southern Counties	S148KNK	The Shires
R419TJW	North Midlands	R619MNU	Fox County	R811YJC	Cymru	S149KNK	The Shires
R420COO	London	R620MNU	Fox County	R812TKO	Southern Counties	S150KNK	The Shires
R420TJW	North Midlands	R621MNU	Fox County	R812YJC	Cymru	S151KNK	The Shires
R421COO	London	R622MNU	Fox County	R813TKO	Southern Counties	S152KNK	The Shires
R421TJW	North Midlands	R623MNU	Fox County	R813YJC	Cymru	S153KNK	The Shires
R422COO	London	R624MNU	Fox County	R814TKO	Southern Counties	S154KNK	The Shires
R422TJW	North Midlands	R625MNU	Fox County	R814YJC	Cymru	S156KNK	The Shires
R423COO	London	R626MNU	Fox County	R815YJC	Cymru	S157KNK	The Shires
R423RPY	North East	R627MNU	Fox County	R816YJC	Cymru	S158KNK	The Shires
R423TJW	North Midlands	R628MNU	Fox County	R817YJC	Cymru	S159KNK	The Shires
R424COO	London	R629MNU	Fox County	R818YJC	Cymru	S160KNK	The Shires
R424RPY	North East	R630MNU	Fox County	R819YJC	Cymru	S161KNK	The Shires
R424TJW	North Midlands	R631MNU	Fox County	R821YJC	Cymru	S169JUA	London
R425COO	London	R632MNU	Fox County	R903BKO	Southern Counties	S170JUA	London
R425RPY	North East	R633MNU	Fox County	R904BKO	Southern Counties	S171JUA	London
R425TJW	North Midlands	R634MNU	Fox County	R905BKO	Southern Counties	S172JUA	London
R426COO	London	R635MNU	Fox County	R906BKO	Southern Counties	S173JUA	London
R426RPY	North East	R636MNU	Fox County	R907BKO	Southern Counties	S174JUA	London
R426TJW	North Midlands	R637MNU	Fox County	R907JNL	Northumbria	S175JUA	London
R427COO	London	R638MNU	Fox County	R908BKO	Southern Counties	S176JUA	London
R427RPY	North East	R639MNU	Fox County	R908JNL	Northumbria	S177JUA	London
R427TJW	North Midlands	R640MNU	Fox County	R909BKO	Southern Counties	S178JUA	London
R428COO	London	R641MNU	Fox County	R909JNL	Northumbria	S179JUA	London
R428RPY	North East	R642MNU	Fox County	R910BKO	Southern Counties	S180JUA	London
R428TJW	North Midlands	R643MNU	Fox County	R910JNL	Northumbria	S181JUA	London
R429COO	London	R701KCU	Northumbria	R911JNL	Northumbria	S182JUA	London
R429RPY	North East	R701MHN	North East	R912JNL	Northumbria	S183JUA	London
R429TJW	North Midlands	R702MHN	North East	R913JNL	Northumbria	S202JUA	London
R430COO	London	R703MHN	North East	R914JNL	Northumbria	S203JUA	London
R430RPY	North East	R704MHN	North East	R915JNL	Northumbria	S204JUA	London
R431COO	London	R705MHN	North East	R916JNL	Northumbria	S205JUA	London
R431RPY	North East	R706MHN	North East	R917JNL	Northumbria	S206JUA	London
R432RPY	North East	R707MHN	North East	R918JNL	Northumbria	S207DTO	Fox County
R433RPY	North East	R708MHN	North East	R919JNL	Northumbria	S207JUA	London

S208DTO	Fox County	S350YOG	North Midlands	SCK692P	North West	SPY210X	Northumbria
S208JUA	London	S351KHN	North East	SCK693P	North West	SRC114X	Fox County
S209JUA	London	S351YOG	North Midlands	SGR777V	Northumbria	SVL830R	Fox County
S210JUA	London	S352KHN	North East	SGR783V	Northumbria	SVS617	London
S211JUA	London	S352YOG	North Midlands	SGR784V	Northumbria	SVV588W	The Shires
S212JUA	London	S353KHN	North East	SGR788V	Northumbria	TCH118X	Fox County
S213JUA	London	S353YOG	North Midlands	SGR789V	Northumbria	TCH120X	Fox County
S214JUA	London	S354KHN	North East	SGR795V	Northumbria	TCH121X	Fox County
S215JUA	London	S354YOG	North Midlands	SGR797V	Northumbria	TDC854X	North Midlands
S216JUA	London	S355KHN	North East	SGS497W	The Shires	TFN979T	OLST
S217JUA	London	S355YOG	North Midlands	SIB1278	Fox County	TFN982T	OLST
S218JUA	London	S356KHN	North East	SIB1279	North East	TFN985T	OLST
S219JUA	London	S356YOG	North Midlands	SIB1280	North East	TFN986T	OLST
S220JUA	London	S357KHN	North East	SIB1281	North East	TFN987T	OLST
S221JUA	London	S357YOG	North Midlands	SIB1282	North East	TFN988T	OLST
S223JUA	London	S358KHN	North East	SIB1283	North East	TFN989T	OLST
S224JUA	London	S462GUB	Yorkshire	SIB1284	North East	TFN991T	OLST
S225JUA	London	S463GUB	Yorkshire	SIB1285	North East	THX202S	Southern Counties
S226JUA	London	S464GUB	Yorkshire	SIB1286	North East	THX291S	Southern Counties
S227JUA	London	S465GUB	Yorkshire	SIB1287	North East	TIB4873	The Shires
S228JUA	London	S466GUB	Yorkshire	SIB1288	North East	TIB4886	The Shires
S229JUA	London	S467GUB	Yorkshire	SIB4846	The Shires	TIB5901	Southern Counties
S230JUA	London	S468GUB	Yorkshire	SIB6705	North East	TIB5903	Southern Counties
S231JUA	London	S469GUB	Yorkshire	SIB6706	North East	TIB5904	Southern Counties
S232JUA	London	S470GUB	Yorkshire	SIB6707	North East	TIB5905	Southern Counties
S233JUA	London	S471GUB	Yorkshire	SIB6708	North East	TIB5906	The Shires
S234JUA	London	S472ANW	Yorkshire	SIB6709	Southern Counties	TIB7835	The Shires
S235JUA	London	S473ANW	Yorkshire	SIB6710	North East	TNR812X	Cymru
S236JUA	London	S474ANW	Yorkshire	SIB6711	Southern Counties	TOF685S	North Midlands
S237JUA	London	S475ANW	Yorkshire	SIB6712	North East	TOF693S	North Midlands
S238JUA	London	S476ANW	Yorkshire	SIB6713	Southern Counties	TOF698S	North Midlands
S239JUA	London	S477ANW	Yorkshire	SIB6714	Southern Counties	TOF701S	North Midlands
S240JUA	London	S478ANW	Yorkshire	SIB6715	North East	TOF702S	North Midlands
S241JUA	London	S479ANW	Yorkshire	SIB6716	North East	TOF704S	North Midlands
S242JUA	London	S480ANW	Yorkshire	SIB7480	The Shires	TOF705S	North Midlands
S243JUA	London	S481ANW	Yorkshire	SIB7481	The Shires	TOF719S	North Midlands
S244JUA	London	S482ANW	Yorkshire	SIB7689	North Midlands	TOJ592S	North Midlands
S245JUA	London	S483ANW	Yorkshire	SIB8529	The Shires	TOU962	North Midlands
S246JUA	London	S484ANW	Yorkshire	SIB8583	North Midlands	TPC101X	North Midlands
S247JUA	London	S485ANW	Yorkshire	SIB9492	North Midlands	TPC102X	North Midlands
S248JUA	London	S486ANW	Yorkshire	SJI5066	Southern Counties	TPC103X	North Midlands
S249JUA	London	S487ANW	Yorkshire	SJI5569	Fox County	TPC104X	North Midlands
S250JUA	London	S488ANW	Yorkshire	SJI5570	Fox County	TPC107X	North Midlands
S251JUA	London	S489ANW	Yorkshire	SJI5571	Southern Counties	TPC114X	North Midlands
S252JUA	London	S490ANW	Yorkshire	SJI5572	Southern Counties	TPD101X	The Shires
S253JUA	London	S491ANW	Yorkshire	SLT59	Southern Counties	TPD102X	The Shires
S254JUA	London	S610KHN	North East	SLU261	The Shires	TPD106X	Scotland West
S255JUA	London	S611KHN	North East	SMK658F	London	TPD107X	The Shires
S256JUA	London	S612KHN	North East	SMK660F	London	TPD108X	Southern Counties
S257JUA	London	S613KHN	North East	SMK666F	London	TPD109X	The Shires
S258JUA	London	S614KHN	North East	SMK675F	London	TPD110X	The Shires
S259JUA	London	S615KHN	North East	SMK678F	London	TPD113X	Southern Counties
S260JUA	London	S616KHN	North East	SMK682F	London	TPD114X	Southern Counties
S261JUA	London	S617KHN	North East	SMK684F	London	TPD115X	The Shires
S262JUA	London	S618KHN	North East	SMK685F	London	TPD116X	Scotland West
S263JUA	London	S619KHN	North East	SMK688F	London	TPD117X	The Shires
S301JUA	London	S620KHN	North East	SMK692F	London	TPD118X	Southern Counties
S302JUA	London	S621KHN	North East	SMK708F	London	TPD119X	Cymru
S303JUA	London	S622KHN	North East	SMK715F	London	TPD121X	Southern Counties
S304JUA	London	S623KHN	North East	SMK716F	London	TPD122X	Cymru
S305JUA	London	S623KHN	Cymru	SMK718F	London	TPD123X	The Shires
S306JUA	London	S624KHN	North East	SMK726F	London	TPD124X	Southern Counties
S307JUA	London	S624KHN	Cymru	SMK730F	London	TPD126X	Cymru
S308JUA	London	S625KHN	North East	SMK741F	London	TPD127X	Fox County
S309JUA	London	S625KHN	Cymru	SMK742F	London	TPD128X	Southern Counties
S310JUA	London	S626KHN	North East	SMK746F	London	TPD129X	Fox County
S311JUA	London	S626KHN	Cymru	SMK747F	London	TPD130X	Scotland West
S312JUA	London	S644KJU	Fox County	SMK750F	London	TPE159S	North Midlands
S313JUA	London	S645KJU	Fox County	SMK753F	London	TPE163S	North Midlands
S314JUA	London	S646KJU	Fox County	SMK754F	London	TPE166S	North Midlands
S315JUA	London	S647KJU	Fox County	SMK758F	London	TSJ35S	Scotland West
S316JUA	London	S648KJU	Fox County	SMK759F	London	TSJ36S	Scotland West
S317JUA	London	S649KJU	Fox County	SND296X	Northumbria	TSJ38S	Scotland West
S318JUA	London	S650KJU	Fox County	SNS824W	Cymru	TSJ47S	Scotland West
S341KHN	North East	S651KJU	Fox County	SNU384R	North Midlands	TSJ52S	Scotland West
S342KHN	North East	S652KJU	Fox County	SNV932W	The Shires	TSJ54S	Scotland West
S343KHN	North East	S653KJU	Fox County	SNV933W	The Shires	TSJ59S	Scotland West
S344KHN	North East	S701VKM	Southern Counties	SNV934W	The Shires	TSU636	Northumbria
S345KHN	North East	S702VKM	Southern Counties	SNV938W	The Shires	TSU642W	Scotland West
S345YOG	North Midlands	S703VKM	Southern Counties	SPC279R	North West	TSU644	Southern Counties
S346KHN	North East	S704VKM	Southern Counties	SPY201X	Northumbria	TSU645	Southern Counties
S346YOG	North Midlands	S705VKM	Southern Counties	SPY202X	Northumbria	TSU646	North West
S347KHN	North East	S706VKM	Southern Counties	SPY203X	Northumbria	TVC402W	Fox County
S347YOG	North Midlands	S822MCC	Cymru	SPY204X	Northumbria	TVP837S	North West
S348KHN	North East	S823MCC	Cymru	SPY205X	Northumbria	TWY7	Yorkshire
S348YOG	North Midlands	S824MCC	Cymru	SPY206X	North East	TXA114K	Cymru
S349KHN	North East	S825MCC	Cymru	SPY207X	North East	UBR110V	Northumbria
S349YOG	North Midlands	SBF233	North Midlands	SPY208X	North East	UBR113V	Northumbria
S350KHN	North East	SCK688P	North West	SPY209X	North East	UDM447V	Cymru

Reg	Fleet	Reg	Fleet	Reg	Fleet	Reg	Fleet
UDM448V	The Shires	WAE192T	North East	WPH126Y	North Midlands	XVS851	London
UGE388W	Scotland West	WAO395Y	North East	WPH130Y	The Shires	XWA72X	North East
UGE389W	Scotland West	WAO399Y	North East	WPH130Y	The Shires	XWA73X	North East
UGR698R	North East	WDC211Y	Northumbria	WPH139Y	North Midlands	XWA74X	North East
UHG724R	North West	WDC212Y	Northumbria	WRA224Y	North East	XWA75X	North East
UJI2337	Southern Counties	WDC213Y	Northumbria	WRA225Y	North East	XWY477X	North East
UJI2338	Southern Counties	WDC214Y	North East	WRC833S	Southern Counties	XWY478X	North East
UJI2339	Southern Counties	WDC215Y	North East	WSU441S	North West	XWY479X	North East
UJN335V	London	WDC216Y	North East	WSU442S	North West	XYJ418	London
UJN430Y	North Midlands	WDC217Y	North East	WSU450S	North West	XYS596S	North West
UKA20V	OLST	WDC218Y	North East	WSU475	Scotland West	YAU126Y	Fox County
UKA21V	OLST	WDC219Y	Southern Counties	WSU476	Scotland West	YAU127Y	Fox County
UKA22V	OLST	WDC220Y	Cymru	WSV565	Northumbria	YAU128Y	Fox County
UKA23V	OLST	WDS199V	Scotland West	WSV566	Northumbria	YCS91T	Scotland West
UOI772	North Midlands	WDS220V	Scotland West	WSV567	Northumbria	YCU961T	Cymru
UPB331S	Southern Counties	WDS234V	Scotland West	WSV568	Northumbria	YEL98Y	Northumbria
UPB335S	North West	WDS241V	Scotland West	WSV569	Northumbria	YFM1M	North West
UPK135S	Southern Counties	WIB1113	The Shires	WSV570	Northumbria	YIB2396	The Shires
URP946W	The Shires	WIB1114	The Shires	WSV571	Northumbria	YIB2397	The Shires
URP947W	The Shires	WKO125S	Southern Counties	WSV572	Northumbria	YLX281	North East
UWW13X	North East	WKO133S	Southern Counties	WTU467W	Cymru	YMB500W	Cymru
UWW14X	North East	WKO137S	Southern Counties	WTU468W	Cymru	YMB501W	Cymru
UWW515X	North Midlands	WKO138S	Southern Counties	WTU470W	North Midlands	YMB503W	Cymru
UWW517X	North Midlands	WKO139S	Southern Counties	WTU475W	Cymru	YMB510W	Cymru
VAY879	Northumbria	WLT348	London	WTU478W	Cymru	YMB512W	Cymru
VBG89V	North West	WLT370	OLST	WYV60T	Scotland West	YMB516W	Cymru
VBG91V	Cymru	WLT372	London	WYW 6T	London	YMB517W	Cymru
VBG93V	North East	WLT385	London	WYW 7T	London	YMB518W	Cymru
VCA458W	North Midlands	WLT438	OLST	WYW10T	London	YMB519W	Cymru
VCA459W	Cymru	WLT479	OLST	WYW14T	London	YNO78S	The Shires
VCA460W	North Midlands	WLT531	London	WYW24T	OLST	YNO80S	The Shires
VCA461W	Southern Counties	WLT545	OLST	WYW38T	London	YNO81S	The Shires
VDB916	North West	WLT554	London	WYW40T	London	YNO82S	The Shires
VDV112S	OLST	WLT664	London	WYW49T	London	YNW401S	Southern Counties
VDV125S	Northumbria	WLT676	London	WYW51T	London	YOT607	Northumbria
VLT5	London	WLT710	OLST	WYW60T	London	YPB820T	Southern Counties
VLT6	London	WLT719	London	WYW63T	London	YPH407T	Southern Counties
VLT12	London	WLT751	London	WYW66T	London	YPJ207Y	North Midlands
VLT13	London	WLT752	OLST	WYW69T	London	YPL420T	Southern Counties
VLT25	London	WLT753	OLST	XOR841	North Midlands	YSU870	Northumbria
VLT27	London	WLT807	London	XPA110	Fox County	YSU871	Northumbria
VLT32	London	WLT859	Northumbria	XPG172T	Southern Counties	YSU872	Southern Counties
VLT47	London	WLT882	London	XPT686R	North Midlands	YSU873	Southern Counties
VLT143	OLST	WLT884	London	XPT802V	Northumbria	YSU895	Southern Counties
VLT163	OLST	WLT888	London	XPT803V	Northumbria	YSU896	Northumbria
VLT173	London	WLT892	London	XRR50S	Scotland West	YSU897	Southern Counties
VLT235	OLST	WLT895	London	XSV689	Northumbria	YSU953	North Midlands
VLT237	OLST	WLT896	London	XSV691	Northumbria	YSU954	North Midlands
VLT242	OLST	WLT897	London	XTE221V	The Shires	YTU986S	North West
VLT244	London	WLT901	London	XTE222V	The Shires	YUM515S	Southern Counties
VLT275	London	WLT916	London	XTE223V	The Shires	YVV893S	The Shires
VLT281	OLST	WLT954	London	XTE224V	The Shires	YVV894S	The Shires
VLT295	London	WLT970	London	XTE225V	The Shires	YVV895S	The Shires
VTV168S	OLST	WLT997	London	XTE226V	The Shires	YWX401X	Cymru
VVV956W	The Shires	WPH118Y	North Midlands	XTE227V	The Shires	YWX402X	Cymru
VVV957W	The Shires	WPH121Y	North Midlands	XTE228V	The Shires	YYE290T	Southern Counties
VVV960W	The Shires	WPH122Y	North Midlands	XTE229V	The Shires	YYJ955	North Midlands
VYJ806	London	WPH123Y	North Midlands	XTE230V	The Shires		
VYJ808	London	WPH125Y	North Midlands	XUA76X	Cymru		

The 1999 Arriva Bus Handbook

ISBN 1 897990 72 3

Published by British Bus Publishing Ltd
The Vyne, 16 St Margarets Drive, Wellington,
Telford, Shropshire, TF1 3PH